Marketing Modernisms

Self-Promotion, Canonization, Rereading

Kevin J. H. Dettmar
and Stephen Watt, Editors

Ann Arbor

THE UNIVERSITY OF MICHIGAN PRESS

Copyright © by the University of Michigan 1996
All rights reserved
Published in the United States of America by
The University of Michigan Press
Manufactured in the United States of America
⊗ Printed on acid-free paper

1999   1998   1997   1996   4   3   2   1

A CIP catalog record for this book is available
from the British Library.

Library of Congress Cataloging-in-Publication Data

Marketing modernisms : self-promotion, canonization, rereading / Kevin
    J. H. Dettmar and Stephen Watt, editors.
        p.   cm.
    Includes index.
    ISBN 0-472-09641-9 (cloth). — ISBN 0-472-06641-2 (paper)
      1. American literature—20th century—History and criticism.
    2. Modernism (Literature)—United States.   3. English
    literature—20th century—History and criticism.   4. Authors and
    publishers—History—20th century.   5. Literature publishing—
    History—20th century.   6. Authors and readers—History—20th
    century.   7. Modernism (Literature)—Great Britain.   8. Authorship—
    Marketing.   9. Canon (Literature)   I. Dettmar, Kevin J. H., 1958–   .
    II. Watt, Stephen.
    PS228.M63M375   1996
    810.9'0052—dc20
                                                            96-35073
                                                                CIP

to Robyn and Nonie

Acknowledgments

We wish to thank Ross Wagner, LeAnn Fields, and Kristen Lare, with special thanks to all of the essayists who contributed to the volume who time and time again have demonstrated their patience and collegiality as *Marketing Modernisms* was reaching completion.

.

Contents

Introduction: Marketing Modernisms

Kevin J. H. Dettmar and Stephen Watt

> One day while I was composing, the telephone rang. A lady's voice said, "Is this John Cage, the percussion composer?" I said, "Yes." She said, "This is the J. Walter Thompson Company." I didn't know what that was, but she explained that their business was advertising. She said, "Hold on. One of our directors wants to speak to you. . . ." Then suddenly a man's voice said, "Mr. Cage, are you willing to prostitute your art?" I said, "Yes."
>
> —John Cage, *Silence* (1966)

> Thank you for your invitation; but I don't feel moved to contribute. The phrasing [of the prospectus] betrays a concept that belittles. Joyce, Woolf, Ford, et al. were after all not junior academics with a way to make.
>
> —A senior academic declining our
> invitation to write an essay for this anthology

According to the models by which most of us were taught modern literature, the title of this volume, *Marketing Modernisms,* seems almost oxymoronic. That is to say, critical accounts of modernism and modernist writing frequently excavate, or are theorized across, a chasm or "great divide" between modernism, however multifoliate its ambitions and productions, and the larger marketplace as intimated by the title of Andreas Huyssen's *After the Great Divide: Modernism, Mass Culture, Postmodernism* (1986). For Terry Eagleton, this chasm looms between the first two terms of Huyssen's subtitle: between an "autonomous, self-regarding, impenetrable modernist artefact, in all its isolated splendour"[1] and a world of more easily consumed products in mass culture, the putative object of modernism's "relentless hostility."[2] The suasive power of this distinction, with its modernist work of purposefully "thickened textures" intended to "forestall" its "instant consumability" (Eagleton's phrasing), is so formidable that both an advertising director from J. Walter Thompson and a well-known explicator of this literature—a veritable director himself of nearly two generations' study of Anglo-American modernism—acknowledge it. The difference, of course, is that both Cage and the anonymous advertising executive lack any reverence for the binarism in which the well-known scholar so fervently believes. "Junior academics" may "have a way to make," he demurs, but "Joyce, Woolf, Ford, et al." never did—nor, presumably, did he or those of his contemporaries who helped canonize these "wilfully inaccessible" Barthesean Author-Gods and justified their ways to us.[3] To borrow a phrase from Walter Benjamin, in the secular or "negative theology" such scholars have practiced, any suggestion that modernist art is not pure is read as a "concept that belittles."[4] This is so because, following Benjamin's argument, a concept that shatters the aura of authenticity also brings the unique and distant into the realm of the transitory and the commensurate—into the world of the commodity and its nearly limitless reproducibility.

Belittlement, however, is not our intention, nor is it the project of any contributor to *Marketing Modernisms*. Rather, the aims of this volume are, first, to demonstrate that its title, however provocative, is not at all oxymoronic; and, second, to understand *marketing* as embracing both material *and* intellectual—finally ideological—practices. These include a wide ambit of activities that have as their goals both the facilitation of transactions between the producers of cultural goods and their consumers, and the elaboration of criteria to define both the relative value of these goods and the aesthetic experience of apprehending them. Our latter ambition—to consider the ways in which critical constructions of modernism have inflected the reception and canonization of certain texts—is vitally connected to, indeed may be regarded as the effect of, the "great divide" adverted to above. A properly "literary study," as Antony Easthope historicizes it, was founded on an "opposition between high and popular culture" in the 1930s and 1940s, on "well-wrought urns" and "verbal icons" one might say, and promoted specific pedagogical and reading practices (the identification of canonical texts and the presumption of such texts' unity, for example).[5] Other more political suppositions about these texts and their reception by the reading public were formulated by Benjamin, Theodor Adorno, and Max Horkheimer, hypotheses that in significant ways supplemented those advanced by the Southern Agrarian and New Critical movements in America. In their famous critique of the culture industry, Horkheimer and Adorno indict mass culture for its "negation" of individual "style" and ruthless "exclusion of the new"; here, Pound's "Make It New" is perverted, and any distinction between part and whole is dissolved.[6] One result of such processes is the formation of an audience from whom "no independent thinking might be expected," one that "uncritically" enjoys the conventional and greets the "truly new" with deep "aversion."[7]

All of the essays in this volume are concerned specifically with Anglo-American modernists and their potential readers in both the popular audience and the academy. *Marketing* in this sense, therefore, occurred in the advertising departments of publishing houses, the editorial offices of literary magazines where the great divide was often bridged, and, yes, also in the minds of modern writers; it continues in the classroom, in the compilation of the anthologies undergraduates read, and in the practices of literary criticism where the divide has typically been formed and deepened. The essays that follow address, in one fashion or another, one of these domains where modernisms were marketed to and ideologically marked for consumers, and several of them—Barbara Green's, for instance, and Cary Nelson's, with which *Marketing Modernisms* concludes—attempt to identify writers and writing, ideas and politics, that have for too long been relegated to the margins of what we regard today as modernism. Hence the dual trajectory of this book both to reconsider the critically suppressed relationship between canonical modernists and the commercial marketplace, and to provide a metacommentary on other exclusionary and political effects devolving from such a pristine conception of modernist poetics, its dense and mysterious "purity."

The durability of the notion of an impassable gulf between modernist writing and the popular audience has been nothing short of remarkable, however, and its powerful effects have been felt by thousands of undergraduate students. Changes in the contents of *The Norton Anthology of English Literature,* for example, first published in 1962 and by 1993 in its sixth edition, corroborate the assertion in this most recent version's preface that a "vital literary culture" is indeed "always on the move."[8] In the latter edition, Virginia Woolf and Katherine Mansfield, the only two women writers included in Norton's inaugural volume, are joined by May Cannan, Edith Sitwell, Stevie Smith, Doris Lessing, Nadine Gordimer, Edna O'Brien, Fleur Adcock, and Susan Hill; moreover, post-colonial writers, totally absent from earlier editions, are included as well, as is a greater, albeit still inadequate sampling of drama, which in 1962 was represented only by Bernard Shaw's *Mrs. Warren's Profession.* And the brash promise in the first edition (part of its own discourse of self-promotion) to have included within its covers the most characteristic writing not just "of some, but of *all* the great writers (other than novel-ists), and in sufficient quantity to allow the instructor considerable lati-tude of choice" has yielded in 1993 to more modest claims.[9] Yet for all its expansiveness of selection, the *Norton Anthology* in 1993 advances pre-cisely the same view of modern writing's relationship to the popular mar-ket as it did in 1962; hence, this recurrent sentence in the introduction to the twentieth century in all six editions: "Although in earlier periods there had been different kinds of audiences for different kinds of writing, the split now developed with unprecedented speed and to an unprece-dented degree because of the mass production of 'popular' literature for the semi-literate." This "gap" was "widened," the essay goes on to assert, by the modern(ist) "artist's war on the Philistine."[10] One can only conclude from the persistence of this and similar gestures in all six edi-tions of *The Norton Anthology* that while a "vital literary culture" is indeed "always on the move," explanations of this culture are not always so mobile or supple.

This is not to suggest that the notion of a great divide misses the mark completely. The establishment of literary magazines and the so-called "Little Theatre Movement" in America during the early decades of this century, among other events associated with modernisms of various gen-res and media, are merely two moments in the formation of such a cul-tural rift. In helping found the Irish Literary Theatre, later the Abbey Theatre in Dublin, William Butler Yeats expressed this sensibility about as clearly and directly as it can be put: "We have," he claimed in an 1897 letter to John O'Leary, "a literature for the people but nothing yet for the few."[11] Following Yeats's lead, Maurice Browne opened Chicago's Little Theatre in 1912, producing plays by Yeats, Henrik Ibsen, August Strindberg, John Millington Synge, Maurice Maeterlinck, and Arthur Schnitzler for a select audience that included Eugene Debs, Emma Gold-man, and Theodore Dreiser. As theater historian Charles Lock observes, by "shunning the masses the Little Theatre fascinated the few: as often in the culture of Modernism, the term 'little' began as a plea for the mar-ginal, the suppressed, the impoverished, and turned to describe an elite."[12] Margaret Anderson's naming her 1914 Chicago periodical *The Little Review*—and her choice of the masthead "Making No Compro-mise with the Public Taste," as Timothy Materer discusses later in this volume in regard to Ezra Pound's influence on the magazine—intimates a similar turning away from the world of consumer goods. These facts notwithstanding, however, it is demonstrable that never before in Western literary history have marketing forces exerted so strong a force over artists in all media than during the first four decades of this century. Advertising is arguably the modern(ist) art form par excellence; and recent legal battles over copyright, fair use, and permissions from literary estates have served to heighten our awareness that whether or not their creators intended them to be so—and in many cases they certainly did—modernist texts are valuable commodities in contemporary culture. A first-edition, first-printing copy of *Ulysses* on verge d'Arches paper (limited edition of 150) today costs about thirty-five thousand dollars, a signed copy of the Hogarth Press edition of *The Waste Land* about forty-six hundred dollars. More surprisingly, perhaps, a signed first edition of *Old Possum's Book of Practical Cats* now goes for seven thousand dollars.[13]

Part of this market success is attributable, of course, not to these modernists, but rather to American culture's seemingly insatiable appetite for celebrities and materials (epiphenomena) associated with them: the poetry of Leonard Nimoy, the paintings of Tony Bennett and John Cougar Mellencamp, for instance. But so-called "high modernists" have indeed *had* a "way to make" in this world; and rather like the alternatives Shakespeare's Maria outlines in her gull-catching letter to Malvolio in *Twelfth Night,* some modernists actively "achieved" or sought the acceptance of a wider popular audience, while others have more innocently and more recently had such greatness "thrust upon 'em." Our concern here, for the most part, is the former group—and a large one it is. As Michael Kaufmann has pointed out, for instance, by 1922 Gertrude Stein had contributed more often to *Vanity Fair* than to the *Little Review;*[14] and, showing that the modernist him- or herself required as careful promotion as the mysterious and dense modernist text, Enda Duffy and Maurizia Boscagli later in *Marketing Modernisms* contemplate the complex negotiations Joyce achieved between sophisticated European artiste and native Irishman in photographs taken for *Time* magazine in the late 1930s. More recently, T. S. Eliot has appeared on a postage stamp, and Yeats and Joyce on Irish banknotes; as Jennifer Wicke maintains in her essay for this anthology, "Bloomsbury" has become a lifestyle, a commodity one can buy from Laura Ashley; and the films of Merchant and Ivory have made E. M. Forster a household name among people who have never read a word he wrote. How can writers who "can no longer accept the claims of the world" in some cases court its patronage and, in others, come to be embraced by this world?[15] How, to alter Huyssen's title slightly, do these writers make it *across* this great divide?

One answer seems obvious: namely, the positing of such a gulf, such a guarantor of Romantic isolationism for modernisms of various form and political inflection, is not only inaccurate, but also exceptionally damaging insofar as it influences matters of canonization and reception.[16] Albeit a "general article of belief" in many critical assessments of modernist projects, the concept of a rigid opposition between "past and present, art before and art now," and the modernist artifact and its tawdry counterpart in popular culture will not stand up to an accounting of the myriad "fretful details" that contradict it.[17] Neither will a monolithic or inflexible conception of modernism; thus, our attempt throughout to recognize a plurality of modernisms, whether or not they are canonized or sanctioned by the academy. In the process of discussing or, as he puts it, "demystifying the ideology" of a capital-M Modernism, Fredric Jameson posits the existence of numerous modernist projects. Following Deleuze and Guattari's lead, he identifies signs of intellectual "fatigue" in the later nineteenth century with capitalism's "decoding" of "earlier types of realities or code-constructions";[18] therefore, "the moment of the emergence of modernism, or, rather, of the various *modernisms* [our emphasis], for the subsequent attempts to *recode* the henceforth decoded flux of the realistic, middle-class secular era are many and varied." Like Jameson, "we cannot hope even to give a sense of their variety here," even given the restriction of our collective attentions to Anglo-American literary modernisms.[19] Given this focus, the modernisms or varied attempts at recoding we *are* able to discuss, emergent during commerce's primacy, not surprisingly reveal their inevitable incorporation within an exchange system to which many modernists were staunchly opposed.

If one were to privilege this view of commodification as a cultural process, however, modernists would inevitably be portrayed as the unfortunate victims of a mechanism outside of their control or ken. Forster can no longer block Merchant and Ivory adaptations of his novels; Monet, Magritte, and Dalí are not able to prevent the display of their paintings on dormitory walls in the company of images of James Dean and Madonna. But modernists were more deeply complicitous in this marketing than such an account would allow. Lawrence Rainey's influential essay "The Price of Modernism: Reconsidering the Publication of *The Waste Land*," for example, outlines quite clearly Eliot's involvement in and concern over the price and placement of his poem.²⁰ Indeed, Eliot was shrewd enough to distinguish between the book and periodical formats, withholding the infamous notes until *The Waste Land* was securely located between hard covers, in part as an incentive for periodical readers to pay for the clothbound package. In this collection, Leonard Diepeveen's essay investigates Eliot's strategies for the instruction and construction of his reading public, a requisite part of every successful promotional campaign.

As Michael FitzGerald has recently demonstrated, Pablo Picasso was every bit as shrewd an entrepreneur as Eliot, and certainly other parallels might be adduced between Fitgerald's account of Picasso's evolving understanding of the marketplace for his painting and the tenor of the essays in part 1 of *Marketing Modernisms,* "Modernist Self-Promotion." Not surprisingly, FitzGerald begins his *Making Modernism: Picasso and the Creation of the Market for Twentieth-Century Art* (1995) by recalling Picasso's initial (and temporary) disdain for art dealers ("Le marchand— voilà l'ennemi") and art historians' similar antipathy to considering seriously the relationship between modernist art and the commodity form: "artists," FitzGerald remarks, "have generally been studied in isolation from the dealers who represented them and the marketplace that judged their work."²¹ Picasso soon revised his opinion and art historians, following the lead of commentators like FitzGerald, are slowly revising theirs. Like the advertising-minded Pound whom Timothy Materer discusses and the William Carlos Williams later described by Daniel Morris, Picasso is placed by FitzGerald "at the center of the promotional enterprise"; and, like a poem's or story's inclusion in an important periodical or anthology, a painting's exhibition in a well-known museum became a significant form of "accreditation."²² Modernist painters acted upon the precedent of the impressionists, who had earlier cultivated what FitzGerald terms a "critical and commercial system" to support them, and by the time of World War I the "aesthetic and financial confluence of the avant-garde and the mainstream" was a *fait accompli.*²³ Unlike many of the contributors to this volume, especially those in its second section, "Voices at the Margins/Rereadings," however, FitzGerald evinces little interest in delineating the ways in which this "critical system" operated, shaping enthusiastic "readers" of Picasso, Matisse, and other painters who flourished after the celebrated La Peau de l'Ours auction in 1914 to which he devotes such considerable attention.

Like the more orthodox art historians to whom FitzGerald alludes, modernist writers and many of their first-generation proponents in the academy wanted for us not to think too deeply about their work in light of marketing and market concerns. For such an interrogation would tend to contradict notions of the aesthetic purity of the modernist artifact, undermining the credibility of what in his essay Walter Kalaidjian terms a "classist and androcentric" high-modern canon that required a "denigrated and feminized version of the mass-cultural market" (a gendered, commercial Other in effect) against which it could be defined. To follow their bidding in this matter though—to replicate some thirty years of a history as told by the *Norton Anthology*—would constitute, as Cary Nelson has phrased it in reference to the "highly forgetful" nature of the received canon of modern American poetry, a kind of deliberate suppression of evidence "so that more selective histories can be retold."[24] Or, to put it differently, in the first sentence of his magisterial biography of Joyce, Richard Ellmann writes, "We are still learning to be James Joyce's contemporaries, to understand our interpreter";[25] and while that is true, we nevertheless need to claim the interpretive power inherent in being Joyce's—and Lawrence's, Woolf's, Barnes's, Pound's, Eliot's, and Stein's—successors. In an unpublished letter to Richard Aldington, Eliot writes of Aldington's sympathetic review in *Vogue* of his work, "It says just what I should like to be said!" And although there is nothing wrong with a critic saying what an author would have liked to have said, there's always a good bit more to query, modify, even refute.

What follows *does* say more on the topic of modernist writing and the marketplace, but of course not nearly enough. Important writers, genres (drama, following the example of its marginal status in literary anthologies, is regrettably absent from this volume), movements, parallels on the continent, and many analogues in the other arts have been left out; others might surely have been elaborated further. Many writers deserving of critical attention—William Faulkner, John Dos Passos, Katherine Mansfield, Nella Larsen, Djuna Barnes, Yeats—will not receive such here. We wish it were otherwise.

The seven essays comprising the first section of *Marketing Modernisms*—"Modernist Self-Promotion"—examine a wide range of strategies modernists and their publishers employed to market their work, fashion themselves as artists or celebrities, and, not infrequently, bridge the gap between an elite avant-garde and the popular reader. For Timothy Materer in "Make It Sell! Ezra Pound Advertises Modernism," modernists seemed paradoxically to accomplish the goal of emancipation from the popular at the same time that they also unwittingly abetted an incipient advertising industry eager to develop more effective promotional schemes. Pound's "campaign" to find a venue for his, Eliot's, and Joyce's writing at *The Little Review,* therefore, raises questions about the poet's resultant "contamination by the advertising techniques he manipulated so well"; and Materer goes on to speculate that one of Leopold Bloom's promotional schemes in *Ulysses* signals Joyce's recognition of a "close parallel between the techniques of modern advertising" and the precepts of imagism. Paradox is at the heart, as well, of D. H. Lawrence's self-promotional project, one of the most interesting gestures of which, according to Joyce Wexler, was to "defend erotic fiction as art while selling it as smut." Subsequent essays in this section treat such canonical figures as Eliot, Woolf, Joyce, and William Carlos Williams within a context of similar concerns. And several essays, Michael Murphy's on *Vanity Fair* in the 1920s, for example, and Daniel Morris's on Williams's negotiations with New Directions over the marketing of his later fiction, illuminate two responses to the often vexatious issue of targeting a popular audience for modern literary art. That is, while *Vanity Fair* in the 1920s endeavored to keep its "upper-middle-class readership culturally up-to-date" by "mediating the vagaries of high modernist art" to its subscribers, the founding of New Directions in 1935 brought with it "conflicting imperatives" about its "meaning and value," about the methods of conducting a "literary business." In the midst of such deliberations and strategizings, both that "mysteriously autotelic object" Eagleton describes—"the commodity as fetish resisting the commodity as exchange"[26]—and the reverential, almost priestly reader-critic who served it so well recede sharply from view.

The second section of *Marketing Modernisms*—"Voices at the Margins/Rereadings"—has several goals. The initial essays in this section, taken as a whole, suggest the difficulties women, African-American, and gay writers confronted both in gaining acceptance and in representing through their characters the racial, sexual, and gendered realities of their lives. In one case, that of the suffrage movement in Britain as described by Barbara Green, the worlds of commercial advertising and militant feminism merge as the "pageantry of the suffragettes" worked to make feminism "visible and organized itself through display and direct engagement with commodity culture." For Green, therefore, hunger strikes, spectacular demonstrations, and women's autobiography become important modern genres, the former two dependent upon the appropriation of tactics from commercial discourses if the suffrage movement was to be politically successful. In the cases of Harlem Renaissance and lesbian writers, as discussed by Christopher Mott and Corrine Blackmer, the problems of self-representation are both different and equally vexing, as the "purity" of art inevitably confronted the realities of censorship and racism.

The essays in this section, finally, in one way or another, offer commentary (or, as we have mentioned, a metacommentary) on the academy's acceptance and intellectual packaging of Anglo-American modernism: of its historical account of avant-garde literary magazines, of its construction of such writers as Joyce and Langston Hughes, of its highly gendered and ideological quality as communicated both by the canon of writers valorized within the academy and, specifically, by the New Critics. For Cary Nelson, the canonization of American modernist poetry is equally a concretization of the "misogynistic stances" of such poets as Pound and Eliot; hence, "any conclusions we might reach about how gender plays itself out in modern poetry are complicated and enriched by wide reading in the forgotten poems of American modernism." *Marketing* in these later essays thus takes on a meaning quite different from the process described in the first section of this volume, for it targets a rather different consumer from the one who paid an annual three-dollar subscription fee in 1920 to read *Vanity Fair*. That consumer typically attends colleges or universities and reads the literary critical products (and their intellectual "takes" on modernist aesthetics) academics create.

Marketing Modernisms: Self-Promotion, Canonization, Rereading is intended finally to provoke further dialogue on these and other matters related to art and the marketplace. How is the modernist artifact altered or, even, reduced by articulation with the discourse of the commodity? How is our sense of textuality affected by this? What role does reading and canonization play in this relationship? To what extent are literary anthologies and little magazines analogous to museums, valorizing certain aesthetics and excluding or ignoring other? After reading *Marketing Modernisms*, we hope you will be moved to contribute to this conversation.

NOTES

1. Terry Eagleton, *Against the Grain: Essays, 1975–1985* (London: Verso, 1986), p. 140.

2. Andreas Huyssen, *After the Great Divide: Modernism, Mass Culture, Postmodernism* (Bloomington: Indiana University Press, 1986), p. 188.

3. The phrase "wilfully inaccessible," to describe modern writers' effrontery to both the "established guardians of culture" and the "most cherished sentiments" of bourgeois audiences, comes from Irving Howe's "The Idea of the Modern," in *Literary Modernism,* ed. Howe (New York: Fawcett, 1967), p. 13. Roland Barthes discusses the "Author-God" in "The Death of the Author," in *Image—Music—Text,* trans. Stephen Heath (New York: Hill and Wang, 1977). Of course, the concept of an author as "god" is at least as old as classical notions of a poet as "maker." It is equally familiar to students of Romanticism and such high modernist figures as Joyce. In *James Joyce and the Making of "Ulysses"* (1934), Frank Budgen suggests that Joyce, like the Old Testament God, "looks on his handiwork and finds it good." In *The Books at the Wake* (New York: Viking, 1960), James S. Atherton asserts that "underlying" the axioms of *Finnegans Wake* is the "fundamental assumption that the artist is God-like in his task of creation" (27). Atherton seems to agree with this, claiming that in *Finnegans Wake* Joyce is attempting "nothing less than to create a third scripture" (28). Although the "sway of the author" remains central to several of the essays in *Marketing Modernisms,* these essays in no way regard the modernist "work" as a single "message," "theological" or otherwise, from the Author to the reader (p. 146).

4. Walter Benjamin, "The Work of Art in the Age of Mechanical Reproduction," in *Illuminations,* ed. Hannah Arendt, trans. Harry Zohn (New York: Schocken, 1969), p. 224. The metaphors of a modernist "purity" and postmodernist "impurity" are usefully developed by Guy Scarpetta in *L'Impureté* (Paris: Bernard Grasset, 1985). So, for example, "Le modernisme du début du siècle visait, lui, à isoler la spécificité et la *pureté* des différents codes: peinture sans représentation, poésie sans anecdote, cinéma sans théâtricalité" (p. 34). In " 'One Hundred Per Cent Bohemia': Pop Decadence and the Aestheticization of Commodity in the Rise of the 'Slicks' " later in this volume, Michael Murphy reads in an issue of *Vanity Fair* the clear sense that at least by 1920 the "problems inherent" in the " 'modernist' notion of aesthetic 'purity' " were becoming quite obvious.

5. Antony Easthope, *Literary into Cultural Studies* (London: Routledge, 1991), pp. 19, 11.

6. Max Horkheimer and Theodor W. Adorno, *Dialectic of Enlightenment,* trans. John Cumming (1944; New York: Continuum, 1993), pp. 129–30, 134.

7. Horkheimer and Adorno, *Dialectic of Enlightenment,* p. 137; Benjamin, "Work of Art," p. 234.

8. M. H. Abrams, general editor, "Preface to the Sixth Edition," *The Norton Anthology of English Literature,* 6th ed. (New York: Norton, 1993), 2:xxxv.

9. Preface, *The Norton Anthology of English Literature* (New York: Norton, 1962), 2:xxix.

10. *Norton Anthology,* 6th ed., 2:1683.

11. *The Letters of W. B. Yeats,* ed. Allan Wade (London: Rupert-Hart-Davis, 1954), p. 286.

12. Charles Lock, "Maurice Browne and the Chicago Little Theatre," *Modern Drama* 31 (March 1988): 110.

13. These figures have been culled from recent annual volumes of *Bookman's Price Index: A Guide to the Value of Rare and Other Out-of-Print Books,* ed. Anne F. McGrath (Detroit: Gale Research Press).

14. Kaufmann made this observation in a paper given at the 1991 Modern Language Association meeting in New York, "Gertrude Stein's *The Autobiography of Alice B. Toklas:* Alternative Marketing Strategies for the Modernist Author."

15. Howe, "Idea of the Modern," p. 18. Ezra Pound's ill-fated scheme to get Eliot out of Lloyd's Bank so that he might write poetry full time—the Bel Esprit scheme—is a prime example of how modernist writers attempted to finesse their way out of this predicament. Eliot was not in principle opposed to the "patronage by subscription" that Pound was attempting to establish; Pound in a letter to Richard Aldington explained that it is "just as honourable to sell one's stuff, or to receive one's pay from thirty people as from thirty thousand, or from twenty intelligent people as from one newspaper owner (now in a lunatic asylum)" (Pound to Aldington, n.d. [1922]; Harry Ransom Humanities Research Center, University of Texas, Austin). At the same time, however, Eliot was anxious that his employers not learn of the plan, thereby imperiling his continued employment should the project fall flat (as, in the event, it did), and was also extremely concerned that he not appear wise to Pound's machinations on his behalf. Pound, in his gruff way, dismissed Eliot's concerns: "There is no affront to his [Eliot's] bloody pride. Only people who want his poetry, and who are willing to pay for it are in on this deal. There is no question of his being an object of charity. We are restarting civilization, and have devised a new modus of making art and lit. possible" (Pound to Aldington, 16 March 1922; Harry Ransom Center). For more details of Pound's Bel Esprit scheme, see Humphrey A. Carpenter, *A Serious Character: The Life of Ezra Pound* (Boston: Houghton Mifflin, 1988), pp. 409–12.

16. It is also, as Woolf suggests in *A Room of One's Own,* crippling for writers, and particularly for women writers whose material resources are seldom as ample as those of their male counterparts. Although only the "room" makes it into Woolf's famous title, she of course argues for both "five hundred a year and a room with a lock on the door" (New York: Harcourt, Brace, and World, 1957), p. 109. As she puts it quasi-syllogistically toward the close of the lecture, "Intellectual freedom depends upon material things. Poetry depends upon intellectual freedom. And women have always been poor" (p. 112).

17. Malcolm Bradbury and James McFarlane, eds., *Modernism: A Guide to European Literature, 1890–1930* (London: Penguin, 1976), p. 21.

18. Fredric Jameson, "Beyond the Cave: Demystifying the Ideology of Mod-

ernism," in *The Ideologies of Theory, Essays 1971–1986* (Minneapolis: University of Minnesota Press, 1988), 2:125.

19. Ibid., 2:129.

20. See Lawrence S. Rainey, "The Price of Modernism: Reconsidering the Publication of *The Waste Land*," *Yale Review* 78 (Winter 1989): 279–300.

21. Michael C. FitzGerald, *Making Modernism: Picasso and the Creation of the Market for Twentieth-Century Art* (New York: Farrar, Straus and Giroux, 1995), p. 3.

22. Ibid., p. 5.

23. Ibid., p. 18.

24. Cary Nelson, "Modern Poems We Have Wanted to Forget," in *Cultural Studies*, ed. Nelson, Paula A. Treichler, and Lawrence Grossberg (New York: Routledge, 1992), p. 170.

25. Richard Ellmann, *James Joyce* (New York: Oxford University Press, 1959); the same sentence opens the 1982 revised edition.

26. Eagleton, *Against the Grain*, p. 140.

PART ONE
Modernist Self-Promotion

Make It Sell! Ezra Pound Advertises Modernism

Timothy Materer

> The flow of images carries everything before it . . . like some perpetual, arbitrary surprise, leaving no time for reflection.
>
> Guy Debord, *Comments on the Society of the Spectacle*

In 1914 D. H. Lawrence told Amy Lowell that Ezra Pound's imagism was "just an advertising scheme."[1] He might have added, "but what an advertising scheme!" As we will see, his suspicions of Pound the propagandist were justified. But Amy Lowell appreciated the importance of imagism better than Lawrence did because she was still a relatively unknown artist. Pound coined the term *imagism* in 1912 to help market some poems by H.D. (Hilda Doolittle) that he was sending to *Poetry* magazine. Since H.D. had published nothing to date, Pound shrewdly reasoned that her work would be more readily accepted if she were identified with a group of poets. Pound appended to the manuscript the words "H.D., *Imagiste*" and explained to *Poetry*'s editor, Harriet Monroe, that H.D.'s poems were written "in the laconic speech of the Imagistes."[2] When Amy Lowell read H.D.'s poems in the January 1913 *Poetry,* she felt her own identity as a poet had been defined. Not only Lowell but all aspiring poets, including some hostile to Pound's movement such as Conrad Aiken, now had to define themselves in relation to this new literary phenomenon. Harriet Monroe referred to the "battle for Imagism" to indicate the central importance the movement had in the pages of her journal.[3] More important to Pound, however, was the larger battle to establish what he called "our modern experiment" (*SL* 180). The rapid rise and fall of imagism provided the context in which Pound developed his conception of modernism.

In addition to inventing a catchy name for the movement, Pound used two additional advertising strategies. When Lowell first heard of the movement, she was intrigued that its name was French. She was thus seduced by an old but still powerful technique for publicizing cultural movements—using the cachet of a French name. Pound intended the term *les Imagistes* to help distinguish the movement from the "mushiness" of *les Symbolistes,* but to Amy Lowell and others the name instead suggested a glamorous association with French poets such as Baudelaire and Mallarmé.⁴ The second additional strategy was to suggest that the movement had a secret or mysterious ingredient or quality (as advertisers may refer to "secret ingredient X," "xylitol," or "Fahrvergnügen") that only the user of the product can appreciate. In imagism the secret ingredient was referred to in the March 1913 *Poetry* as a "certain 'Doctrine of the Image,'" which the imagists had not "committed to writing" and which "did not concern the public."⁵

Pound's definition of the image as "that which presents an intellectual and emotional complex in an instant of time" takes nothing away from the intriguing mystery of the imagist secret doctrine. Pound explains that he uses the term *complex* "rather in the technical sense employed by the newer psychologists, such as Hart." For even the best-informed reader, this hint that complex is being used in a psychological sense (as in the term *Oedipus complex*) would have clarified nothing about the nature of the image—but it would imply its modernity. Moreover, the generality of the term *thing* in the imagist principle of "Direct treatment of the 'thing' whether subjective or objective" is even more mysterious or obscure than "complex."⁶ Whether this obscurity was calculated to intrigue, or whether it was just a product of Pound's natural ability to mystify, these product descriptions were brilliantly successful.

From the success of imagism as a movement, however, there emerged a problem that even Pound's advertising genius could not surmount. He had invented a name for a new poetic technique, but of course he could not patent, franchise, or in any way control its use. Would-be imagists who wrote bad verse were more of a problem for the movement than those who attacked it for its obscurity or free-verse rhythms. Again, Amy Lowell illustrates the dynamics of the movement. Armed with an introductory letter from Harriet Monroe, Lowell sailed to England in 1914 principally to meet Pound and learn about the imagists. Pound initially welcomed her, introducing her to W. B. Yeats and Ford Madox Ford, and publishing one of her poems in his anthology *Des Imagistes* (1914). But Pound did not feel that Lowell's poetry was direct and concise enough to exemplify imagist technique.

Nevertheless, to give a sense of a new and influential "movement" Pound was willing to expand the original imagist group of Richard Aldington, H.D., F. S. Flint, and himself. The expansion was a mistake because it gave anyone who appeared in the anthology, including mediocre poets such as Lowell, Skipwith Cannell, and John Cournos, an authoritative claim to the title of imagist poet. (The title of Pound's next collection, *The Catholic Anthology* of 1915, was meant to suggest no specific literary orientation.) With the authority of appearing in *Des Imagistes,* Lowell next used her wealth and literary connections to publish further imagist anthologies and take over leadership of the movement. Pound could not match the resources Lowell put into play when she invited a writer like D. H. Lawrence to dine at her first-class hotel and offer to pay him for a contribution to a new anthology. Pound admitted her superior propaganda ability when he conceded to Margaret Anderson in 1917 that she "would advertise us like HELL. It is her talent" (*P/LR* 141). As William Pratt put it, "at the crucial stage of Imagist development one master propagandist was vanquished by another."[7]

Pound dropped the term imagism and dubbed Lowell's movement "Amygism," rudely dismissing her as a "hippopoetess." He of course refused to contribute to Lowell's proposed second "imagiste" anthology. Lowell's suggestion that a committee choose the poems increased rather than lessened Pound's opposition because, as he wrote to her, he wanted "the name 'Imagisme' to retain some sort of meaning. It stands, or I should like it to stand for hard light, clear edges, I can not trust any democratized committee to maintain that standard" (*SL* 38). Ignoring Pound's suggestion that her anthology be called "Vers Libre or something of that sort" (*SL* 39), Lowell published *Some Imagist Poets* (1915), which included a publisher's blurb implying that she was leader of the imagist movement. In a complaining letter, Pound rejected Lowell's apology for her publisher's advertisement, noting that it was still appearing: "I don't suppose any one will sue you for libel; it is too expensive. If your publishers 'of good standing' tried to advertise cement or soap in this manner they would certainly be sued" (*SL* 44).

Yet it was not the Madison Avenue ruthlessness of Amy Lowell that soured him on imagism as much as his realization that by expanding the number of imagists he had lost, to use another marketing term, quality control over the new poetic product. He changed the title of an article he was writing in 1914 from "Imagism" to "Vorticism" once he decided the earlier movement no longer served his purpose. Vorticism publicized the newest developments in painting and sculpture as well as literature. But Pound's description of literary vorticism in *BLAST,* the vorticist journal, demonstrates that the new movement was simply an improved version of imagism. Although he now describes the image in painterly terms as the "primary pigment" of verbal art, the imagist principles of "hard light, clear edges" (which well describes Lewis's geometric paintings) are the same; and once again he presents H.D.'s poetry as the epitome of the movement.[8] As Hugh Kenner has observed, the real difference between imagism and vorticism was that the latter movement distinguished Pound from the mediocre artists that had overtaken imagism. Vorticism "implied his alliance with his own kind," which included a brilliant sculptor like Henri Gaudier-Brzeska and the painter Wyndham Lewis.[9] He rejected Lowell's "democratized committee" because it would mean accepting "a certain number of people as my critical and creative equals" (*SL* 38) who didn't deserve the honor. Although World War I spoiled his plans by dispersing his allies, he was by 1914 determined to keep what he called "our little gang" (*SL* 27) an elite group.

This principle of allying with a clearly defined group of first-rank artists also guided Pound's dealings with the periodicals in which literary modernism developed. In 1914–15 he still hoped to found a periodical that would review not only literary events but also cultural and political ones. However, the financial problem of supporting such a wide-ranging effort was overwhelming, and so was the problem of finding a sufficient number of cohesive and first-rate contributors. (T. S. Eliot was later to face this problem with *The Criterion.*) Pound soon saw that only a "little magazine" could remain uncompromised by its financial support, including its dependence on subscriptions, to publicize a new movement in arts. Even when, as late as 1915, he was still hoping to establish a general review, Pound looked for a way to sharpen his focus. His most remarkable plan was to eliminate half the human race by founding a "Male Review," or at least placing on the masthead "No woman shall be allowed to write for this magazine."[10] Admitting that this plan would eliminate some good writers ("about six"), he argued that the "ultimate gain . . . in vigour" would be worth it (*P/Q* 54).

Aside from his obvious misogyny, his plan for a male review was inspired by his difficulties with Dora Marsden and Harriet Monroe and what he called the "damd female tea parties who . . . committeeize themselves" (*P/Q* 27). Marsden had founded *The New Freewoman* as a suffragette journal. Pound and others convinced her that it would have a wider appeal with a less militant title. It was changed to *The Egoist,* and, beginning in August 1913, Pound was in charge of the literary side of the paper. Its achievements in publishing imagist poets (a special imagist number in May 1915) and serializing Wyndham Lewis's novel *Tarr* and James Joyce's *A Portrait of the Artist* were considerable. Yet Pound was never satisfied with the journal because he felt that Marsden's contributions to it compromised its quality. He thought that his band of writers would be "smothered under Miss Marsden's outpourings" on such topics as the "origin of mind" or "the philosophy of the 'real.'"[11] He supported the magazine on condition that Marsden guarantee fifty pounds a year to both James Joyce and Wyndham Lewis and also employ Eliot as an editor (*P/Q* 60). (Under this arrangement, Pound himself contributed twelve articles for free.) But he told John Quinn that "Miss Marsden is some sort of fool, I haven't found out precisely which sort. The blob of her stuff on the front pages would always prevent the paper from being really satisfactory" (*P/Q* 71).

The writers he was associated with in Harriet Monroe's *Poetry* were even less satisfactory than those in *The Egoist.* Monroe's idea of a great poet was Vachel Lindsay or Carl Sandburg. Concerning such poets, Pound advised her that although the "'Yawp' is respected from Denmark to Bengal . . . we can't stop with the 'Yawp'" (*SL* 11). It took Pound months to convince Monroe to publish Eliot's "The Love Song of J. Alfred Prufrock," which she wished were a more positive and energetic poem in the Vachel Lindsay manner. Although he sent her "Prufrock" in October 1914, it was not published until June 1915. Pound accused Monroe of asking Eliot to "write down to an audience" and refused even to send her Eliot's address to prevent her interference. Moreover, Monroe's way of running the journal seemed too democratic to support an elite band of writers. Monroe had solicited, mostly from businessmen, more than one hundred small pledges of from twenty-five to fifty dollars for five years in order to start the magazine. To Pound, her dependence on such support, as well as committees to award poetry prizes, inevitably undermined *Poetry*'s usefulness. As "little magazines," *The Egoist* and *Poetry* were able to "break the phalanx of a lot of stupidity."[12] But now he needed to find a type of little magazine that would be as aggressive and focused as Lewis's *BLAST.*

Early in 1917 Pound learned that he could take over *The Little Review,* a Chicago literary magazine that desperately needed more financial backing. Pound's literary projects were already being supported by a wealthy

New York lawyer, John Quinn. Quinn fit Pound's conception of the ideal patron, like the Sigismundo Malatesta of the *Cantos*, because he was a man of affairs with an independent and discriminating taste in the arts. Pound had already funneled some of Quinn's money to *The Egoist*, and Quinn was prepared to support the cultural review that Pound dreamed of founding. When he realized that Quinn's resources and the available talent would not support a full-scale review, Pound decided that shaping an existing journal to his purpose would be a more realistic plan. He did not want to sever his ties to *The Egoist* and *Poetry*, however, since they were continuing to support some of his friends—often at higher prices (especially in the case of *Poetry*) than the *Little Review* could pay. Moreover, he felt obligated to continue sending his new poems to *Poetry*.

In letters to Quinn, he tried to sort out how he might make the best use of each of the magazines he helped to edit. In September 1916 he was planning a "compact fighting sheet," and in May 1917 he told Quinn he wanted to make *The Little Review* a "single punch" by sending "more active matter" to them: "I want the Little Rev. to make things grow."[13] Critical prose, such as his essays on Elizabethan literature, went to *The Egoist*; but more imaginative prose, such as his satiric sketch on Rabindranath Tagore ("Jodindranath Mawhwor's Occupation") went to *The Little Review*. Although he was still dealing with female editors, Margaret Anderson and her associate Jane Heap, he felt they were free of a "fixed mania like Dora Marsden['s]" (*PQ* 97). Moreover, he admired their courage in printing fourteen blank pages in the September 1916 issue under the announcement that they hoped to edit "a magazine of Art. The September issue is offered as a Want Ad" (*PQ* 97). This was a publicity gesture worthy of Pound himself that convinced him that Anderson had high standards. In taking on the new magazine he still thought in terms of a "movement," but he did not characterize it through a name, like imagism or vorticism, but through individual writers. A letter to Anderson in March 1917 explains that he wants "an 'official organ' (vile phrase). I mean I want a place where I and T. S. Eliot can appear once a month . . . and where James Joyce can appear when he likes, and where Wyndham Lewis can appear if he comes back from the war" (*P/LR* 6).

After the arrangements had been made, and Quinn agreed to pay for the material Pound solicited for the magazine, Pound announced his position as "Foreign Editor" of the review in what he called his "opening manifesto" (*P/LR* 20) in the May 1917 issue. After announcing that

Lewis, Eliot, and Joyce would be core contributors, he attacked *Poetry* as a means of defining his editorial position:

> *Poetry* has never been "the instrument" of my "radicalism." I respect Miss Monroe for all that she has done for the support of American poetry, but in the conduct of her magazine my voice and vote have always been the vote and voice of a minority. . . . *Poetry* has shown an unflagging courtesy to a lot of old fools and fogies whom I should have told to go to hell.

He continued by attacking *Poetry*'s frequent censoring of its poems, especially when submissions offended Christian morality. *The Little Review,* on the contrary, would not bow to local "codes of propriety." He held up the works of Joyce, Lewis, and Eliot as a standard because "they are practically the only works of the time in which the creative element is present, which in any way show invention, or a progress beyond precedent work." His principle of fostering individuals rather than a movement is stated in the closing sentences of the manifesto: "There is no misanthropy in a thorough contempt for the mob. There is no respect for mankind save in respect for detached individuals."[14]

Pound had decided that avant-garde literature could only be marketed though a magazine that appealed to an elite, which in turn enforced his conception of modernist literature. In his view, Monroe's failing as an editor was to try to market poetry that appealed to a wide, democratic audience. He complained constantly about the Walt Whitman quotation on *Poetry*'s masthead: "To have great poetry we must have great audiences." The July issue of *The Little Review* began carrying on its masthead the contradictory slogan: "Making No Compromise with the Public Taste." Similarly, Pound disliked the policy of the American journal *Seven Arts,* which claimed it wanted to express the spirit of the "community." He wrote to Quinn that "Great Arts is [*sic*] NEVER popular to start with. They [*Seven Arts*] want to be popular and good all at once,,????!!!!!!!!" (*P/Q* 93).

The material Pound sent *The Little Review* of course made few compromises with the community or public taste. In the May 1919 issue, Pound's "manifesto" is followed by T. S. Eliot's prose sketch "Eeldrop and Appleplex," in which two characters based on Eliot himself and Pound "mingle with the mob" in order to record its habits with Flaubertian contempt. A typical Eeldrop observation is that the "majority of mankind live on paper currency . . . they never see actual coinage."[15] In the same issue, the first of Lewis's "Imaginary Letters" (of a soldier to his unfaithful wife) explores the difficulties of the artist who must live among the "herd" of ordinary people. In the following June issue Pound's imaginary dialogue with Rabelais ("An Anachronism at Chinon") reflects on the relative freedom of expression in Rabelais's era in comparison with ours. When Lewis's service in France interrupted the flow of his "Imaginary Letters," Pound took up the series in September 1917 with a letter on "The Nonsense about Art for the Many." As he told Anderson, he wanted "to start off the new order of things with a bang" and publish something "to catch edgeways on the public ivory" (*P/LR* 15).

If he indeed wanted to set the public's teeth on edge, he got his wish when the October issue brought the first of five suppressions of *The Little Review* by the U.S. Post Office. Wyndham Lewis's short story "Cantleman's Spring-Mate" (the echo of the word *cattleman* in the title suggests Lewis's protagonist is above the "herd") narrates a casual affair of a soldier with a country girl before he returns to the war. Although it was suppressed because of its alleged obscenity, the cynicism it expresses toward the Darwinian struggle in the trenches was probably even more offensive to the judge who made the obscenity ruling. Margaret Anderson's editorial response to the suppression was as defiant as Pound could have wished: "*The Little Review* was founded in direct opposition to the prevalent art values in America. It would have no function or reason for being if it did not continually conflict with those values."[16]

After publishing blank pages in her magazine rather than compromise her standards, Anderson had now in effect published a blank issue, since the "Cantleman" issue could not be mailed to subscribers. She was caught up in the dilemma that a continual conflict with prevalent values would mean that no one would read her magazine. Pound considered it a good sign if a poem or story would "irritate a number of people" (*P/LR* 21). But how long could such a magazine survive, and what could it accomplish?

The answer is that it could not survive for long (*BLAST* lasted two issues), but what it could accomplish is the early publication of the central work of modernist literature, *Ulysses*. Joyce's work did more than set people's teeth on edge. It excited hostile and well-organized opposition from people like John Sumner of the New York Society for the Prevention of Vice and Judge Augustus Hand. Anderson and Heap suffered through four separate suppressions for publishing *Ulysses*. The obscenity trial concerning the "Nausicäa" episode in the July–August 1920 issue almost sent them to prison and resulted in the loss of Quinn's subsidy, even though John Quinn supported them with money and legal representation through all the suppressions. Quinn admired *Ulysses* as much as Pound did and supported the magazine principally because it was supporting Joyce. It is impossible to imagine Harriet Monroe, with her group of businessmen backers, publishing even one chapter of a work like *Ulysses*, much less supporting the publication through numerous legal difficulties. Nevertheless, both Pound and Quinn wanted to stop publishing the episodes before the editors did, because the prosecution jeopardized the publication of *Ulysses* in book form. Soon after the court decision that prevented further serial publication of *Ulysses,* the magazine was indeed suspended in early 1921 until it was reorganized as a quarterly—ending its career in 1929 as a Parisian journal. Nevertheless, when looking back on the *Little Review* era, both Anderson and Pound felt that it was *Ulysses* that justified the magazine's existence. As Pound wrote to Quinn even before the final suppression of the magazine, "the Little Rev. may have been crazy, but it had a definite and calculable madness" (*P/Q* 196). The "craziness" in Pound's campaign for the modernist experiment was that it limited its audience and finally burned itself out.

Yet Pound's campaign seems at least "calculable madness" once one appreciates the kind of modernism he was publicizing. So far the term *modernism* has been used historically to identify the literature written from the first imagist poems (1912) until the publication of two works championed by Pound, *Ulysses* and *The Waste Land* (1922). What Pound meant, however, when he used the term "modern experiment" (*SL* 180) or "ultra-modern" (*SL* 11) is best defined by the term *avant-garde*. Pound's modernism implies experimentation and originality, and it finds its natural expression in short-lived journals such as *BLAST*. Although *The Little Review* was designed as a conventional literary review, Pound turned it into an avant-garde one and so necessarily shortened its life. Pound's constant emphasis, as in his *Little Review* "manifesto," is upon works that "show invention, or a progress beyond" earlier works. He founded a literary movement so contemporary that it needed renovating and even a name change within the year of its birth. The relation of Pound's modernism to its audience is also avant-garde in that its purpose is either *épater le bourgeoisie* or to give its readers a radically new perspective on the world. Certainly *The Waste Land* was such an innovative and shocking new work, and it was the kind of poem *The Little Review* was meant to publish. However, with John Quinn's help, Pound placed Eliot's poem in *The Dial* rather than in *The Little Review* because the *Dial* payment was far better.

Considering Eliot's conception of modernism, it may be appropriate that it appeared in a less avant-garde publication. Eliot, like D. H. Lawrence and W. B. Yeats, may be distinguished as modernists from the essential *Little Review* authors, Joyce and Pound. Stanley Sultan does so in *Eliot, Joyce, and Company*, saying that their modernism is illuminated by

> Pound's imperative, "Make It New," and by [its] second historical for-mulation—involving "leaps from vanguard to vanguard" in Harold Rosenberg's phrase. . . . It is a uniquely modernist development because Joyce and Pound turned the means of the revolution in art into its end. Neither the generation of Conrad and Yeats, nor Joyce's and Pound's contemporaries, including Eliot, shared their emphasis on innovation for its own sake.[17]

Thus Pound and Joyce continue creating, in *The Cantos* and *Finnegans Wake*, innovative and difficult works for little magazines like *The Little Review* (Paris), *The Transatlantic Review, Transition,* and *The Exile* and publishing them through private presses such as Shakespeare and Co. *(Ulysses)* and Three Mountains Press *(A Draft of XVI Cantos)*. As entrepreneur and advertiser, Pound went from marketing a broad-based product such as imagism to radically experimental works for a select audience.

Our metaphor of marketing modernism, which compares artworks to commodities and literary movements to advertising campaigns, illumi-nates Pound's role in the development of modernism. But the trope is of course limited because anyone who markets a product that appeals to the few and antagonizes the many does not belong in the world of commer-cial advertising. Pound's motives were obviously more idealistic than those of a Madison Avenue executive. Yet his literary campaigns do raise the question of whether Pound avoided contamination by the advertising technique Margaret Anderson manipulated so well. He considered this issue himself when he assured her that he was not "particularly propa-gandist" (*P/LR* 9) but admitted to her some months later that he should "get out of the big stick habit" (*P/LR* 65) in supporting his favorite writers. To William Carlos Williams he admitted he had "to work hard enough to escape, not propagande, but getting centered in propagande" (*SL* 123).

There is in fact a close parallel between the techniques of modern advertising and imagist techniques. James Joyce seems to notice this parallel in *Ulysses*. Joyce's Leopold Bloom is an advertising canvasser who has designed an advertisement using crossed keys to promote a tea and wine merchant named Alexander Keyes. The image of the keys also refers to the crossed keys of the parliament on the Isle of Man. Since this British island has an independent parliament, the crossed keys carry a reference to Home Rule, as well as the "keys to the kingdom" of the Catholic Church. This intellectual and emotional complex has no other purpose than to dispose prospective Irish customers favorably toward Keyes's wine, spirit, and tea shop. Each night before sleep Bloom meditates on the perfect advertisement in terms of Pound's imagist principles: "Some one sole unique advertisement to cause passers to stop in wonder, a poster novelty, with all extraneous accretions excluded, reduced to its simplest and most efficient terms not exceeding the span of casual vision and congruous with the velocity of modern life."[18]

Pound himself disapproved of just such a "poster novelty" when he wrote to John Quinn in 1917 about a war bond poster he saw at the London town hall.

> Vision. Poster reproducing Whistler's portrait of his mother. Half covered with inscription
>
> OLD AGE IS COMING
> BUY WAR BONDS.
>
> This is, I suppose, the supreme honour democracy can pay to an artist.[19]

The honor of appropriating the artist's visual and verbal techniques has now gone so far that the image in poetry has been swamped by the flow of images in advertising. Marjorie Perloff deplores what has happened to what is virtually "Imagist doctrine" in modern advertisements: "Exact treatment of the thing, accuracy of presentation, precise definition—these Poundian principles have now been transferred to the realm of copywriting."[20] Her comment implies no criticism of Pound. Her critical doubts about how the image is being used in contemporary poetry has to do

"with the actual production and dissemination of images in our culture."
For example, advertisements no longer carry much narrative or descriptive information. Perloff observes how advertisements from the American 1930s reveal the "predominance of text over image," and a narrative
(for example, how a woman never attracted a mate because she had
neglected to use Listerine) was more important than the illustration.[21]

Yet the emphasis of image over text, or slogan over narrative, actually
developed much earlier, and just as Pound's poetic career was beginning.
As early as the 1890s slogans that followed the second imagist principle of
"using no word that does not contribute to the presentation" were recognized throughout the English-speaking world: for example,
"Absolutely Pure" in a baking powder commercial, or "the Beer that
made Milwaukee famous." A slogan like "He won't be happy til he gets
it" is the caption for a picture of a baby reaching for Pears' soap.[22] When
Pound spoke of "direct treatment of the thing," he meant the poet should
present "concrete things" (*SL* 49) or particulars rather than generalize.
But the "thing" as commodity was culturally pervasive since at least
"The Great Exhibition of Things" at the Crystal Palace (1851).[23] As noted
earlier, *The Little Review* was sophisticated enough about advertising to
run blank pages to serve as want ads for true art. Another innovation was
an advertisement that solicited ads from Chicago businesses by compli-
menting or insulting them. Anderson's most reliable advertisers were
Mason and Hamlin pianos, which, true to the *Review*'s elite spirit, were
endorsed by the greatest pianists of the day (fig. 1). Some advertisements
did carry substantial verbal descriptions—for example, concerning the
quality of Goodyear no-skid tires. But the Goodyear advertisement's
main feature was the image of a tire as a rainbow that poetically presaged
good driving weather (fig. 2). And some *Little Review* advertisements
were as purely imagistic as any in a modern magazine. As B. L. Reid
observed, the most sexually provocative thing published by *The Little
Review* was not *Ulysses* but the endorsement by Mary Garden for
Crane's Chocolates (fig. 3), which simply presented the opera singer's
décolleté image with a brief quotation.[24]

The problem Perloff analyzes is not a matter of the commercializing of
the poet's craft but of both popular and elite culture responding to the
same emphasis upon the "thing." Advertising images and a consumerist
culture were already powerful enough in Pound's time to transform the
poet's technique into the advertiser's trick. Joyce's gentle satire of
Bloom's poster and *The Little Review* advertisements shows how perva-

Mason & Hamlin advertisement. The Little Review, 2
(March 1915): 64.

The Promise of A Better Tire Day

Goodyear Fortified Tires came, years ago, to promise men a better tire day. And that promise was fulfilled.

They made Goodyear the largest-selling tire in the world, a place it has held ever since. Last year men bought 1,479,883—about one for each car in use.

Not Magical

Don't expect in the Goodyear a magical tire. It is not exempt from mishap and misuse.

It won top place because it averaged best. It did that because, in five great ways, it excels every other tire. It combats in five ways, exclusive to Goodyear, these six major troubles—

Rim-Cuts	**Insecurity**
Blowouts	**Punctures**
Loose Treads	**Skidding**

One way—our "On-Air" cure — costs us $450,000 yearly. One comes through forming in each tire hundreds of large rubber rivets. One compels us to vulcanize in each tire base 126 braided piano wires.

One comes through our double-thick All-Weather tread, with its sharp, tough, resistless grips. These things together mean a super-tire.

Lower Prices

Yet these costly-built tires, in the past two years, have been thrice reduced in price. Our last reduction—on February 1st—brings the two-year total to 45%.

Never has a tire given so much for the money as Fortified Tires do now. We ask you, for your own sake, to prove it. Any dealer will supply you.

The Goodyear Tire & Rubber Company, Akron, O.

Crane's
Mary Garden Chocolates

"Your Chocolates are really the finest I have ever tasted anywhere in the World"

Mary Garden

Crane's Mary Garden Chocolates advertisement. The Little Review, 6 (April 1920): 64.

sive imagistic advertising techniques were early in the century. In the case
of Pound's image as well as the advertising image, authority is derived
from its "direct treatment of the thing." The thing or commodity is present so convincingly—for example, a frosty bottle of ice-cold Coke—that
it appears unquestionably "The Real Thing©".

An advertisement does not reason one into the conviction that Coke,
say, is better than Pepsi. It simply "presents," as the imagist recommended. The image is the argument. Pound made this point clearly in his
"Vorticism" essay: "An image, in our sense, is real because we know it
directly."[25] This notion of a direct, unmediated access to reality takes the
poet's philosophical naïveté to its limit. The qualification "in our sense"
does hint that Pound knows he is overstating for effect. Yet in Pound's
poetry, as in advertising, the assumption is indeed that the vividly present
image is the truth—intensity is all. Vincent Sherry notes that in Pound's
work "the radical particularity of the Image underwrites the autonomy
of the Self, a kind of heroic individuality. Antistatist and libertarian as
this sign may be, it may serve the designs of the tyrannical, self-
authorizing ego."[26] Daniel Bell's criticism of modernism's preoccupation
with the "autonomous self" supports Sherry's criticism of Pound's development. In *The Cultural Contradictions of Capitalism,* Bell connects the
capitalist entrepreneur and the artist in a way that seems entirely relevant
to Pound: "In the economy, there arises the bourgeois entrepreneur. . . .
In the culture, we have the rise of the independent artist. . . . The impulse
driving both the entrepreneur and the artist is a restlessness to search out
the new, to rework nature, and to refashion consciousness."[27] Bell notes
the contradiction that the entrepreneur's view of the self is radical in its
commitment to absolute freedom and continuous innovation, yet dependent on a conservative, bourgeois society. The same clash of avant-garde
tendency and cultural conservatism defines Pound.

Pound's development from a rebel against all authority to a fascist
supporter of Mussolini is so contradictory that the poet's critics are only
now beginning to analyze, rather than dismiss or ignore, the link between
his art and his politics. Bell makes the same point about modernist techniques in art that Perloff develops at length in *Radical Artifice:* "The
impulse to rebellion has been institutionalized by the 'cultural mass' and
its experimental forms have become the syntax and semiotics of advertising and haute couture. As a cultural style, it exists as radical chic."[28]
Perloff shows how the decadence of imagist style dominated poetry in the

second half of our century. However, the cultural contradictions that led to this stylistic corruption were already full-blown in Pound's art.

The mysterious "doctrine of the Image" did indeed develop, given Pound's own "big-stick habit," into the authoritarian rhetoric that Vincent Sherry describes. Pound presents his images with a directness and certitude that is unquestionably vivid. In *Hugh Selwyn Mauberley*, brief notations such as "The tea-rose tea-gown etc. / Supplants the mousseline of Cos" present his condemnation of modern culture against a backdrop of classical culture. "Quick eyes gone under earth's lid" vividly notes the loss of young men in the war. A setting of "pickled foetuses and bottled bones" characterizes a failed poet, and the "cream gilded cabin of his steam yacht" a successful novelist.[29] Although Pound's judgments on a decadent society are certainly harshly authoritative, such images do not raise any special problems in his early poetry. For example, no one would disagree that luxurious yachts suggest an inauthentic writer, though in fact Pound later admitted that he had judged the novelist in question, Arnold Bennett, too harshly; and *Mauberley*'s caricature of Max Beerbohm seems based on the mistaken assumption that Beerbohm was Jewish.[30]

Pound's judgments are deeply troubling as he takes fascist positions and continues to use his imagistic technique, renamed the "ideogrammic method," in *The Cantos*. The famous image that opens *The Pisan Cantos* implies a judgment on Mussolini and fascism that is movingly expressed and deeply felt, yet totally unacceptable to almost any poetry reader one can imagine.

> The enormous tragedy of the dream in the peasant's bent shoulders
> Manes! Manes was tanned and stuffed,
> Thus Ben and la Clara *a Milano*
>   by the heel at Milano
> That maggots shd/ eat the dead bullock
> DIGONOS, Δίγονος, but the twice crucified
>   where in history will you find it?[31]

Pound refers to the newspaper photograph of Mussolini and his mistress Claretta Petacci, their bodies hanging from their feet in Milan, to express his judgment on the tragic course of the war. Pound is absolutely sure of his judgment that Mussolini is yet another heroic individual, like

Dionysus or even Christ, whose noble designs have been betrayed. There is not the slightest suspicion here that Mussolini, on the contrary, was in any sense responsible for the peasant's misery. The image presents the judgment, and the judgment is based on nothing more than Pound's ability to present it so intensely. Pound's imagistic rhetoric here functions as Guy Debord says that "spectacular discourse" (the "flow of images" in our culture) functions in isolating an image from its context. In Pound's case, it rather involves presenting a false context for the image by comparing Mussolini to Christ and the twice-born ("Digonos") to Dionysus. Debord's statement that "spectacular discourse leaves no room for any reply" is also true of Pound's image of Mussolini's fall.[32] As Sherry and Bell note, nothing more than the authority of the artist's ego validates this kind of artistic discourse. In the terms of Pound's "Vorticism" essay, the image is intense, vivid, "direct"—and therefore "in our sense . . . real."

Along with Vincent Sherry, Philip Kuberski is a recent critic who explores this link between Pound's imagism and his political views. Like Stanley Sultan, he too defines Pound's modernism in terms of technique, experiment, and innovation and shows how Pound's art reflects "the nascent forms of technological and mass discourse; the splintering of the subject and syntax, the use of the single 'image,' montage, and collage all indicate ways in which Pound's poetry mirrors the age of telegraphy, radio, cinema, and advertising."[33] Although he appears to find a direct link between Pound's poetics and his fascism, Kuberski's own analysis quoted above rather supports Sherry's view that Pound's "radical Image stand[s] poised . . . between opposite possibilities; between a turn to the left and a slide to the right."[34] Pound himself misapplied imagist poetics when they served fascist propaganda; they are now misappropriated by capitalist society. Pound's impulse to advertise and propagandize for a radically new movement was crucial to the birth of modernism in the arts. But imagist technique in the service of an authoritarian spirit was inevitably corrupted by a society preoccupied with the direct treatment of things.

NOTES

1. As quoted in Jean Gould, *Amy: The World of Amy Lowell and the Imagist Movement* (New York: Dodd, Mead, 1975), p. 137.

2. *Selected Letters of Ezra Pound: 1907–1941*, ed. D. D. Paige (New York:

New Directions, 1971), p. 11. Subsequent references appear parenthetically in the text, abbreviated *SL*. H.D.'s description of Pound's naming of her as an imagist is in her *End to Torment: A Memoir of Ezra Pound,* ed. Michael King (New York: New Directions, 1979).

3. Harriet Monroe, *A Poet's Life: Seventy Years in a Changing World* (New York: Macmillan, 1938), p. 267.

4. *Pound/The Little Review: The Letters of Ezra Pound to Margaret Anderson* (New York: New Directions, 1988), p. 155. Subsequent references appear parenthetically in the text, abbreviated *P/LR*.

5. "Imagisme" quoted in Monroe, *A Poet's Life,* p. 297. This note was technically written by F. S. Flint, who "sought out an Imagiste" (Pound) for the information in his note.

6. Pound, "A Few Don'ts by an Imagiste," in *Literary Essays of Ezra Pound,* ed. T. S. Eliot (New York: New Directions, 1968), p. 4.

7. William Pratt, ed., *The Imagist Poem* (New York: E. P. Dutton, 1963), p. 20.

8. Pound, "Vortex," in *BLAST,* no. 1, ed. Wyndham Lewis (1914), p. 153.

9. Hugh Kenner, *The Pound Era* (Berkeley and Los Angeles: University of California Press, 1971), p. 191.

10. *The Selected Letters of Ezra Pound to John Quinn: 1915–1924* (Durham, N.C.: Duke University Press, 1991), pp. 71, 53. Subsequent references appear parenthetically in the text, abbreviated *P/Q*.

11. Ezra Pound to John Quinn, 17 August 1917 (John Quinn Archive, New York Public Library; see also *P/Q*, p. 61. I am grateful to the New York Public Library for permission to quote from the unpublished letters of Ezra Pound to John Quinn.

12. Ezra Pound to John Quinn, 30 May 1916; John Quinn Archive, New York Public Library.

13. Ezra Pound to John Quinn, 3 September 1916 and May 1917; John Quinn Archive, New York Public Library.

14. Pound, "Judicial Opinion (Our Suppressed October Issue)," *Little Review* 4 (May 1917): 3–6.

15. T. S. Eliot, "Eeldrop and Appleplex," *Little Review* 4 (May 1917): 7, 10.

16. Margaret Anderson, "Editorial," *Little Review* 4 (December 1917): 48.

17. Stanley Sultan, *Eliot, Joyce, and Company* (New York: Oxford University Press, 1987), p. 111.

18. James Joyce, *Ulysses,* ed. Hans Walter Gabler et al. (New York: Random House, 1986), p. 592.

19. Ezra Pound to John Quinn, 29 December 1917; John Quinn Archive, New York Public Library.

20. Marjorie Perloff, *Radical Artifice: Writing Poetry in the Age of Media* (Chicago: University of Chicago Press, 1991), p. 94.

21. Ibid., p. 57.

22. Frank Presbrey, *The History and Development of Advertising* (Garden City, N.Y.: Doubleday, Doran, 1929), pp. 365, 368.

23. See chapter 1, "The Great Exhibition of Things," in Thomas Richards, *The Commodity Culture of Victorian England* (Stanford: Stanford University Press, 1990), pp. 1–72.

24. B. L. Reid, *The Man from New York* (New York: Oxford University Press, 1968), p. 454.

25. Pound, "Vorticism," in *Gaudier-Brzeska: A Memoir* (New York: New Directions, 1974), p. 86.

26. Vincent Sherry, *Ezra Pound, Wyndham Lewis, and Radical Modernism* (New York: Oxford University Press, 1993), p. 46.

27. Daniel Bell, *The Cultural Contradictions of Capitalism* (New York: Basic Books, 1976), p. 16.

28. Ibid., p. 20.

29. Pound, "Hugh Selwyn Mauberley," in *Personae: The Shorter Poems of Ezra Pound,* rev. ed. (New York: New Directions, 1990), pp. 186, 188, 190–91.

30. See Pound's footnote on Bennett in *Literary Essays,* p. 429.

31. *The Cantos of Ezra Pound,* eleventh printing (New York: New Directions, 1989), p. 439.

32. Guy Debord, *Comments on the Society of the Spectacle,* trans. Malcolm Imrie (New York: Verso, 1990), pp. 28–29.

33. Philip Kuberski, *A Calculus of Ezra Pound: Vocations of the American Sign* (Gainesville: University Press of Florida, 1992), p. 186.

34. Sherry, *Radical Modernism,* p. 46.

"I Can Have More Than Enough Power to Satisfy Me": T. S. Eliot's Construction of His Audience

Leonard Diepeveen

That's not your style at all. You let me throw the bricks through the front window. You go in at the back door and take out the swag.

Ezra Pound to T. S. Eliot, ca. 1916

In 1917 T. S. Eliot, beginning to be noticed as one of the new poets in English, published "Reflections on 'Vers Libre,'" his first nonreview essay, in *The New Statesman*. The move seems strategically awkward for someone setting out to reform contemporary poetry. After all, the literary section of *The New Statesman* was significantly more conservative than those of several other magazines in which Eliot could have published at the time. Although socialist in its political pages (employing George Bernard Shaw as one of its two major writers and deriving its initial mailing list of potential subscribers from lists of supporters of the National Committee for the Prevention of Destitution and the Fabian Society), *The New Statesman* presented an equally odd setting for Eliot in its literary pages—although for quite a different reason.[1] Its literary editor was J. C. Squire, promoter of the Georgian poets, and someone whom Eliot was publicly to describe in a few years as a person "whose solemn trifling fascinates multitudes."[2] Together with Robert Lynd, Squire created a chatty, genteel setting for the promotion of conservative writing—both Eliot's "Prufrock" and his emphasis on "professionalism" were out of place in this setting.[3]

But "Reflections on 'Vers Libre'" fits its conservative context, and in doing so it establishes Eliot's conventionality more than it does his radicality; it makes him seem anything but avant-garde. Awkwardly fitting a poet who began his career two years earlier with "The Love Song of J. Alfred Prufrock" and several contributions to *BLAST*, Eliot's Olympian conclusion meets the most conventional expectations: "we conclude that the division between Conservative Verse and *vers libre* does not exist, for there is only good verse, bad verse, and chaos."[4]

Yet in its conservatism "Vers Libre" doesn't simply satisfy suspicions that one can read the purposeful beginnings of conservatism in Eliot's early essays—although that may be true. The oddness of this essay serves a moil of conflicting agendas, including a strategy that does not so much assert a stated argument as insinuate itself by suggestion into many of Eliot's other early essays, a strategy that one can begin to see in "Vers Libre" in an awkwardness that critics have yet to remark on. The essay begins oddly; Eliot starts what purports to be an attack on contemporary *poetry* with an attack on a contemporary *reader*: "A lady, renowned in her small circle for the accuracy of her stop-press information of literature, complains to me of a growing pococurantism. 'Since the Russians came in I can read nothing else. I have finished Dostoevski, and I do not know what to do'" (*SP* 31). As Eliot reports it, his response was measured, confident, one in which he "suggested" that she turn to Dickens, whom Dostoyevsky apparently admired. After hearing in turn the reader's complaint that Dostoyevsky was a realist while Dickens was a sentimentalist, Eliot went on.

> I reflected on the amours of Sonia and Raskolnikov, but forbore to press the point, and I proposed *It Is Never too Late to Mend.* "But one cannot read the Victorians at all!" While I was extracting the virtues of the proposition that Dostoevski is a Christian, while Charles Read is merely pious, she added that she could no longer read any verse but *vers libre.* (*SP* 31)

This is the Eliot that no one likes to have around, the self-assured patriarch who always manages to say something ugly and embarrassing. On the other hand, that Eliot can manage to be embarrassing in this way at the age of twenty-eight, with his first book of poems yet to be published, is a testament to his rhetorical adroitness. While quoting a person whose gender is meant silently to undermine her seriousness, Eliot paraphrases himself, a move that removes the personality and urgency of conversational syntax from the representation of his thoughts. It gives him a calm objectivity in which he "suggests," "reflects," "forebears," and "extracts." This rhetorical control should suggest Eliot's finesse rather than his clumsiness, for this tone, which has since earned him enmity, did not function primarily to eliminate readers from modernism; rather, it had a purpose of winning readers to himself early in this century.

Eliot secured his reputation in the time spanning his first series of literary essays in *The New Statesman* and *The Egoist* in 1916–17 and the essays he was writing for the *Times Literary Supplement* and the *Criterion* in 1926. What happened after that was momentum—by 1926 his major early poems and essays were written, and the momentum created by this point was able to withstand Eliot's literary-political moves from 1927 to 1930. Using Eliot's essays to discuss how a reputation is built, Louis Menand tells part of the story in *Discovering Modernism,* looking at, among other things, how Eliot distances himself from earlier writers. Scholarship has demonstrated the brilliance of Harold Bloom's paradigm: Eliot creates space for himself by separating himself from earlier writers, by rewriting them. But this rewriting has a particular slant that ought to make us suspect its completeness. Eliot's career is accompanied with selective silences foreign to many other modernist writers; he does not enlist the sorts of force he could have. In his biography of Eliot, Peter Ackroyd makes the point that Eliot early in his career had professional associations with a bewildering variety of people, many holding antagonistic literary and political views.[5] This variety does not imply gregariousness; it suggests a useful slipperiness and inscrutability for which Eliot's social persona became famous—in 1930, Pound described Eliot as someone "who has arrived at the supreme Eminence among English critics largely through disguising himself as a corpse."[6] Thus, in 1919 Eliot writes to his mother of his pleasure at being "isolated and detached."[7] Socially and aesthetically aloof, he does not belong to any single set of writers; he separates himself from avant-garde "isms"; he does not write manifestos. In short, he does not make the typical allegiances and antagonisms that many writers of the time used to create a context and elbow room for their writing.

Eliot's selective silence does not mean he was more passive about his reputation than was a writer like Pound. Nor does the silence imply that Eliot's reputation can be accounted for solely by his writing being transparently superior to that of other writers of his generation. Writers don't just clear space by distancing themselves from past writers or by forming allegiances with contemporary writers; they also clear space for themselves by "creating" an audience. And for Eliot this reforming of an audience is a strategy more primary than his often-noticed strategy of rewriting earlier writers, for that rewriting always serves this more general strategy, which appears throughout his essays, and which unites the reviews of contemporary culture with his writing about earlier culture.[8] Apparently believing that one can more efficiently change the literary landscape by directing his attention to changing reading habits than to changing how poets write (lesser poets, after all, will adapt themselves to changed reading habits), Eliot shapes his audience in order to refocus its horizon of expectations, to recreate it in a more useful form. Using primarily the essays Eliot wrote between 1916 and 1926, this essay will show how Eliot clears space for his own poetry by using his own peculiar apparatus—haphazard statements that utilize the language of elitism and exclusion to reform the expectations of and attract readers most useful to the success of his poetry.[9]

The opening quotation from "Reflections on 'Vers Libre'" thus forms part of a pattern. Although they are never the ostensible subject of these early, spectacular essays (including "Lancelot Andrewes," "Andrew Marvell," "The Metaphysical Poets," and "Tradition and the Individual Talent"), references to readers crowd Eliot's writing.[10] These essays, so aggressively illuminating aspects of Eliot's poetry, have consequently hidden what they haphazardly reveal about Eliot's management of his reputation. The chance comments mean something; the fact that they are not systematized does not diminish them, for Eliot was not a systematic aesthetician. With the exception of "Tradition and the Individual Talent," there is no systematizing theory in his essays; theory arrives obliquely, usually as part of a review aimed at the specific demands of a specific work.[11] Generally, scholars have treated Eliot's references to readers in combination with his comments about the literary canon as a mark of Eliot's "tone" or his cultural anxiety.[12] Both theses see the same effect in the references—restriction, securing a place for the author in an exclusive literary club, where Eliot creates the restrictions for membership. Yet his comments about readers reveal more than his peculiar mix of literary and social attitudes. Eliot may in fact be elitist and have an arrogant tone, but an important question that has not been asked is how he *used* these qualities.[13]

An answer to this question will show that "Reflections on 'Vers Libre'" is less an analysis of current writing than it is an attack on public reading habits, presented in a conservative guise that readers will easily swallow. After the opening anecdote quoted above, Eliot continues: "It is assumed that *vers libre* exists. It is assumed that *vers libre* is a school; that it consists of certain theories" (*SP* 31). Eliot's irritation is more with *readers'* assumptions than with poetic craft, an emphasis that continues even when he turns to the ostensible subject of his essay, contemporary poetry: "I am aware that many writers of *vers libre* have introduced such innovations, and that the novelty of their choice and manipulation of material is confused—if not in their own minds, in the minds of many of their readers—with the novelty of the form" (*SP* 32). According to the way Eliot frames the discussion, the problem with the literary marketplace is more with its consumers than its producers. In his critical writings from 1916 to 1926, Eliot more typically vents his spleen at other critics and the general reader (especially the general reader, for reasons that will become clear) than at other poets. The essay genre, although he privately complained about the writing of reviews, gave him the perfect occasion to discuss readers' tastes, both in his selection of a canon, and—more important—in how to read that canon.[14] That opportunity is why Eliot, who was not self-destructive, would apparently turn on a potential audience, for he found the peculiar framing of his attack a useful way to change his audience's expectations about how and whom to read.

Of course, not all of Eliot's awareness of his audience has his unique imprint. Eliot was aware, in the obvious way all writers are aware, how public interpretations of a poet affect a reputation. To John Quinn in 1919 he wrote: "I hear that several weeks ago the *New Republic* referred to me in very flattering terms. I have not seen the paper and do not know the date, but it ought to be of influence with a publisher" (*L* 313). Thanking Richard Aldington for a positive review of *The Sacred Wood*, Eliot hoped that the review would "at least come to the notice of Messrs. Methuen, against whom I have no grievance except that they chose 'La figlia che piange' to print in an anthology because it is the mildest of my productions" (*L* 468). Eliot was also ordinary in noticing the negative power a periodical publisher could wield. Thus, in referring to his favorite enemy of the early 1920s, J. C. Squire, Eliot writes: "*The London Mercury,* which started with a great deal of advertisement, will, I hope, fail in a few years' time. It is run by a small clique of bad writers. J. C. Squire, the editor, knows nothing about poetry; but he is the cleverest journalist in London. If he succeeds, it will be impossible to get anything good published" (*L* 358). Eliot went on to argue that Squire, whose *London Mercury* had a large readership that neared ten thousand in 1921,[15] controlled through his influence an additional five or six literary periodicals—all but the *Athenaeum* and the *Times Literary Supplement,* where

Eliot did virtually all of his London publishing from 1920 until late in 1922, when the pages of the *Criterion* became an additional site.

But some of Eliot's awareness of reputation was not so obvious and was much more active than the above anecdotes, in which Eliot portrays himself as he did to his family, as "isolated and detached," as the passive recipient of notice. Eliot's letters to his family also reveal in these years someone anxious to give his relations evidence of how well he was doing as a writer, someone who was aware of the forces that he could use to shape his reputation. To his mother in March 1919 he wrote about the select audience he was attracting by publishing in journals with extremely small circulation, such as *The Egoist*, through which he was "getting to be looked up to by people who are far better known to the general reader than I." Eliot went on to claim other forms of awareness of how to shape his public.

> There is a small and select public which regards me as the best living critic, as well as the best living poet, in England. I shall of course write for the *Ath. [Athenaeum]* and keep my finger in it. I am much in sympathy with the editor, who is one of my most cordial admirers. With that and the *Egoist* and a young quarterly review which I am interested in, and which is glad to take anything I will give, I can have more than enough power to satisfy me. (L 280)[16]

Characterizing himself as the most *influential* (he italicizes the term) American critic in England since Henry James, Eliot concludes: "I know a great many people, but there are many more who would like to know me, and I can remain isolated and detached" (*L* 280). Eliot's demarcation of his audience, his awareness of the consequent forms and locations of power he can mobilize, and his awareness of his influence: these sorts of overt speculations should shape how we read his public writing.

Of course, Eliot's interest in his own reputation doesn't trumpet itself in his published writing, where the tone is calculated to establish his objectivity. The difference between his published and unpublished writing does not have to suggest, however, that his published writing was dishonest or that it has no linkage with his letters; rather, the public and private writing naturally correspond to the same vaguely stated but powerful interests.[17] The difference between his essays and his letters is in methods used to accomplish a single strategy. In *The Invisible Poet* Hugh Kenner argues that the tone of Eliot's essays changed according to the journal in which the essay appeared. Kenner also argues that Eliot's Olympian, pompous tone in his essays is a subversive form of humor, humor that an in-the-know audience would catch, but Kenner does not examine further ways in which it might function.[18] Further, this plausible theory doesn't quite handle why Eliot uses an identical tone to castigate readers both at Squire's fusty *New Statesman* and at Harriet Weaver's *Egoist,* with its more sophisticated, au courant readers—while the *Egoist* published installments of Joyce's *Ulysses* (and in the process got into some exhilarating legal trouble), Squire's review of the book complained that Joyce "has sunk a shaft down into the welter of nonsense which lies at the bottom of the mind, pumped up this stuff and presented it as criticism of life."[19] Such similarities in tone suggest that irony is not Eliot's dominant mode in essay writing and make more plausible Sumany Satpathy's rethinking of Kenner's thesis, in which Satpathy examines analogues to Eliot's tone and arguments in earlier issues of the *Times Literary Supplement* and argues that Eliot cultivated the *TLS* tone as a strategy for getting published.[20]

But Eliot's tone has a function beyond this, for it does not stop its work once it has helped him to get published. The further possibilities lie in the subversion of Eliot's language. Consider the following example from one of Eliot's "London Letters" to the *Dial,* whose audience probably was not as uniformly sympathetic to the avant-garde as were readers of the *Little Review,* but who also were more sympathetic to the sort of poetry Eliot wrote than were readers of the *New Statesman:* "Looking back upon the past season in London—for no new season has yet begun—it remains certain that Strawinsky was our two months' lion. He has been the greatest success since Picasso."[21] This passage uses the language of the society/arts page of a provincial newspaper to describe artists that Eliot admired and thought part of modernism's transformation of contemporary culture. Eliot uses clichés comfortable to his audience but applies them to a modern subject that he believes in. We are meant to take the substance of the assertion straight, but what about the form of the assertion? In conjunction with the substance, the form is subversive, but not subversive in the sense that Eliot is exchanging a knowing wink with his readers. Rather, the tone calms suspicions so that an unstated assertion slips in: Stravinsky is socially acceptable *and* modern.

Eliot's rhetorical strategy divides his readers into two useful groups that serve as the focus of his discontent: critics and the reading public. His discussion of critics is overt, specific, and useful, while not ingenious for establishing his power. According to Eliot in his 1920 "A Brief Treatise on the Criticism of Poetry," bad critics—frequently the same people as bad poets—have no method;[22] as he was to grumble more specifically in the next year, they read for the wrong things.

> There is Mr. Clutton-Brock, whose attention is not focussed upon literature but upon a very mild type of philosophic humanitarian religion; he is like a very intelligent archdeacon. There is Mr. Robert Lynd, who has successfully cultivated the typical vices of daily journalism and has risen to the top of his profession; and there is Mr. Squire, whose solemn trifling fascinates multitudes.[23]

In contrast to his discussion of the general reader, Eliot's discussion of literary criticism is directed at a specific, quotable cultural institution, one that cannot mistake that it is being assaulted, while his discussion of readers attacks people with broader but less specific manifestations of cultural power. His discussion of critics is ostensibly directed at specific individuals, and it is respondable—it appears to have the possibility of becoming a discussion. But, as is the case with his discussion of general readers, Eliot's discussion of the opinions of J. C. Squire, Robert Lynd, and others is directed not to these writers but to an equally useful group that is listening in. These readers of the *Dial*, familiar with the opinions of these well-known critics, would read Eliot's blasts against what were at that time reasonable opinions held by the general literary public (and probably by many of the readers of Eliot's essay). But these attacks on these readers' own opinions were deflected by being attributed to other, specifically cited, individuals.

Eliot frequently complains of critics' effect on the general reader. Bad reviewing has bad consequences not so much because it is wrong, but because the reading public accepts what it is told: "If the public which reads reviews possessed any critical faculty of its own this would not much matter."[24] According to Eliot, cultural power proceeds from the top down, and powerful and inept critics stand in the way of the literary paradigm shift that Eliot and others were to effect in the coming years.

> We have, then, a large number of writers giving the public what it likes; and a large body of reviewers telling it that it is right to like what it likes; and the *Morning Post* to tell it that everything new is a symp-

tom of Bolshevism; and the *London Mercury* to tell it that it is already such an enlightened public that what it does not like cannot be really good.[25]

When Eliot discusses good criticism, his model of the top-down flow of power becomes benign, and less passively accepted. Good criticism differs from bad because it is objective, and the objectivity allows it to be put to a very different use than the coercion of the public. Eliot argues, "Every form of genuine criticism is directed toward creation. . . . The poetic critic is criticising poetry in order to create poetry."[26] In the same essay Eliot examines the question of literary criticism through his construction of the career and reputation of an imaginary poet, and he asserts that not only is good criticism directed toward creating poetry, but, like bad criticism, it is directed toward readers. Eliot ends his essay, somewhat—but only somewhat—archly: "So great is the value of good criticism, which is discreet advertisement."[27] Readers are directed through the "discreet advertisement" of the competent critic rather than through the "it is told" of bad criticism. Eliot, of course, implicitly defines his criticism as the former—discreet, but with a product to sell.

In using critics to clear space for himself, Eliot addresses their power as it is manifested in a public stance and typically positions himself as one who does not hold the power over the general reading public that these critics do. However, his rhetorical stance toward his public construction of "readers" is quite different. By setting up the "reader" as someone who has not given a written response, Eliot makes it easy for himself to conjecture opinions and activities to this reader, responses that always differ from Eliot's beliefs. Although occasionally he identified himself as a reader, Eliot never identified himself with the generic group *readers*— for Eliot, as for many modernists, groups are uglier than individuals (hence the problems with his tone). Eliot's readers don't necessarily correspond to reality; indeed, it may be in Eliot's interest that they don't. In referring to "the public" Eliot always constructs the reading public as a homogeneous group, a move that makes his discussion strategically much simpler, but probably less accurate. In any case, on Eliot's terms whether or not the reader is real is an untestable proposition—one cannot have a dialogue with Eliot's reader.

Eliot most often refers to what might be described as general readers. His readers, though, are always subject to qualitative analysis; they never just *are*—a curious move for someone intent on making literary criticism the domain of the objective statement, whose true object is always the poem and not something else. Lazy and confused, general readers are bad readers. Eliot argues that "the majority of men . . . seek the sense of ease which the sensitive man avoids."[28] Using a damning passive voice and a vague referent, Eliot writes, "It is assumed that *vers libre* exists" (*SP* 31). Readers have "prejudice"; they "have merely assimilated other people's personal tastes" (*SP* 209; *L* 317). And laziness is dangerous, he argues in a startling periodic sentence whose tone, when isolated from the pattern developing in Eliot's writing as a whole, could seem out of place and functionless in his *TLS* lead article on Lancelot Andrewes.

> To persons whose minds are habituated to feed on the vague jargon of our time, when we have a vocabulary for everything and exact ideas about nothing—when a word half understood, torn from its place in some alien or half-formed science, as of psychology, conceals from both writer and reader the meaninglessness of a statement, when all dogma is in doubt except the dogmas of sciences of which we have read in the newspapers, when the language of theology itself, under the influence of an undisciplined mysticism of popular philosophy, tends to become a language of tergiversation—Andrewes may seem pedantic and verbal. (*SP* 183, 184)[29]

For Eliot, the lazy reader is the confused reader. "Confused" is a term that he uses abundantly and with zest; confusion is a sin more heinous (but more easily corrected) than bad taste. Eliot argues, "In the common mind all interests are confused, and each degraded by the confusion."[30] Readers get their confusion from bad poets and bad critics. They get it, for example, from bad vers libre poets, whose "novelty of . . . choice and manipulation of material is confused—if not in their own minds, in the minds of many of their readers—with the novelty of the form" (*SP* 32). And they get it from critics: "If we attend to the confused cries of the newspaper critics and the susurrus of popular repetition that follows, we shall hear the names of poets in great numbers; if we seek not Blue-book knowledge but the enjoyment of poetry, and ask for a poem, we shall seldom find it" (*SP* 40). When it comes to specific works of poetry, confused readers have trouble recognizing good work. Readers of Pound "are apt to confuse the maturing of personality with desiccation of the emotions."[31]

Eliot's confused reader is not just a contextless psychological being;

Eliot gives the reader what can seem to be a gratuitous sociological characteristic as well. His reader is invariably middle class. In public, Eliot writes of "the English middle-class Grin";[32] in private he encourages Schofield Thayer, editor of the *Dial,* to "dart forth [his] scorn and pour the vials of [his] contumely upon the fair flat face of the people. Be Proud, but Genial, Affable, but Inflexible; be to the inhabitants of Greenwich Village a Flail, and to the Intellect of Indianapolis a Scourge" (*L* 236). Indianapolis was a safer (and much more typical) bet to make in public than Greenwich Village, as is clear when Eliot in a 1923 essay condemns "The possessors of the inner voice [who] ride ten in a compartment to a football match at Swansea, listening to the inner voice, which breathes the eternal message of vanity, fear, and lust."[33] In a review of Harold Monro's *Some Contemporary Poets,* Eliot ties to the middle class a useful if predictable quality: "at this very moment it enjoys the triumph, in intellectual matters, of being able to respect no other standards than its own." It is complacent aesthetically and socially: "Culture is traditional, and loves novelty; the General Reading Public knows no tradition, and loves staleness."[34]

Eliot's characterization of the reading public is, of course, hardly an original stance. What is ingenious about Eliot, however, is the use to which he puts this description. When Eliot wrote of the "General Reading Public," when he referred to "readers," or when he used a damning "they" or "it is said," the referent of these terms was clear in the minds of his readers. However, for the most part Eliot could also be sure that the readers of his indictments did not identify themselves with the indicted group. In their original form most of Eliot's essays reached a very small audience, and these readers' awareness of being part of an elite audience encouraged them to think of themselves more as individuals than as part of a mass audience, and certainly not as part of the general reading public. In 1922, Eliot, writing his London Letters to the *Dial,* was writing to a circulation of nine thousand per month; during the same year, *The Egoist* (where in 1919 he published "Tradition and the Individual Talent") reached two hundred subscribers per month.[35] Harold Monro's *Chapbook* announced its circulation as one thousand and the *Little Review* reached two thousand readers in April 1916, although its numbers were typically smaller, underscoring the motto that appeared on its cover: Making No Compromise with the Public Taste.[36] Even when Eliot reached the peak of his essay-writing career, in his editorship at the *Cri-*

terion, the circulation of that journal was usually around four hundred.[37] For all their differing aesthetic presuppositions, then, these journals' small circulations demanded of their readers a conscious act of literary/ sociological separation and identification. And when Eliot did write for a journal that had a large middle-class readership, the *Times Literary Supplement* (which announced sales of around twenty-three thousand when he wrote his articles "Andrew Marvell" and "The Metaphysical Poets" in 1921, and around thirty thousand when he wrote his pieces on Andrewes and Bradley in 1926 and 1927), he never gave his examples of bad readers a class designation.[38] As Eliot's letter to his mother shows, there is a useful public. This was not the public that Eliot referred to in his essays; it was the public that read these essays. At this stage in his career Eliot didn't want the general reader; he wanted his version of the literary world.

Other than a rough idea of their numbers, what can we know about this literary world, the actual public that read Eliot's essays?[39] The essays and letters themselves give imprecise clues, for to a large degree Eliot gave his actual readers the same sort of inexact designation but precise function that he gave to his characterization of middle-class readers. Eliot assigned his varying readers a single function: a group of readers that he wanted to nudge through a series of logical moves. Despite their single function, Eliot's audience was extremely varied in literary taste— there probably wasn't a lot of ideological crossover between the readers of *The Egoist* and *The New Statesman*. Yet many of Eliot's readers had a similar identity because they read these small literary magazines. Their small numbers identifies readers of all of these magazines as people with a committed, often professional, interest in literature. This professional interest does not completely disappear when Eliot wrote for the much larger audience that read the *Times Literary Supplement*. While the *TLS* had a large middle-class readership, it also, by virtue of this and its extensive reviewing, also attracted a professional audience composed of writers, critics, and publishers. That recurring audience in the midst of this variety should tell us something. While it is hardly ingenious detective work to claim that the audience for Eliot's literary criticism that appeared in literary magazines was partly a professional audience, it is striking that Eliot never mentions them in public as his audience. As one might expect, that silence is strategically useful. First, Eliot wants to keep up the *fiction* that he is writing for a general public (and he probably wants to some degree to directly influence this general audience). Second, the group of publishers and published writers who read Eliot's essays were extremely important, for by changing their reading habits Eliot could hope to achieve a greater change in the general literary community. Eliot thinks of critics as readers; Arthur Clutton-Brock, an extremely influential critic for the *Times Literary Supplement* and other journals, does not have his attention "focussed upon literature but upon a very mild type of philosophic humanitarian religion."[40] This group of publicly known figures (but as readers of Eliot's essays, quite anonymous) is Eliot's most desired and useful audience; as Eliot writes to his mother, "I am getting to be looked up to by people who are far better known to the general reader than I" (L 280). Changing the reading habits of these influential writers (and, along the way, some of the less powerful literary reading public) would do most to facilitate the advent of a public for modern texts.

The first stance Eliot wishes his readers to assume is a passive one: Eliot's references to the general reader did not encourage *his* readers to imagine themselves to fall in the group of general reader. Eliot constructed this general reader that his audience did not identify with because this mythical reader was a useful construct to convince his actual audience of the following attitudes. First, it suggested to his readers that there was a large group of bad readers. Second, it implied that there was a small audience of good readers for modern writing—this audience is not the "fashionable" audience. To describe this small audience Eliot coins a term new for literary history—the qualified audience. The qualified audience is not composed of ordinary people who look into their hearts for affirmation of what they see in the text. But neither is the qualified audience Milton's "fit but few," for Eliot's term implies a *professional* setting of standards that had nothing to do with morality and little to do with unconscious aesthetic sensitivity, a setting of standards that might be congenial to those who saw themselves, by virtue of the journals they read, as part of an elite.

In doing so, Eliot was explicitly attempting to change the form of elitism that governed British publishing life, to redirect the notion of poetry and reading as a gentlemanly pursuit. The idea of writing and reading as a gentlemanly, amateur activity was utilized as a rallying cry by critics sympathetic to Georgian writers, such as Harold Monro, publisher both of Eliot and the volumes of the anthology *Georgian Poetry*. Monro wrote the following derisive lines about the professionalism of many contemporary poets and their consequent emphasis on marketing:

And the poet? So far, what is he? A young man with a lively enjoyment of natural or artificial beauty, a sensitiveness for the right word, a vast instinct for self-advertisement.

It will be, as his career progresses, the business of the young professional to maintain strict appearance of such an attitude of scorn for the common public as is supposed by that common public to be natural to those who write verse or paint. He must freely display all the typical characteristics of the rôle he has adopted. Actually he is much in love with that public. . . .[41]

Eliot went one further and attached ideas of professionalism to his reading public. In a telling description of an ideal audience, Eliot claims that F. H. Bradley's books "come to the hands only of those who are qualified to treat them with respect"; the sermons of Lancelot Andrewes are similarly "only for the reader who can elevate himself to the subject" (*SP* 197, 181). Eliot creates an equally small audience for poetry. In "Tradition and the Individual Talent" he argues that of many readers "very few know when there is an expression of *significant* emotion, emotion which has its life in the poem and not in the history of the poet" (*SP* 44). The qualifications for reading modern texts can be laid out as a program, an apprenticeship to an eventual "mastery," a professional setting of standards that can require one to go back and redo explicit parts of the course:

We will leave it as a test: when anyone has studied Mr. Pound's poems in *chronological* order, and has mastered *Lustra* and *Cathay,* he is prepared for the *Cantos*—but not till then. If the reader then fails to like them, he has probably omitted some step in his progress, and had better go back and retrace the journey.[42]

These claims about the shape of the modern audience made some other claims easier to accept. First, the claim that reading modern literature is hard work. Eliot sets off with asterisks the last line of an article tellingly entitled "Professional, or . . .": "But we must learn to take literature seriously."[43] Good and bad readers are separated by their willingness to undertake this work. Thus, Eliot privately complains that Conrad Aiken's review of *The Sacred Wood* "was rather grudging and not the result of a conscientious study of the book"; in contrast, Eliot writes to

Virginia Woolf that *Jacob's Room* "requires very careful reading" and that he will have more to write "after I consider that I have really mastered the book" (*L* 448; 606, 607). The work of Donne and Cowley "requires considerable agility on the part of the reader" (*SP* 60), as does the work of St.-John Perse if one intends to discover its quality: "it is to be expected that the reader of a poem should take at least as much trouble as a barrister reading an important decision on a complicated case."[44]

When Eliot lectures Eleanor Hinkley that understanding French literature is "hard work," but that "no one can ever have a really trained taste with English alone," his use of "trained" is neither accidental nor limited to a specific context or person (*L* 228). What is true for the reader of Lancelot Andrewes, who must "elevate himself to the subject," is equally true for one who reads the poems of Ezra Pound, which "require . . . a trained ear, or at least the willingness to be trained."[45] The good reader is the trained—or at least the trainable—reader. To be trained admits of outside influence, of power that moves from the top down. Thus, training is possible with anthologies, in which "the reader's vision [is] clarified and his mind instructed, when bad poems of totally different types are set off against each other."[46] To train, instruct, and improve the technical (not moral) competence of readers, Eliot argues, is the function of criticism and the literary review: "Its [*The Criterion*'s] great aim is to raise the standard of thought and writing in this country by both international and historical comparison" (*L* 551).

The last step in Eliot's scattered argument is crucial to the management of his audience and the success of his own poetry. Good critics need to train readers because modern literature is necessarily difficult. In dozens of passages Eliot argues that the difficult form of modern writing is essential. Early in his career (1915), feeling enough rapport with Pound to interlard his own writing with Pound's capitalized nouns, Eliot writes: "It might be pointed out again and again that literature has rights of its own which extend beyond Uplift and Recreation. Of course it is imprudent to sneer at the monopolisation of literature by women" (*L* 96). What lies beyond is the right to difficult writing: "To say that an involved style is necessarily a bad style would be preposterous. But such a style should follow the involutions of a mode of perceiving, registering, and digesting impressions which is also involved."[47] Here, as it is in many essays, the defense of difficulty is pointed toward accurate psychological representation, but Eliot was to make grander claims for difficulty's necessity.

It is not a permanent necessity that poets should be interested in phi-losophy, or in any other subject. We can only say that it appears likely that poets in our civilization, as it exists at present, must be *difficult*. Our civilization comprehends great variety and complexity, and this variety and complexity, playing upon a refined sensibility, must pro-duce various and complex results. The poet must become more and more comprehensive, more allusive, more indirect, in order to force, to dislocate if necessary, language into his meaning. (*SP* 65)

This argument is strategically elegant because it doesn't seem self-serving; as part of the zeitgeist, difficulty is inevitable, not useful. Further, Eliot doesn't look at difficulty's effects; he looks at the reasons for its exis-tence.

Eliot gives his own difficult writing more authority by discussing difficulty in many of his reviews of earlier literature. *All* good poetry that is difficult is *necessarily* difficult: "But a degree of heterogeneity of mate-rial compelled into unity by the operation of the poet's mind is omnipresent in poetry" (*SP* 61). Thus, in *Anabasis* the difficulty is neces-sary: "Any obscurity of the poem, on first readings, is due to the sup-pression of 'links in the chain,' of explanatory and connecting matter, and not to incoherence, or to the love of cryptogram. The justification of such abbreviation of method is that the sequence of images coincides and concentrates into one intense impression of barbaric civilization."[48]

Eliot's claims about reading follow a useful road both for the readers of his essay and for the success of his own poetry. In contrast to the large group of bad readers, there is a small, qualified audience of good readers for modern writing. They form part of a small group who are willing to undergo the hard work and training required for reading modern writ-ing, which is difficult, but necessarily so. The purpose of this narrowing down is not first of all to exclude readers (although it certainly does do that), for the maligned audience is not present. Rather, it is to encourage a small group of readers in a tendency that was encouraged by the sorts of magazines they read: to imagine themselves as part of a professional elite, as included in the appreciators of good writing, writing that looks remarkably like *The Waste Land*.[49]

This method has much to encourage its success, first of all because it is not presented systematically. What seems crass stated as a series of propositions seems much less so when presented haphazardly. Eliot's arguments for readers work precisely because they are scattered, unorganized, unsystematic—it is easy to agree with a quip whose consequences aren't systematically worked out. To argue with Eliot's haphazardly presented terms would be both to change the tone of the argument, giving a systematic response to an unsystematic argument, and to ponderously ally oneself with a genteel dullness or a populist Philistinism—and few readers of little magazines in the 1920s were ready to do that. It's no wonder Eliot swept Cambridge but not Kensington.

As the ad hoc nature of Eliot's argument might suggest, he achieves assent frequently without the use of an explicit logical proposition. At times he uses cultural codes that contain an implicit assertion but because of their highly elliptical and metaphoric nature do not admit of a logical rebuttal. One may dislike the following statement, but, without ponderously unpacking the assumptions presented in a metaphoric quip that is not central to the argument of the essay in which it appears, one cannot easily enter into an argument with it: "The possessors of the inner voice ride ten in a compartment to a football match at Swansea."[50] Eliot's use of passive voice also encourages a form of reader's assent in which Eliot typically does not identify, but assumes that his readers know, the implied agent. When granted by his readers, such a move gives him an objectivity and a sense of judgmental power. Eliot also uses what sounds like an objective voice to speak for a *genre* of writing—not his particular writing. While, as many critics have shown, Eliot carefully selects qualities in these writers that are transferable to his own poetry, Eliot's argument purports to be a universal argument, with the specific examples being Dante, Donne, and others.[51] And, of course, his often-remarked Olympian tone has a coercive function. He begins his essay "Criticism in England" with "We generally agree in conversation that the amount of good literary criticism in English is negligible."[52] The unrestricted "we" marks an audience identification and is usually the subject of a sentence that posits a generalized opinion that Eliot finds momentarily fecund for his reading audience to hold, and for which he wishes to deflect audience resistance by identifying also himself as someone who holds that position. As does his unstated passive voice, the use of "we" and "one," besides giving Eliot the passive and authoritarian tone that he cultivated both with his anonymous reviewing at the *Times Literary Supplement* and his polemical writing at *The Egoist,* makes readers complicit with his judgments. Not to go along with the argument swept along by these techniques is to ally oneself with amateurism, sloppiness, and "women." What is so interesting about these comments is not so much their unattractiveness, but that they succeeded. Although these comments (and their underlying arguments) were presented by one who was only beginning to have the cultural power he desired, their success depends upon readers granting the writer an authority that does not require him to spell things out.

A further reason for Eliot's success is that his demands aren't as hard as they look, for he creates requirements that are easy to misread. While he often requires his audience to work hard, Eliot qualifies that work by making it easy *for some:* "Some can absorb knowledge, the more tardy must sweat for it. Shakespeare acquired more essential history from Plutarch than most men could from the whole British Museum" (*SP* 40). While modern literature is difficult, Eliot offers a genteel way out: one could be an absorber rather than a sweater (and be in good company in the bargain). Eliot's requirements are much less threatening than those of Pound. At his most ambitious, Pound attempted to set up his own "College of Arts" in which to instruct the culturally incomplete; more typically, he gave out copious reading lists that included Confucius, Homer (perhaps using a Latin crib or a French translation), and Cavalcanti. Eliot didn't even demand that his readers know Weston's *From Ritual to Romance,* which in his notes to *The Waste Land* he claimed "will elucidate the difficulties of the poem much better than my notes can do."[53] Second, employing a Romantic argument about the primacy of the intuitive, Eliot continually argued that readers needed to understand less than some thought they did. This argument is made most insistently in his 1929 essay on Dante, where Eliot argues, "It is a test (a positive test, I do not assert that it is always valid negatively), that genuine poetry can communicate before it is understood" (*SP* 206). He repeats this argument at several points in the Dante essay. (The Dante essay is important enough for Eliot to repeatedly anthologize despite its lack of clear connection to modern literature. This is not solely because it puts Dante in the canon, but because of its extensive discussion of difficulty.) He also makes it for Ezra Pound, by constructing an imaginary reader once again. This reader, confronting difficult poetry, has this reaction.

> "This," he will say of some of the poems in Provençal form or on Provençal subjects, "is archaeology; it requires knowledge on the part of its reader, and true poetry does not require such knowledge." But to display knowledge is not the same thing as to expect it on the part of the reader; and of this sort of pedantry Pound is quite free.[54]

Eliot, always easier than Pound was in his requirements for readers' knowledge of specific texts and facts, would go on to argue for Pound that "though *Personae* and *Exultations* do exact something from the reader, they do not require a knowledge of Provençal or of Spanish or Italian."[55]

Pound would not have as easily made such a statement, a contrast that shows that Eliot, by rarely making his requirements specific, knew how to work his readers in a way Pound never did, and gives some clue as to why, unlike Eliot's assessment of Pound's career, Eliot did not "have to retire to obscurity or Paris like Ezra" (*L* 541–42). Eliot's prose shows that writers solidify their place not just by writing poetry, not just by rewriting earlier writers, but also by changing the reading habits of a crucial audience. This can be done only through the complicity of one's audience. Eliot's construction of modern poetry through his attack on contemporary reading habits does not just demonstrate Pound's assertion, at the beginning of Eliot's reviewing career, that Eliot's style was to "go in at the back door and take out the swag." It shows that he convinced a large group of readers to hold the door open for him.

NOTES

1. Edward Hyams, *The New Statesman: The History of the First Fifty Years, 1913–1963* (London: Longmans, 1963), p. 17.

2. Louis Menand, *Discovering Modernism: T. S. Eliot and His Context* (New York: Oxford University Press, 1987), p. 61; T. S. Eliot, "London Letter," *Dial* 70, no. 6 (June 1921): 690.

3. See Hyams, *The New Statesman,* pp. 37–38, 155–57 for more details on the tone of the literary pages of the *New Statesman.*

4. T. S. Eliot, *Selected Prose of T. S. Eliot,* ed. Frank Kermode (New York: Harcourt Brace Jovanovich; Farrar, Straus and Giroux, 1975), p. 36; subsequent references appear parenthetically in the text, abbreviated *SP.* See Menand pp. 61–62 for a more complete account of the conservatism of Eliot's argument in this essay.

5. Peter Ackroyd, *T. S. Eliot* (London: Hamish Hamilton, 1984), p. 89.

6. Ezra Pound, "Credo," in *Selected Prose, 1909–1965,* ed. William Cookson (New York: New Directions, 1975), p. 53.

7. T. S. Eliot, *The Letters of T. S. Eliot,* ed. Valerie Eliot, vol. 1 (London: Faber and Faber, 1988), p. 280; subsequent references appear parenthetically in the text, abbreviated *L.*

8. For a typical example, see Ronald Bush on Eliot's reading of Lancelot Andrewes (*T. S. Eliot: A Study in Character and Style* [New York: Oxford University Press, 1983], pp. 113–14). In a 1942 article, Eliot makes the same admission about his own critical writing: "I can never re-read any of my own prose writings without acute embarrassment. . . . Especially when he [the poet] is young, and actively engaged in battling for the kind of poetry which he practices, he sees the poetry of the past in relation to his own. . . . What he writes about poetry, in short, must be assessed in relation to the poetry he writes" (Eliot, "The Music of Poetry," *Partisan Review* 9, no. 6 [November–December 1942]: 452–53).

9. While this is an argument about attempts to shift power and how power is produced, I am not trying to create a melodrama in which Eliot manipulates his readers through devious and exclusionary means. Rather, I am convinced by Michel Foucault's contention: "We must cease once and for all to describe the effects of power in negative terms: it 'excludes,' it 'represses,' it 'censors,' it 'abstracts,' it 'masks,' it 'conceals.' In fact, power produces; it produces reality; it produces domains of objects and rituals of truth." According to Foucault, "power produces knowledge (and not simply by encouraging it because it serves power or by applying it because it is useful)" (*Discipline and Punish: The Birth of the Prison,* trans. Alan Sheridan [New York: Random House, 1979], pp. 194, 27). Eliot's use of power created reality; it produced a useful form of modernism.

10. The public comments about readers decrease in number drastically after the mid-1920s, after Eliot has a less awkward sense of his space.

11. See Hugh Kenner, *The Invisible Poet: T. S. Eliot* (New York: Citadel Press, 1959), pp. 82, 88, for a more complete analysis of how this ad hoc approach to theory works.

12. Grover Smith, for example, describes Eliot's essays as having "a pedagogical tone and waspish temper that still have power to delight or irritate" (*The Waste Land* [London: George Allen and Unwin, 1983], p. 43). B. L. Reid writes that in *The Sacred Wood* "the familiar ex cathedra tone, the disingenuous apologetic air, is already infuriatingly obvious" ("T. S. Eliot and *The Sacred Wood,*" *Sewanee Review* 90, no. 2 [spring 1982]: 229). For a description of the varieties of Eliot's tone, see Roger Sharrock, "Eliot's Tone," in *The Literary Criticism of T. S. Eliot,* ed. David Newton-De Molina (London: Athlone Press, University of London, 1977).

13. One needs to be careful in defining the target of Eliot's elitism, for as David Chinitz argues in "T. S. Eliot and the Cultural Divide," Eliot's attitudes to class and mass culture are remarkably complex. Early in his career Eliot believed that the gulf between the upper and lower classes was a mark of "social disintegration" that threatened art. Eliot saw the particular usefulness of the lower classes to be their engagement with popular culture. That accounts for his dislike of the middle class, and for the presence of popular culture in a poem like *The Waste*

Land (*PMLA* 110.2 [March 1995, 236–47]). As I argue in this essay, Eliot's elitism is conceptually set up as one of professionalization. Elitism's practical consequences of course reach to social classes, particularly the middle class, but it is important to note that Eliot's version of professionalization did not entail a specific class alignment.

14. In a forgettable essay published in Harold Monro's *The Chapbook,* Eliot reveals himself at his most nervous about the institution of reviewing: "If it were only possible first to abate this nuisance of reviewing, we might hope for some improvement in the condition of verse. If it were more difficult for young poets to spring into brief and meaningless notoriety, they might be more self-critical. There should be no reviewing of poetry in daily newspapers. In the periodicals which appear less frequently, no work should be discussed except from one of the several critical points of view approved: the historical, the philosophical, the expert-professional. From the last point of view, only the absolutely first-rate should be discussed at all" (Eliot, "A Brief Treatise on the Criticism of Poetry," *Chapbook* 9 [March 1920]: 8).

15. Patrick Howarth, *Squire: Most Generous of Men* (London: Hutchinson and Co., 1963), p. 136.

16. Although presenting himself to his mother as self-assured, Eliot at times gets nervous in the control of his isolated power. Regarding his participation in the *Criterion,* Eliot writes to Richard Aldington: "You know that I have no persecution mania, but that I am quite aware how obnoxious I am to perhaps the larger part of the literary world of London and that there will be a great many jackals swarming about waiting for my bones. If this [the launching of the *Criterion*] falls flat I shall not only have gained nothing but will have lost immensely in prestige and usefulness and shall have to retire to obscurity or Paris like Ezra" (*L* 541–42).

17. Neither do I assert that there is a peculiar candor in his letters that is missing from his essays and that only in his letters do we get the "real" Eliot. Eliot is more harsh in his private letters than in public writing, but that is because his harshness is not directed to the reader of the letter. There are too many different audiences and functions for his audiences to get a single read on his letters.

18. Kenner, *The Invisible Poet,* pp. 94–106. For critics who are nervous about Eliot's tone, yet do not wish to attack the writer, such an approach has enduring popularity. In a 1982 essay Linda Shires makes the same point as Kenner, arguing that Eliot learned to "mimic British journalistic idioms so that he could mock the very establishment for which he wrote" (Linda Shires, "T. S. Eliot's Early Criticism and the Making of *The Sacred Wood,*" *Prose Studies* 5, no. 2 [September 1982]: 230). While this assertion makes Eliot a more attractive writer, it doesn't address the exclusionary tone of many of his comments. It also does not adequately account for either the heterogeneous audience that he addressed or his apparent admiration for many of the practitioners of this tone.

19. J. C. Squire, [Affable Hawk, pseud.], Rev. of *Ulysses,* by James Joyce, *The New Statesman* (April 7, 1923): 775.

20. See Sumany Satpathy, "Eliot's Early Criticism and the *TLS,*" *Literary Criterion* 23, no. 3 (1987): 33–40.

21. Eliot, "London Letter," *Dial* 71, no. 4 (October 1921): 452.

22. Eliot, "Brief Treatise," p. 1.

23. Eliot, "London Letter," *Dial* 70, no. 6 (June 1921): 690.

24. Eliot, "Brief Treatise," p. 1.

25. Eliot, "London Letter," *Dial* 72, no. 5 (May 1922): 511.

26. Eliot, "Brief Treatise," p. 3.

27. Ibid., p. 6.

28. Eliot, "Contemporanea," *Egoist* 5, no. 6 (June–July 1918): 70.

29. In this setting, bad poets cater to bad readers, and, in a reversal of the power structure Eliot sets up for bad criticism, readers are perhaps the more to blame. In Sandburg's "more ambitious verse . . . there is just the same surrender as in England, to what the people want" ("London Letter," *Dial* 72, no. 5 [May 1922]: 512).

30. Eliot, "The Function of a Literary Review," *The Criterion* 1, no. 4 (July 1923): 421.

31. Eliot, *Ezra Pound: His Metric and His Poetry* (1917), rpt. *To Criticize the Critic and Other Writings* (London: Faber and Faber, 1965), p. 173.

32. Ibid., p. 174.

33. Eliot, "The Function of Criticism," *Criterion* 2, no. 5 (October 1923): 35. As these examples may show, Eliot does not characterize his middle class with the precision of a sociologist. Rather, inhabitants of Indianapolis and Greenwich Village, soccer fans, and readers of Georgian poetry are Eliot's shorthand terms for readers who share the same confused and complacent reading habits. Different actual audiences require different shorthand terms—the accuracy of these terms is not so important for Eliot as their function—they are always presented as a damning quip.

34. Eliot, "London Letter," *Dial* 70, no. 4 (April 1921): 451. In his essay Eliot does add a qualifier to this statement: "And it must not be supposed that this great middle class public which consumes Georgian poetry corresponds to the public of Mrs Ella Wheeler Wilcox. I intend no disrespect to that lady, whose verse I have read with ease and some pleasure. The Georgian public is a smallish but important public, it is that offensive part of the middle class which believes itself superior to the rest of the middle class; and superior for precisely this reason that it believes itself to possess culture" (451–52).

35. Lawrence Rainey, "The Price of Modernism: Reconsidering the Publication of *The Waste Land,*" *Yale Review* 78, no. 2 (Winter 1989): 298, 296. These figures vary slightly from source to source, but the ones I cite probably come quite close to actual circulation. Joost comes up with a slightly larger number of *Dial*

readers—13,440 early in 1923 (Nicholas Joost, *Schofield Thayer and "The Dial": An Illustrated History* (Carbondale: Southern Illinois University Press, 1964). About 600 of these readers were given free copies. The Lidderdale and Nicholson biography of Harriet Weaver lists the circulation of *The Egoist* as low as 160 copies in 1915 (Jane Lidderdale and Mary Nicholson, *Dear Miss Weaver: Harriet Shaw Weaver, 1876–1961* [New York: Viking, 1970], p. 106).

36. Joy Grant, *Harold Monroe and the Poetry Bookshop* (Berkeley and Los Angeles: University of California Press, 1967), p. 157; Ian Hamilton, *The Little Magazine: A Study of Six Editors* (London: Weidenfeld and Nicolson, 1976), p. 21; Frank Luther Mott, *A History of American Magazines* (Cambridge: Harvard University Press, 1968), 5:171.

37. Hamilton, *Little Magazines,* p. 69.

38. An interesting point about Eliot's articles for the *TLS* is that they clearly position him at the center of English literary power. Eliot, in close connection with *TLS* editor Bruce Richmond at the time, wrote these articles as lead articles. Each issue of the *TLS* had only one lead article of 3,000–4,500 words, positioned on the front two pages and allowing the author to write a piece that addressed not just the book itself, but the book's subject matter more generally. The rest of the reviews were smaller, 750–1,000 words, and focused on the individual book's merits.

39. Some largely ineffective attempts at target marketing tell us something about editors' anticipations of who their readers might be. As mentioned earlier in this essay, the *New Statesman* sought readers of a similar political affiliation and created a list of some twenty thousand potential readers (Hyams, *New Statesman,* p. 17). Joost gives an account of a creation of a mailing list of thirty thousand for the *Dial,* cobbled together from publishers and private club membership lists. Returns were small—only one hundred positive replies (*Schofield Thayer,* pp. 40–41).

40. Eliot, "London Letter," *Dial* 70, no. 6 (June 1921): 690.

41. Harold Monro, *Some Contemporary Poets* (London: Leonard Parsons, 1920), p. 14. In his first editorial in his *London Mercury* J. C. Squire used a similar idea to characterize the current avant-garde: "Young men, ignoring the fundamental truth in the maxim, 'Look in thy heart and write,' have attempted to make up poems (and pictures) 'out of their heads' " ("Editorial Notes," *London Mercury* 1, no. 1 [November 1919]: 4).

42. Eliot, *Ezra Pound,* p. 182.

43. Eliot, *Egoist* 5, no. 4 (April 1918): 61.

44. Eliot, preface to *Anabasis,* by St.-John Perse, trans. T. S. Eliot, rev. ed. (1931; London: Faber and Faber, 1959), p. 10.

45. Eliot, *Ezra Pound,* pp. 166, 167.

46. Eliot, "Reflections on Contemporary Poetry [III]," *Egoist* 4, no. 10 (November 1917): 151.

47. "Philip Massinger," *Times Literary Supplement,* 27 May 1920; rpt. as part 1 of "Philip Massinger" in *The Sacred Wood* (London: Methuen, 1928), p. 131. This is not Eliot's carte blanche for all manifestations of difficult writing. To Leonard Woolf, Eliot writes about his own work, "I feel that there is much in the book [*The Sacred Wood*] which ought to have been completely rewritten, which is unnecessarily difficult or obscure" (*L* 427).

48. Eliot, preface to *Anabasis,* pp. 9, 10.

49. Much of the logic of this analysis is indebted to Louis Menand's discussion of literary professionalism (*Discovering Modernism,* pp. 97–132).

50. Eliot, "Function of Criticism," p. 35.

51. Eliot rarely refers to his own writing publicly, although once, in an anonymous essay in the *Athenaeum,* he refers to himself as an aging poet.

52. Eliot, "Criticism in England," *Athenaeum,* 13 June 1919, p. 456.

53. Eliot, *Collected Poems, 1909–1962* (New York: Harcourt, Brace and World, 1963), p. 70.

54. Eliot, *Ezra Pound,* pp. 165, 166.

55. Ibid., p. 166.

"One Hundred Per Cent Bohemia": Pop Decadence and the Aestheticization of Commodity in the Rise of the Slicks

Michael Murphy

A man-about-town entry in a 1919 issue of *Vanity Fair,* coyly mourning the loss of "real" bohemianism in the era of modernism—when starving artists, it seems, had become too popularly accepted as spectacles for bohemian watching to any longer be a *really* voguish pastime—pauses for a moment to meditate with mannered cynicism on the workings of the fledgling industry of avant-garde culture:

> Maria's was the scene of so much merriment in the old days that it is with honest regret that I record the melancholy fact that professional bohemianism had its beginning there. Persons whom we called "floor-walkers" came to see the animals feed, and to listen to their jokes. The increased patronage enabled Maria to enlarge her premises and straightway there appeared on the scene fake bohemians who performed for the benefit of the visitors, earning for themselves an occasional drink or cigar or meal. In the face of this infliction those who were able to pay for the meals that they preferred to eat unobserved scattered and became a nomad race, while a survival of the unfittest led in due time to the colonization of Greenwich Village and Washington Square. As practised here to-day, bohemianism is no longer a profession but a business which draws its trade chiefly from the suburbs and upper west side of the town. Its marts are in rookeries and damp, candle-lighted catacombs, before whose doors stand rows of automobiles—a warning to the wary. [1]

On one level, of course, this is what much contemporary cultural theory would recognize immediately as classic market-phobic modernist dis-

UNIVERSITY OF HERTFORDSHIRE LRC

course. Pining with dandyish nostalgia for the good old days of authentic artistic suffering, free of the "infliction" of popular acceptance and support, the article speaks with pained disapproval of the growing commodification of the artistic personality—or better, "temperament"—in the age of mass culture. Indeed, according to the article, such developments have led to a tawdry, merchandized "survival of the unfittest" and a gross "colonization" of even the purest, most market-resistant bohemias.

But ultimately more striking than the article's obvious market phobia, it seems to me, is the carefully mannered *coyness* of its expression of that phobia. Indeed, this coyness might well be taken to suggest a certain self-consciousness not only about the elaborate system of patronage that modernism had clearly begun to invent for itself by 1919—the article is clear about that much—but even about the article's *own* implication in the "business" of bohemianism. Of course, we must assume that its author cannot be unaware of *Vanity Fair*'s important and explicit role in this "business"—its function as promoter and even market planner for the new art, its careful targeting of a suburban or wealthy urban readership to patronize that art who could afford the stylish automobiles and personal items it advertised, and its especially skillful appraisal of and traffic in the celebrity values of the most important "bohemian" figures, photographed stylishly by serious "art" photographers for display in regular full-page portraits. It is clear to even *Vanity Fair*'s most casual reader that the main purpose of "One Hundred Per Cent Bohemia" was to publicize the apparently burgeoning bohemian nostalgia industry, of which the article itself can be taken as a clear manifestation. Simply, it was written to instruct potential "bohemian-watchers" just where to find both the monuments of bohemianism's past "glory days" and the real bohemians' contemporary impersonators now "performing" there.

Of course, the sort of tour-guide function performed by the article only supplemented *Vanity Fair*'s ultimately more important and more general curatorial function. Self-appointed Armory Show publicist Frank Crowninshield, unimpeachably devoted to the cause of avant-garde art, was adamant about this dimension of the magazine's purpose when he took over *Vanity Fair*'s editorship in 1914. The inaugural issue declared the magazine to be "a record of current achievements in all the arts"[2] and dedicated itself to the reproduction of what we would now generalize as "modernism" through the regular publication of work by such important modernist figures as Picasso, Gauguin, Matisse, T. S. Eliot, André Gide, e. e. cummings, Gertrude Stein, D. H. Lawrence, and Colette, among many others. In fact, Crowninshield even professed a conscious intention to appropriate both the spirit and general look of avant-garde journals. His statement of editorial vision in the first issue spoke glowingly of creating a mass-circulation magazine that would be "a trifle more fluent, fantastic, or even absurd," more like "the French periodicals"[3] than most popular American magazines of the day. This would prove especially true in *Vanity Fair*'s use of particular futurist, vorticist, dadaist, and surrealist visual effects. Indeed, some of the most striking of *Vanity Fair*'s covers were actually commissioned works by such avant-garde luminaries as futurist painter and writer Fortunato Depero and cubist-dadaist fellow traveler Marie Laurencin.

Simply, then, *Vanity Fair*'s clear social function (one with which the great proliferation of "slicks" has made us quite familiar these days) was to keep its mass upper-middle-class readership culturally up-to-date. For three dollars or so a year, it would mediate the vagaries of high-modernist aesthetics to a popular audience. A 1919 subscription ad resolved fairly typically (though with *undeniable* panache) to keep "the Tired Business Man" "in touch with the newest and liveliest influences of modern life."

He is chain-lightning in his office. He knows all about the bank-statement, the corn crop, the freightcar shortage. . . . But *SOCIALLY!* great Beatrice Fairfax! He is lost at a dance: swamped at a dinner; helpless when confronted with hostesses, buds, dowagers, visiting French generals, literary lions, Hindu musicians, Japanese dancers; dumb at discussions of Eli Nadelman's sculpture. . . . All he needs is to tear off that coupon and spend three insignificant dollars for a year of the forward-marching magazine of modern American life. . . . There is more joyous fun-making and mental stimulation in one single copy than in fourteen yards of Bergson or Ralph Waldo Emerson.[4]

In fact, we should remember, this mediation would happen *not only* by bringing businessmen who risked philistinism Eli Nadelman and Hindu musicians, or by keeping even the most careful track of where to find their exhibitions and performances, but also, somewhat less specifically, through the magazine's *own* service as a *model* of sophisticated cultural modernity. Indeed, *Vanity Fair* cut an unmistakable cultural figure—in the mannered, all-gods-dead high civility of its staff writers, in its dedication to a leisure at once both gentlemanly and decadent (encompassing both Josephine Baker and golf), in the striking sleekness of its layout, in the bold overstylization of its paid advertisements, in its dramatic and technologically innovative use of color, and so on. That is: *Vanity Fair* would market modernity not only by transcribing it, but by *embodying* it as well. In a sense, the magazine simply *became* modernism for many of its readers. Indeed, from the moment we try to imagine the early modern reader spotting bold art deco covers on the newsstand alongside slowly dying nineteenth-century "family" magazines, it is easy to see the early-twentieth-century glossy magazine as both enabled by and participating in the proliferation of an especially self-conscious and important sense of what it meant to be modern—and even modern*ist*.

And yet much of the experience of those readers, I argue, was most evocative of precisely the qualities that current critical convention asks us to *dissociate* from modernism. Indeed, the strange double-bind of *Vanity Fair*'s declared purpose—popularizing an aesthetic based largely on a demonstrated scorn for popular appeal—called for a strange doubleness of approach and sensibility, and this doubleness helped accommodate a startling complicity with precisely the sort of mass-market-driven forces and impulses we normally imagine modernism denouncing. What it seems to me that *Vanity Fair* suggested to its readers *most powerfully,* that is, was that being modern—and by extension even being modern*ist*—was not about market *phobia* at all, but precisely about market *savvy.*

Of course, as I have begun to suggest, this is not the conventional way to understand modernism. Instead, according to what has become an increasingly familiar cultural-theory commonplace, modernism's founding ethos of heroic originality produced a naive modernist phobia about all things smacking of too close an association with the mass market and with marketplace values—what Andreas Huyssen, in perhaps the most important and widely read book on modernism published in the last twenty years, has called an overpowering and disabling "anxiety of contamination."[5] That is: any acknowledgment of the literal economics of art's production and consumption would suggest too clear an ideological imprint for the maintenance of the "purist" epistemology of "originality" and "creativity" so important to modernism. To recognize the exchange value of art objects would be to fly in the face of modernism's foundationalist assumptions about art's "eternal" and "timeless" value. And, of course, to capitalize on that exchange value in any way would be to "contaminate" the creative accomplishment of the "genuine" artwork unthinkably.

This is an understanding of modernism, it's worth remembering, in no way limited to Huyssen, though I have taken his term to describe it generally. In fact, this understanding is shared *not only* by the different factions of the contemporary left, who of course all invariably dismiss the "contamination anxiety" they associate with modernism as elitist and naive—from sober neo-Marxists like Huyssen and Fredric Jameson to glib, end-of-the-political "simulacrists" like Arthur Kroker and David Cook. Indeed, the assumption that modernism invariably shunned mass audiences also animates many of the arguments made by the contemporary neohumanist Right like Hilton Kramer and Roger Kimball, who want to restore what they see as a glorious modern tradition after the much-proclaimed "fall" into a "debased" postmodernism celebrating the mass-cultural and (worse!) multicultural. It was also, what's more, always the standing commonplace on both the modernist left (Adorno) and right (Greenberg), who in fact both championed it enthusiastically, if for reasons they each phrased somewhat differently. Terry Eagleton's assessment of modernism, though, is suggestive of the central assumptions behind all these positions:

> Modernism is among other things a strategy whereby the work of art resists commodification, holds out by the skin of its teeth against those social forces which would degrade it to an exchangeable object. . . . To fend off such reduction to commodity status, the modernist work . . . thickens its textures and deranges its forms to forestall instant consumability, and draws its own language protectively around it to become a mysteriously autotelic object.[6]

Indeed, *none* of the critics cited above, no matter what their orientation in the spectrum of cultural-theory positions—in fact almost no one writing today[7]—will disagree that one of the fundamental characteristics of "modernism" was its inclination to "thicken its textures and derange its forms to forestall instant consumability" out of an utter and explicit aversion to "those social forces which would degrade it to an exchangeable commodity."

On one level, the problem with this consensus understanding of modernism is simple: it has come to seem too neat a narrative, too general and unqualified a diagnosis of the astonishingly multiple, dynamic, and complicated phenomenon that we agreed a long time ago it was something of a reduction to generalize as "modernism." It is a simple misrepresentation of the multiplicity of early-twentieth-century culture, and it demands qualification. Though "contamination anxiety" indeed aptly describes one of the ideological cornerstones of the general modernist ethos, *not all individual "modernists" were equally "contamination anxious."* On another level, however, the problems with our conventional understanding of "modernism" may also reveal something about the shared preoccupations, expectations—and needs—of contemporary cultural theory. Indeed, while generalizations about marketplace phobias in the first sense clearly serve to provide a convenient way to package and consume history, I wonder if they have become such popular cultural-theory truisms for other reasons as well—*particularly for those of us working from a perspective we imagine defined somehow by the exhaustion of the modernist tradition.* That is, it seems to me that such generalizations *also* work conveniently to legitimate some of our happiest and most urgent assumptions about the possibilities for an enlightened contemporary aesthetic practice—about a postmodernity that can be called "postmodern" because it has indeed finally solved and dispensed of modernity's defining problems. These days, this very popular narrative of modernist contamination anxiety implies, after the much-elaborated lessons of pop art and the ever-escalating prices paid for fetishized art objects at auction, we are far too aware of and enlightened about the commodity function of our art and our ideas to ever again be surprised or threatened by it. Further, this very reassuring sense of having graduated from modernist naïveté, from a contamination-anxious state of innocence, has come largely to define our sense of what constitutes our "postmodernity," and our need for this sort of reassurance, it seems to me, has exerted a powerful influence on our reconstructions of modernism. So if we will avoid risking complicity with some very self-serving historical misrepresentations, I argue, we need to resist our inclination to allude casually and dismissively to an unfairly stereotyped modernism as a way to suggest that we have now all learned to deal with the problems of art's commodification in duly sophisticated and enlightened ways. At its worst, this stereotype seems to me not only a crude underestimation of the past; it also implies a dangerous overestimation of the present.

But the very term developed to describe magazines like *Vanity Fair,* on the other hand—which in fact filled such a new market niche that they required the invention of an entirely new publishing category for themselves—is suggestive of the sort of market savvy normally thought of as anathema to the modernist aesthetic. Of course, in one sense, the term *slicks,* said to come into common use around 1930, forms a simple allusion to the newly invented glossy paper on which the slicks were printed. And yet in another sense, it is difficult to ignore how the term resonates with the marketplace-related connotations of *slickness*—especially if we suppose that readers recognized how deftly the slicks themselves had been marketed. Indeed, if *Vanity Fair* did serve as an important *model* of modernity for its readers, it is easy to imagine that those readers must have felt called to become something like "slick" consumers of culture themselves.

What's more, as we have already begun to notice, this dimension of *slick*ness is readily apparent in "One Hundred Per Cent Bohemia." In fact, in this context, the article's provocative title could perhaps be seen *not only* to describe the purity of the nineteenth-century starving artist (the obvious straight reading), but *also* to use the language of advertising cliché—with profoundly *slick* irony—as a sort of tongue-in-cheek certification of its *own* embodiment of avant-garde modernism. "One Hundred Per Cent Bohemia," that is, would seem in this sense calculated to assure its customers with a sort of Warholian panache that the article served to re-present radical modernity for them in readily consumable form with a high degree of faithfulness, that readers anxious about how to be modern would get their money's worth—that the text advertised in the title *would indeed be "one hundred per cent bohemian."* In sum, the text's own slickness, its mannered, even vaguely decadent self-consciousness about its reproduction of modernist "contamination anxiety," is unmistakable. Following from the advertising associations of its title, for example, the article itself participates wryly in the language that would turn bohemianism into a circus sideshow, describing bohemiangazers as those who "came to see the animals feed." And it exaggerates the discourse of contamination anxiety to a point that even approaches gentle self-parody, speaking playfully of a "survival of the unfittest" and issuing "warn[ings] to the wary" with mock gravity about the "infliction" of bohemianism's new popularity. In this sense, it seems to me difficult not to recognize that "One Hundred Per Cent Bohemia" actually has no more than an *ironic* investment in what it seems to celebrate as "real" bohemianism—while *Vanity Fair*'s very literal investment as a magazine of contemporary arts and letters in the new, apparently "compromised" bohemianism, on the other hand, should be obvious.

Indeed, the article's author seems entirely unsettled by inconsistencies that a "contamination-anxious" modernist would find wholly disabling. The article goes quite happily on in its implicit contradictions, effectively supplying consumers with just the pretense of a distaste for consumption and the consumable that it has taught them to desire, even if with a hint of self-mockery ("Bohemians were once regarded as a race apart from other folk," it complains wryly, "like Californians or musicians.")[8] "One Hundred Per Cent Bohemia," moreover, is positively unflappable in its zealous and playful marketing of what it would have us believe is the antithesis of marketplace values.

As I have already begun to suggest, however, what seems surprising about all this, given the prevailing cultural-historical wisdom, is the suggestion that an ironic acknowledgment of one's own status as commodity—or at least *a general consciousness of the mixed nature of "bohemianism" in a world in which art's function as business was becoming ever more apparent*—might actually serve as a striking signifier of modernity for "high" aesthetic modernism. Or more exactly, perhaps, that the spirit of playful light irony enacted in "One Hundred Per Cent Bohemia" appears so very easily to accommodate and mediate what we might expect to be a really debilitating inconsistency—between *Vanity Fair*'s status as a piece of market-driven mass culture and the self-consciously "high" modernism it would reproduce for its consumers. But this same ease of reconciliation—between modernism and "slickness"—seems to hold for the slicks' *general* reproduction, outside the narrow limits of "One Hundred Per Cent Bohemia," of the spirit of modernism. *Vanity Fair*'s clear association with commodity, for example, never seemed at all a problem but in fact was a source of pride for gentleman-editor Crowninshield. Though his enthusiastic advocacy of avant-garde modernism was tireless, as we have noted, Crowninshield could at the same time use the pages of the magazine itself to defend the powerful "glamour and color" of ads as therapy for the "monotonous and humdrum lives" of "most American women,"[9] as he did in one 1934 editorial satirically titled "Thoughts on Sin—and Advertising." Indeed, *Vanity Fair*'s sense of affiliation with the popular vogue in the world of mass-market modernity never railed against but seemed entirely consistent with its founding interest in Art. The language of such manifestos of self-consciously "high" culture as D. H. Lawrence's 1928 "Deserted Battlefields: A Polemic against Mass Thinking and Men's Modern Indifference to the Ancient Rewards" or Jean Cocteau's 1922 "The Public and the Artist" could sit without apparent contradiction alongside such mass-cultural frivolities as the magazine's twin "Nominated for the Hall of Fame" and "We Nominate for Oblivion" features, which clearly paid playful tribute to the whimsicality and ephemerality of media-constructed tastes. Even single articles, like André Gide's 1928 "The Too General Public," could be significantly mixed. On the one hand, the Gide article invoked the language of high-cultural elitism so as to denounce the effect of "the mob" on the prospects for what Gide conceived as the nobly "disinterested" "pure work of art"[10]—in what finally amounts to a very faithful reproduction of modernist "contamination anxiety." And yet at the same time the article insists, explicitly *against* what it calls the "degeneration" of art under the doctrine of "art-for-art's-sake," on restoring art to the natural "social necessity" that according to Gide characterized its function and identity in the premodern world.[11] This, of course, is the same fundamentally mixed nature that would allow publisher Conde Nast to imagine *Vanity Fair*—which was committed enough to its avant-garde tastes even to consciously accept losing readers to it[12]—at the same time close enough in concept and audience to the fashion-oriented *Vogue* for the two to merge in 1936.

The most conspicuous connection of *Vanity Fair* and its reproduction of "elitist" high modernism to the mass market, though, was almost certainly through its great penchant for advertisement, examples of which appeared in a dizzying barrage of colorful art deco graphics through the first thirty, sometimes even fifty, pages of each issue. The magazine substantially exceeded all its contemporaries in total amount (and almost certainly, one must assume, *percentage*) of advertising space per issue—including even big sellers like *Vogue*, which actually earned far more in total revenues.[13] Maybe for the first time in the history of publishing (though standard practice in contemporary glossies), *ads in the slicks became as clearly important a part of what a magazine might offer its readers as anything else.* More importantly, not only did *Vanity Fair* define its identity significantly through association with the particular commodities it advertised (cars, high-fashion clothing, ocean passage to Europe), but its ads themselves were clearly intended to be appreciated *aesthetically.* Typically, that is, *Vanity Fair* ads quickly began to appropriate the *look* of the modern art the magazine was devoted to reproducing—so that given advertisers developed associations with different trademark styles, like what clearly became Sak's Fifth Avenue's signature expressionism, for example. Some even went so far as to capitalize calculatedly on the established conventions of *Vanity Fair's* graphic presentation of that art (again, relatively common practice today) so that it became difficult even to tell without looking closely whether certain pages were features or ads (figs. 4–8). They might even be some new hybrid of the two, like designer- and boutique-specific fashion announcements—the illustrations for which, similarly, were *always* displayed in exactly the same form as the magazine's regularly featured fine-art engravings and etchings. Simply, the slicks began to look *uncannily* like their ads, even using the ads' typically garish color and stylization to *announce themselves for sale*—as with, say, the tuxedoed and bobbed-haired Charleston dancers who formed the *V* and the *F* for one 1927 *Vanity Fair*, which often integrated the subjects of its cover art into the letters of its masthead. The slicks and their ads, then, came to form what readers could only experience as a powerfully seamless single tissue.

Certain ads even mimicked the magazine's curatorial function as tastemaker, sometimes crudely. This was very much the case, for example, with the long-running series of front- and rear-leaf Steinway piano ads that featured oil paintings commissioned for "the Steinway Collection." These, I should note, were typically prepared by commercial artists with mixed reputations like Rockwell Kent, who as professional "illustrators" had no qualms about reproducing on demand particular avantgarde styles to which they had no special aesthetic allegiance, but would also bring to those reproductions respectable art-school and museum exhibition credentials (along very often with *conspicuously* European-sounding names, like Nicholas Remisoff, F. Luis Mora, and Sergei Soudeikine). Still other ads that, less coy about their commercial function, marked themselves more clearly *as* ads of course became always progressively bolder and more striking, all the time claiming their radical modernity more explicitly and as a more central part of the magazine's identity. Certain ads even went beyond the blurring of ad and feature to explicitly violate the ostensibly sacrosanct modernist line between art and commodity itself, comparing their products to the great "achievements" in art in what can now only seem positively comic combinations—like the Goodyear *Portrait of a Man by Titian* ad in one 1931 issue, part of a long Goodyear series based on camparisons with great museum masterpieces (fig. 9).

Men's Footwear
by Alan McAfee,
of London

an embodiment of bench workman-
ship that has been characteristic of
british boot-making for more than
two centuries. made in *london,*
expressly for *saks-fifth avenue*
under the personal super-
vision of *mr. alan mcafee.*
models for all occa-
sions are presented.

SAKS-FIFTH AVENUE
New York

Vanity Fair, *May 1928.*

Cover, Vanity Fair, *January, 1929.*

STEINWAY
THE INSTRUMENT OF THE IMMORTALS

LE SACRE DU PRINTEMPS, *painted for the* STEINWAY COLLECTION
by SERGEI SOUDEIKINE

While there are still differences of opinion regarding Stravinsky's famous ballet, it is interesting to note that in 15 years the critical fraternity has come to accept it almost to a man. The public estimate is scarcely less enthusiastic. Its influence upon contemporary music has been widespread and profound.

THERE is such a wealth of enjoyment in the ownership of a fine piano . . . such a plenitude of power, and companionship, and beauty, that in cultivated homes it is numbered among the necessities of life.

Such people realize that music is as vital to the soul as air and food are to the body. They find in the piano the most personal and intimate means of ministering to that need. And in the Steinway they find the most exquisitely responsive, the most superbly endowed of all pianos.

For more than 75 years the Steinway has been the acknowledged leader among pianos, wherever good music is performed. Its extraordinary qualities of tone and sensitivity have placed it in a class by itself. Virtually every musician of note, from Wagner to Igor Stravinsky, has chosen it both for personal and concert use.

Yet despite its striking superiority, the Steinway is actually among the most economical of pianos. For 50, 40, and even 50 years or more it will serve you well, as only the best and finest things can do.

Calculated on the basis of cost-per-year, it is less expensive than any other instrument. . . . And you need never buy another piano.

There is a Steinway dealer in your community, or near you, through whom you may purchase a new Steinway piano with a 10% cash deposit, and the balance will be extended over a period of two years. Used pianos accepted in partial exchange.

Prices: $875 *and up—plus transportation*

10% down *balance in two years*

STEINWAY & SONS, Steinway Hall
109 West 57th Street, New York City

Vanity Fair, *February 1929, rear leaf.*

Fredric March

The maddest member of "The Royal Family" is at present appearing in a new picture opposite Claudette Colbert

■ Fredric March graduated from the University of Wisconsin in 1920, and shortly afterward made his stage début in Sacha Guitry's *Deburau*. After appearing in *The Rogue, Tarnish*, and *The Devil in the Cheese*, young Mr. March accepted an engagement in California with a road company of *The Royal Family*, that play by George S. Kaufman and Edna Ferber which, upon its opening in New York, was instantly hailed as a hilarious parody of the Barrymore family—hailed, that is, by everybody except, possibly, the Barrymore family themselves. It was at this time, two years ago, that Fredric March was enticed into the moving pictures, appearing in *Manslaughter, Laughter* and other films; but curiously enough, his greatest triumph in the talkies has been as the same *Tony* in *The Royal Family* which he once played in a road company on the Coast. He is married to Florence Eldridge, and his current film is tentatively entitled *Honour Among Lovers*

Etching, Vanity Fair, *December 1928.*

■ For a light-weight suit with outright *class*—*Nurotex* rang the bell long ago. But this season it breaks its own record for true quality. ■ Designed in bedford cord and embossed weave effects—in pure whites, tans and greys...newly distinctive—superb. ■ It has longer life than most suits at twice its price. It is feathery light, with the sort of good looks that stay put, no matter how great the wear. ■ Readily washed or cleaned—yet it has a way of shedding the dirt that helps to keep it clean. ■ And if you want a *sporting Nurotex*, there are suits with knickers and extra tennis trousers that will add real zest to your game. ■ Say "Nurotex" to your clothier...He'll produce. ■ Goodall Worsted Company Sanford, Maine. Selling Agent, A. Rohaut, 229 Fourth Avenue, New York

THE SURPRISE OF THE SEASON IN
THESE UNUSUAL NUROTEX SUITS

Advertisement, Vanity Fair, *March 1931.*

In fact, at moments the modernist ethos itself even came to be defined explicitly and without apparent contradiction—*seamlessly,* even—as a manifestation of market savvy in very practical terms. For example, in what was then a fairly revolutionary piece of slickness—though one that now characterizes, at least in part, pretty standard glossy-magazine verve—literary and arts figures were normally recommended to readers not only in terms of the relative spectacles of their successes ("because her play . . . is a success on Broadway and her novel is the most popular one of the year"),[14] but even in terms of the facility with which they combined the separate realms of art and business ("because though a *Fortune* editor he still writes poetry").[15] And the formats in which they were featured (like the famous monthly *Vanity Fair* "Hall of Fame") mixed artists and writers so freely with actors, singers, dancers, musicians, athletes, and businesspeople as to make them significantly indistinguishable. The all-the-world's-a-marketplace associations invoked from Thackeray's title and Bunyan's allegory—and exploited explicitly in *Vanity Fair*'s own "Kaleidoscopic Review of the Modern World" ads—made this gesture complete. Truly modern aesthetic success in essence, it turns out, simply *is* marketplace success, nothing more or less. Those ads quote Bunyan: "and In That Town There Is A Fair Called *Vanity Fair* and In It Are All Such Merchandise Sold as Places, Honours, Preferments, Titles, Lusts, Pleasures and Delights of All Sorts . . . and They That Reep This Fair Are The Men of This World."[16] The magazine was worth its three dollars a year, then, above all, because it knew the current market values of the celebrities, styles, aesthetics, and ideas it featured, and because it would guide its reader through the kaleidoscopic market of modernity with all the instincts of the sharpest shopper—the same instincts, it suggested, necessary to negotiate that market as a modern *artist* as well.

And this, it seems to me, is no small point, even if we have become somewhat accustomed to the art-and-commodity-blurring publishing practices initiated by the slicks. In fact, I think, it could be argued that nowhere else in all of modern culture is the theory of art-as-commodity explored more immediately than it is in the slicks, so oddly situated between high art and mass culture. Indeed, in their playful negotiation of the very difficult contradiction at the heart of their cultural function—the mass popularization of defiantly elite art—the slicks develop a peculiar sort of cultural market savvy. And, all the customary truisms about "elitist" modernism and its "contamination anxiety" notwithstanding, it seems to me precisely this savviness that the slicks offer their readers as

Portrait of a Man by Titian

The
DOUBLE EAGLE
by
GOOD YEAR

APPRECIATION is the fruit of merit. The work that is sound and durable in quality is sound and durable in fame. Thus the Goodyear Double Eagle Tire, introduced as being almost needlessly fine, today is far richer in public appreciation than at any earlier time. It stands alone. It has no rival in popular or critical esteem. Of all the super-tires it is the archetype and masterpiece — first not only in reputation, but also in sales.

Vanity Fair, *June 1931, rear leaf.*

the essence of what it means to be a "modernist"—what it means to be kept, as *Vanity Fair*'s ad department says, "in touch with the newest and liveliest influences of modern life."

Of course, the phenomenon of commodity's aestheticization in the modern world has been observed quite often, especially in Frankfurt School critiques of mass culture, conceived by way of Marxist theories of commodity fetishism. Especially powerful, for example, are the brilliant opening paragraphs of the "Culture Industry" chapter of Horkheimer and Adorno's *Dialectic of Enlightenment,* in which the authors very incisively explicate the powerful tautology through which slick culture had by the 1940s so thoroughly legitimated art's commodification. I do not mean to suggest that we should be blind to the power with which these critiques describe the brazen capitalization and colonization of modern mass culture and consciousness. In one sense, the rise of the slicks and their insistence on seeing art as a business can be seen as the simple sign of a thoroughly commodified culture, representing the co-option—and even the vulgarization—of an art making a serious attempt to resist an oppressively conventionalized mainstream. And yet in their zeal for political and cultural sobriety these critiques also seem to me regularly to fall short of acknowledging the potential radical suggestiveness of certain self-conscious forms of commodity culture like the slicks. In short, those forms implicitly serve to point out the inherent difficulties of the very notion of commodity fetishism itself, which depends directly on a foundationalist theory of value: if all value were culturally constructed, that is, then how could any value be understood as "fetishized"? On one level, then, commodity culture clearly reinforces highly naturalized—*commodified*—ideologies. But on another, it serves as a potentially quite powerful *denaturalizing* force. To recognize one's own embeddedness in commodity culture is not only to risk encouraging resignation to dominant social forces; it is also, at least potentially, to call self-conscious attention to the terms of one's own ideological and historical construction.

In this sense, the slicks' embrace of the mass marketplace serves powerfully to undermine what a Marxist would call the "use value" theory on which foundationalist aesthetic sensibilities are based, particularly if we understand it as a metaphor for what Jean Baudrillard calls the "political economy of the sign." For the slicks, what counted for good art was not by any means absolute and eternal—as it was, of course, for the modernism of "contamination anxiety" theory—but was profoundly relative and culturally constructed, the product of complexly layered meanings taken on through the play of culture around it. That is, if art is necessarily commodity and commodity begins to look so provocatively like art—as it does in the slicks—then whatever currency either achieves can be based on no naturalized aesthetic gold-standard, but only on its appeal to culturally situated and interested audiences. Indeed, the slicks became 150-page monthly advertisements and were both attractive (as art) and consumable (as commodities) because of it. And there was no need for the slicks' reader-consumers to expect any more tangibly concrete return on their investments than that. In fact, by making all the art they published recognizable only in terms of an acknowledgment of its function as commodity, and by in turn making commodification itself their most conspicuous aesthetic value, the slicks insisted upon a system in which no other form of tender could possibly make any sense. Exchange value, that is, came to wholly supersede use value for the slicks: the glossy magazine had a currency all its own, instantly recognizable and negotiable, though impossible to *cash in*—as, say, the reader of an 1890s *Century* might "cash in" on an article by Henry Cabot Lodge, which would provide a certain amount of "real" information with which one could form an opinion, for instance, on politics or economics. It is hard to imagine that the sleek little piece of literate civility that constitutes "One Hundred Per Cent Bohemia," on the other hand, could offer its reader the performance of any "function" other than the supply of raw materials for cultural barter—exactly the sort of empty, Eli-Nadelman-and-Hindu-musicians cocktail party banter, that is, that we have in fact seen *Vanity Fair* explicitly advertise to prospective subscribers. This, of course, is the principle difference between the twentieth-century "slicks" and the premodern nineteenth-century "pulps," their mass-cultural predecessors. *Vanity Fair* simply *had no use,* a fact clear to everyone involved with either its production or its consumption, and its value was in fact based squarely—and openly—on that uselessness. The slicks' readers weren't interested in securing from the magazines any knowledge that they could value as information, as irreducible *truth,* but only very relative and arbitrary knowledge produced in a specific historical context as an exchange object, knowledge that they could in turn continue to trade on for its exchange value—*slick* knowledge. With the rise of the slicks, that is, it no longer mattered what was *in* a magazine, only what *brand* it was.

To be sure, many contemporary inheritors of the foundationalist left tradition, often writing in the shadow of the Frankfurt School, resist recognizing the potential denaturalizing dimension of the commodity aesthetic quite explicitly—even though they tend to be significantly more discriminating and qualified in their judgments on mass culture and the politics of the high/low distinction than their Frankfurt School predecessors. Jürgen Habermas's famous denunciation of postmodernism's breaking of faith with the noble modernist project of "enlightenment" in a "Dyonisiac" submission to the postindustrial milieu of "disillusionment" that "furthers [dangerously anticritical] capitalist modernization processes"[17] stands, of course, as an especially important and obvious example, as does Fredric Jameson's related inclination to equate postmodernism with what he calls "the cultural logic of late capitalism." In fact, at times these theorists even denounce an inclination in the Frankfurt School's founders themselves to get too close to a rethinking of the commodity aesthetic. Huyssen, for example, objects to Theodor Adorno's theory of "culture industry" on the grounds that the commodity aesthetic's apparent defiance of use value provides for no possibility of effective political intervention—no possibility of "an emancipatory cultural production."[18]

But theorizing such a possibility—an outside the "marketplace" of cultural construction—proves always irreducibly problematic. It is for this reason that Huyssen, for example, is moved to call Adorno's "black-hole theory of capitalist culture" both "too Marxist and not Marxist enough."

> Culture and commodification have been collapsed in this theory to the extent that the gravitational pull of the culture industry leaves no meaning, no signification unscathed. . . . [But i]f cultural products were commodities through and through and had only exchange value, they would no longer even be able to fulfill their function in the processes of ideological reproduction. . . . Culture industry, after all, does fulfill public functions; it satisfies and legitimizes cultural needs . . . it articulates social contradictions in order to homogenize them.[19]

Undeniably, texts have social "functions." Certainly, for example, the slicks themselves reproduced and reinforced some very important class distinctions, and *Vanity Fair* subscribers undoubtedly used the magazine as a signifier of some desired or newly attained social-class standing. But this attempt to make such function stand in for what Jean Baudrillard has called the epistemological "alibi" of unproblematically real "use" is unmistakably flawed. For Baudrillard, whose early works formed some of the founding documents in the still ongoing struggle between post-structuralism and Marxism, the notion of such use always meant, very specifically, a rock-bottom essential utility unconstructed by the cultural marketplace through which commodities attempt a false metaphysical justification for their market-determined prices.[20] But social function in the sense in which Huyssen means it—the power of a commodity to reproduce the ideology oppressing its consumer—of course clearly never works to convince any prospective consumers of that commodity's value. This sort of "use" has nothing to do with the semiotic "alibi" justifying a sense of some text's "inherent" worth or meaning. What's more, it is no rigorous theoretical fine point to observe that one's understanding of a text's social function is itself inescapably constructed. The attempt to "bracket" off (as Heidegger would say) a site from which to speak with pseudo-objectivity can never be understood as anything more than a hermeneutically necessarily compromise. And the length to which Huyssen appears willing to go in this sort of bending of the term *use value* in order, as he says, to find some signification "unscathed" by marketplace exchange, to find a *pure use* that defies commodification, to escape the "black hole" of ideology, seems to me only to reveal the clarity of the extent to which such "purity" simply makes no sense within the now dominant system of accelerated exchange suggested by the commodity aesthetic, a system the slicks clearly helped inaugurate. Once the "alibi" of use is suspended, once the notion of ideology as "false consciousness" is finally abandoned, ideology itself must be measured and accounted for differently—and the slicks, I think, call our attention powerfully to that difference. The only "function" left to perform in the kind of modern world the slicks suggest is exchange: nothing between the covers of any given issue of *Vanity Fair* (no—including the covers especially) has any "use" for its reader except as an item of exchange.

In this sense, then, the rise of the slicks can be said to have ushered in the age—provocatively—of what Baudrillard calls "pure sign exchange value," in which all pretenses of a rock-bottom, essentialized use value are finally forgone. Of course, this is an age we normally think of as radically *post*modern. And in fact, if any realm of modernist consciousness could be said to have had a truly generative influence on postmodernism's fascination with mass culture and cultural "economics," it indeed seems to me not—as is always assumed—the avant-garde's militant clashing of high and low, which always ends up only reifying those categories, but *slick culture*, in which these categories are mixed in a significantly more provocative way. This is why the cultivation of a sort of ultimate slicks experience was such a vital pillar of Andy Warhol's pop project, for example—resulting in such an important piece of budding postmodernity as *Andy Warhol's Interview* magazine, the ever more trendily photographed and laid out, self-consciously substanceless homage to mass-media celebrity—a coyly, almost grotesquely accelerated slick—published by Warhol until his death. It should come as no surprise, that is, that *Interview* became the focus of Warhol's attention and the center of what can be thought of as the sort of Warhol arts empire after the slow dissolution of the frenetic 1960s Factory scene in the early and middle 1970s. Only through such a vehicle—begun in 1969, and in fact still in publication and even heightened financial health (it may yet turn out to be Warhol's most enduring legacy!)—could Warhol move pop most rigorously toward postmodernity.

And yet it is also in this way that the slicks are "bohemian" in the *fullest* modernist sense, I think. The cultural climate of what Baudrillard calls "pure sign exchange value," that is, is perhaps less *unqualifiedly* foreign to the modernist imaginary than we might—or than we have been taught to—expect. Of course, I do not mean to suggest that modernism is not in any way characterized by a phobia of "contamination" by what Huyssen has rightly called its mass-cultural "Other." Or that this phobia has not had "exclusionary" and "elitist" socioeconomic effects. But it also seems to me that if modernism's margins can be marked so clearly by a sensitivity to the cultural construction of meaning—manifested in a powerful blurring of the lines between art and commodity, aesthetic sophistication and market savvy—then perhaps the *general cultural imaginary activating* what we have come to think of as "high" modernism might even be seen to be in some way preoccupied with commodification, at least as an issue. In fact, we might imagine that sensibilities on the margins of modernism had even begun to intuit the marketplace, with all its potential for calling attention to the cultural construction of meaning, as a potentially important site of cultural resistance. Perhaps "slick" culture can be seen to have moved modernism powerfully to the brink of something it had long been working through, at least subconsciously, but could never entirely resolve. For the new glossy magazine, at least, bohemia was itself a marketplace, and marketplaces turned out to be the ultimate bohemias.

Indeed, through its thinly ironic reenactment of the traditional bohemian *l'art pour l'art* scorn for commerce ("bohemianism is no longer a profession but a business"), which serves to accentuate a more subtly ironic and culturally incisive enactment of the capitalist culture industry itself (as we have seen, the article does nothing so effectively as advertise bohemians to prospective patrons), "One Hundred Per Cent Bohemia" (and the slicks in general) created an extraordinarily pervasive cultural posture that seems to me especially wise to the politics of the culture industry. The slicks, that is, were endowed with a strange, almost campy sort of *pop decadence* that allowed them, among other things, to appropriate the prevailing cultural forms (like "contamination anxiety") while maintaining (like "One Hundred Per Cent Bohemia") an extremely high degree of self-consciousness. They enacted a mode of cultural participation—or perhaps a mode of aloofness—that enabled a peculiar savvy about perceiving and negotiating the exchange-constituted currencies of particular texts (or even styles of textualizing) in the cultural marketplace. So if the slicks suggest the rise of a new form of cultural economics, one based on the ultimate dissolution of the epistemological foundation of use, then they also can be seen to have offered their readers a powerful model for negotiating those economics. The slicks, I argue, not only popularized the stereotypical *forms* of modernism, they popularized its implicit, and it seems to me often ignored, sense of cultural savvy—its very *slick*ness—as well. In order to fully participate as a reader in the modernism *Vanity Fair* reproduced, one needed to be slick indeed.

In fact, perhaps "contamination anxiety" itself can be seen in part simply to conceal this preoccupation with the marketplace, this closet *slickness,* even behind what we might think of as a sort of *commodity voyeurism.* Huyssen has already compellingly suggested the ways in which masculinist modernism figured its mass-cultural Other as overwhelmingly female.[21] In this context, then, the sort of repressed desire for consummation in the popular media that we have seen in modernism's representation in the slicks—"One Hundred Per Cent Bohemia"'s simultaneous submerged fascination with the details of the "business" of bohemianism and yet apparent obligation to demonstrate a curt disapproval of that "business" publicly—shouldn't seem surprising. Quite to the contrary, the magazine's position in the aesthetic hierarchy was explicitly implicated in the gendering of art culture as male and mass culture as female, resulting in a simultaneous ambiguity of both gender and aesthetic class. We should remember, after all, that the clearly feminized slicks were first and foremost women's fashion publications—including even arts-oriented *Vanity Fair*, which was originally conceived and published in 1913 as *Dress and Vanity Fair*—and that *Vanity Fair* was in fact marked by a strong identification with a gay fashion subculture throughout its twenty-two-year run, an identification reinforced by the figure of Crowninshield, the magazine's famous dandyish "bachelor" editor.[22] Indeed, it is difficult not to understand the *explicitly* homophobic distaste of *Vanity Fair*'s serious-minded, literary feature-writers like Edmund Wilson for its fashion department in these terms:[23] one imagines the dandyish *Vanity Fair* sensibility as the manifestation as much of a repressed commodity-urge as of a repressed homoeroticism.

So it makes sense to imagine that masculinist modernism's obligatory expressions of disapproval for the mass market might more generally be marked also by the signs of something more like an only partially repressed leer. And one needn't look very hard to find such signs. It is difficult not to notice, for instance, that these sorts of leers form a defining feature of the work of a "high" modernist as notoriously misogynist and aestheticist as Ernest Hemingway, who like all well-known and highly successful fiction-writers in early-twentieth-century America published often in the best-paying slicks, especially *Esquire* and *Colliers*. Indeed, it formed a recurring and notorious Hemingway motif to include a lead female character whose depiction was shaped largely by association to work as a fashion model in glossy magazines—a character based in fact on the figure of Hemingway's own second wife, Pauline Pfeiffer, herself an on-and-off Paris correspondent for *Vogue*. Most notably, these characters include Margot Macomber in "The Short Happy Life of Francis Macomber," temptress and brazen emasculator who "commanded five thousand dollars as the price of endorsing, with photographs, a beauty product which she had never used," and the beautiful, obedient Helen, the "rich bitch" in "The Snows of Kilimanjaro,"[24] who similarly rouses the lazy voyeuristic interest—but dilutes the purer aesthetic potency—of the story's Hemingway figure, Harry. In fact, these slicks-constructed women—having stepped directly off the pages of glossy magazines, *explicitly* the phantasms of masculine/modernist longing—are always at once two things. On one hand, they are the vehicles of an ultimate aesthetic "selling out" that can end only in listlessness and death, figured in "The Snows of Kilimanjaro" as a gangrenous spiritual decay. On the other, they are the site of an irresistible sexual fascination—the artist's flirtation with and seduction by slick culture.

> She looked at him with her well-known, well-loved face from *Spur* and *Town and Country,* only a little the worse for drink, only a little the worse for bed, but *Town and Country* never showed those good breasts and those useful thighs and those lightly small-of-back-caressing hands, and as he looked and saw her well known pleasant smile, he felt death come again.[25]

Hemingway's unmistakable and often-noted squeamishness about what Huyssen rightly identifies as "contamination" by a feminized mass culture, then, is as much matched by its repressed opposite—a leering, voyeurish fascination—as, say, Filippo Marinetti's similar and much-noted embrace of machinery, which of course always ends up simply feminizing and fetishizing the mechanical in brutally misogynist ways.[26] In this sense, then, "anxiety of contamination" theorists of modernism like Huyssen have always been at least *partly* wrong: as Jean Baudrillard has implied in comments on "ascetic" Bauhaus purity-of-function design, modernist contamination anxiety is really at most only the manifested repression of a significant semiotic *fashion fetish.*[27]

Less repressed into this sort of twisted Hemingwayesque voyeurism, a certain modernist preoccupation with the marketplace is even apparent around the edges of modernism's conventionalized construction of the artist. The stereotype of the great modernist literary figure, at least in America, includes "formative" work in advertising, even as a kind of badge of healthy aesthetic apprenticeship that too eager and energetic modernist writers must wear in their youths and repress before they can graduate to "serious" work—the sign of a sensitive but not yet formed talent. The much-chronicled careers of F. Scott Fitzgerald, Sherwood Anderson, Allen Tate, and Hart Crane, for example, all followed this pattern. Perhaps more obviously, modernist works themselves often traded on the styles and rhythms of commodity culture explicitly—even, arguably, in spite of their own formalist "anxieties" about mass culture. This is clearly the case with such landmark pieces of modernism as William Carlos Williams's *Paterson,* certain sections of Hart Crane's *The Bridge,* much of e. e. cummings's poetry, and the "Newsreel" and "Camera Eye" prose poems in John Dos Passos's *U.S.A.,*[28] which are all rife with advertising slogans and mass-media-induced colloquialisms—in fact, are often based prosodically on the rhythms of ad copy. As in the slicks, then, an only slightly submerged fascination with—and indeed, aestheticization of—commodity comes to serve as an important signifier of modernity. And the sort of acute market savvy we have seen this aestheticization of commodity enable is also reflected in a certain modernist tradition of self-promotion (begun to be accounted for, in fact, in "One Hundred Per Cent Bohemia")—from Marcel Duchamp to Salvador Dalí to Stein and Hemingway to even Norman Mailer, whose *Advertisements for Myself* perhaps forms its self-conscious apogee. There is in "One Hundred Per Cent Bohemia," that is—as in what seems to me modernism's self-conscious deployment of the cult of authorial personality more generally—a profound sense of and intent to exploit the outrageousness of the ironic reversal it enacts. Even for segments of recognizably "high" modern culture itself, the ultimate act of bohemianism becomes, as early as 1920—though of course ever more explicitly for the Situationists in the 1950s and Andy Warhol in the 1960s—an immersion in its own marketing process.

But the degree to which this equation between art and commodity, bohemia and marketplace, seems natural for the modernist sensibility generally, weaned at least in part on this pervasive modern *slickness,* may be indicated, I argue, just as clearly by the drawing that appears directly above "100 Per Cent Bohemia" (fig. 10), which has no apparent strictly illustrative relationship to the article but clearly asks to be read as illustration because of its direct proximity to the copy. Drawn by *Vanity Fair* regular "Fish," it is a sort of an orgy of stylization—appropriate enough, it would seem, for an illustration of bohemianism. And yet its subject—a posh jazz-age ballroom, complete with dancing, flirting, drinking, and black jazz musicians—is hardly evocative of the "pure" bohemianism the article seems to champion. But we need to remember how far modernism and its "slicks" may have already begun to take us from the model of the dignified starving artist. That is, the modernist bohemia, unlike the "authentic" Romantic one to which the *Vanity Fair* article's title would seem to refer, can often be seen to have reached the very brink of achieving an acute consciousness of its own commodification. It is not, apparently, the stubborn artistic resistance to the popular, carried out in dirty cafes and cheap studio lofts—but instead the highly ironic, self-consciously decadent *enactment* of the popular, the consuming of consumption, carried out with special effect in ballrooms and magazines of culture—that characterizes "bohemianism" at modernism's outer limits.

L'ENSEMBLE CORDIALE
American jazz music in London has added the final bond to the fraternal union of England and America, according to "Fish," who speaks for both countries

One Hundred Per Cent Bohemia

The Early Days of New York's Bohemian Glory, When Clemenceau Dined at Pfaff's

Vanity Fair, *January 1920.*

Indeed, by this peculiar and much-repressed logic, it is hard to imagine that anything could really be considered fully a *hundred* percent bohemian at the moment of modernism's fullest unfolding without having appeared at least *once* in a glossy magazine.

NOTES

1. James L. Ford, "One Hundred Per Cent Bohemia," *Vanity Fair,* January 1920, p. 108.

2. Frank Crowninshield, reprinted in *Vanity Fair: A Cavalcade of the 1920's and 1930's,* ed. Cleveland Amory and Frederic Bradlee (New York: Viking Press, 1960), p. 13.

3. Ibid.

4. *Vanity Fair*, February 1919, p. 82.

5. Andreas Huyssen, *After the Great Divide: Modernism, Mass Culture, Postmodernism* (Bloomington: Indiana University Press, 1986), p. vii.

6. Terry Eagleton, "Capitalism, Modernism, and Postmodernism," in *Against the Grain* (London: Verso, 1986), p. 140.

7. Very recently, a few scholars have begun to challenge the orthodoxy of contamination-anxiety theory. Aside from the other essays in this collection, see, for example, Jeffrey Weiss's *The Popular Culture of Modern Art: Picasso, Duchamp, and Avant-Gardeism* (New Haven: Yale University Press, 1994); and Paul Mann's *The Theory-Death of the Avant-Garde* (Bloomington: Indiana University Press, 1991).

8. Ford, "One Hundred Per Cent," p. 65.

9. Crowninshield, pp. 259–60.

10. André Gide, reprinted in Amory and Bradlee, *Vanity Fair*, p. 155.

11. In fact, the degree to which this essay anticipates the sophisticated arguments of more contemporary art theorists, from André Malraux to Peter Burger to Douglas Crimp—especially in the historical specificity of its critique of ostensibly asocial *l'art pour l'art* aestheticism—makes it fascinating reading. If, as I will argue here, the general cultural milieu of the "slicks" suggests some unexpected commonalities between modernism and postmodernism around the issue of the ubiquity of the marketplace, then this unexpected kinship between Gide and, say, Crimp would also seem similarly revealing.

12. George H. Douglas, *The Smart Magazines* (Hamden, Conn.: Archon Books, 1991), p. 99.

13. Ibid., p. 101.

14. Amory and Bradlee, *Vanity Fair*, p. 88.

15. Ibid., p. 258.

16. *Vanity Fair*, October 1931, rear leaf.

17. Jürgen Habermas, "Modernity—an Incomplete Project," in *The Anti-Aesthetic: Essays on Post-Modern Culture,* ed. Hal Foster (Seattle: Bay Press, 1983), pp. 14, 13.

18. Andreas Huyssen, "Introduction to Adorno," *New German Critique* 6 (Fall 1975): 5.

19. Huyssen, *After the Great Divide*, pp. 21–22.

20. See especially *Notes for a Critique of the Political Economy of the Sign,* trans. Charles Levin (St. Louis: Telos Press, 1981); and *The Mirror of Production,* trans. Mark Poster (St. Louis: Telos Press, 1975).

21. See "Mass Culture as Woman: Modernism's Other" in Huyssen, *After the Great Divide,* pp 44–62.

22. Douglas, *The Smart Magazines*, p. 112.

23. George Douglas reports in *The Smart Magazines* that though Crowninshield never gave any clear public signals about his sexual orientation,

"Wilson did believe . . . that the atmosphere at *Vanity Fair* had a somewhat vaguely homosexual flavor about it. It was an atmosphere that emanated from the men's fashion department, where the regular staffers were invariably homosexual. . . . Perhaps there was something of a spirit of masculine frivolity and nonchalance that soured some of *Vanity Fair*'s staff members, if seldom the casual reader. Edmund Wilson left after a year to become a literary critic for the *New Republic,* where he told friends that at last he would be able to devote himself to more serious writing projects" (112).

24. Ernest Hemingway, *The Snows of Kilimanjaro* (New York: Scribner), pp. 122, 9.

25. Ibid., p. 18.

26. See, for example, the passage from *War, the World's Only Hygiene* collected for English-speaking audiences as "Multiplied Man and the Reign of the Machine," in *Marinetti: Selected Writings* (New York: Farrar, Straus and Giroux, 1972), where Marinetti writes of the machine aesthetic: "We are developing and proclaiming a great new idea that runs through modern life: the idea of mechanical beauty. We therefore exalt love for the machine, that love we notice flaming on the cheeks of mechanics scorched and smeared with coal. Have you never seen a mechanic lovingly at work on the great powerful body of his locomotive? His is the minute, knowing tenderness of a lover caressing his adored woman" (90). As a result, of course, these male mechanics were to have only "swift, casual contacts" (92) with *real* women.

27. Baudrillard, *Notes*, p. 192. In *Notes for a Critique of the Political Economy of the Sign,* Baudrillard writes: "the Bauhaus' revolution is *puritan.* Functionalism is ascetic. This fact is [what is most] revealed in the sobriety and geometric lines of its models, its *phobia* [my italics] of *decor and artifice*" (192).

28. In a manuscript under composition, tentatively titled *The Great American Dream Machine: John Dos Passos's "USA,"* Anthony Di Renzo has even connected Dos Passos's work to postmodernism, as I do, for similar reasons, especially around his sense of the coy, dime-store "manufacturedness" of Dos Passos's prose style.

Selling Sex as Art

Joyce Wexler

The expansion of the reading public in the nineteenth century made art and money antithetical goals. Protesting against the insidious equation of commercial success with literary value, serious writers defined themselves as artists by repudiating any interest in how much they earned.[1] Modernist novelists could not seek sales directly because they inherited contradictory ideologies of authorship. On the one hand, the Romantic artist as genius was expected to express an inviolable inner vision without regard for its rhetorical effect or market value. On the other hand, the Victorian author as professional was expected to earn a living by writing. In the first model, money was a sign of corruption, but in the second it was a proof of success. Each ideal generated cautionary counterparts: the hack who wrote only for money and the amateur who could not publish anything. In this conflict, art was aligned with writing for oneself, martyrdom, and self-expression, while sales were aligned with writing for an audience, professionalism, and rhetoric. The characteristic difficulty and obscenity of modernist fiction were formal responses to this situation.

The marketing genius of modernist authors inspired them to defend erotic fiction as art and sell it as smut. Turning the period's contradictory ideologies to their economic advantage, many modernists disavowed financial aims while benefiting materially from the erotic aspects of their work. Explicit sex was a protest against materialist social values, but it also increased sales. Once sex was aligned with art against commercial ends, it provided the money serious writers could not admit they wanted. Censorship advertised the work of Joyce and Lawrence far beyond the avant-garde audience.

Commercial publishers were also tangled in these contradictions: they could not publish work that was illegal, yet they knew that erotic fiction would be extremely profitable. Publishers eventually defended this fiction in court on the grounds that it was not erotic, but they wanted to publish it because it was.[2] In the key legal decisions that permitted *Ulysses* and

Lady Chatterley's Lover to be sold openly, courts accepted the argument that artistic necessity justified obscenity. In both cases, judicial opinions inadvertently parodied the "art for art's sake" slogan in their recurring description of pornography as "dirt for dirt's sake."[3] In practice, the distinction between art and dirt often depended on the perceived audience. Throughout the nineteenth century, prosecutors tended to seize material only when it addressed "persons with incomes of less than £500 a year. The law was not invoked against the authors of serious literature nor the morals of the better-off members of the community" (*T* 1–2).

As moral standards became stricter in the Victorian period, courts were asked to establish a new consensus on the meaning of obscenity, but judicial opinions reflected the conflict between the Romantic and Victorian conceptions of art. While defendants invoked the purity of their intentions, prosecutors emphasized the work's rhetorical effect, and they assumed this effect would vary with the social class of the reader. An 1867 decision included a test that was generally accepted as a statement of English common law: "Whether the tendency of the matter charged as obscenity is to deprave and corrupt those whose minds are open to such immoral influences and into whose hands a publication of this sort may fall" (*T* 3). This test protected Thomas Hardy and George Moore from prosecution, though they experienced unofficial censorship by the circulating libraries. Applying this standard, the courts banned Frank Harris's autobiography *My Life and Loves* (1922) as well as Radclyffe Hall's *The Well of Loneliness*, published by Jonathan Cape in 1928. Although the literary merit of *Well of Loneliness* was recognized, and its most explicit passage is "that night they were not divided," it was considered obscene because its subject, however chastely described, was a lesbian relationship (*T* 4). It was not republished until 1948, when its appearance was not contested. In the intervening years, authors' artistic intentions had become a successful defense against obscenity.

Although its difficulty stipulated an elite audience, much modernist fiction violated moral standards too flagrantly to be ignored. Even the briefs for the defense did not dispute the obscenity of certain passages in *Ulysses* and *Lady Chatterley's Lover*. Instead, they argued that the author's intention and the effect of the work as a whole had to be considered. Both sides regarded high sales as evidence of pornography, but the defense assured the court that these books were too difficult to be popular or profitable.

Ruling on *Ulysses* in 1933, Justice John M. Woolsey analyzed both authorial intention and rhetorical effect. The text passed the first test because Joyce's intent was not "dirt for dirt's sake."[4]

> [H]is attempt sincerely and honestly to realize his objective has required him incidentally to use certain words which are generally considered dirty words and has led at times to what many think is a too poignant preoccupation with sex in the thoughts of his characters. (*U* ix–x)

Woolsey exonerated Joyce on the grounds that his intention had been to describe "persons of the lower middle class living in Dublin in 1904" (*U* ix). Thus, if the "theme of sex" recurs in their minds, "it must always be remembered that his locale was Celtic and his season Spring" (*U* x). Underlying Woolsey's opinion was the assumption that highbrow readers would consider vulgar language suitable to lower-middle-class subjects. He allowed mimetic realism to justify any obscenity in the novel.

Applying the second test, he cited the legal standard of obscenity: "tending to stir the sex impulses or to lead to sexually impure and lustful thoughts" (*U* xi). His task, as he defined it, was to consider the book's "effect on a person with average sex instincts—what the French would call *l'homme moyen sensuel*" (*U* xi), that is, a person such as himself. Woolsey said that he found the book too difficult and too disgusting to produce any erotic response: "the effect of 'Ulysses' on the reader undoubtedly is somewhat emetic, nowhere does it tend to be an aphrodisiac" (*U* xii). To be sure he was correct, he devised a test he considered valid: he consulted two of his friends, and they agreed with him. Difficulty was not only a sign of art, but it was also a barrier to any kind of pleasure. As the defense attorneys had argued, "It is axiomatic that only what is understandable can corrupt."[5] If *Ulysses* had been addressed to a wider audience, Joyce would have been guilty of "exploiting obscenity" to increase sales (*U* viii). In aligning pornography and readability against art and difficulty, Woolsey enforced the modernist ideology that art and money were antithetical. As long as erotic fiction addressed an elite audience, it could be defended as art.

The issue of audience was raised in the appeal filed a year later. Although Woolsey's decision was upheld, the dissenting opinion written by Justice Martin T. Manton proposed different tests. He argued that obscenity statutes applied to particular passages rather than to the work as a whole and dealt with the effect of such passages on the most vulnerable segment of the community rather than on the average or elite members. Since the presence of obscene passages had not been disputed, Manton addressed intent and effect. He rejected artistic intention as a defense, because any pornographer could claim that he saw nothing obscene in his own product (*USA* 458). The relevant issue for Manton was the effect of obscenity on the "young and inexperienced" whom the law sought to protect, not on "those who pose as the more highly developed and intelligent" (*USA* 460–61).

Manton insisted that obscenity laws were not written to serve literary interests.

> The people do not exist for the sake of literature; to give the author fame, the publisher wealth, and the book a market. On the contrary, literature exists for the sake of the people. . . . Art for art's sake is heartless and soon grows artless; art for the public market is not art at all, but commerce; art for the people's service is a noble, vital, and permanent element of human life. (*USA* 461)

Although Manton believed that art should idealize rather than imitate life, both he and Woolsey accepted the dichotomy of art and money. While Woolsey concurred with the defense's blandishments that the difficulty of art blocked any "aphrodisiac" response, Manton correctly estimated the market value of modernist fiction in spite of its difficulty. *Ulysses* was in demand as soon as it was banned. Joyce helplessly watched pirated editions reap his profits. An edition of two thousand copies sold out in four days, and another pirated edition printed in monthly installments sold forty thousand copies a month.[6] When Sylvia Beach's 1922 edition appeared, there were not enough copies to meet the demand.

Woolsey's decision became an important precedent in obscenity cases, but *Lady Chatterley's Lover* had to wait more than twenty-five years to benefit from it. In 1959 Grove Press sued to publish the first legal unexpurgated edition. Like Woolsey, Federal Judge Frederick Bryan found that Lawrence's purpose was not prurient: "Thus, this is an honest and sincere novel of literary merit and its dominant theme and effect, taken as a whole, is not an appeal to the prurient interest of the average reader" (*T* 13). He judged the "passages describing sexual intercourse and using phallic language" to be "necessary to Lawrence's development of plot, theme, and character."[7] Evaluating the book's effect on readers, he tried to determine "whether to the average person, applying contemporary community standards, the dominant theme of the [novel] taken as a whole appeals to prurient interest." Like Woolsey, he found that the book was not "dirt for dirt's sake."

In addition to these tests, Bryan explicitly considered the way the book was marketed as a way to assess its effect: "A work of literature published and distributed through normal channels by a reputable publisher stands on quite a different footing from hard core pornography furtively sold for the purpose of profiting by the titillation of the dirty-minded" (*T* 13). Since it was written as art and sold as art, the novel was declared not to be obscene. Persuaded that aesthetic value outweighed erotic appeal, Bryan also reinforced the dichotomy between art and money. The novel's aesthetic value must have been great indeed, because this edition sold 3,225,000 copies in the first eight months.[8]

Hardly anyone calls this fiction obscene today, but Joyce thought *Lady Chatterley* "a piece of propaganda in favour of something which, outside D. H. L.'s country at any rate, makes all the propaganda for itself," and Lawrence considered *Ulysses* "the dirtiest, most indecent, obscene thing ever written."[9] The testimony of Joyce, Lawrence, and more than three million readers suggests that these books were not merely the aesthetic objects that publishers' lawyers claimed. Obscenity had a powerful rhetorical effect and a predictable economic value.

The mutual effort of authors and publishers to exploit the commercial value of this fiction without admitting mercenary motives vexed their negotiations. Lawrence's publishing experiences illustrate how modernists used obscenity as a weapon against social conventions, defending it as art, while they profited from it. Lawrence's correspondence also demonstrates that publishers were interested in avant-garde fiction because of its erotic content. From the beginning of his career, the eroticism of Lawrence's fiction attracted and frightened publishers, but contradictory ideologies of authorship dictated the terms of Lawrence's responses to editors' requests for revisions.

Although Heinemann accepted the manuscript of *The White Peacock* (1911), Heinemann's editor, Sidney Pawling, required extensive revisions. Like novice authors of the preceding generation, Lawrence was pleased at Pawling's interest and accepted his advice: "A good deal of it, including the whole of the third part, I have re-written. To be sure, it needed it. I think I have removed all the offensive morsels, all the damns, the devils and the sweat."[10] Although he complied with Pawling's suggestions,

Lawrence implied that only the threat of censorship made revisions necessary. Indecency, however, was not the main objection; Pawling also
asked him to condense the manuscript to tighten the structure (*L* 1:158).
This professional advice did not destroy Lawrence's originality; it
significantly improved the book. More intervention, not less, was needed.
Reviewers praised the descriptive passages, especially natural scenes, but
objected to glaring structural weaknesses that remained.[11] Pawling
accepted this manuscript in spite of its narrative faults because he perceived its literary and commercial value.

From this point on, the only obstacle to publication Lawrence faced
was censorship. He believed that his frankness was far more moral than
the evasions publishers encouraged, but publishers knew that certain passages were actionable. They also knew, however, that the eroticism in
Lawrence's work would make it extremely profitable. Heinemann was
reluctant to publish Lawrence's second novel, *The Trespasser,* still called
"The Saga of Siegmund," because it was "erotic," but he also wanted to
prevent any other firm from bringing it out. Rather than refuse the book
and thus lose his option, Heinemann tried to persuade Lawrence to with-
draw it and submit another manuscript. Warned that publication could
permanently damage his reputation as a serious writer, Lawrence turned
to Edward Garnett, an editor for Duckworth, for advice.

> I shall like to hear your opinion of the work. Hueffer called it "a rot-
> ten work of genuis" [*sic*], but he was prejudiced against the inconse-
> quential style; said that erotic literature must be in the form of high
> art.
>
> This Saga, on the contrary, is based on brief notes made from actu-
> ality. Nevertheless I swear it has true form. (*L* 1:330)

Since Hueffer (later Ford Madox Ford) was a writer as well as an editor,
his opinion was worth considering. Despite Lawrence's tone, he soon followed Hueffer's advice. Adopting the modernist aesthetic of impersonal
form, Lawrence began to argue that the erotic elements in his work were
necessary to both his art and his moral purpose.

When Lawrence decided to leave teaching and earn his living as a professional writer, he became more concerned with his audience. As a
result, a characteristic modernist conflict between money and art
erupted. Permitting Duckworth to make additional cuts in *The Trespasser* for decency's sake, he now also justified revision as a financial

necessity: "I don't mind if Duckworth crosses out a hundred shady pages in *Sons and Lovers.* It's got to sell, I've got to live" (*L* 1:526). Yet believing art had an inviolable core, Lawrence could not write novels directly for the marketplace.

> I could do hack work, to a certain amount. But apply my creative self where it doesn't want to be applied, makes me feel I should bust or go cracked. I *couldn't* have done any more at that novel [*Sons and Lovers*]—at least for six months. I must go on producing, producing, and the stuff must come more and more to shape each year. But trim and garnish my stuff I cannot—it *must* go. (*L* 1:501)

Distinguishing his own desire to "shape" his work from others' demands that he "trim and garnish" it, he proposed an ethic of revision: the reason for making changes determined their legitimacy. If the aim was to increase sales, revision was a sellout, but he could accept the need to seek a wide audience for his prophetic mission. In 1914 he explained his attitude to his audience in a letter to John Middleton Murry: "Don't give up feeling that people *do* want to hear what you say: or rather, they don't *want* to hear, but they need to, poor things" (*L* 2:171). Pleasing one's audience was pandering, but changing it was a writer's duty.

After the critical and commercial success of *Sons and Lovers,* the primary dispute between Lawrence and publishers was how "honest" he could be without risking prosecution. Attempting to satisfy publishers' requests for similar novels, Lawrence promised that "The Sisters," the forerunner of *The Rainbow* (1915) and *Women in Love* (1920), would be "impeccable" (*L* 1:526). But as he progressed, the material lost its innocence: "I did 200 pages of a novel—a novel I love [*The Lost Girl*]— then I put it aside to do a pot-boiler ['The Sisters']—it was *too* improper. The pot-boiler is at page 110, and has developed into an earnest and painful work—God help it and me" (*L* 1:536).

Begun as a "pot-boiler" to meet publishers' specifications, "The Sisters" became an "earnest and painful work." He wanted to proclaim a sexual gospel for the times, if people would only listen.

> Pray to your Gods for me that *Sons and Lovers* shall succeed. People *should* begin to take me seriously now. And I do so break my heart over England, when I read the *New Machiavelli.* And I am so sure that only through a readjustment between men and women, and a making

free and healthy of the sex, will she get out of her present atrophy. Oh Lord, and if I don't "subdue my art to a metaphysic," as somebody very beautifully said of Hardy, I do write because I want folk—English folk—to alter, and have more sense. (*L* 1:544)

The "readjustment between men and women" and a freeing "of the sex" was a selling theme. Editors had appreciated the erotic qualities in his fiction since *The White Peacock,* but Lawrence had to find a way to make sexuality part of his artistic intention. Following Hueffer's advice, he used aesthetic and moral justifications as his books became more explicit.

After publishing three books, Lawrence was less responsive to publishers' formal criticism and censorship. His resistance was not a sign of new indifference to readers but was instead a mark of increased confidence in his own judgment. With experience and critical recognition, Lawrence was in a position to argue with editors more forcefully. The main points of friction continued to be legal issues of obscenity and libel that publishers could not afford to ignore. Always fully appreciating Lawrence's literary and commercial value, publishers tried to convince him to eliminate actionable passages, but their requests conflicted with his specific rhetorical goal—to jolt his readers into new lives—and they made him feel that he was being asked to sacrifice art for profit.

Lawrence knew that violating contemporary moral standards was financially risky. Determined to be explicit where others were suggestive, he broke the code governing what could be implied but not stated. He felt his honesty was thoroughly moral, and he believed this justification would be sufficient for his publisher as well. He urged his first agent, J. B. Pinker, to enlist Methuen's support for *The Rainbow.*

Do you think Methuen is ready to back up this novel of mine? He must make some fight for it. It is worth it, and he must do it. It will never be popular. But he can make it known what it is, and prevent the mean little fry from pulling it down. Later, I think I must go and see him. There will be a bit of a fight before my novels are admitted, that I know. The fight will have to be made, that is all. The field is there to conquer. (*L* 2:294)

Lawrence tried to reassure Pinker that *The Rainbow* would be acceptable: "Therefore tell Methuen if he asks . . . that there shall be no very flagrant love-passages in it (at least, to my thinking)" (*L* 2:270). Although he promised Pinker he would cooperate with Methuen, he also warned that he would not mutilate his book.

> I hope you are willing to fight for this novel. It is nearly three years of hard work, and I am proud of it, and it must be stood up for. I'm afraid there are parts of it Methuen won't want to publish. He must. I will take out sentences and phrases, but I won't take out paragraphs or pages. So you must tell me in detail if there are real objections to printing any parts. (*L* 2:327)

Although Lawrence frequently protested that he had done nothing illegal or immoral, he fully intended to violate legal and moral codes. Like other modernists, Lawrence based his rhetorical stance on opposition to contemporary society. He felt blind rage: "For I am hostile, hostile, hostile to all that is, in our public and national life. I want to destroy it" (*L* 2:328). The public knew it was being attacked and defended itself through censorship. Despite the early support of publishers, critics, and readers, Lawrence's work became unpublishable because it was illegal. In November 1915, *The Rainbow* was declared obscene, and Methuen was ordered to destroy all copies. The immediate result was that the price rose sharply.

> That was a ridiculous affair, instigated by the National Purity League, Dr Horton and Co, nonconformity. Of course I achieved a good deal of notoriety, if not fame, am become one of the regular topics. But the whole thing is nasty and offensive. —I heard that Hatchard's had sold their last copy of the *Rainbow, sub rosa,* for four guineas. (*L* 2:477)

Lawrence's agent believed the prosecution could be fought. According to Ezra Pound, Pinker blamed Methuen for caving in to a mere magistrate:

> [Pinker] put the whole blame on Methuen. Some crank went to a magistrate and said the book was immoral. Methuen admitted it. Then the magistrate gave various orders, *in excess of his powers.* If Methuen had declined to obey, or if they had denied that the book was immoral, *NOTHING* could have been done until the Home Office moved. The

Home Office had inspected the book (Mr Birrell being asked for an opinion said the book was too dull to bother about) and decided that they would do nothing.[12]

Although Pound had no legal expertise, he was also correct in predicting that *The Rainbow* prosecution would make publishers wary of new fiction, especially in wartime. Sales had guaranteed publishers' support until the war agitated authorities in unpredictable ways. Before the war, even libraries had circulated *Sons and Lovers,* but after *The Rainbow* was suppressed, publishers themselves censored explicit sexual passages.

Lawrence tried to rally powerful friends to defend his book, but nothing could be done in wartime. Amy Lowell frankly proposed compromise to make his work publishable, but he refused on the grounds that any tampering would destroy what was distinctive.

No, Amy, again you are not right when you say the india-rubber eraser would let me through into a paradise of popularity. Without the india-rubber I am damned along with the evil, with the india-rubber I am damned among the disappointing. You see what it is to have a reputation. (*L* 3:296)

Lawrence's refusal illustrates how ideology distorted the issues. Pretending to be contemptuous of the "paradise of popularity," he claims that the public will either consider him evil or disappointing, erotic or boring, and he rejects both characterizations. He implies that "popularity" requires him to sacrifice his originality. But publishers' sustained interest in his work indicates that literary popularity was not at issue. Once revision was demanded by censors rather than editors, Lawrence regarded compliance as an ethical and political issue. To change his work in response to a threat would be moral cowardice.

Commercial publishers, for their part, felt he abandoned them, not the reverse. Although only the threat of prosecution checked their enthusiasm, Lawrence's response to censorship was to turn against publishers. They were an ideal target because they were intermediaries between writers and readers, and they handled the money. Publishers recognized the quality and value of Lawrence's writing, yet they could not violate the censor's standards. Despite the seizure of *The Rainbow,* they competed to buy manuscripts they could not openly publish. In England Martin Secker wanted to release *Women in Love* under its old title, "The Sisters"

(*L* 3:391), but negotiations broke down when Lawrence insisted that *The Rainbow* had to be included in the agreement. Secker offered two hundred pounds for all rights to *The Rainbow,* but Lawrence declined these terms in favor of Duckworth's willingness to offer royalties. Secker refused to match Duckworth's offer, arguing that Lawrence's books were unprofitable. Nevertheless, he was willing to offer substantial sums— three hundred pounds for *Women in Love* and two hundred for *The Rainbow*—if Lawrence would relinquish royalties. Secker told an intermediary: "But I am a little tired of the whole thing and, now Duckworth is in competition, am quite ready to retire in his favour. Lawrence's books are not worth competing for from a money making point of view (*L* 3:460 n. 1). Secker's offers indicate that he was weighing risks against potential profits. The risk was worth taking for a high rate of return but not for shared gains. Meanwhile, Duckworth withdrew his offer when Lawrence refused to delete a potentially actionable chapter from *The Rainbow.* Lawrence frankly told Secker what had happened and asked to reopen negotiations. This time Secker agreed to royalties and a one-hundred-pound advance on both *The Rainbow* and *Women in Love* (*L* 3:499).

B. W. Huebsch, who bought the American rights, explained publishers' interests and affirmed the value of steady sales.

> The degree of my interest is not to be measured by the extent of the sales, but I think that my methods will probably be advantageous to you in the long run even though the immediate results may seem rather meager. The demand for your books, though not large, is persistent. I much prefer this to the more rocket-like success. (*L* 3:356 n. 1)

Although Huebsch was unable to publicize *The Rainbow* because he feared prosecution, he quietly sold out an edition.

> I withheld the book when the ghouls were lying in wait for me to publish it, and a few months ago I quietly distributed the edition that I had prepared in the autumn of 1915 without advertising or any other publicity, so that at least the book is not buried. (*L* 3:356 n. 1)

As news of *The Rainbow* prosecution spread, the demand for copies increased. Lawrence saw that privately printed editions of illegal books could be profitable (*L* 2:449, 462). He did not exploit this phenomenon successfully until he wrote *Lady Chatterley's Lover,* but he saw its possibilities at once. In collaboration with Middleton Murry and Philip Heseltine, he developed a proposal for authors to publish their own books. They had two main goals: to rescue worthwhile manuscripts rejected by other publishers and to bring this work to the public's attention.

Calling their venture "The Rainbow Books and Music," they intended to begin with Lawrence's *The Rainbow* because they understood the value of its "renown" (*L* 2:542). Attributed to Heseltine but echoing Lawrence's letters, the circular attacked the link between profits and publishing decisions in the literary market.

> The present system of production depends entirely upon the popular esteem: and this means gradual degradation. Inevitably, more and more, the published books are dragged down to the level of the lowest reader.
>
> It is monstrous that the herd should lord it over the uttered word. The swine has only to grunt disapprobation, and the very angels of heaven will be compelled to silence. (*L* 2:542 n. 1)

Descending to crude epithets, their rhetoric revealed the elitism underlying their complaints against commercial publishers. In contrast, their statement of aims was vague: to "unseal those sources of truth and beauty which are now sterile in the heart." They had two criteria for publication. They would issue privately "such books as would either be rejected by the publisher, or else overlooked when flung into the trough before the public." Although neither event was responsible for the suppression of *The Rainbow,* the second had more justification. As the number of books rapidly increased to address the varied segments of the potential market, the "best" books, those addressing the most educated readers, were easily overlooked in the deluge of titles. Private publishing was a way to certify work Lawrence and his partners approved.

The cooperative venture appealed to Lawrence's lifelong desire for a community of like-thinking people, but his own publishing experiences did not support the first part of its rationale. He knew that *Sons and Lovers* had not earned its advance, yet Duckworth offered to publish *The Rainbow* on the same terms (which Lawrence rejected as paltry), and Methuen tripled this offer. Both publishers recognized the aesthetic quality and commercial value of Lawrence's writing and were willing to invest their money to support their literary judgment. In contrast, seven hundred copies of the cooperative venture's advertising circular produced only thirty replies (*L* 2:605). Lawrence's hope that private publishing would preserve the purity of his vision from editorial compromise and commercialism proved fruitless at this time, but it flourished after the war. In the 1920s, private presses eager to publish banned books emerged to fill the gap between conventional morality and avant-garde taste.[13]

Lawrence's restless postwar period of self-imposed exile ended when he found a way to establish an intimate connection with a select group of readers and still earn money from his writing. Learning from others in his position, he developed private publishing arrangements to circumvent editorial judgment and legal restraints. He thought private publishing would overcome both of his objections to commercial firms: the taint of money and the market of "common" readers: "I think there ought to be some system of private publication and private circulation. I disbelieve *utterly* in the public, in humanity, in the mass. There should be again a body of esoteric doctrine, defended from the herd. The herd will destroy everything" (*L* 3:143).

Reviving plans for private publishing, he finally discovered how to reconcile art and professionalism. He intended to follow a model Norman Douglas had developed: "I'm thinking I shall publish my novel *Lady Chatterley's Lover* here in Florence, myself, privately—as Douglas does—700 copies at 2 guineas. It is so 'improper,' it could never appear in the ordinary way—and I won't cut it about. So I want to do it myself—and perhaps make £600 or £700" (*L* 6:225). Knowing the book would be considered immoral, Lawrence defended it on moral grounds: "My new novel is three parts done, and is so *absolutely* improper, in words, and so really *good*, I hope, in spirit—that I don't know what's going to happen to it" (*L* 5:638). He vehemently defended the purity of his motives in his 1929 essay "A Propos of *Lady Chatterley's Lover*": "And this is the real point of this book. I want men and women to be able *think* sex, fully, completely, honestly and cleanly." He shifted the charge of immorality to his opponents: "Obscenity only comes in when the mind despises and fears the body, and the body hates and resists the mind."[14] Despite this rationale, he conceded that he wanted to shock the public: "I want subtly, but tremendously, to kick the backsides of the ball-less" (*L* 6:72). Although Lawrence offered aesthetic justifications for violating conventional morality, his purpose was to change society. The "pariah" did not write for himself: "As for writing pariah literature, a man has to write what is in him, and what he *can* write: and better by far have genuine pariah literature than sentimentalities on a 'higher' level" (*L* 7:226).

Independence from publishers made *Lady Chatterley's Lover* possible.

Lawrence's rhetorical aims changed in the course of writing the novel when he developed a plan for private publication. Having written the first draft to "open a chink of the tomb for the young and for future generations through the therapy of exposure to the doctrine of tenderness and touch," in the final draft "this purpose had become subsidiary to the wish to shock the castrated consciousness of an older generation of middle and upper-class readers."[15] Citing Lawrence's wife, John Worthen demonstrates that "the mode of its production was a final and decisive influence on the kind of novel it became."

> Frieda Lawrence summed up the development by suggesting that the first version "he wrote as she came out of him, out of his own immediate self. In the third version he was also aware of his contemporaries' minds." . . . Such a distinction very properly stresses the public quality of the third version.[16]

Rhetorical decisions replaced self-expression: it became a "bomb" for the society Lawrence came to loathe. Although written with flagrant disregard for contemporary standards of propriety, *Lady Chatterley's Lover* was also one of his most blatantly didactic books. He felt he modified his inner voice less than he had in any other work, yet his rhetorical purpose was stronger here than anywhere else. Paradoxically, the novel became more public because it could be published privately.

Thanks to the publicity censorship provided, he could make more money by printing illegal manuscripts privately than by publishing openly. He thought of his project as a mission to reform publishing: "I hate middle-men, and want to eliminate them as far as possible. If I can carry this thing through, it will be a start for all of us unpopular authors. Never let it be said I was a Bennett" (*L* 6:343). Curtis Brown's, his current literary agency, was among the middlemen who would not share in the profits of private publication. Brown's office warned Lawrence not to destroy his "at last respectable reputation" (*L* 6:353). Lawrence dismissed his agent's irritation: "Curtis Browns [*sic*] seem very huffed with me for making money on the private editions, apart from them. But they had such a scare over *Lady C.* how can they possibly handle the stuff I do in private" (*L* 7:518). Knopf and Secker also encouraged him to make the manuscript publishable, but Lawrence hoped to earn more and compromise less than they expected.

Lawrence appreciated the ironies of the market for limited editions. Increasing the price could increase the demand: "But this shows you the insanity of the modern collector of books. And a good author can't even get his work printed. Makes me tired! I hate this expensive edition business" (*L* 7:304). Lawrence could now afford to mock commercial publishers' timidity because he had finally found a more profitable alternative. He knew he had a viable public:

> [T]here is a big public waiting to get anything which they think is not orthodox, does not come via the "good" publishers. There is the enormous "proper" public, of Heinemann or Gollancz. But I believe the "improper" public is almost as big, if not bigger, so long as they are fairly safe. . . . But then I am amazed to realise how huge, and how much more potent the "improper" public is. (*L* 7:448)

Here Lawrence was truly prophetic. He saw that alternative publishing for an "improper" minority public could produce a good income, and he foresaw that larger publishers would want to capture this market too.

In fact, *Lady Chatterley* was Lawrence's most profitable book. It was published in June 1928, and by the end of August gross receipts were £980 (*L* 6:533). His chief problems were filling orders before customs inspectors seized the books and then collecting money from people who falsely claimed they had not received their copies. Lawrence attempted to halt this situation by urging Secker to publish an expurgated version to secure copyright (Britton, 261). Demand was so great that the book was pirated, forcing Lawrence to print a second edition cheaper than the pirated copies.

Yet Lawrence's financial motives trouble many critics. Derek Britton tries to apologize for them.

> The desires to preserve his own and the novel's artistic integrity and to "take in the badly-needed shekels" . . . were of more or less equal status. Mercenary as the latter motive was, and at odds with the novel's teachings against money-lust, which are given greater prominence in the final version, it seems unreasonable to find fault with Lawrence in this; though it must also be acknowledged that in the importance he attached to the money-making aspect of private publication he fell short of his own high-minded principles.[17]

Lawrence's attention to marketing the novel was an aspect of his rhetorical intention, and other signs of his concern with readers' responses also disturb Britton. He locates the value of the novel in its sources—"the initial rush of inspirational creativity which brings a work into being, followed by a process of struggle in which it is made to grow to completion" (183). He concedes that revision was Lawrence's usual habit, yet he argues that in this case the results were "detrimental" because Lawrence replaced "tenderness" with hostility to the middle and upper classes: "The novel was no longer Lawrence's compassionate gift to the world, it was the instrument of the wart-hog's revenge" (251). The Romantic ideology of the author as artist predisposes Britton to prefer the "more emotional" early drafts, even though Lawrence decided their Blakean "lyricism and mysticism" were not fit for the public (249).

Despite his Romantic bias, Britton recognizes that the first version was "too diffuse and unstructured," and he acknowledges that revision made it the "most well-crafted of all Lawrence's novels."[18] Dismissing this evidence of Lawrence's artistic intentions, Britton attributes the revisions to Lawrence's mood: "Reluctance to face charges of mysticism, fear of self-exposure and a compulsion to engage himself in a fight—these seem to have been the principal motives which led Lawrence to reject *John Thomas and Lady Jane* [the second version of the novel]" (251). Britton adheres to the Romantic logic that spontaneous writing is closer to deep feeling and that deep feeling is the primary source of literary quality. Lawrence's decision to move away from personal feeling toward form and from self-expression toward rhetorical aims does not sway Britton. He pits his judgment against Lawrence's:

> as far as the novel was concerned, Lawrence's decision to carry out a thorough reworking was ill-judged. Several of the motives which his current mood dictated made for stridency of expression and rigidity of thought. More importantly, perhaps, illness had blunted his sensibilities. (252)

Britton's argument begins and ends with Lawrence's feelings. Refusing to credit Lawrence's artistic intentions or the novel's rhetorical effect, Britton cannot help condemning financial aims.

The central irony of Lawrence's career was that being unpublishable made him profitable. Thanks to private publishing ventures, both limited de luxe editions and illegal printings earned him a better income than his more reticent books had provided. Unfairly blaming publishers for government censorship, he found a way to circumvent editorial and commercial restraint. As a result, he felt he could communicate with his readers directly. His most acclaimed and most profitable works were written when he believed his readers urgently needed his message; his sales were greatest when readers believed the books were illicit. Like other modernists, Lawrence found that erotic content guaranteed an audience, and aesthetic intentions exonerated him for seeking one.

NOTES

1. But the dichotomy between art and money was no truer then than it is now. In fact, Richard Ohmann shows that the novels that have entered the contemporary canon have enjoyed both critical acclaim and high sales. Thus the canon omits writers who were merely popular (Puzo, Wouk, Krantz) as well as those who were merely praised (Coover, Wurlitzer, Sukenick). Instead, it includes writers of bestsellers which also received critical acclaim—Heller, Pynchon, Bellow, Mailer, Roth, Updike, Kesey. See Richard Ohmann, "The Shaping of a Canon: U.S. Fiction, 1960–1975," *Critical Inquiry* 10 (September 1983): 199–223.

2. See John Sutherland, "Fiction and the Erotic Cover," *Critical Quarterly* 33, no. 2 (1991): 3–36. He shows that when these works were issued in paperback format, publishers deliberately tried to sell serious literature through sexy cover art: "Predictably, the back cover stresses the obscenity and persecution of the Author of *Ulysses'*" (14), and "The back cover of *Women in Love* harps predictably on the banned-book aspect of the novel" (16).

3. Montgomery H. Hyde, *The Lady Chatterley's Lover Trial* (London: Bodley Head, 1990), p. 13. Subsequent references appear parenthetically in the text, abbreviated *T.*

4. John M. Woolsey, "Decision," in *Ulysses,* by James Joyce (New York: Modern Library, 1961), p. x. Subsequent references appear parenthetically in the text, abbreviated *U.*

5. Michael Moscato and Leslie LeBlanc, eds., *The United States of America v. One Book Entitled "Ulysses" by James Joyce* (Frederick, Md.: University Publications of America, 1984), p. 258. Subsequent references appear parenthetically in the text, abbreviated *USA.*

6. See James Joyce, *Selected Letters,* ed. Richard Ellmann (New York: Viking, 1975), pp. 292, 315.

7. Michael Squires, *The Creation of "Lady Chatterley's Lover"* (Baltimore: Johns Hopkins University Press, 1983), p. 201.

8. Jeffrey Meyers, *D. H. Lawrence* (New York: Knopf, 1990), p. 387.

9. Ibid., p. 362.

10. See *The Letters of D. H. Lawrence,* ed. James T. Boulton et al., 7 vols. to date (Cambridge: Cambridge University Press, 1979–), 1:158. Subsequent references appear parenthetically in the text, abbreviated *L.*

11. See R. P. Draper, ed., *D. H. Lawrence: The Critical Heritage* (London: Routledge and Kegan Paul, 1970), pp. 33–34.

12. See *Pound/Joyce: The Letters of Ezra Pound to James Joyce, with Pound's Essays on Joyce,* ed. Forrest Read (New York: New Directions, 1967), p. 283.

13. Hugh Ford, *Published in Paris* (New York: Macmillan, 1975), p. 352.

14. *Phoenix II,* ed. Warren Roberts and Harry T. Moore (New York: Viking, 1968), pp. 489, 490. See *Lady Chatterley's Lover,* A Propos of "Lady Chatterley's Lover," ed. Michael Squires (Cambridge: Cambridge University Pres, 1993), pp. 308, 309.

15. See Derek Britton, *Lady Chatterley: The Making of the Novel* (London: Unwin Hyman, 1988), p. 251.

16. See John Worthen, *D. H. Lawrence and the Idea of the Novel* (Totowa, N. J.: Rowman and Littlefield, 1979), pp. 175, 178.

17. Britton, *Lady Chatterley,* p. 242.

18. Ibid., pp. 251, 252.

Coterie Consumption: Bloomsbury, Keynes, and Modernism as Marketing

Jennifer Wicke

The temptation in writing about markets and marketing is that we think we know what we are writing—or thinking—about. After all, perched as we are in the catbird seat above the roiling ship that is the modern economy, we consider ourselves adepts of the market, alert to its schemes, prescient to the touch of its invisible hand. *The market* as such is a term stretched beyond a viable attenuation, though, in modern capitalist economies where it is a synonym for civil society. We loosely gesture in our speech toward "the marketplace" as if alluding to a venue around the corner, or to some agora-like trading ground whose parameters are discernible. If what *the market* means is the abstract space of the exchange of goods, commodities, and finally money, or its phantom representation in futures, then it has no location, since the abstract space of the exchange of goods is all-pervasive, even in our dreams. "Marketing" as a practice has a specific set of techniques and a vocabulary dedicated to its mysteries: direct mail, targeted marketing, market managers, and so forth; still, despite the seeming empiricism of the practice, what we mean when we talk about marketing in general is also diffuse, since it has reference to the shadowy transubstantiality of "the market." In what follows, I want to stand back from the two linked terms and heighten their defamiliarization. Rather than recounting a particular marketing or publicizing strategy designed to promote specifically modernist work, I will worry the concepts of the market and of marketing—a name and a habitation I hope to make very strange—by trying to show how modernism altered our ideas of "markets" and the practices of marketing. I ask my readers to entertain the notion that modernism contributed profoundly to a sea change in market consciousness, a consciousness we all tend to share, with sharp disputes about what implications should flow from that shared consciousness. This means that modernism (writ large) is neither separate from market consciousness, not just a Johnny-come-lately in putting to use market procedures to advance aesthetic goals. The connection is much more intense, more salient, more peculiar, if I am to be believed: aspects of modernist practice made possible the transformations in the understanding of that secret sharer, "the market," and as a result changed the nature of modern markets for once and all. While the architecture of this argument is on a grand scale, the part of it I sketch out here has a comfortably familiar and less opulent setting—the site is Bloomsbury, the writer Virginia Woolf, and the market theorist John Maynard Keynes.

This essay approaches the issue of modernism (in literary terms, primarily the modernist writing of Virginia Woolf) as it takes form, in part, within a self-defined marketing segment, the world of Bloomsbury. The free-floating social ties of Bloomsbury constituted a particular site of production and consumption, and Woolf's affinities with Bloomsbury are not just aesthetic matters of taste or the style of her work. Rather, Bloomsbury can be seen as an invented community, in intention almost a utopia of and for consumption, following on problems delineated by William Morris and Oscar Wilde, among others, about the production of art in an inequitable, and capitalist, society. "Lifestyle" is a dimension of modern art production and social tastes articulated by contemporaries like Wilde, James, and even Nietzsche, and despite the anachronistic terminology, lifestyle is what Bloomsbury was selling. This aspect of Bloomsbury—that is, its implicit relation to art, to labor, and to modernity—remains current in the cultural imagination, as the line of fabrics and wallpapers, desk accessories, and greeting cards with links to Bloomsbury attests. More than an episode in marketing, this continued fascination reflects the unique status of Bloomsbury as a modernist imaginary indubitably associated with socioeconomics. This essay investigates the degree to which Woolf's writing is inflected with and by its Bloomsbury context as an experiment in coterie consumption, which means both the consumption of art by a coterie, the "Bloomsberries," and the marketing and consumption of their art (and thought and lifestyle) as produced by a celebrated coterie. Such an investigation can help us sort out our conflicted responses to the inevitable marketing and self-marketing of modernism, especially where so much emphasis is placed on obscuring or occluding the commoditization of modernist literature.

What accounts for the rapturous survival of Bloomsbury as an artistic and social movement, a fashion, a deeply desirable lifestyle? Quite recently the *New York Times* "Home" style page devoted a long, illustrated article to several descendants of the Bloomsbury circle (obviously none of them directly sprung from Virginia Woolf) who have taken up an artist's calling. These grand-nieces and great-grandsons have returned to the mode of artisanal/artistic production made famous by Vanessa Bell and Duncan Grant in creating their house, Charleston. Charleston is now being restored as the national monument it indubitably is: indeed, if my argument is persuasive, a veritable *international* monument to the fluid modern market. The descendants have opened a gift shop on the premises of Charleston where they ply the vibrantly colorful artistic trades of the Bloomsburyites, from painted pottery to enameled firescreens to in-home fresco application and textile weaving. Profits from the shop not only support their considerable artistic and craft achievements, but make it possible to continue the restoration work on the house, which entails precisely the same intricate arts-and-crafts techniques as are being copied to make the wares for the shop. A neat circulating loop is thereby set up, one that helps serve as a gloss on the transformations of modern market consciousness via modernism I am exploring, serving also as a conduit to the work of Virginia Woolf and her "Charlestonian" effect on John Maynard Keynes's economic theories. Woolf's books are sold in the shop, and her image appears throughout the house as well, since her sister and assorted other Bloomsbury confreres drew, painted, and photographed her to record her strong presence at Charleston.[1]

The Charleston gift shop is only the very latest in a chain of Bloomsbury-style revivals that began almost with the beginning of Bloomsbury, as when in the 1920s the editor of British *Vogue* consulted her Bloomsbury friends for style tips, and Virginia Woolf contributed fiction to its pages. On my desk as I write is a small box decorated in a "Bloomsbury" pattern, a reworking of a Vanessa Bell painting whose rose, ocher, and silvery blue-green are meant to (and do) conjure the two sisters. Laura Ashley fabrics went through a passionate Bloomsbury phase a few years ago, offering exact replicas of Charleston designs on a range of curtains, bedspreads, rugs, and sheets. An immensely popular home-decorating book by the aptly named Jocasta Innes features the colors, patterns, and bold energies of Bloomsbury and suggests a trip to Charleston as the ultimate inspiration for "the thrifty home artist-decorator." Ebullient pictures in her text show the lampshades, cupboards, and garden gates of the extraordinarily productive and imaginative Bloomsbury artists, and their flair for nuanced, radical color and discordant design.

I may seem to have made a detour down a hedgerow to land at Charleston. However, the nexus of style, artistry, domesticity, and modernism that Charleston reflects and currently refracts in our present lifestyle market is an intricate *market* nexus. In a sense, Bloomsbury was the modernist inheritor of the William Morris social and aesthetic market niche. While Morris had an ostensibly far more detailed political program, in the sense that the craft patterns and plans he devised at his country seat were meant to (and did) transform middle- and lower-middle-class design in a period of overwhelming industrial ugliness, Bloomsbury too had an outreach program for the dissemination of style. As in the case of Morris, literature and book publishing was intertwined with high-art painting and sculpture, with home design, wallpaper and picture frames and so on, ad infinitum, in the Bloomsbury *lebenswelt*. The *lebenswelt* was also a *lebensraum,* as perhaps is most powerfully incarnated in Virginia Woolf's *A Room of One's Own* and in her *Jacob's Room,* as well as in the stunning interiors of Charleston's rooms. I mean by this that the overall ambiance of Bloomsbury was also concretized as a design for living, a way of life that could and did boil down to what one did with, and in, the rooms allotted to one.

The Bloomsbury lebensraum, or life space, was a new marketing model. To return to William Morris momentarily, by way of contrast, is to see that where Morris resolutely opposed the capitalist mass production and structures of social living he nonetheless tapped into for his audience (and his customers), Bloomsbury was not so flagrantly antitechnological nor nostalgic for what amounted to the craft production techniques of a far distant Merrie Olde England. Bloomsbury style did not preach against or evade modernity as such; what remains so entrancing about Charleston, for example, is that it celebrates the shabby, the rarefied, and the new with equal fervor. Morris thought that the lush vines and flowers of his textile designs were in harmony with a medieval worldview that could instruct people to resist industrial ugliness and thereby resist capitalism. Instead, his gorgeous designs were technologically mass-produced and disseminated their beauty squarely within a capitalist market. Bloomsbury style, and Bloomsbury writing, acknowledges technology and capitalism with relaxed acceptance, although not with complacency. What it does not do, and this is, I think, the key to its longevity and its perennial fascination, is to throw out the baby with the bathwater of obsolete Edwardian mores. Charleston's modernism, for example, is not the minatory fierce modernism of form following function. Instead, startling painterly innovations coincide with rickety kitchen chairs, rusty radiator covers, and upholstery with fuzzy worn patches. Low-tech and relatively high-tech artistry coincide and counterpoint, and no color combinations are deemed impossible. Where Morris's missionary position led him to abjure manufactured goods, Bloomsbury is perfectly happy with the compromises to manufacture we all must continually make—to plumbing, to furniture, to dishes and housewares and mass-produced books, to wireless sets and contraceptives and toiletries of all sorts. Morris was distressed that people have to buy things, rather than make them or have them made by hand; Bloomsbury takes up a position out of Morris by way of Wilde's "The Soul of Man under Socialism." In that glorious essay Wilde exalts a socialism that can be derived only from harnessing capitalist modernity, those aspects of contemporary production and consumption that offer cheaper goods and services, machines to do work, and advances in hygiene and health brought about by manufactured items and improved living and working conditions. The point for Wilde is to reach the stage where everyone can spend her or his time making art, or consuming art, whereas for Morris it was to return to cottage production where people made all their own goods, some of which would then have artistic or high-craft beauty. Wilde's essay teeters on various brinks of naïveté about machine labor, the absence of politics, and the preponderance of art, but it is incredibly salient, and modern, in proposing that we accept the inability of going back to excruciatingly labor-intensive craft production, sans machines, and that we face up to the major role of consumption in modern markets. Wildean socialism adapts John Stuart Mill's utilitarian formula to the following: "The greatest goods [note plural] for the greatest possible number," where said goods could be art, or chocolates, or embroidered waistcoats, or sexual pleasure. In a rhetorical riff that alludes to Morris without naming him directly, Wilde writes of the revolution in taste literally imposed on an unwilling public.

People have been to a very great extent civilized. It is only fair to state, however, that the extraordinary success of the revolution in house-decoration and furniture and the like has not really been due to the majority of the public developing fine taste in such matters. It has chiefly been due to the fact that the craftsmen of things so appreciated the pleasure of making what was beautiful, and woke to such a vivid consciousness of the hideousness and vulgarity of what the public had previously wanted, that they simply starved the public out. It would be quite impossible at the present moment to furnish a room as rooms were furnished a few years ago, without going for everything to an auction of second-hand furniture from some third-rate lodging house. The things are no longer made. However they may object to it, people must nowadays have something charming in their surroundings. Fortunately for them, their assumption of authority in these art matters came to grief.[2]

The essay on socialism is a veritable ode to individual joy, insisting that a significant portion of the joy that is to come derives from the creative exercise of taste, in other words, consumption in a market economy that embraces aesthetics as well as machines. Wilde vents spleen, as in the passage just cited, against the terminal philistinism of the bourgeois Public, led to aesthetic value as the proverbial horse, this time made to drink the water of beauty instead of simply balk before it. His argument requires a little vilification of the Mass, in order for the Individual to shine forth that much more brightly, and the artist with an especial luster. Still, the emphasis falls on how individualism as a creed can be folded back into an ineluctably social and material world where individuals lose their peace to create by the pervasive suffering of others. In order for all of us to partake freely of the creative goods and desires of modernity, economic justice is required as an almost aesthetic necessity. Bloomsbury updates Wildean socialist individualism in that it proffers a mode of living that people can, and do, emulate, creating what is essentially a coterie canon of consumption. Oscar writes as an Individual concerned for the social: "The Ideals that we owe to Christ are the ideals of a man who abandons society entirely, or of the man who resists society absolutely. But man is naturally social."[3] By the time Bloomsbury arrives as an inchoate social group, a *public* secret society, the oxymoron serves to underscore the strength of the Bloomsbury idea—Wildeanism lived in a coterie fashion, Oscar as a *group*.

E. M. Forster bashed away at Bloomsbury for just this coterie aspect, summing up its coterie nature as "Academic background, independent income." We can be perfectly content to grant the accuracy of the barb but need to look at the special modernist configuration of this coterie to understand its relevance to market theory. Given that Bloomsbury constituted a coterie on the basis of a shared upper-middle- to upper-intellectual-class position, what is remarkable is the degree to which such a rarefied group was both elite and emblematic. If in the nineteenth century "our" valets did "our" living for us, Bloomsbury modernism was about a design for living being carried out first by the Bloomsberries and then, perhaps, by a new unvaleted "us."

As a market economist writing at the same time as Keynes but in virtual obscurity, Hazel Kyrk establishes that there is a phenomenon reshaping markets in the twentieth century. In her excellently comprehensive *A Theory of Consumption* (published in 1923), Kyrk describes the fuzzy end of the economic lollipop—consumption.

> The conduct of business affairs can be reduced to principles; it has a definite end, and each operation can be measured in terms of that end; there is an exact test of efficiency. Hence business policy can be formulated rather definitely, and followed with some exactness. The consumer, however, has no definitely formulated policy, no clear-cut ends. Often it would be impossible for him to describe specifically what he is seeking in the market. There is no exact standard or measure for most of the things he buys, no measure of their suitability for his purpose; there is no criterion for success.[4]

Kyrk here shows us what is easy to forget: the market looms large and amorphous from the reception end, however well delineated it may appear to be on the production side. There are two different maps of the "market," one a vague landscape the consumer ponders over and marks on, the other the crisply folded cartographic grid of the producers. Somewhere in the intersection lies the modern market, which can no longer be envisioned as a giant, if tidy, bazaar of goods. Kyrk goes on to batten this down in her lucid fashion.

> In other words, consumption is largely non-rationalized; the consumer does not know what he wants in such a way that he can select with exactitude when it is displayed upon the market. . . . It is obvious that the more general and the more vague are the consumers' standards and aims the more easily the producer can control his demand and guide it into specific lines. The book agent can sell the old farmer an encyclopedia of universal knowledge in one volume because, although he wants wisdom and information via the printed page, he has no

means of discrimination or of discovering the proper instrument to serve his purposes. For the same reason the seeker after health without the rudiments of medical knowledge buys freely of patent mixtures, and the family trying to beautify the home "decorate" the parlor floor with a red and green atrocity called by the dealer an art square. Examples are legion. . . . Unfortunately, many of the purposes consumers seek to carry out upon the market are general and vague.[5]

An additional blurring of the market region comes about because most consumers are atomized buying units, which puts them at great disadvantage in knowledge, wealth, and clout with respect to producers. And here is where Bloomsbury also comes in, as a mystified answer to this vexing disadvantage: Bloomsbury is a group, a coterie, and it "consumes," or chooses from the market, in a concerted effort of knowledge, taste, and power. Bloomsbury is an example of the way consumers now must, and will, "acquire definite codes for material living." Kyrk suggests many avenues for the acquisition of these codes, including public education and other such measures, but she falls back on the mysterious "forces" that guide and direct a consumer. Surely one such force, and it is quintessentially modernist, is the beckoning image of coterie lifestyle. What makes Bloomsbury unique in this event is that Bloomsbury was a coterie of and for consumption, a force within the market that made a market. It is to this rather vague or seemingly circular marketeering I now turn.

The supreme modernist economist is John Maynard Keynes, and he is supreme because he retheorizes the market explicitly along the fuzzy, chaotic lines I have been traversing above. The expansion and contraction of the economic system, that is, the market, cannot be explained, as it had been, as a matter of equilibrium between saving and investment. As Keynes put it: "The old-fashioned quantity-theory tutor, who only looks at the quantity of the kitchen-bills, has . . . nothing to learn from dyspepsia!" Keynes's modernist refashioning in his two major works, *The Economic Consequences of the Peace* (1919) and *The General Theory of Employment, Investment, and Money* (1936), is in dialogue with the economic precepts of the great Alfred Marshall, or perhaps it is more accurate to say that Keynes felt himself to be demolishing the classical, or "orthodox," economic theories of his predecessors. For the ordered, rationalist image of the market and its laws Keynes substitutes an insistence on the chaotic nature of the market, no longer chartable in regularized terms, but recognizable as a preternaturally sensitive organism ready to ramify the smallest shock throughout its limpid, limbic system. Keynes's biographer, the economist Robert Skidelsky, refers to the "modernist/collectivist mindset" operative in Keynes's theories, and to the latter's belief that "order was not natural. It had to be created."[6]

The nature of the order created by the economist was provisional, momentary, and intertwiningly intricate, a cast of mind overlaid on the blooming, buzzing confusion of the market. William James's phrase for the nature of consciousness has always been apt as an analogue of the many instances in Virginia Woolf's fiction where massing, transitory phenomena are captured in a web or net (even of words) to hang suspended, ordered for a fraction of time in their blooming, buzzing confusion. Rooks sparkle out of shaken trees, bees buzz within an embracing gauze, flowers erupt pollen contained in the cistern of their own petals, clouds melt and re-form under a collective, binding gaze of misprision. We take these moments in Woolf's fictions to be the oblique rendering of consciousness, where modern consciousness is assumed to be chaotic, fleeting, frangible, bound only by the arcs of words that trace it metaphorically on the page. Consider, though, how well this trope of consciousness (as blooming, buzzing, dispersed, and displaced) and the modernist strategies of writing Woolf invents and deploys to display it conjoin with the new view of "the market"—that is, of human beings caught up in their buzzing, blooming socioeconomic system. Like consciousness, the market has come to defy description, in that it is no longer equatable with realist or entirely rationalist models of representation. This puts the modernist economic theorist like Keynes in the position the modernist writer like Woolf also confronts—a position where the imperative is to represent what is acknowledged beforehand to be resistant to representation, at least by traditional (realist, rationalist) means.

Consciousness in Woolf's writing is, oddly, what I would call social consciousness, in the sense that absolute privacy of consciousness is unobtainable, and the thoughts, images, and refrains of consciousness take collective forms. Consciousness is telekinetic (to use Hillis Miller's delightful term for Woolfean narrativity) and telepathic, not necessarily in any mystical way, but in a sociomaterial unfolding of a wide social net within which consciousness buzzes and blooms.[7] People may not *know* one another's thoughts in telepathic communication, but they *are* one another's thoughts; whatever order there is to consciousness arrives in the momentary interconnections of inchoateness. It may be objected that this is all produced by writerly sleight of hand, that it is Woolf's linguistic artistry that makes a single consciousness seem to shimmer and fall in the interconnected minds of her characters as if a firework rocket had burst, blossomed, and then dispersed its evanescent traces. And this would be correct, as far as it goes, which isn't particularly far. If Woolf can indeed "write consciousness" or represent it in this novel manner, that is because, bracketing her individual genius for a moment, such a mode of collective consciousness has a role in modern everyday life. To that extent, Woolf is *transcribing* (via modernist experimentalism) a phenomenon of the everyday world, however hard it may be to explain in everyday language. This phenomenon is encountered in everyday life as the experience of "the market," which is not to say that there are not other venues or modes for this experience. I want to focus here, however, on the adjacency of Woolf's modernist writing of consciousness and the expansion and transformation of our notion of the market, given its fullest modernist expression in the economic theories of Keynes. The point is not to link up Woolf and Keynes as fellow modernists plowing different but adjacent modernist plots, influencing one another in genteel Bloomsbury exchanges between artist and economist over the back fence of modernism. Such an "influence study" would be interesting but trivial, in light of the substantially larger claims of my argument, which have to do with a very genuine alteration in the market economy and, correspondingly, in the aesthetic and conceptual representations of our market world. This is not another way of salvaging "economic determination in the last instance," either, so that as market forces change, modernism comes along to, what else, *reflect* them. Au contraire. The argument is that "the market" is at least as much an aesthetic phenomenon as it is anything else, and that neither art nor economics can be separated out of it or given an artificial primacy as instigator or reflector. At the risk of appearing to cash in my chips before I am done playing, I would say that Woolf and Keynes are *doing the same thing,* that is, giving representation to the everyday of the market in the genres and institutional formats appropriate to their quite different formations as literary writer and theoretical economist. And how is it, short of the dull miracle of "influence," that they can be seen to be doing the same thing? By virtue of the highly equivocal status of Bloomsbury as a coterie of consumption, whereby Bloomsbury becomes a market in miniature, a blooming buzzing confusion of consumption and production. The very ductility of Bloomsbury, then, as a loosely knit and loosely netted group of people whose consumption and production caroms off each other, recirculates and then scatters out into a wider marketplace, is similar to the rooks in the net or the bubbles in the hand or the flickering candle flames of Woolfian fiction. Her fiction, as modernist art, might on its surface appear to be antimarket, dead set against the forces of market capitalism that were changing the nature of artistic production, as so many other fields. However, the opposite is true: Woolf's writing offers marketing as modernism, the market as susceptible only to the invisible hand of art or creation to "order" it. No longer could positivist reason or rationalist quantification hold sway in conceiving the market or depicting its "laws": the liquidity and lambency Woolf gives to her narrative skein is the nature of the modern market, too. To write one is to write the other—as a foray into *Mrs. Dalloway* can perhaps show.

Alex Zwerdling calls *Mrs. Dalloway* Woolf's "most searching account of the class isolation of her society." This is undoubtedly true and makes for the overarching patterns of loneliness and estrangement that cut through the novel: Septimus Smith with his clerkly aims at cultivated status, dying at the hands of medical condescension, Clarissa Dalloway stuck wondering what those in the social sphere just above hers actually think of her and her parties, and so on. The book is a head-on collision with class and its minute determinants.[8] In addition, though, it can be read as an extraordinary rendition of the microcomplications of "the market," a market shot through with desire, memory, global history and national tradition, sex, loss, and shopping.

Everybody knows by now that Clarissa goes shopping, indeed, starts the book with her shudder of pleasure poised at the foot of London's gleaming shopfronts. "Mrs. Dalloway said she would buy the flowers herself" is the first sentence of the novel, set off all by itself as if to emphasize the solitary nature of the shopping trip for one of life's most necessary luxuries.[9] The words that come a paragraph later are classic too in their rhapsody: "What a lark! What a plunge!" As readers we are still stepping off the curb to buy the flowers in the early morning air, but what follows disconcerts us, as the plunge takes us back in time to the eighteen-year-old Clarissa in the pristine morning air of her girlhood home, Bourton, where she stands at an open window conversing with Peter Walsh. It is not until she folds up her reminisence of Peter like the pocketknife he always carries that we are returned to the pavement: "She stiffened a little on the kerb, waiting for Durtnall's van to pass." As she crosses the street under the invisible leaden circles of Big Ben's chime, she contemplates her investment in life: "For Heaven only knows why one loves it so, how one sees it so, making it up, building it up round one, tumbling it, creating it every moment afresh." The reverie on life is also a comment on consciousness, where the agency of consciousness as a maker and builder of moments positively sculpts "life" in its plasticity. In other words, consciousness is a seeing that literally makes and remakes life moment by moment. The transition in the rest of the paragraph buttresses this cognitive making but concentrates on the city landscape and its buzz and bloom of market confusions.

> In people's eyes, in the swing, tramp, and trudge; in the bellow and the uproar; the carriages, motor cars, omnibuses, vans, sandwich men shuffling and swinging; brass bands; barrel organs; in the triumph and the jingle and the strange high singing of some aeroplane overhead was what she loved; life; London; this moment of June. (5)

The image of the vortex is not amiss, however, in what it conjures of a received idea of the modernist city. With an emphasis on consumption, viewed as an active, even productive or creative, process, Woolf's text is a prism to point to the multiple strands of the market, the market as a metropolitan space, and consequently how this major emblem of modernism, the city, is "sexed" quite differently. Sexing has to do with the procedures of horticulture and grafting, or with the inspection of plants or animals early on when sexual characteristics can still be modified. Within this difference there is by no means a singular "woman's" city *or* a single "female" modernism—instead, I want to point to the richness of urbanity in Woolf's writing, as it establishes multiple vectors for the women within it. Woolf's market modernism, if we can now call it that, emphasizes fluidity, sexual and social difference, and the active thrusts of consumption. There is no Bloomsbury depicted in *Mrs. Dalloway,* no character who could "be" a Bloomsberrie. Instead of the market as a thematic issue in this work, however, I'm trying to tease out the procedures and strategies of writing that lend themselves to precisely the economic gestures Keynes was to make in his work: a way of conceiving the market comprehensively, dynamically, chaotically, and with a strong rewriting of gender. Here Bloomsbury's comfortable response to homosexuality is integral to the modernist rewriting of market economies—and to the experience of them.

If, as Raymond Williams persuasively demonstrates, modernism is

characterized by an international, cosmopolitan metropole, with a floating bohemia or avant-gardist café society, a migratory modernist workforce, if you will, then Woolf's work decisively fails to register this, opening itself up to the charge of Little Englandism from some quarters.[10] The
positive way to make this charge is to refer ad infinitum to Woolf's lyricism and to the miniature scale—that is, the domestic settings or the
embroidery hoop of narrative circumference within which her texts work
their inscriptions.[11] We may choose, however, to envision her writing as
a material modernism engaged throughout with the dilemmas of the
urban and of modernity, recasting these *avant la lettre* of our understanding of critical modernism. The sexing (female, gay) of the metropole
spins about the core of consumption, its mysteries, its possibilities, its
sacred rites.

We are led to expect shock as the Benjaminian objective correlative for
the modernist urban experience; in *The Transparent Society* Gianni
Vattimo links shock with Heidegger's term for the modernist artwork's
effect, *Stoss,* or the blow, and arrives at a definition for modernist aesthetic experience: "the focal point for art corresponding to this excitabil-
ity and hypersensitivity is no longer the work, but experience. . . . The
phenomenon Benjamin describes as shock, then, does not concern only
the conditions of perception, nor is it to be entrusted to the sociology of
art. Rather, it is the manner of the work of art's actualization." This
Heideggerian formulation nonetheless vaults over one of the primary disputes of modernism, the immediate assumption of the alienating or reifying nature of reproduction, consumption, spectacle. Moreover, Woolf's
work addresses the nature of the commodity itself within such systems, in
ways that give the lie to an overly hasty vilification of commodification.
In my view, this transpires because of the obliquity of Woolf's approach
to the urban and to the European in general: *her* metropole, unlike, say,
Benjamin's, is sexed and thus reconfigures the stage of the commodity,
consumption, and gender. Benjamin's "The Work of Art in the Age of
Mechanical Reproduction," to cite the locus classicus, does valorize film,
for example, for its distillation of the aesthetics of shock, and its seemingly resolute eradication of aura. Emphasis on the term "reproduction"
has to some extent blinded us to the absence of the understanding of consumption, a process that entails a re-auraticization under the sign of personal history, fantasmatic agency, collective desire. The society of the
spectacle is not simply a society of appearance manipulated by power,
where the refraction of goods in myriad shop windows makes a dazzling

skin over the stark reality of hegemony. "This is also the society in which reality presents itself as more fluid, as weaker, as soft, where experience can acquire the characteristics of oscillation, disorientation, and play," Vattimo notes, and since he is speaking of modern social form, or "reality," and not of Woolf or her writing, the adjectives "fluid," "weak," and "soft" are not any summing up or privileging of the "feminine," but descriptive of an alternative understanding of the effects of the advent of mass culture and the media.[12] Essentially, I am claiming, Woolf's writing already contains or enacts just such an exploration. Moreover, the "Copernican revolution" of Keynes's theories of the market exhibit precisely this turn to Vattimo's "disorientation, oscillation, and play," where the market is not a mathematical self-regulating machine but a fluid—indeed soft—interplay of elements where disorder reigns.

The dual possibility of this cultural terrain is brought out in the famous episode of collective transfixation as a skywriting plane emits its puffy, magic script across the sky, "Glaxo . . . Creemo . . . Toffee," writ large for the wonderment and puzzlement of the onlookers in the park. "The clouds to which the letters E, G, or L had attached themselves moved freely, as if destined to cross from West to East on a mission of the greatest importance which would never be revealed, and yet certainly so it was—a mission of greatest importance" (21). The words "West" and "East" are capitalized here, a portentous reminder of the pan-European nature of World War I and the importance of airplane technology to its devastation. Precisely what is not meant, it seems to me, is that this airplane is the mere replica of that other engine of destruction. Here the airplane, for good or ill, is an ineluctable feature of modernity capable of hieroglyphic play, of hierophantic writing. "It was toffee; they were advertising toffee, a nursemaid told Rezia. Together they began to spell t . . . o . . . f . . ." This skywriting, emblematic of all writing under the sign of mass culture, prompts an unfurling of the personal history of various women in this city, especially Mrs. Dempster, a figure left out of most accounts of modernity, urbanism, and shock, but decisively included here with her malleable desires intact:

Ah, but that aeroplane! Hadn't Mrs. Dempster always longed to see foreign parts? She had a nephew, a missionary. It soared and shot. She always went to sea at Margate, not out o' sight of land, but she had no patience with women who were afraid of water. It swept and fell. Her stomach was in her mouth. Up again. There's a fine young feller aboard of it, Mrs. Dempster wagered, and away and away it went, fast and fading, away and away the aeroplane shot; soaring over Greenwich and all the masts; over the little island of grey churches, St. Paul's and the rest till, on either side of London, fields spread out and dark brown woods where adventurous thrushes hopping boldly, glancing quickly, snatched the snail and tapped him on a stone, once, twice, thrice. (40–41)

Mrs. Dempster's experience, if we can provisionally call it that, is not comfortably to be lodged in the vocabulary of reification or alienation, nor simply in the realm of the specular and spectacular. On the contrary: via the unexpected medium of the evanescent toffee advertisement Mrs. Dempster has entered a geopolitical reverie. Her metropole is sexed by way of the skeins of consumption, which are not riveted, mechanical, restricting but offer a cast-out line to another way of envisioning her circumstances.

The narrative complexity of this and other Woolf texts rests on the almost perverse mobility of narrativity, where there are no boundaries or borders to narration. The mobile camera of vision moves at will into and out of the "heads" of a large cast, many only fleetingly the locus of narrating consciousness, never to return in the narration. Narrativity does not just leap from head to head, though, in Woolf's arachnid prose. The filaments of narrative line swoop back in narrative time or penetrate the rhetorical figures of speech already set up, as if moving back behind the counter in a store. An example of the latter swooping motion is worth extended quotation, coming as it does at the point of purchase of the flowers Mrs. Dalloway has gone out to buy, tracing as it does the surface face of consumption only to tunnel back within it.

There were roses; there were irises. And yes—so she breathed in the earthy garden sweet smell as she stood talking to Miss Pym who owed her help, and thought her kind, for kind she had been years ago; very kind, but she looked older this year, turning her head from side to side among the irises and roses and nodding tufts of lilac with her eyes half closed, snuffing in, after the street uproar, the delicious scent, the exquisite coolness. And then, opening her eyes, how fresh like frilled linen clean from a laundry laid in wicker trays the roses looked; and dark and prim the red carnations, holding their heads up; and all the sweet peas spreading in their bowls, tinged violet, snow white, pale—

as if it were the evening and girls in muslin frocks came out to pick sweet peas and roses after the superb summer's day, with its almost blue-black sky, its delphiniums, its carnations, its arum lilies was over; and it was the moment between six and seven when every flower— roses, carnations, irises, lilac—glows; white, violet, red, deep orange; every flower seems to burn by itself, softly, purely in the misty beds; and how she loved the grey-white moths spinning in and out, over the cherry pie, over the evening primroses! (18)

This narrative rodomontade may seem far afield from the modernist revision of the market I am staking out in Woolf and Keynes, but Woolf's looping-the-loop here is the characteristic narrative development (or put another way, characteristic Woolfian modernist aesthetic development) of market consciousness. Clarissa is in the florist's shop, poised to select flowers from Miss Pym; her vision scans the flowers, an anonymous narrative voice declares the items (there were roses, there were irises). Suddenly, momentarily, it is Miss Pym who is the vessel of consciousness as she looks at Clarissa, but then upon "her" eyes (presumably Clarissa's) opening, the language enters the simile, so that the stacks of flowers she is choosing from take on a magical life as girls on a summer night were out picking the flowers they somehow resemble. The simile is by this point stretched to a maximum attenuation, but Woolf gives it more play on the line, as a moment of unspecified narrative consciousness is set up—a moment "between six and seven" in a summer garden laced with grey-white moths. The fitful play and tug of consciousness on the line is motivated in and through objects of consciousness (for reader and character) that are at the same time objects of consumption—and consciousness and consumption are conflated, in confluence with each other.

This is the aspect of the market that operates through metaphor and metonymy to carve out more and more spaces for being. Another technique orchestrating the book resides in the interstices of those spaces, the uncanny ways that experiences and thoughts become shared, collective, or catalytic. Take for example the moment toward the end of the book when Peter Walsh is walking down the street and hears the ambulance's bell as it races too late to the scene of Septimus Smith's suicide. What stirs in Peter is the contrast he perceives to India, the comforting sense that every citizen's disaster matters in London and will be attended to for the public good. Of course there is strong irony in this; Smith's anonymity and estrangement are total, and he commits suicide because he fears an excess of dehumanizing "help" from the medical profession. This, too, is the market in action, however, in that unexpected crystallizing moments unite strangers around sometimes invisible processes of exchange. Peter is revitalized by the moment of Smith's death, since he construes it as an index of how much people should matter to one another in a polity. Smith is still dead, but he has in his suicidal self-sacrifice occasioned many such moments of renewal or at least rethinking on the part of others. Clarissa hears of his death and makes of that moment of anonymous juxtaposition a credo of solidarity with those who are outcast. Wending its way in and through the fragmentary corridors of shared consciousness, or shared narrative space, the narrative voice provides an alternative explanation of social relations. Woolf's style of writing is a paradigm case for a different concept of market relations: expansive, often depersonalizing, fraught and yet ever promising.

To shift to Keynes is to lose the freight of literary tradition, but to retain the emphasis on language. Keynes's style of economic writing is no less a paradigm case of modernism, and of marketing as modernism. Across his major treatises and his many essays flickers the glancing light of the rhetorical, which for Keynes can shape as nothing else can the new conception of the market. As a glimpse of the affinities with Woolf's project, consider his declaration in a review of Bernard Baruch's *The Making of the Reparation and the Economic Sections of the Treaty* (referring, of course, to the economic and political aftermath of World War I, which as it happens is also the framework of *Mrs. Dalloway*): "It is dangerous to treat the living word as dead. Words live not less than acts and sometimes longer. The war, it may almost be said, was fought for words."[13] Language, then, is material, and the material of the market is comprised of language as much as of other stuff. Thus its plasticity, its mobility, its dynamism, its susceptibility.

A pivotal refrain in Mrs. Dalloway is the rather garbled crooning song, "the voice of an ancient spring spouting from the earth," emitted by the chthonic old woman who sits at the park entrance, one of Woolf's old-woman figures, half working-class crone, half mythologized primal earth mother. Language circulates in the market and, in a reversal of the expected, is made to undo the hierarchy of high and low, male and female, art and commerce. The song she sings has thankfully been identitfed for us by numerous commentators as a version of Richard Strauss's "Allerseelen," whose lyrics are a lament for a lost love on All Souls' Day. Elegiac aspects aside, and these have been wonderfully useful in interpretation, what is remarkable is this reversal of the high versus low or popular continuum of art and how it speaks to an alternating current for modernism. Strauss's words are not just filtered through this popular, oral form, they are remade as a feminized British folk culture—an international, or read in this context, a European, high-art fragment recirculates through the old woman, a sexing of the metropole. The old woman's "ee um fah um so, foo swee too eem oo" is the transformation through consumption of the otherwise impregnable modern artifact, and its rearticulation as another form of currency.

Clarissa Dalloway has a privileged relation to the metropolitan market because of her status within consumption. To give the merest sketch of what would be a more protracted argument, this entails that she figures the surplus currency of consumption, or its auratic excess. Her parties, it goes without saying, are bound up in extensive acts of literal consumption, the purchase of flowers and candles and food and clothes. But of greater significance is the placement of Clarissa at the core of the book, a meditation on urban modernity. Clarissa tentatively and tenuously reverses the disenchantment of the world characteristic of modernity by the generosity of her gendered acts of consumption, where consumption is reformulated as the nature of the gift. This appears paradoxical, in that gift-giving looks like the reversal of consumption, the taking in or appropriation of something through an act of exchange. Nonetheless, Clarissa's consumption has this perverse or unexpected valence, and it is linked by the text to the nature of modernist writing and Woolf's writing in particular. "I threw a coin once into the Serpentine," Clarissa famously says, comparing this to the suicide of Septimus Smith as a form of sacrifice, giving the gift of his death to the city of London not as a soldier in the European war, but as an ex-centric denizen of the city itself. And on the verge of his suicide, Septimus is gendered female, when he decorates the party hat as his penultimate creative offering. The sexing of the metropole in this fashion is not meant at all to suggest that, for example, men are unable to take up this relation to the city or to consumption. Rather, this is a way of figuring the dynamics of the modernist city, where, to put it very baldly, shopping is not the root of all evil—nor, one hastens to say, is it utopian. The processes and procedures of modernity, however, are accorded weight and positive possibilities, in contradistinction to the dehumanization often attributed to the modern city. The city of women— Clarissa's London, for instance—is the site not only of all the hierar-

chies and divisions of the gendered social world, but also of their lique-
faction in gifts of consumption.

In *Mrs. Dalloway* the English subjects depicted throughout the book
are eccentric to the metropole in multifarious ways, whether by dint of
having spent twenty years in India like Peter Walsh, repatriating as a
World War I veteran in the case of Septimus Smith, being Italian, coming
down from Scotland in hopes of escaping poverty there, or in less tangi-
ble ways, as for Richard Dalloway, pillar of the metropolitan establishment, but secretly a farmer manqué, a man with rural longings. This corresponds to Woolf's sexing of the metropole in her own right; the city is
never univocally, monolithically singular, but stratified, residual, disparate. In these works and others Woolf surveys the terrain of a European culture delegitimated by its descent into repeated warfare, predicated on a network of metropolitan capitals in ghostly alliance with the
peripheral places of their imperial economies, and yet despite this,
becomes the architect of provisional cities of women, where consumption
retains aura, enchantment, and even the possibility of the gift.

There is a resonance to the refiguring of the market in all this, too, as
Keynes's economic theory insists on the fractured global rhythms that
give rise to the multiple oscillations of the market on any given day.
Keynes's "banana parable" follows the logic of Woolf's prose in an
uncanny way. Seeking to describe the relation between saving and investment in the modern economy, and their unexpected failure to link up in
straightforwardly "efficient" ways, Keynes gives the example of a society
predicated economically on the banana alone.

> Imagine a community, initially in a state of equilibrium, which pro-
> duces only bananas. A thrift campaign is started, as a result of which
> people start saving more and consuming less, the rate of investment in
> banana plantations initially staying the same. The price of bananas
> then falls by the amount of the increased saving. Virtue is rewarded:
> people get the same amount of bananas as before for less money, and
> they have "saved" as well. But the producers of bananas have now
> made an unexpected loss, since they have been forced to sell their
> bananas at below cost price. They cannot, of course, "hoard" them,
> because they will rot. The increased saving has not increased the
> aggregate wealth of the community at all: it has simply transferred
> part of it from the producers to the consumers of bananas. So nothing
> has happened to reduce their excess saving.[14]

Events cascade from this point in the parable, where the traditional medicine of "thrift" or saving has disastrous or at least unwonted effects. The invisible hand of a self-regulating market will fail and fail decisively. Keynes goes on: "you could always cure the trouble by lowering the rate of interest. But that is a matter for the banking system. In a closed economy, like banana-land, there would be no problem in doing this. But as things now are in Britain, if the Bank of England were to lower the interest rate, money would go abroad and we would lose gold, forcing up the rate of interest again."[15] The unexpected solution is to save less or to invest more, but not to save more or invest less. While not as effulgent rhetorically as "I threw a coin into the Serpentine," there are still powerful bonds between these modernist parables of the market. Consuming (a synonym for "saving less") is stripped of its stigma, is in fact a means of defying what Keynes called "the evangelicized economics of the Victorians" and Woolf calls, in her novel, "Conversion and Proportion." The latter two monstrous erectile principles of force are countered throughout the text by acts of market consumption—and even the deliberate "wasting" of money, as when the gold coin is tossed into the park pond by Clarissa, or, as many would moralize, when she puts together a party. Another way of putting my point here is that a modernist economic understanding of the market had to be fought for with an equivalent effort to the aesthetic battle waged by modernists like Woolf against those she summarized as "Mr. Bennett." Moreover, the modernist market is an aesthetic artifact as truly as it is an economic "model," and a design for living in both cases.

For both Keynes and Woolf this activity of the market, or within the market, has an aura of enchantment, as debased coins are taken into a private economy of exchange. Keynes grapples with the "quantity theory" of money and its relation to a psychosocial process: "The orthodox theory assumes that the only reason people save money—refrain from consumption—is in order to invest it. This seems reasonable enough—after all, you can't consume bits of paper or gold. But then you have the King Midas problem. I don't think he was completely mad, though he certainly seems to have been an extreme case of an anal-sadistic personality."[16] Clarissa is surely an anti–King Midas figure in *Mrs. Dalloway,* not so much because we can confidently attest to her lack of anal sadism, of course, but because she continually traverses the route between hoarding and investing and offers a "magical" solution to these antinomies—sacrifice through spending. Keynes's work set itself against the mystification of the market as a self-regulating machine, but it does this by acknowledging the mystificatory potential inherent in the market, what Woolf's writing conveys by its magicality and poetic infusion. Essentially, this is a countermagic of the market. Recall that it was Ronald Reagan who, in a burst of anti-Keynesianism with long-lasting effects on most of the Western industrial economies, triumphally declared a return to "the magic of markets." This particular magic harkened back to the neoclassical economic faith in the regulatory order of the market system, where "things" would get sorted out as if by magic. Keynesian and Woolfian modernist magic is the antithesis of Reaganite or Friedmanite (as in Milton) or Marshallian (as in Alfred) monetarist magic. As such, it is an understanding of the market as magical in a complex, fluid, unpredictable, social, emotional, and sacrally consuming fashion—everything that the hierarchized wizardry of classical market magic would repudiate. This is a "soft," a fluid magic, feminized, anarchic, yet interconnected, playful at its best. Woolf and Keynes as modernists have to find a vocabulary for the momentary, the oscillating, the everyday, for a market transfused by a collective magic, one always at great risk of breaking down. Both comprehend that the market can be a battlefield, or a minefield, or a liquid terrain of experience, choice, agency and desire exquisitely sensitive to all the ripples that play across its surface. And for them consuming is at the heart of this rough magic.

If this is the habitus of modernism, then there is an analogy in the urban room of one's own of Woolf's eponymous essay. Without delving into the complex political terrain of this text, it is worth noting that the production of writing for the modern woman writer is tied inextricably to the procedures of consumption, to the assurance of such a room. It is not often mentioned that this polemical piece of modernist feminism is a city text, where the modernist urban environment is rewritten as a city of women and in a sense for them. Coming full circle, it is possible to see how Woolf sexes the metropole with a vengeance in this instance. "Publicity is what is necessary," she says, in a stroke restaging the commonplaces of our take on the commodified public sphere of modernity, whose quintessence is supposed to be the city. Leonard Woolf once commented on the relief it gave Virginia Woolf to have her books published by their own Hogarth Press, as she was free of "constantly worrying about public taste and the pressures of the marketplace."[17] This is another sense of the market, a specialized one restricted to literary production. However antipathetic Woolf, and other modernists, may at times have been toward that small subset of the larger market, Woolfian modernism does not target publicity or consumption per se as problems—if anything, as I hope I have shown, the market is perceived to be a shadowy common room within which acts of much creative magic or transforming potential can be performed.

A circle back to Bloomsbury completes the circuit of this argument. The magic of Bloomsbury is related to the "magic" these modernists discerned in the market. Certainly, it can and must be admitted that the persistent fascination with Bloomsbury and its acolytes owes something to our envy at their glamour and élan, their class position, their quasi-bohemian freedoms in the relative lap of luxury—but this is a minor, if human, all-too-human note. The enchantment of Bloomsbury is more seriously and intensely related to its sui generis market position, if you will. The members of Bloomsbury (however fractious they may have been as a group), and in particular Woolf and Keynes as I have singled them out here, lived a version of the modernist market, created a version of the possibilities of that market, and apprehended the modernist logic of the market anew. Cause and effect are ineffectual categories for analyzing this process, in fact are far too aligned to the rigid cause/effect economic theories of the socioeconomic that Bloomsbury modernism rejects. The lines of demarcation between and among consumption and production, use value and exchange value, art and commerce, male and female, gay and straight, are unsettled and whirled about by Bloomsbury. Debt, saving, and spending are refigured, rewritten, relived. Not only did Bloomsbury become a laboratory of lifestyle, it contributed to the famous turn to "deficit spending" that is now the hallmark of the bourgeois liberal state, and, in comparison to the brutalities of supply-side economics, is a veritable state of grace. Bloomsbury's very existence forecloses the temptation to see art and "the market" on two utterly divergent paths, or on paths that can only intersect with muddy, or smutty, results for both sides. Woolf and Keynes needed the crucible of Bloomsbury to reconstruct the modern parable, and to enact it. The intriguing allure of Woolf's sweater sets, or the glow hovering over Keynes's male lovers in retrospect, or the nimbus of glamour permanently ensconced at Charleston is not of an entirely other order than the attentive efforts we make to read, think, and see modernity. Within this modernist moment, art remade the market, and the market made modernism.

NOTES

1. For an exceptionally thorough iconography of Bloomsbury artifacts, see Elizabeth P. Richardson, *A Bloomsbury Iconography* (Winchester: St. Paul's Bibliographies, 1989). The book catalogs each and every photograph, painting, and literary or journalistic reference to major and minor members of Bloomsbury, giving a sort of proof to my thesis that it is impossible to sort out Bloomsbury "art" from Bloomsbury "market"—they are one and the same.

2. Oscar Wilde, "The Soul of Man under Socialism," in *De Profundis and Other Writings* (New York: Penguin, 1979), p. 46.

3. Ibid., p. 510.

4. Hazel Kyrk, *A Theory of Consumption* (Cambridge: Riverside Press–Houghton Mifflin, 1923), p. 119.

5. Ibid., p. 120.

6. All Keynesians and all those interested in modern economics (which includes most of us) are indebted to Robert Skidelsky for the two published volumes of his projected three-part intellectual biography of John Maynard Keynes, *Hopes Betrayed, 1883–1920* (London: Allen Lane, 1990) and *The Economist as Saviour, 1920–1937* (New York: Viking Penguin, 1994). These remarks of Skidelsky's are taken from p. 410 of the second volume. See also his immensely helpful and learned essay "Keynes and Bloomsbury," in *Essays by Divers Hands,* ed. Michael Holroyd (London: Royal Society of Literature, 1982), pp. 15–27.

7. See Miller's chapter on Woolf's *Mrs. Dalloway* in his *Fiction and Repetition: Seven English Novels* (Cambridge: Harvard University Press, 1982), pp. 176–202, for a discussion of the telekinesis of her narrative voice. Equally relevant is Geoffrey Hartman's now classic article, "Virginia's Web," reprinted in *Beyond Formalism* (New Haven: Yale University Press, 1977), pp. 71–84. The essay is highly formalist in the best sense, as it uncovers a Woolfian technique of language we can then put to additional material use.

8. Overall, *Virginia Woolf and the Real World* (Berkeley and Los Angeles: University of California Press, 1986) is a terrifically judicious and solid book; its insights for this argument come thick and fast in the chapters "Class and Money" and "Mrs. Dalloway and the Social System," chapters 4 and 5 respectively.

9. All quotations are taken from the 1953 Harvest–Harcourt Brace Jovanovich reprint of Virginia Woolf's 1925 Hogarth Press edition of *Mrs. Dalloway*. This first sentence and following comes on page 3.

10. Raymond Williams, *The Politics of Modernism: Against the New Conformists* (London: Verso, 1989).

11. The modernist critic Michael Levenson, for one, has made just such a formalist, gendered aesthetic case, with which my argument takes complete issue.

12. See Gianni Vattimo, *The Transparent Society,* trans. David Webb (Balti-

more: Johns Hopkins University Press, 1992), especially chapter 4, "Art and Oscillation," pp. 45–61.

13. John Maynard Keynes, *The Collected Writings of John Maynard Keynes,* gen. eds. Austin Robinson and Donald Moggridge (London: Macmillan, 1971–89), vol. 17, *Activities, 1920–1922: Treaty Revision and Reconstruction,* p. 97.

14. As cited in Skidelsky, 2:323–24.

15. As quoted in Skidelsky, 2:325.

16. Skidelsky, 2:322–23.

17. The phrase is Zwerdling's, *Virginia Woolf,* p. 106.

Joyce's Face

Maurizia Boscagli and Enda Duffy

> . . . every face bears the mark of writing.
>
> Russell Berman

It may come as a shock to some to find that James Joyce, great modernist writer and arch-priest of high art, appeared on the cover of the May 8, 1939, edition of *Time* (fig. 11), and within, was "profiled"—that is, sub-jected to the indignity of having his identity sifted through the stereotypes and banalities of the mass-market American media. The shock of seeing his face there merely allows one to grasp the depth of contradiction at work in representing the "great modernist artist" in *Time's* cover photo-graph. Here is the writer who, even more than Kafka, Eliot, or Woolf, worked in his writing to disrupt and delegitimize the notion of a discrete and unified modern subject; through bricolage constructions from Molly to Bloom to HCE, he fashioned instead complex models of multiply interpellated and fragmented subject effects. Gisèle Freund, the most illustrious portrait-photographer of artists and writers in Europe in the interwar years,[1] took the *Time* photograph at the moment when Joyce had completed *Finnegans Wake*,[2] the text in which the activity of decen-tering subjects is most intense. In this photograph, however, Joyce allows himself to be presented to the world as a highly conventional centered subject.

This ready assumption of conventional subject status, and the slippage it implies between the image of the artist and the implications of his art, is enabled, we would like to suggest, by the photograph's negotiation of two more fundamental contradictions in Joyce's self-representation as artist. First, we hope to show that in this photograph and in the accom-panying *Time* photo-essay Joyce manages to juggle a suggestion of his Irish origins with the actual evidence that he now lives elsewhere. Second, we suggest that he intentionally stages his image as an advertisement: the photographs are the place where Joyce "makes a spectacle" of himself as

Joyce's Face *(1938). Photograph by Gisèle Freund.*

a commodity. At the same time, he appears deeply uneasy with his self-display, and throughout Freund's photo-essay the viewer witnesses Joyce's attempt to defuse and deny his self-fetishization through strategies of self-distancing. In vain: the aura of Joyce the famous modernist and internationally recognized artist is indistinguishable from the aura of the fetish-presence of the star (an unsuccessful fetish, as we will see). His face, notwithstanding the photographer's insistent and professed attempt to capture "the man" and his human depth, produces, we will claim, an identity instantly fabricated at the behest of consumerist imperatives to advertise *Finnegans Wake*, to market the highest of high-modernist productions to the consuming masses. By looking closely at the *Time* cover and accompanying article, and at a series of Gisèle Freund photographs of Joyce and his friends taken for *Time* and for another assignment for *Life* magazine, and since published in Freund's *Three Days with Joyce*,[3] we will explore how these posed photographs suppress and gloss over the contradictions that make them interesting: their ambiguous negotiation of Irishness *versus* cosmopolitanism, and of unique individuality *versus* the depersonalized status of the commodity embodied by the figure of the star. At stake is the relation between Joyce's art and his particular status as an international celebrity in popular culture.

The fable of origins and the history of the subject as celebrity, the two tropes renounced but hardly evaded in Joyce's languidly self-assured poses in these photographs, are to be discerned first, we wish to claim, around the notion of the artist's Irishness. Joyce as shown by Gisèle Freund is the Irish native who went on, by way of his role as exiled artist, to become a popular-culture star. As such, his photo on the cover of *Time* in 1939 might even be said to mark an epistemic break in representations of Irish faciality, between on the one hand the long history of imagining faces encoded by nationality within the context of physiognomic readings, where the face was read as a synecdoche of Irish national character, and on the other, the internationalization of such a face, as an image of a Western everyman, a model of the modern nomadic subject. Joyce's modernist representativeness in this latter sense comes from his avowal of this transnational quality; this in turn implied a triumphant overcoming of the claims of locality and origin. Any trace of an origin is what seems to be obliterated in the cosmopolitan face of Joyce, but it remains as the necessary foil to the face's international (Western) anonymity, as its uncanny. It is the indelible trope of origin that one is invited to bring to a reading of the face of the author. Making possible Joyce the cosmopolitan, haunting these photographs, is Joyce's Irish face.

In his poem "In Memoriam Francis Ledwidge," about the Irish poet killed in World War I, Seamus Heaney thinks of Ledwidge's appearance: "A haunted catholic face, pallid and brave."[4] To Heaney, meditating on the public image of an Irish poet, Ledwidge's Irishness and his Catholicism are written all over his face. Such an Irish face, if it ever existed, was the one invented historically by tropes of Irishness that became prevalent in the context of British colonizing efforts in Ireland in the sixteenth and seventeenth centuries, and reached a crescendo in collusion with the study of physiognomy and the "science" of phrenology in the nineteenth. Such physiognomic studies as the physical descriptions of the folk in Trollope's Irish novels were implicated in racial and national stereotypes that owed their existence to a colonial regime they served to legitimize. In the nineteenth century, the study of faces, made easier with the technology of the camera, worked in collusion with the study of racial characteristics; defining the appearance the "natives" of every colony had become the goal.[5] The Irish face, as the feared visage of the terrorist, became a given after police photos of Fenians were used in Victorian police files.[6]

Scientists also focused on the Irish head and face; as late as the 1930s, not long before Freund was photographing Joyce, Harvard scientists were photographing thousands of faces in the West of Ireland to discern a quintessential Irish type. All this recording, whether by police, scientists, or photographers, may be said to have represented Irishness within a matrix already laid down as a given by colonial descriptions of the Irish generally. These, as L. Perry Curtis has shown in *Apes and Angels*,[7] which focuses on the infamous *Punch* cartoons of the Irish, saw the Irish within a thoroughly Manichaean division. The Irish were portrayed either as barbarians, ultimately as terrorists, or as civilians, acquiescent figures who might be redeemable as collaborators with the British regime. Seamus Deane has documented the persistence of these images of the Irish from colonial times to the present.[8] Postcolonial theorists, such as Homi Bhabha writing on the hybridized subjectivities of colonial subjects,[9] have demonstrated that this habit of reading the colonized other was general in colonialist discourse. We can read Heaney's two adjectives, "pallid" and "brave," to describe Ledwidge's face, as a shade of this same Manichaean allegory: "pallid," as in wan, docile, meek, that is, the civilian face; and "brave," as in courageous, willing to fight, and potentially a wild barbarian visage. Ledwidge's face shows him to Heaney as the almost wholly interpellated subaltern native.[10] If we detect Irishness in Joyce's face, pallid and brave in its own way, we are reading into it elements of civility and barbarity set up as the codes by which Irish subjectivity is read.

The Irish face, however, exists only as an illusion, one developed by a racist discourse of colonialism; there is nothing necessarily Irish about looking either brave or pallid. Signs of frailty and determination are nevertheless subtly encoded as Irish in Joyce's portraits. This Irish face, in Freund's photographs, is barely discernible; rather, it may be said to exist as an erasure, not present in any specifically quotable form, but nevertheless offered to the viewer as an ineluctable zero-degree of Joyce's subjectivity, and around which his "star quality" is in fact constructed, as the implied narrative of his heroic rejection of this origin. *Time* states this directly: "No observer of his life and works can fail to note that James Joyce is a typical Irishman" (84). One strategy of representing Joyce in Freund's photographs is based on subverting this topos of Joyce as Irishman, and Joyce's face as an Irish one. But in order for us to collude with and take pleasure in that subversion, the images assume too that we will first read these as Irish faces, and imagine in a turn of the raised, defensive hand, the dry, stretched skin, the line of mouth and thinning hair a combination of bravery and pallidness that somehow, to readers of *Time* in the late 1930s and to potential purchasers of the new novel *Finnegans Wake,* will be inescapably Irish.

In Joyce's uses of profile, in the poses where he twists his limbs, and finally in the spectacle of his worn hands and face, there are subtle concessions to the "Irishness" of Joyce's body. These portraits, then, hint at the elements of barbarity, mystery, and servitude key to colonist-inspired stereotypes of Irish subjects; as such, they mingle the civilian and barbarian elements that the stereotype kept apart. Specifically, while presenting suggestions of the barbarian under erasure, they refuse the topos of the civilian as that which defines Joyce's present cosmopolitanism. For example, Joyce is often shown in these photographs in half or full profile. The profile, in nineteenth-century photographs, was a topos of mysteriousness, as in Julia Cameron's most famous portrait of Tennyson. It was common too in images of the barbarian other, and Irish rebels were often shown in profile to suggest both mystery and danger. In the Irish painter Sean Keating's paintings from the Irish War of Independence, *Men of the West* (mentioned in Yeats's poem "The Municipal Gallery Revisited") and *Men of the South,* both showing posses of peasant guerrillas,[11] the fighters are shown in profile. The most famous Irish rebel almost always shown in profile was Patrick Pearse; he was photographed thus, it appears, because of a squint he wished to hide. In these contexts, Joyce's averted face (he almost never looks directly at the camera) places him in a tradition that we can read, however unconsciously, as one often deployed to show the Irish as barbarian. That this pose was used too to show the poetic and mysterious qualities of sitters generally allows the photographs to pit the barbarian stereotype against the civilian, for mysteriousness was a quality that, since the Romantics and especially with Arnold's writing on the Celts as "tumultuous, passionate . . . prone to revolt," had always been ascribed to the Irish but was also ascribed to Romantic artists in the home country. The effect is to show this attribution of attractive tumultousness as no more than a liberal recasting of the old stereotype of the native as devilish.

Next, in the peculiarly twisted limbs of Joyce's body in one of the most arresting of Freund's photographs (*TD* 28) one can discern an echo of the leprechaun-like Irish body familiar in representations at least since the *Punch* cartoons; this is a body that, even when still, seems to be simultaneously casting about in a rage or frenzy. Again, see Freund's image of Joyce's worn hands (*TD* 53), and the imperfections of his face in the close-up photograph (fig. 12) which we will consider later in relation to the professed realism of Freund's portrait work. Here, beneath the polished and bedecked cosmopolitan citizen of the world, is the work-worn servant, an echo of the images of peasants that became common photo and postcard subjects as tourism grew apace in Victorian Ireland. The Irish barbarian was almost always the peasant (the merit of Sean Keating's paintings of guerillas is to metamorphose the peasants into heroes), and Stephen Dedalus himself, recalling a dream of such an Irish rustic, had admitted at the end of *A Portrait of the Artist:* "I fear his redrimmed horny eyes." To the extent that he allows imperfections, or suggestions that he might be a worker or a servant, to show, Joyce reminds the viewer that what haunts these photographs is an uncanny trace of the Irish peasant-barbarian stereotype they suppress.

These intimations of Irishness in the photographed face and body of the writer are tenuous, and it is precisely this tenuousness that is key to their effect. They are allowed to exist as traces that are almost, literally, effaced. From the earliest physiognomic discourse, it was never claimed that this science had more than a statistical validity; from the viewpoint of the believer in the scientific basis of racial stereotyping, however, such pronouncements, perversely, made physiognomic investigations all the more totalizing, as exceptions could be cited to prove the general rule. "His face is thin and fine, his profile especially delicate," noted *Time* (82). These portraits of the artist in Freund's photographs often present themselves as exceptions; the thin lips, refined nose, and hidden eyes, for example, confound the images of Irish faces from the Victorian *Punch*

Joyce's Face *(1938). Photograph by Gisèle Freund.*

cartoons that gave the Irish thick lips, snub noses, and bulging eyes so that they might seem more completely simianized in keeping with post-Darwinian versions of phrenological discourse. Joyce's dandified clothes and cane, his two ostentatious rings, all give the lie to any easy characterization of Joyce's face as an Irish one in the ways that it had been described by colonial stereotypes. More fundamentally, Joyce's self-representation in these photographs, first as a reader, then in the interior settings of the home and bookshop, and then with particular exact gender configurations (a man his secretary, two women his friends) all serve to play with the same notion of his Irishness and ultimately to subvert the viewer's expectations regarding it, so that a space for Joyce as the "exile" into cosmopolitanism is opened up. In almost all of his photographs taken after leaving Ireland, Joyce effected a determined dandyism as a means to imply an involved cosmopolitanism; photographed by Berenice Abbott in Paris over a decade before the *Time* pictures, for example, he had posed in profile with his hand to his forehead in a gesture at once languid and contemplative, and sported a bow tie, which, as Brenda Maddox notes, was daring daytime wear for the 1920s. In the Freund photographs, the zeal of the cosmopolitanite seems overcome; Freund's textured images appear to bring to the surface that desire to suppress suggestions of his Irishness that the Abbott and other photographs had worked to conceal.[12]

A series of photographs that catch Joyce himself in the act of looking and reading invite the viewer into this game of eradicating while they incite, of subverting even as they hold on to a trace of Joyce's Irish origin, inviting one to revel in the writer's glamorous transnationalism. The photograph on the cover of *Time* shows Joyce reading. What is foregrounded is an excessive gaze on his part upon the book: he stares through thick glasses and through another glass held over the page, and we find ourselves gazing at a man gazing at a book. In this gesture Joyce problematizes the act of looking itself (the viewer realizes that Joyce's own eyesight, his ability to see, is very poor); he implies to his readers, sympathetic watchers, that they must gaze with care. Joyce, not returning our gaze as he squints at the page, seems to accept us as voyeurs. Yet his very act of reading itself disrupts the representation of the Irish subject as (illiterate) barbarian. "Joyce's curious glasses give him a somewhat Martian appearance," says *Time* (82), implying that his gaze at once others him ("somewhat Martian") and also drawing attention to that othering (it is his glasses and his eyes that lead the *Time* writer to consider him as other in the first place). Joyce's representation in the act of seeing calls upon his readers to go beyond looking as a form of physiognomic surveillance and works to involve them in the act of looking as a way of understanding strangeness, of annotating the eccentricities of the star who has been elevated by a populace "without qualities."

The deflection from the face turns one's attention to Joyce's space, to the settings in which he is presented. The first of these is the home; in the first instance, this space stands for the original home, Ireland. Yet if anything, the Joyces' best room resembles a hotel room: there is little individualization here. The hotel is a starred locus in modernist fiction, from the Grand Hotel des Bains where a modern subject faces desire and death in Thomas Mann's *Death in Venice* to the hotel in Virginia Woolf's first novel, *The Voyage Out*, where the heroine discovers desire before dying also. Joyce's drawing room as hotel suite is the perfect setting for the modernist artist who is heroic precisely in being away from home, in exile. Here Joyce, like a traveling businessman, is working (*TD* 22, reproduced in *Time*, 78). This turns out to mean correcting proofs, so that he is still looking, rather than writing; actual composition is thereby retained as an activity related to origins.

Notice in this photograph (*Time*, 78) that the typical iconography of the writer's setting, his study desk, is absent; work, for Joyce, is recast as leisure, in a modernist version of the Elizabethan poet's *sprezzatura*. This negligent indolence derives its interest, as it did with Sir Philip Sidney, from a class register. Joyce is casting himself here as a gentleman. The rich gown he wears, the elegant slippers, the rugs and good furniture of the room all bear this out; the general air is one of solid, and anonymous, luxury. As such, Joyce is the émigré (i.e., the upper-class emigrant) who has prospered abroad. *Time* reminds us of how this relates to images of Irishness when it quotes Joyce naming Ireland as "the little brown bog" (84). Gentility, the setting implies, means access to the cosmopolitan. The only personal items in the setting that could render up clues to Joyce's identity are the books, the titles of which are obscured, and a series of other portraits, of Joyce's son Giorgio and his family and others, and a drawing of Joyce himself. These merely set up the possibility of portraits within portraits ad infinitum, a regression of clues toward a significance that, even if discovered, could never be pinned down to the represented subject. Joyce the gentleman, in his hotellike drawing room, surrounded by portraits, reaches an apogee of bourgeois anonymity. Leisured, well dressed, yet occupied, he manages to be anything but the imaginary Irishman who might have been dreamed up by a *Time* reader in 1939; rather, he comes very close to being a copy of the figure that a male *Time* reader might have imagined as his ideal self. This quietly assured "man without qualities" could be admired as a "success" by such a reader to the extent that he was tacitly imagined to have overcome the debilitating distinctiveness, and lower-class characteristics, that, to such a reader, his Irishness would have implied.

If the home, then, signifies the Irish home but does not get to represent it in any of its baleful particularity, the bookshop that is the setting of the central photographs turns out to be a much more richly encoded space. In these pictures Joyce is shown sitting at a table opposite Sylvia Beach, who had published *Ulysses*, and Adrienne Monnier, surrounded by books and by images of writers who are famous and English and mostly male: Shakespeare, Keats, Shelley, Lawrence (fig. 13). Here again, the representational potential and limitations of photos of the author are foregrounded, for in the main picture, we are given three images of Joyce: himself, and the two images of him on the wall behind the two women. In the game of "find Joyce in this picture," we cannot be sure which one might be the real Joyce; the actual author's face looks less substantial than the "characteristic" Joyce (with eye patch, white jacket, looking dapper) of one of the photographs. Further, these images of famous authors next to their books reiterate the role of the author's image in bolstering book sales.

Such hints are subdued in the bookshop because of its intimacy. The shop works as an ambiguously public space, half home, half salesroom. The fireplace and chairs suggest home; the portraits over the fireplace might be family pictures. It is appropriate that Joyce, who as Stephen Dedalus in *Portrait* and *Ulysses* portrays himself as a would-be alienated exile, is deeply uncomfortable in this space. He looks it: "I was struck by the paleness of his features and the fatigue of his face," notes Freund (*TD* 43), and the photos show him shifting, scratching his head, placing his hands before his face. Freund notes that there was a "bitterness" (41) between the author and booksellers in the past. Yet it is here too that Joyce smiles: "For the first time, I saw Joyce smile," says Freund (49). The context is an anecdote that associates *Ulysses* with the *Odyssey* (Joyce has been reminded of Henri Matisse's mistake in assuming that he was to illustrate Homer's epic rather than *Ulysses*), but this is more than a smile of self-satisfaction. In *Ulysses* Stephen, looking at the Britisher Haines, had remembered a saying about the three things an Irish person should never trust: "Hoof of a horse, horn of a bull, smile of a Saxon."[13] The subaltern native's smile also, as some postcolonial writers have noted, is not to be taken at face value: the lineaments of servility are often covered by a smile. Joyce's smile, then, may be said to mark his most ambivalent moment, about his fame, about his relation to the photos on the wall and his books behind him, but above all toward the two women who helped publish and publicize his work as a marketable commodity. Joyce had

James Joyce with Sylvia Beach and Adrienne Monnier.
Photograph by Gisèle Freund.

smiled when the talk was about a "deluxe American edition of *Ulysses*" (*TD* 49). These women, posed between the author and portraits that publicize him, are his promoters. His smile before them is the closest he came to letting slip his mask of reserve at this promotion, that involves nothing less than apparently feigning an old friendship. It is the smile of the former subaltern who has become a star, but who is aware that this has been achieved by presenting a subjectivity—the formal, successful author—acceptable to a mass audience.

That these friends, the promoters who are included in the representation of the author's milieu, are women, adds the currency of gender to the representational economy of these images. At home, and in the images from Giorgio's home (*TD* 56–69), Nora Joyce, the artist's wife, is notably absent, and Freund feels that she must account for this: "Joyce did not insist that his wife appear in the photographs, although he was very attached to her" (63). Nora, as Galway native and as woman, would signify the domestic aspect of the Joyce household and, more particularly, the Irish element of such domesticity all too strongly: her absence allows the image of the artist as alienated exile to operate more successfully. The two women booksellers, then, enter the photographs as the figures who replace Nora and have a different significance; they are representative of us, the viewers. Looking on as they do from a small distance, they empathize with Joyce's modernist alienation and glorify it as guarantee of his greatness. As such, the gender stereotypes that are prone to develop in the imperial versions of the native subject get reversed. In colonist images, the men often get cast as the barbarians, the women as the civilians who, from the colonist's viewpoint, must be protected from the native men. Gayatri Spivak expresses this construction in her phrase "White men saving brown women from brown men."[14] In the natives' nationalist counterdiscourse, this gender split is often exacerbated: the male is seen as reformable, while the female figure comes to represent the nation symbolically. In Ireland, this was the pattern of nationalist discourse,[15] and Irishwomen were often shown as the pure symbols of the state, as in Yeats's Countess Cathleen. In these photographs, such a gender coding is reversed; it is Joyce, the male figure, who is rendered as a symbol of greatness, while the women, American and French, are shown as the defenders and promoters of his reputation. In the same way, reversing the usual attribution of purity to the women, it is the male Joyce who is desexualized here, while there is perhaps a hint of the sexual in the closeness of the two women who sit opposite, watching him. They are shown as workers, traders, and consumers and are shown as such within a realist idiom; it is Joyce, rather, who is raised to the level of reified symbol. Joyce as *divo* emerges here through the setting up of a contrast with the two women; when one remembers too that the photographer is a woman, then the scenario that enables Joyce to be figured as the international "star" author is clearly one based also on the familiar story of the abnegation of the women and their roles.

In a note for Stuart Gilbert, Joyce wrote of Dubliner's "Cult of the divo, carried to a degree unknown even in Italy. All the great singers came to Dublin, and the names Campanini, Joe Mass, Maria Piccolomini . . . were household words. . . . many of the great modern singers . . . John Sullivan . . . John McCormack, Margaret Sheridan for example are Irish."[16] Here Joyce is imagining the version of popular fame, and an early model of stardom, from which he would be able to go on to cast himself. He is also keen to imagine that such fame is possible for an Irish person, suggesting that Gilbert could all too easily forget these singers' Irishness when noting their fame. This effacement of Irishness, while all the time keeping reminders of it alive, is the process that Joyce too undergoes in Freund's photographs, and especially on the cover of *Time*. In order for Joyce to be more than a bourgeois without qualities, he had to convey a version of the anomie of the modern cosmopolitan subject. Yet Freund as photographer also worked to "capture" in his portrait depths of significance befitting a great artist. In Joyce's case, the first trope was that of the exile, the man not at home. Each photograph, then, had to retain, as its haunting uncanny, a trace, however tentative, of the home, which for Joyce was Ireland; in suppressing and subverting this trace Joyce makes possible his image as an alienated cosmopolitan author.

As the troubled face in the cover photo (fig. 11) and the accompanying *Time* article make clear, this subject as modernist artist is defined by his alienation; he allows himself to be presented to the public here as a modernist, "obscure" author who can be recontained within popularly accepted categories around the ideologeme of exile. As the modernist in exile, his is the stance of the restless artist who is always moving: all the Paris addresses to which Joyce moved are suggested in the restlessness of the figure in these photographs. The irony of this presentation is that implicit in the image of the artist who is not at ease is an embedded memory of the fixed abode he has left, which in his case was Ireland. "His friends believe that nothing short of a European war could drive him back to the 'little brown bog' and the haunting Liffey," concluded the *Time* article,[17] redrawing its readers' attention to Joyce's role as alienated artist; the allusion to his reasonable friends, lesser mortals, implies that the great artist alone situates his greatness in his gesture of refusal. The contradiction that exists here, then, between Joyce's representation as transnational exile and the retained traces of his Irish origins, is precisely what enables us to envision him as an exile. Every one of the Freund photographs incorporates an awareness of this sense of alienated homelessness, and therefore every one of them is haunted too by the other place— Ireland—from which the artist has escaped to make this glamorous version of homelessness possible. And notice that all this is suggested while the artist is shown seated mostly in a Parisian drawing room.

Because a disavowal of homelessness is his initial defining trait, Freund's photographs of Joyce in the street, as *flâneur*, are the most characteristic. Walking up the Rue de l'Odeon, Joyce seldom looks less than lost, ill at ease, befuddled. Freund notes that this specific series of images was taken without his permission; knowing he would arrive, she set up her camera in the street. She points out that in doing this she was anticipating the *paparazzi* of the post–World War II years, capturing the star as he entered the public street. Thus at the moment when Joyce is most transparent, when he is most evidently the modernist alienated artist as *flâneur,* he is also most the star, the object of the *paparazza*'s intrusive camera. These are the most "revealing" of Freund's photographs in that in them we see signs of a depth of suffering on Joyce's face—and among them we find one where Joyce is holding out his purse. Here most clearly, but no less comprehensively than in the posed images, we can discern the second contradiction, between the humanist model of the subject whose enormous depths of affect guarantee his humanity and the new "star" celebrity subject catering to the dreams of popular culture. These photographs, after all, were advertisements, promotional material allowed—with the reluctance of the star—because their publication would push sales of *Finnegans Wake.*

It took Freund a whole year to convince Joyce to pose for these photographs. In the end, he consented through the intercession of a mutual friend, the writer Louis Gillet: "I asked him to explain to Joyce that a photo-essay about him could do well to aid the distribution of the latest book, which was written in a language even more difficult than that of *Ulysses,*" wrote Freund in *Three Days with Joyce.* To understand the other contradiction that marks Joyce's images—that between the individual and the star—as well as the semiotic ambiguity that characterizes the photographs, we need to examine carefully not only the model's but also the photographer's intentions and claims.

Joyce regarded the photo-essay primarily as an advertisement and consented to be photographed to publicize himself and his work. Yet for Freund, the advertising motive was only a pretext: she "tricked" Joyce into being photographed by using the difficulty of *Finnegans Wake* as a bait, but what she was really interested in was what was expressed by his physiognomy, the "truth" of his face. In *Gisèle Freund, Photographer,* Freund makes clear that the motivation for her famous gallery of portraits of writers and intellectuals is her own pleasure at contemplating "the inexhaustible panorama of the human face" (*GF* 59). Nonetheless, she was aware that without retouching and beautifying the model to make him resemble a movie star, there would be no professional success. Refusing to comply with these conventions, she needed to become an *amateur* portraitist, while she turned to photo-reportage for a living: "that is what I did, while taking portraits for my enjoyment" (59).

If we compare the photographer's aim (her "dilettantism," disinterestedness, private enjoyment in reproducing faces) with that of the model (his interested professionalism, his desire to display himself for reasons of literary propaganda), we realize that the photos are marked by two very different intentions: while Joyce did want to pose as a star ("Joyce had a keen sense of how he wished to present himself to posterity. Fiction was his business and he kept to it," Ellmann asserts [preface to *TD* n.p.]), Freund is confident that the camera will reveal Joyce as he really is. Without any retouching, she feels, his gestures and his face will point to a human depth that can be deciphered by the reader, and as such they will provide insights both into his character and his work.

Further, the relation between the book and the face is understood differently by the photographer and the model. For Freund the face is the necessary complement to the book, that which the audience wants to see after reading the literary text: "When we read a book whose content moves us, we are interested in looking at the author's face: it is generally printed on the jacket, since the publisher is aware of our wish to see if these features correspond to the idea we have formed of the author. This image is thus very important for the man of letters" (*GF* 59). The temporality of the link between author, audience, and text sketched by Freund is in open opposition to the actual "timing" of the photo-essay. In this case, first comes the face and then the book: its temporality is that of advertising, particularly of the advertising of a film through the popularization of the star.[18] The different understanding of this temporality in Freund's own writing signals once again a contradiction between Joyce's and Freund's reading of the function of the photos. While for the latter they are almost a humanistic accessory, demanded by the audience's desire after its consumption of the text, the former is urgently aware that without the face, without the photograph, there might be no book at all. It's not the text that produces the desire for consuming the face, therefore, but vice versa. In other words, for Freund the "great man" is an a priori, a human essence that can be captured by the eye of the camera, and for Joyce—fearful of not being able to sell *Finnegans Wake*—the author is a commodity whose hypothetical essentiality is dispersed and destabilized through its image; as such, he is a very volatile substance, which owes its identity and role to the laws of the market. His image, as Freund writes, is indeed very important for the man of letters, and her words can be read in two different ways. On the one hand, Joyce needs a certain physiognomic copyright over his production, so that his self—

through the face—can be stamped on the text both as a mark of owner-ship and as evidence of the author's existence. On the other hand, once the man (of letters) is signified by an image—a photo, as an actor is—he becomes a staged icon, a commodity.

By turning himself into a saleable image, an image that promotes sales, the writer reiterates the fate of the commodity in consumer capitalism, where desire and consumption are produced through commodity aes-thetics. Yet, the fear of having been reduced to the status of the com-modity is counterbalanced by the awareness, on the author's side, of the necessity to market himself and his work. Paradoxically, for the mod-ernist to maintain his self (authorship, subjectivity), he has to "give it away" and have it reproduced in the modern media through a form of costuming. Joyce's wears his "masks"—the rings, the velvet house jacket, the book he's reading—with the fear that nothing might be left under the costume, and yet the costume is necessary to sell, and therefore to sur-vive, as an author.

Freund's photographs portray this unresolved tension between Joyce the star and Joyce "the man," and as such they inscribe an unmediated relation between the opposite categories of fetishism and naturalism, use value and exchange value, public and private, intimacy and com-modification. The conflict these oppositions imprint in Joyce's image can be analyzed by inserting its iconography into two critical constellations: Horkheimer and Adorno's critique of the culture industry in *Dialectic of Enlightenment*, and Roland Barthes's revision of naturalism vis-à-vis the construction of photographic "truth" in *Camera Lucida*.[19] If neither constellation can resolve the conflicts that mark Joyce's face, both can at least help us explain how this photo-essay can be regarded indeed as a game where nobody wins, where any possibility of a coherent and unified meaning is continually undermined. Joyce discounts Freund's claim to realism by actively working at becoming an image; at the same time, his attempt at playing the modernist star is compromised by his desire for (self-)authorship. Once his authorial self and his self-made, staged image seem to collapse one into the other and his self-display (his self displayed) becomes threatening for him, Joyce grows more and more diffident in front of the camera. That is, he seems simultaneously to respect and violate the rules of the culture industry, to retreat into the sphere of an impenetrable interiority, by displaying his world without allowing intimacy.

Because of the complex semiotic and aesthetic relations in which his image is caught, Joyce does not succeed in representing himself as the fetishized star. The dialectic of revelation and concealment, intimacy and distance, remains unsolved, so that the photographs function as a frustrating memorial to loss and lack—as a text that offers no catharsis to the viewer. The problem is how to read such "nothingness," what value to attribute to Joyce's directionless gaze and to its lack of address.

By letting his image be reproduced and circulated serially, Joyce is contravening one of the crucial imperatives of modernist authorship: the silent elision of the author from the text, the choice to assume the spectatorial position of the indifferent god paring his fingernails created by Joyce himself in *A Portrait of the Artist as a Young Man*. In *Portrait* the spectatorial position is not yet that of the consumer, but that of the producer—he who refuses to be the object of the gaze, but who rather creates this very object and has the power to position the audience and to manipulate its response. With the *Time* photo-essay Joyce enters the terrain of mass culture by becoming himself the object of the gaze whose reified subjectivity Horkeimer and Adorno study with a vengeance in *Dialectic of Enlightenment*. Their analysis of the effects of mass culture, particularly those concerning the work of art and the author, have an immediate resonance in Joyce's case, as a brief recapitulation of their critique will show.

The culture industry, in Horkheimer and Adorno's terms, exposes and makes recognizable to the critic the mystified status of the bourgeois work of art—it makes evident that the work of art had always been a commodity—while at the same time sanctioning the standardization of every form of individuality. In this way, mass culture decrees the end of style in favor of "nothing but style"—an imitative textuality and a surrogate identity. For Horkheimer and Adorno identity as well as individual style are defined negatively: to have an identity is to say no to power, to refuse to be identified by, and made identical with, the social hierarchy. In the same way, style becomes the rejection of conformity in favor of aesthetic and ideological dissonance. The artist who conforms to the dictates or to the seductions of power loses his individual style and rather inaugurates a regime of pseudoindividuality. Such pseudoindividuality is signified by the cult of the film star, in whom

What is individual is no more than the generality's power to stamp the accidental detail so fully that it is accepted as such. . . . The peculiarity of the self is a monopoly commodity determined by society: it is falsely represented as natural. It is no more than the moustache, the French accent, the deep voice of the woman of the world. (*DE* 154)

The artificially produced individuality, the fetishized detail that comes to signify the person, or the "synthetically produced physiognomies" of the Hollywood star are commodities that the culture industry creates and circulates not as use values, but as exchange values. The cinema star, the media personality—and equally the work of art in the age of mechanical reproduction—is cultural capital, not to be actually "used," but to be exchanged among prestige seekers: "the prestige seeker replaces the connoisseur. . . . One simply 'has to' have seen *Mrs. Miniver,* just as one 'has to' subscribe to *Life* and *Time.* . . . No object has an inherent value: it is valuable only to the extent that it can be exchanged. The use value of art, its mode of being, is treated as a fetish; and the fetish, the work's social rating (misinterpreted as its artistic status) becomes its use value—the only quality which is enjoyed" (*DE* 158). Presumably, it is this exchange value that the *Wake* will assume after having been publicized, via its author, in the pages of *Time.*

One way this prestige-seeking audience can be drawn to consume art is through "the shallow cult of the leading personality," as Horkheimer and Adorno phrase it. Joyce's self-advertising seems aimed exactly at pursuing and perpetuating this cult. In a passage that sounds like an uncanny description of Freund's photo-essay, the two critics write: "In the most influential American magazines, *Life* and *Fortune,* a quick glance can now scarcely distinguish advertising from editorial picture and text. The latter features an enthusiastic and gratuitous account of the great man (with illustrations of his life and grooming habits), which will bring him new fans, while the advertisement pages use so many factual photographs and details that they represent the ideal of information which the editorial part has only begun to try to achieve" (*DE* 163). Here the critics' anxiety about the misplacement of "editorial picture and text" with advertisement can help us understand Joyce's own perplexities with his own photographic representation. The advertisement is the designated space of images, where the phantasmagoria of the commodity produces desire in the consumer—the desire not for the commodity's use value, but for the object as fetish, for its image *as* value. The editorial article, instead, is conceived as the writerly space of language, *ratio,* realism, and use value. Horkheimer and Adorno's distinction between the editorial text and the advertisement is reiterated in film theory in the distinction between diegesis and the "song and dance" number. This distinction is made by Laura Mulvey in "Visual Pleasure and Narrative Cinema," where she theorizes how cinema produces identification for the male and female spectator. In classical Hollywood film, the narrative is interrupted by the appearance in the frame of a fetishized female presence, which delays and suspends suture—that is, the viewer's desire for closure, wholeness, identification. By appearing in an editorial article that looks like an advertisement, Joyce is placed in a role analogous to that of the cinematic fetish, and thus displaced into a feminine role that jeopardizes his authority as masculine subject. On the pages of the magazine the famous writer, the *producer* of diegesis in his work, stands for that which interrupts and prevents the narrative. Deprived of his voice, he merely "makes a spectacle" of himself in order to sell. In the very images that are supposed "to tell," Joyce is condemned to silence, and confined to the dangerous position of the author turned commodity in a system of exchange.

Joyce's own gaze and body language suggest that he is aware of this danger and rather looks for strategies that can defuse and counteract his self-fetishization as a guest star in *Life*. His pictures are both self-revelatory and self-denying, showing the image of a man faking his self, and at the same time jealous of the fiction he has authored. This is signified by the way in which Joyce averts his eyes from the camera, in an attempt to negate his state as the object of the photographic gaze. At the same time, he tries to defuse his status as a fetish to to make himself only indirectly available, by displacing and projecting his aura onto the objects that surround him. These objects become his stand-ins, at times the only tools he offers to the viewer to carry on her hermeneutical work.

In the same way that these backdrops might be read as spaces haunted by Joyce's once-upon-a-time and now superseded Irishness, so too Joyce's present "self" is narrated, more than anything else, by the spaces within which he was photographed: his home, Giorgio's house and garden, Rue de l'Odeon, the bookstore, and by the "things" with which his image is staged. Often these objects function as emblems, each pointing to a preexisting, transcendent substantiality (Art, Music, Literature, Aristocracy, Leisure, Family)—an auratic reservoir of meaning that Joyce's accoutrements evoke, so that he can be signified without signifying in the first person, or, we could say, he can let himself be seen and yet remain detached, not be there.

By making himself readable in the first instance through his objects, by remaining aloof, enigmatic, and yet visible, Joyce seems to realize Roland Barthes's desire to express interiority while retaining one's intimacy, even within the space of photographic exposure:

> The Age of Photography corresponds precisely to the explosion of the private into the public, or rather into the creation of a new social value, which is the publicity of the private: the private is consumed as such, publicly. . . . But since the private is . . . the condition of an interiority which I believe is identified with my truth . . . I must . . . reconstitute the dimension of *public* and *private:* I want to utter interiority without yielding intimacy.[20]

Is this interiority without intimacy what we see in Freund's photo-essay? Given Joyce's strategies for manipulating his image and fabricating his interiority, what is given to the viewer to see? The photographs continually oscillate, without any possibility of "stopping" their semiotic instability, between a benign legibility and a mystifying obscurity, realistic evidence and mere opacity.

As a persona Joyce is entirely legible, both physiognomically and allegorically. His body language is expressive, as much as his enigmatic face is: it announces, in turn, detachment from earthly affairs, benevolence, mildness, self-absorption, absentmindedness, shyness. At the same time his rings, his robe, the books around him announce, allegorically, the qualities that he wants his audience to read. Here, however, realism is nothing more than the effect of *techne:* both the seamless visibility and the realistic transparency of Joyce's images are predicated upon the exclusion and invisibility of other crucial elements of his life. For instance, when the writer is photographed in his home, Nora—the key figure in his domestic universe—is absent. Similarly, the immediacy of the photographs, claimed by Freund in her introduction, has been achieved, it turns out, by excluding the image that to her appeared least immediately legible, and that in fact Freund never showed to Joyce himself: "Nor did I show Joyce the color portrait in which he is seen head-on. I found it too revealing and tragic, and I did not wish to upset him. It appears here for the first time in color," she writes (*TD* 17; see fig. 12). Here Freund herself seems to share her model's perplexity regarding self-exposure. The "truth" that emerged in the photo-essay had been concealed for many years, and his "real self" was never shown to Joyce. At the same time these images testify to the photographer's will to pierce through her subject's staged and fully available impenetrability, to give the viewers at last what they really want: an image of the author treacherously extorted or elicited through a sort of candid-camera technique.

We might say that Freund truly misread the images that she chose not to show to Joyce, particularly that of Joyce "head-on" (fig. 12). Her decision not to show this photo to the model implies that photography *does* tell the truth, independently of photographer's intentions and model's pose. The camera allows the appearance of what otherwise could not be seen with the naked eye. In this case, as Freund's censorship seems to imply, it reveals even more. In fact, the photo is striking precisely because it reveals nothing; it might even have been discarded in the first instance because of its refusal to reveal. Similarly, it is not tragic because it allows no catharsis to the viewer.

In this portrait (fig. 12), the camera eye painstakingly pans on each detail: the wrinkles, the opaque color of Joyce's eyes, the grey of his moustache, the dry, thin lips. Joyce is holding a magnifying lens but is not absorbed in the activity of reading: the book is not included in the photographic frame, and neither are the velvet robe, the objects, the papers that throughout the photo-essay had made his image decipherable. What is available is the image of an aging man with an uncertain, almost fixed expression—the gaze of an ill person, perhaps (indeed, Joyce was to be dead in less than two years). The myopic eyes, swimming inside the thick lenses and unfocused on any object, represent the writer as an almost blind man, a man who allows others to see what he could hardly see himself. At this extraordinary moment the total transparency of Joyce's face suddenly turns into total opacity. What was expected to produce a perfectly naturalistic representation of the subject—to make him speak, confess—produces silence. When Joyce is really shown "as he is" without having his face retouched, in the absence of the accoutrements that had come to signify him in the other photographs, he ceases to be—to be "Joyce." The transparency of this image, together with his seeing nothing, makes him in this final instance unavailable as the object of the gaze, at last unreadable through any cultural code.

If Joyce in these photos constitutes himself quite consciously as the commodity on display, what does the absolute transparency *and* opacity of this image mean? Does it function as a form of resistance to reification? Or rather does it capture the effect of modern reification on the subject? Is Joyce the commodity itself, or is he the manager of the commodity and of its image? To answer these questions we must turn once again to *Dialectic of Enlightenment,* where Horkheimer and Adorno conclude their critique of the culture industry with these words: "personality scarcely signifies anything more than shining white teeth and freedom from body odor and emotions. The triumph of advertising in the culture industry is that consumers feel compelled to buy and use its products even though they see through them" (*DE* 167). What if the consumer cannot see through the product? What if they can see through it, but there is nothing to see? Does this opacity make Joyce an unsaleable commodity? And does his unsaleability work as an instance of unreified subjectivity?

The photograph of Joyce "head-on" remains illegible, and, if the photo-essay were to maintain its compensatory and explanatory value, this photo had to be excluded and remain unpublished. Here the fetishistic projection of the viewer, of the photographer, and of the model himself is baffled. No revelation is given: the clarity, visibility, and comprehensibility that might compensate for the obscurity of the *Wake* are not there. In fact the particular transparency of this image makes the hermeneutical model of depth/surface suggested by Freund obsolete, or, at least, impracticable. This photograph is nothing but surface: one's gaze alone cannot pierce through it. One needs a caption, a title, a name to make sense of it, to know who, what it means. Paradoxically, Joyce is even more elusive when he is "caught" unawares by the camera. What Freund proposes as the ultimate ground for the truth about the writer (surprise, spontaneity), and the revelatory visibility that should provide full suture for the viewer's gaze and full possession of the object is exactly what rips the visual continuum open again and disrupts the narrative with which the audience tries to appease its fetishistic desire for suture. While as a fetish Joyce's face should provide a sense of presence and fulfillment (however aleatory), the photo "head-on" offers nothing to see. Rather, like the female genitals that terrify Freud's little boy in "Medusa's Head," Joyce functions as the sight (the site) that has caused the need for the fetish in the first place.

Thus Joyce the fetish, in this particular photograph, manages to frustrate the desire signified by the gaze, the desire for suture, for the uninterrupted circulation of narrative and meaning. His face remains undecipherable: not only does it mean nothing, but in particular, had it been published, it would not have meant "Joyce" for the audience of *Life.* With the cessation of representation comes the cessation of individuation, the end of the subject's being. This aging man could be anybody and could be thinking anything: the photo provides no element that could anchor his unstable identity. As such, it constitutes a curious counterpart to another famous snapshot of Joyce, taken when he was not yet Joyce, the author of *Ulysses*. This is the image of a young man—shaven face and cap on his head—with the hands defiantly in his pockets, and his legs apart. Years after the photo was taken, Joyce was asked what he was thinking at that moment. With this question the interlocutor was hoping to obtain a *meaningful* answer, perhaps a literate anecdote that could confirm to the viewers that this young man *is* Joyce, that Joyce had always been himself, merely the early version of the famous future author. With his desire for identification, the photographer wants to demonstrate that the signifier and the signified are directly connected and that together they coherently point to the referent. Joyce's answer intentionally disrupted this semiotic coherence, and, by destabilizing the continuity between the face and the book claimed by Freund, he once again displaced the self: "Asked about what he was thinking about when C. P. Curran photographed him, Joyce replied, 'I was wondering would he lend me five shillings.'"[21]

As in the "head-on" color photograph taken more than thirty years later, here Joyce was teasing his interlocutor's desire for depth, interiority, and revelation. Yet this image, with its anecdote, has a caption, even a narrative that can help us, ironically, to make sense of what we see. In Freund's close-up, once the props through which his subjectivity had been elusively signified in the other photographs are gone and the emblems of his staged upper-class, cosmopolitan, and implicitly Irish literary identity taken away, the face of the artist is emptied of any representativeness, of any individuality. Once the objects in the background disappear—the objects that had made Joyce readable as a text—his meaning fades too.

The most disquieting element of this portrait, however, what really takes the viewer aback, is the lack of address that characterizes Joyce's gaze. In the other pictures of the photo-essay, Joyce's eyes never meet ours, but at the same time he is always engaged in a recognizable activity, reading a book, looking at Sylvia Beach in a conversation, "caressing" his grandchild and his son with his gaze. However quizzical and aloof his expressions, his own scopic activity works as a hermeneutical means for the viewer—and allows us to read him physiognomically as revered genius, benevolent personality, almost blind man, dandy, international Irishman, famous writer, father. His intentional averting his eyes from the camera, his choice to represent himself as a disengaged presence, truly occupied in his own activities, truly self-absorbed, is the most salient quality of Joyce's self-fetishization, the true aura of his image. In the close-up this aura is entirely dispersed: Joyce's gaze is no longer absorbed in a particular activity, holding a child or a book. No longer self-absorbed either, his gaze is totally open and available. It's the lack of address of this gaze that makes it inaccessible. Its directionless quality makes it impossible for the viewer to master it, exactly because it refuses to master our own. Ultimately, Joyce's gaze is unable to give the viewer's eye a point of view with which to identify, and a direction to follow the traces of its own desire to know, the desire for suture.

Joyce's iconography in Freund's photo-essay in general is suspended between the editorial article and the advertisement, between the space of diegesis and meaning-production and the space of the fetish, but when one reads back from the key "withheld" photograph, one senses that it is deeply reticent in both cases. As a fetish, his face has no compensatory value, no apotropaic power. Instead of suturing the gaps that lack and desire open in the reader, like a Medusa's head without snakes it produces more desire, and more fear. A pervasive silence emerges from the interstices of this, the most vivid of Joyce's "poses," so that, instead of narration, a story, disclosed secrets, we are left with a mute immobility, and the final undecipherability of his face.

What can we read in the empty silence of Joyce's face? The two critical constellations through which we have structured our own critique—the Frankfurt School negative dialectic and Roland Barthes's poststructuralist reflection—do not help us to formulate any final judgment. Is the silent immobility of his face the same as the "intense immobility," the "ecstasy" that Barthes recognizes as the power of photography? Is the lost coherence between signifier, signified and referent the "absolute realism" that in *Camera Lucida* defies meaning and any cultural reading of the image, to show that photography really renders reality for what it finally is—catastrophe? And if so, does Joyce succeed in preserving his privacy while still giving away his interiority? Is what we (don't) see what Barthes calls "one's truth," "the Intractable" of which one consists? Or: Is the cessation of being (Joyce) to which this image points, an example of Adornian negation, the denial of a reified self that utters protest against (capitalist) conformism? Does the photograph exemplify the resistance that alone can confer identity to the standardized subject of mass culture? Or does this portrait rather bear the scars of mass culture in its lack of individuality, in its foreclosing individuation, even the meaningless detail that the generality stamps on the subject? And what is tragic about this new way of producing *and* denying subjectivity?

The fact is that the traces of Irishness that Joyce had summoned only to submerge them seem merely archaisms in the context of this higher-stakes play of the reified subject and his mass consumption. If Joyce's face is tragic, it testifies to the tragedy of the dispersal of all bourgeois subjectivity through the exhaustion both of allegorical and hermeneutical ways of reading: the evasion of Irishness in these images might be read as a masquerade covering the evasion of traditional forms of subjectivity altogether. If historically, the face has been that part of the body that more than any other has signified reason, the spirit, the subject, Joyce's once Irish face shows that physiognomy bears no longer the inscription of the logos, but that, rather, it provides the elements that allow a commercial logo to be composed. The tragedy Freund read in what she considered her greatest Joyce photograph is nothing less than the decline of the logos in favor of the logo. We have moved from an allegorical reading of the man as the pattern of his Irish origins, to a hermeneutical reading that inquires physiognomically into the "depths" of the character's interiority as a cosmopolitan bourgeois subject, to the end of reading. Joyce's face turns out not to be a text to decipher and make sense of, to recall its national origins and envision its bourgeois depths; rather it is the representation of the elements that can evoke, in a stylized form, the represented Joyce as a trademark: the stylized silhouette—round glasses, spare moustache, sleek hair combed back—that has appeared, in recent years, in the brochures and publicity materials of the International Joyce Symposium, for instance. In this stylized silhouette Joyce's individuality both as the Irish subject and as the modernist *auteur* are relentlessly effaced, even as they appear to be accentuated, by the imperatives of a transnational commodity culture.

The tragic element that Joyce's image speaks for Freund is the (humanist's) necessary renunciation of the self, and the equally tragic loss of signification to the arena of commodity aesthetics. In this context, the face cannot tell, but only sell—T-shirts and, why not, as happens at the Joyce Symposium, culture. Tragic, but déjà vu: Horkheimer and Adorno had already made it clear, in 1947, that culture is, and had always been, a commodity. In this context, Irishness itself becomes a constellation of signifiers to be deployed only if they are judged to awaken consumer nostalgia and desire. In fact, this discovery and the way it is articulated through the reading that Joyce's photograph does not allow, is quite comic, and in line with Joyce's own desires: if the photo-essay wanted to "sell" the book, the mass of Joyce's readers—fifty years later—are still there to buy, both the *Wake* and the face.

NOTES

1. On Gisèle Freund, see Gisèle Freund, *The World in My Camera*, trans. June Guicharnaud (New York: Dial, 1974); Hans Puttnies, *Catalogue de l'oeuvre photographique Gisèle Freund* (Paris: Editions de Centre Pompidou, 1991); Gisèle Freund and Rauda Jamis, *Gisèle Freund, Portrait* (Paris: Des Femmes, 1991); Hans Joacim Neyer, *Gisèle Freund* (Berlin: Aragon, 1988).

2. The photograph was taken in March 1939; *Finnegans Wake* had been completed by November 13, 1938 and the book was published on May 4 1939. See Richard Ellmann, *James Joyce*, rev. ed. (Oxford: Oxford University Press, 1982), pp. 714–22.

3. See "Night Thoughts," *Time*, May 8, 1939, pp. 78–84; Gisèle Freund, *Three Days with Joyce, Photographs by Gisèle Freund* (New York: Persea Books, 1985). Subsequent references to *Three Days with Joyce* will be given in parentheses in the essay, abbreviated *TD*.

4. Seamus Heaney, "In Memoriam Francis Ledwidge," in *The Faber Book of Contemporary Irish Poetry*, ed. Paul Muldoon (Boston: Faber and Faber, 1986), pp. 262–64.

5. See, for example, "The Roman and the Celt," *Anthropological Review* 5 (1867): 151–75; and "Knox on the Celtic Race," *Anthropological Review* 6 (1868): 175–91.

6. A striking example of such police photography of the Irish face that relates to Joyce's own family milieu in Dublin is cited in Peter Costello, *James Joyce: The Years of Growth, 1882–1915* (New York: Pantheon Books, 1992). In the photographs given after p. 150 is an image of John Kelly, a model for Mr. Casey in *A Portrait of the Artist*, "photographed on a Dublin street by the secret police in August 1892." Costello notes (109) that this photograph seems to be the only existing one of John Kelly.

7. L. Perry Curtis Jr., *Apes and Angels: the Irishman in Victorian Caricature* (Washington: Smithsonian Institution Press, 1971).

8. See Seamus Deane, "Civilians and Barbarians" in *Ireland's Field Day*, ed. Seamus Deane et al. (Notre Dame, Ind.: University of Notre Dame Press, 1986), pp. 33–42.

9. See Abdul R. JanMohamed, "The Economy of Manichaen Allegory: The Function of Racial Discourse in Colonialist Literature," and Homi K. Bhabha,

"Signs Taken for Wonders: Questions of Ambivalence and Authority under a Tree Outside Delhi, May 1817," both in *"Race," Writing and Difference,* ed. Henry Louis Gates (Chicago: University of Chicago Press, 1986), pp. 78–106 and 163–84.

10. In the poem as a whole, this description of Ledwidge's face is at the center of more complex questions about how the poet's appearance, his poetry, and his imagery relate to his peculiar position as a Catholic nationalist who went to fight in the British Army in World War I, and, in the statue seen by the young Heaney, is now being commemorated in mainly Protestant Northern Ireland as an Irish, a Northern Irish, and also a British hero.

11. See Jeanne Sheehy, *The Rediscovery of Ireland's Past: The Celtic Revival, 1830–1930* (London: Thames and Hudson, 1980), pp. 179–81. *Men of the South* is reproduced on p. 181.

12. See the Berenice Abbott and other photographs of Joyce and his family in Brenda Maddox, *Nora: The Real Life of Molly Bloom* (Boston: Houghton Mifflin, 1988), following p. 204.

13. James Joyce, *Ulysses* (New York: Random House, 1986), p. 19.

14. Gayatri Spivak, "Can the Subaltern Speak?" in *Marxism and the Interpretation of Culture,* ed. Cary Nelson and Lawrence Grossberg (Urbana: University of Illinois Press, 1988), p. 297.

15. One of the most forceful descriptions of this discourse of Irish nationalism is to be found in David Lloyd, *Anomalous States: Irish Writing in the Post-Colonial Moment* (Durham, N.C.: Duke University Press, 1993).

16. See Costello, *James Joyce,* p. 48.

17. The *Time* cover shows a photographic portrait of Joyce reading, taken by Gisèle Freund, which is reproduced in Freund, *Gisèle Freund Photographer,* trans. John Shepley (New York: Harry N. Abrams, 1985), p. 88. Subsequent references are given in the text, abbreviated *GF.* The *Time* photo is a cropped version of the one produced in *Gisèle Freund Photographer.*

18. Richard Dyer studies the specific ways in which a star is used to advertise a film in *Stars* (London: British Film Institute, 1979).

19. Max Horkheimer and Theodor W. Adorno, *Dialectic of Enlightenment,* trans. John Cumming (New York: Herder and Herder, 1971), and Roland Barthes, *Camera Lucida: Reflections on Photography,* trans. Richard Howard (New York: Hill and Wang, 1981). Further references to *Dialectic of Enlightenment* will be given in the text, abbreviated *DE.*

20. Barthes, *Camera Lucida,* p. 98.

21. Ellmann, *James Joyce,* photograph and caption on plate VIII, following p. 110.

A Taste of Fortune: *In the Money* and Williams's New Directions Phase

Daniel Morris

In his *Autobiography* (1951) William Carlos Williams embraced a classic tenet of modernism by separating the literature of "contemplation" from the literature of "pulp"; he claimed he set his writing against the "calculated viciousness of a money grubbing society."[1] As Herbert Leibowitz writes, Williams presented himself in *The Autobiography* as "amiably virtuous," a "pure" poet unaware of the inner workings of how reputations were made among the expatriate "insiders" in Paris and disinterested in making the commercial appeal in New York. In another recent study of *The Autobiography,* Ann W. Fisher-Wirth describes Williams's Franklinesque innocence as his "word for the source of his power."[2] In the Paris chapters of *The Autobiography,* which Williams based on his visit there in 1924, Leibowitz writes that he presented himself "as Doc Williams from Rutherford, a suburban yokel cutting a sorry figure in the modish world of art and wealth." Leibowitz, however, shrewdly points out that this impersonation of "the artless provincial rogue" was a "ruse" that enabled him "to get literary business done." Leibowitz understands Williams's claims to innocence in psychological terms as a prop that allowed Williams, like a child, to take "the royal road to approval and reward." It was like a "second skin that shields a person from attack."[3] While allowing this psychological interpretation to stand, I would like to follow up on Leibowitz's suggestion and take literally the premise that "innocence" was a mask that enabled Williams to "get his literary business done." In this essay I will consider Williams's account of himself in the context of his complex, at times paradoxical, relationship to the literary marketplace(s)—both "avant-garde" and "commercial"—in the period when his self-fashioning as a "literary innocent" took place in the fictional narratives he published with New Directions beginning in 1937.

To think of a high-modern poet such as Williams in the context of publicity and the literary marketplace might come as a surprise to generations of readers trained not to look beyond the individual text for its significance. Modern poetry has since its inception been perceived as an institution that stood outside of and opposed to market conditions. Lawrence S. Rainey, however, has shown that even such an archetypal modernist impresario as Ezra Pound was trying to transform modernism from a "minority culture" to "one supported by an important institutional and financial apparatus" when he sought to help T. S. Eliot publish *The Waste Land* in such popular magazines as *Vanity Fair* and *The Dial.*[4] We have also been taught to think of market pressures as somehow distracting writers away from literary creativity. By reconsidering an overlooked, but, I think, intriguing part of the Williams canon, the second installment of the Stecher Trilogy of novels, *In the Money* (1940), I hope to adjust these commonplace assumptions. I will argue that the tensions between the poet and his publisher, James Laughlin, as well as the pressures Williams faced in resuscitating his career as a poet, generated authentic creativity at a time when Williams was unclear about his literary direction. As we shall see, *The Autobiography* was not the only narrative in which Williams presented an "innocent" main character in order to conceal his own professional ambitions.

Williams's shift of emphasis during his first years with New Directions from "impersonal" lyrics toward didactic fiction, and his attention to telling stories that mirrored the way he wanted his literary reputation to be known by ordinary readers, occurred at a time when he most acutely sensed his lack of renown in comparison to other modern poets. Since Laughlin could provide the funds to print his works but, for ideological and personal reasons that I will soon describe, could not fully accept Williams to be an author interested in reaching ordinary readers through commercial appeals, Williams reacted to Laughlin's separation of the literature of "contemplation" and the literature of "pulp" by promoting his own image as a poet through covert depictions of himself and his literary competitors *within* his New Directions writings. The ruse of "innocence" described by Leibowitz and Fisher-Wirth that allowed Laughlin to think of Williams as a "literary saint" for whom commercial interests were a "sin" is mirrored in the screen of innocence foisted by Joe Stecher in his quest to overcome the firm that holds a monopoly over the printing of money orders in *In the Money*. The ruse of "innocence" in Williams's self-characterizations is also a structural feature of the novel insofar as Williams wrote ironic fictions for New Directions. He discussed one thing (printing money orders) while on another level he was discussing something of greater personal importance (printing literature for money). The novels that Williams wrote for New Directions were supposed to catapult him to a stronger market share. But they were, in content, themselves about his conflicted relationship to what he calls in *White Mule* "the United States of America—money," and about how his literary identity as what Anne Janowitz has called "a thoroughly American, though not usually poetic type, the indigenous 'tinker,' or inventor" should be inscribed.[5] Williams's ambivalence toward his new contract with Laughlin, his transition from obscurity to fame, his break with his former friend and ally, Pound, his shame about making money from his allegedly anti-commercial writing, and his doubts, at age fifty-five, about his own literary powers, all factored into his decision to write the veiled autobiography, *In the Money,* and became the basis for the novel's deep structure.

Before interrogating Williams's situation as a professional author as represented in *In the Money,* I want to take a closer look at the relationship between Williams and Laughlin. We shall see that the two men, to a degree that now seems almost farcical, held conflicting imperatives about the meaning and value of founding New Directions in 1935.

To begin, Laughlin did not believe that advertising and publicity were acceptably decorous ways to present modern letters. In founding New Directions, Laughlin, the son of a Pittsburgh steel magnate, wished to develop a stable of obscure experimental writers whose production showed through example the freedom of self-expression, as Laughlin writes in the introduction to the *New Directions Annual* of 1939: "We *must* affirm the right of the artist to create in freedom and the right of the citizen to enjoy the things of the mind and the spirit in freedom. *New Directions,* in its small way, is, and has always been such an affirmation."[6] Laughlin believed Williams to be a "pure" writer not interested in what Laughlin called the "sin" of hype that only appealed to the "crude" instincts of a large readership. Laughlin, therefore, subscribed to Margaret Anderson's point of view when she said that her *Little Review* would "make no compromise with public taste." Laughlin's initial strategy in dealing with Williams's willingness to "compromise with public taste" was to persuade him of the nobility of obscurity.

It is hard to conceive of a new social order except by revision of verbal orientation. And it is the writer alone who can accomplish that reorientation. But it will not be the slick paper writers who cater to inferiority complexes, or the editor who will print nothing "unfamiliar to his reader" or the commercial publishers' hair-oil boys. It will be men like Cummings or Carlos Williams who know their business well enough to realize the pass to which language has come and are willing to endure obscurity and poverty to carry on their experiments.[7]

In contrast to Laughlin's wish to ignore the "sinful" side of letters, Williams remained throughout the 1930s and until the end of World War II frustrated with his own failure to overcome the shadow of the other contenders for control of American poetry, particularly the expatriate "traditionalists," Eliot and Pound, as well as the better established "nativist" poet, Hart Crane, and the chief mature rival on the eastern seaboard, Wallace Stevens. Williams hoped that the New Directions contract would be his springboard toward greater sales as well as an increased respect from other writers. If only Laughlin could think of his writing as merchandise.

"You are young at the game of publishing," wrote Williams to Laughlin in January 1938. "[It] was distressing to me to have people asking as they still ask: Where can I get [*White Mule*]? Nobody seems to have heard of it."[8] Over the course of their correspondence, Williams presented to Laughlin a tutorial in shrewd salesmanship. This education in the "publishing game" ranged from advice about book design, to information about why Laughlin should publish writers such as Louis Zukofsky in order to insure a distinct identity for the new firm, to why the poet felt publishing firms such as Random House and Harcourt Brace could better present his work than New Directions, to instructions about which journals to place his lesser poems in a way that he said would serve as "good advertising" for the anticipated major effort, *Paterson*.[9] Here is one typical example of Williams acting as salesman for his poetry: "So, in the end, make your arrangements for distribution as complete as possible, especially make more detailed arrangements for advertising my stuff than you did with *White Mule*. I think inadequate management of sales cost us plenty that time" (*SL* 28). At issue in this case is the production of the *Complete Collected Poems (1906–1938)*, which, after a flirtation with its publication at Oxford University Press that Williams said "would have meant a certain prestige for me which I have wanted, not too seriously, all my life," eventually appeared in 1938 with New Directions.[10] This *Complete Collected Poems (1906–1938)* was part of the publication strategy developed by Laughlin and the poet to recover, as a set, out-of-print Williams work. Eight Williams titles appeared in the New Directions catalog from 1937, when Williams published *White Mule*, the first self-proclaimed "winner" with New Directions that sold out of its initial run of fifteen hundred copies, until 1946. While this collection of books marked by far the most concentrated attempt by any publisher to make Williams available to ordinary readers in a uniform edition, he did not believe they were marketed aggressively enough by Laughlin for him to reach a greater market share.

Laughlin said he published writers such as Williams and e. e. cummings in order to enhance the public's taste for serious work. "I'll get a writers' press started that will be a force able to fight the New York bastards," Laughlin wrote to Williams, referring to the commercial publishing houses (*SL* 22). Although Williams's poetry was set in opposition to commercial writing in that he wanted readers to perceive everyday objects from an aesthetic, rather than a utilitarian, point of view, Laughlin's vision of a united group of experimental writers did not take into account divisions among the modern poets. It was about T. S. Eliot, and not about the New York publishing houses, that Williams wrote to Laughlin,

> Eliot is a cultured gentleman and cultured gentlemen are always likely to undersell the market. . . . I'm glad you like his verse but I'm warning you, the only reason it doesn't smell is that it's synthetic. Maybe I'm wrong but I distrust that bastard more than any writer I know in the world today. He can write. Granted. But—it's like walking into church to me. I can't do it without a bad feeling at the pit of my stomach: nothing has been learned there since the simplicities were prevented from becoming multiform by arrest of growth—Birdseye foods, suddenly frozen at 50 degrees below zero under pressure at perfect maturity, immediately after being picked from the canes. (*SL* 40–41; March 26, 1939)

The eliding of the difference between literary authors and name brand goods in this passage suggests the fluidity with which Williams moved between "high" and "low" culture. More importantly, it shows that he perceived his struggle for literary acknowledgment as a simulation of a struggle among competing brands of nationally marketed goods in an unconcealed market economy.

Later in the same letter Williams directs Laughlin to "plan to print" a second impression of *In the American Grain* (1925) as the first in a series called the New Classics, which would make out-of-print modernist titles again available for a dollar apiece (*SL* 43). Williams explains that he has chosen to repackage old work rather than to offer Laughlin the second installment of *White Mule* (*In the Money*) because he regrets that he is "not writing these days" (*SL* 41). The bitter critique of Eliot for disrupting the organic growth of poetry by pressuring it into an easily-consumed but now frozen or deadened form shows that Williams perceived with regret the direction his own creative energies had taken him: repackaging and selling old work as the result of his struggle for literary acknowledgment. Williams believed that the cultural war he waged against Eliot, presented as a struggle among competing brands of nationally marketed goods in an unconcealed market economy, had restricted his freedom to grow in "multiform" directions as a poet. Williams felt that not only his path toward literary creation—a path that he described as originating "hot from the blood" as opposed to that stemming from "the tradition of literature purely"—was more difficult to perform than Eliot's and Pound's, but also that their "camp" actively sought to sabotage his production.

> [The "hot from the blood" technique] is always under the great handicap of monumental invention for its content and form. But the pimps of literature [Eliot and Pound] seize the position due great imagination and all its prerogatives and puff themselves up at the true artist.
>
> This wouldn't be so bad if they did not at the same time actively, very often, drive down the already sufficiently harassed man seeking to rescue and build up a present world in his creation. . . . By this they are actively the enemies of the highest reaches of the artist's imagination and will always be the ones to keep the artist down, seldom to help him up. (*SL* 44)

Williams's paranoid version of international modernist literary culture as a hostile underworld in which Eliot and Pound were the primary conspirators in a plot to sabotage his bid for literary renown is reflected in the printing wars that take place in *In the Money*. The independent outsider, Joe Stecher, must, like Williams against "the enemies of the highest reaches of the artist's imagination," struggle against an international firm that conspires against his professional success, Wynnewood and Crossman.[11]

Although Williams decided in 1937 to stay on with New Directions for the time being, he remained a pushy and disgruntled author. He consistently scolded Laughlin for failing to treat his writing as merchandise. His New Directions fiction, especially *In the Money,* became a complicated fusion of his conflicted relationship to art and commerce, as Williams reflected in the novel on his professional concerns about the publishing contract, and on his ambivalence about yoking financial profit for the maker to the work of designing and printing a culture's signs of symbolic and economic value.

Williams composed *In the Money* in a nine-month period between August 1938 and the bleak winter of 1940, as World War II escalated with Russian involvement and Japan's war on China. It was published by New Directions on October 29, 1940. Williams discussed its composition and initial publication with Laughlin in a number of letters, two of which I wish to quote from at some length. These letters suggest Williams's ambivalence about commercial publishing, for even though he curses the big firms he still urges Laughlin to do business with them. The letters also reveal his hopes that the novel will be a moneymaker, as well as confirm his growing disenchantment with the politics of Ezra Pound. The juxtaposition in these letters of discussion about *In the Money* and Pound's politics will provide evidence that when Williams was composing his fictive "business battle," he was also planning his argument, in displaced form, against Pound's dominant status in letters by attacking his economic views. In the novel, paradoxically, Williams will adopt his own version of Pound's Social Credit theory as his own argument in favor of his receipt of a form of social credit (the Laughlin contract) for the work he had already done on behalf of modern letters. On June 7, 1939, Williams mentioned to Laughlin that he "must get at the new *White Mule.*"

> By the way, I've decided on the title for volume two: *A Taste of Fortune.* It has a somewhat musty flavor at that but it goes, I think, with the story. I did think of using *In the Money.* Like that better? The second is snappier and more up to date. . . . Suppose you go into the plant? How about having somebody like Simon & Schuster or the other bastards buy up the sheets of the original *White Mule* and bind the new volume up with them into one glorious whole. Just an idea. This time it's got to be pushed hard. (*SL* 49–50)

In the same letter, Williams mentioned that Pound had spent the night of June 5 with the Williamses. He "spread himself on the divan all evening and discoursed to the family in his usual indistinct syllables," Williams wrote. While he grants in the letter that Pound's views are "important" and "inspiring," Williams's also feels that Pound is "sunk . . . unless he can shake the fog of Fascism out of his brain during the next few years which I seriously doubt that he can do" (*SL* 49). Williams had supported the Loyalists against Franco in Spain, and it was about this event that his split with Pound became indelible: "You can't argue away wanton slaughter of innocent women and children by the neo-scholasticism of a controlled economy program. Shit with a Hitler who lauds the work of his airmen in Spain and so shit with Pound too if he can't stand up and face his questioners on the point" (*SL* 49). In a letter written on December 14, 1940, less than two months after the novel's publication, Williams argued that Pound's political views proved he could not be trusted as a public writer in the United States. Williams reported to Laughlin of his wife Flossie's happiness "with her check," the initial royalty from *In the Money:* "[I]t will buy her a good coat with a fur collar! If there's to be more so much the better, good for you too." The rest of this letter shows that while Pound did not implicate Williams in his "fireside chats" over Rome Radio until July 30, 1941, Williams was becoming riled with Pound's letters to him from Rome in 1939 and 1940, the period when he composed the novel that spoke of a separation from an earlier professional allegiance. Pound's views, particularly in their unabashed anti-Semitism and in their support of Franco's crushing of the Loyalists, were abhorrent and worthy of censorship, even from old friends and supporters of his theories on monetary reform. Williams's criticism of Pound, however, went beyond this political critique in order to merge Pound's political ideas with his literary position in relationship to Williams.

> Ezra is an important poet, we must forgive him his stupidities. . . . But I prefer not to have to do with him in any way. He wants to patronize me. Don't tell me this isn't so for I know better. His letters are insults, the mewings of an 8th grade teacher. That's where he thinks I exist in relation to his catastrophic knowledge of affairs, his blinding judgments of contemporary values. . . . [M]y perceptions overtook him twenty years ago—not however my accomplishments. When I have finished, if I can go on to the finish, there'll be another measuring. (*SL* 58–59)

Williams understood Pound's arguments on behalf of Mussolini to be evidence that the original literary and intellectual "measuring" of Pound as the great teacher versus Williams as the naive pupil, demanded the reversal supplied by the *In the Money* plot.

Although he believed the focus on economics, rather than on poetry, diminished Pound's concern for the craft of poetry, Williams, as early as 1934, had turned his attention to the relationship between economic governance and the making of poetry. In a review of George Oppen's *Discrete Series* called "The New Poetical Economy," Williams argued that a new social order could be detected and implemented through attention to the details of crafts and industries, including the way poems were written.

> An imaginable new social order would require a skeleton of severe discipline for its realization and maintenance. Thus by a sharp restriction to essentials the seriousness of a new order is brought to realization. Poetry might turn this condition to its own ends. Only by being an object sharply defined and without redundancy will its form project whatever meaning is required of it. . . . [Oppen's] poems seek an irreducible minimum in the means for the achievement of the objective, no loose bolts or beams sticking out unattached at one end or put there to hold up a rococo cupid or a concrete saint, nor either to be a frame for a portrait of mother or a deceased wife.[12]

In *In the Money* Williams, similarly, will adopt the language of economics as a vehicle to discuss his relationship to literary forms. The *economic* aspect of the "irreducible minimum" of his imagist lyrics becomes the criterion through which Williams wanted his own reputation as poet judged. In his description of *In the Money*'s Joe Stecher, Williams celebrates a pragmatic economic reformer whose philosophy of printing money orders resembled Williams's own theories about literary precisionism and his conception of the poem as a well-designed machine. Such a conception of the poem, according to Alec Marsh, claims to reduce the usurious aspect of poetic language through its antimetaphoric materiality.[13] That is to say, Williams's objectivist poetry reduced poetic language's ability to extend reality through the meaning-expanding process of metaphor. Williams's antimetaphoric, mimetic version of poetic language allowed him to perceive his poetry as a relatively nonrhetorical object. It could reflect the actual world without distorting its value in the process of representation if the proper design were achieved by the poetry craftsman. The poet's political function, Williams implicitly argued, was to remain focused upon repairing the line and the idiom of the poem so that it reflected, rather than distorted, the image of actual contemporary life. He abhorred the making of critiques of social systems extraneous to the poem, which was the practice of Pound, who in 1939 was lobbying the United States Congress and trying to meet with President Franklin Roosevelt and Henry Wallace to discuss money theory.

The model for Joe Stecher has traditionally been identified as Paul Herman, a printer and the father of Williams's wife, Floss. Paul Herman died, apparently accidentally, of a self-inflicted gunshot wound on March 26, 1930. According to Paul Mariani, Stecher's story constituted a "sympathetic living portrait of Paul" (*NWN* 304). This is true enough, but it does not account for the nearly ten-year gap between Paul Herman's death and Williams's composition of the novel. Why was Herman's professional story on Williams's mind around 1940? One approach toward answering this question is to notice Williams's own identification with Herman as a betrayed member of a literary community that he believed he had once served faithfully.

Paul Herman's alienation from his literary community of Rutherford, New Jersey, began in 1914, when he supported Germany against England as World War I began. Herman became ostracized for his pro-German stance from fellow members of a locally prestigious literary club known as the Fortnightly Reading Club. Herman, who had just been named president of the club, lost the respect of its members when in 1916 he cast the only negative vote in favor of sending a letter to President Woodrow Wilson that claimed support for the British cause. From that point on, Mariani writes, "many of his closest friends refused to have anything more to do with him. . . . The Hermans were ostracized from the community for all practical purposes, and they soon left Rutherford for Monroe" (*NWN* 22).

Williams implicated himself in his father-in-law's problems by joining the Carlstadt Turnverein, a gymnastics club that was rumored to be in support of the Kaiser. Mariani mentions that in a 1916 editorial in the *Rutherford American,* another doctor condemned "a certain young doctor in town who was openly supporting the Kaiser" (*NWN* 120). At the start of World War II, Williams was equally unsure about supporting England against Germany since he felt that America had not yet completed its "revolution of the word" against England, the formerly dominant imperial power and the new seat of authority for the despised Eliot. That Paul Herman's most important conflict occurred within the domain of letters, the reading club, allows us to link this ostracism to that felt by Williams in the 1920s and afterward, when he was refused admittance to the avant-garde literary circle in London and in Paris, the community headed by Eliot and by Pound, and the one from which Williams fled back to his native ground of Rutherford after his flirtation with expatriation in 1924.

Mariani's indispensable biographical commentary aside, *In the Money* has not received sufficient critical attention from many of Williams's critics. In his essay on the Stecher trilogy, Neil Baldwin has come the closest to linking Williams's professional struggles with Joe Stecher's. Baldwin correctly claims that the novel "moves closer to personal history and documentary [than] *White Mule*" and that it "is a record of Williams's encounter with his changing time."[14] Instead of pursuing the "encounter with his changing time" by understanding the relationship between Williams's attitudes toward his New Directions contract and what Baldwin describes as "Joe's preoccupations about the approaching competition for a contract he needs to gain," however, Baldwin links Stecher's attempt to start a printing firm to Williams's struggle in the first decade of the twentieth century to start a medical practice. "Joe is frustrated as he finds out just how difficult it is to be a small businessman with large expectations. It must have been equally difficult for a country doctor with two young sons to function at the outset of his career," Baldwin writes.[15]

Other critics have discussed the novel, but their interpretations do not come so close as Baldwin's to connecting Stecher's professional situation to Williams's. Linda Wagner and James E. B. Breslin have discussed the novel as symptomatic of the poet's general absorption in the late 1930s on issues of business, and as an example of Williams's working in the 1930s and 1940s in a genre lower down on the scale than poetry. Working in prose, Breslin argued, allowed Williams to experiment with naturalistic techniques while waiting for liberation as a poet.[16] While these observations are reasonable, these critics, like Baldwin, neglect the market conditions under which Williams wrote the novel, and, therefore, they do not pay attention to the resonances of Williams's professional situation in Stecher's story. Wagner, however, is correct in her assessment of the manifest content of *In the Money*.

In the daring of Joe's business venture lies the thread of plot. . . . Trying to win the government printing contract away from his present employer, Joe confronts black lists, sabotage, possible murder. . . . [H]eld down by his present employers, disillusioned by the greediness of the unions, Joe feels he has no recourse but to go into business for himself. In becoming a capitalist, Joe seemingly denies the years he has worked actively in the printers' union.[17]

I will now speculate about how Williams's construction of "the business battle" in the novel was in part shaped by his struggle to assert his identity as an author with an independent voice in a saturated market. Williams's description of the contest for printing a form of money between Stecher and Wynnewood, the "Old Man" whose name resonates with T. S. Eliot's through his allegiance to the "Sacred Wood," and Crossman, whose name reminds us of Williams's accusations that Ezra Pound had engaged in double-crossing by abandoning America and placing his allegiance with Eliot, mirrors Williams's complex relationship to literary culture in the late 1930s. In reading about Joe Stecher's founding of a small but powerful printing house using a fifty-thousand-dollar loan made by someone named Lemon—"If it hadn't been for Lemon of course I couldn't have done anything, he lent me the money"—we cannot forget that Williams was, essentially, founding his own small printing company after 1935 with someone else's cash (the Laughlin steel money) by becoming the cornerstone and "head man" at New Directions. Lemon's willingness to loan Stecher the money to start his new firm resonates with Laughlin's commitment to credit Williams's promise to produce the anticipated long poem, *Paterson,* the biography of his mother later to be called *Yes, Mrs. Williams,* and his own life story. There is a direct relationship between Laughlin's New Directions and Gorham Munson's Social Credit journal *New Democracy.* As Wendy Stallard Flory notes, "Pound had given James Laughlin an introduction to Munson, who put him in charge of the Social Credit and the Arts department which Laughlin chose to call New Directions."[18] Laughlin's commitment to Williams, based on a record of past accomplishments in the art, stand as examples of Social Credit, the economic theory advocated by C. H. Douglas and Pound. In the novel, Social Credit theory is adopted by Williams to justify his own benefits from his new relationship to the commercial literary marketplace.

The "business battle" between Stecher and the firm to which he once belonged begins in chapter 3, "Boss's Party." Stecher, the master printer who at the outset of the novel works for Wynnewood and Crossman, manages to underbid his old firm for the prestigious and lucrative contract to print United States money orders. He underbids them by presenting himself to them as a simple craftsman who is "innocent" of any interest in owning his own firm. This mask of professional innocence and commercial disinterest, we recall, resembles the persona Williams constructed in order "to get literary business done."[19]

In chapter 3, Stecher leaves for Washington, D.C., to make his bid without anyone else from the firm of Wynnewood and Crossman knowing about it. By having a pressman who lives in his neighborhood return his desk key to the office, Stecher is able to give other members of the firm the false impression that he had been in the building, rather than in Washington, on the day he delivered his bid. Wynnewood's lawyer, named Stevens, reported this news to Wynnewood and Crossman. News of this key becomes the first evidence that Wynnewood was mistaken not to lower his bid so that he could compete with Stecher for the Washington contract. In spite of his apparent lack of interest in owning his own firm, Stecher is, in fact, shown in chapter 3 to be a cunning businessman. He is willing to use Lemon's funds to defeat the hold on the printing monopoly by "the organization." Stecher's apparent nonchalance ("Said he just found [the key] in his pocket," Stevens tells Wynnewood) veils his desire to win what the novel describes as "the final showdown" between the two sides that once were one.

Williams's decision to name the lawyer who finds the key Stevens is significant in terms of the submerged criticism of modern writers that informs many of the characterizations in the novel. Wallace Stevens wrote the important and controversial preface to the first edition of Williams's *Collected Poems,* printed in 1934 by Louis Zukofsky and the Objectivist Press. Williams knew he had taken a risk by asking Stevens to write on his behalf, but he needed a "name" author and allowed Stevens to go ahead. "It may sell the book yet—especially if the right Sunday Supplement guy sees it and falls for it," Williams wrote (qtd. in *NWN* 339). To some extent the idea backfired because Stevens was the first critic to call Williams's poetry "anti-poetic," a description Williams abhorred. Stevens described Williams in the preface.

He who insists that life would be intolerable except for the fact that one has, from the top, such an exceptional view of the public dump and the advertising signs of Snider's Catsup, Ivory Soap and Chevrolet Cars; he is the hermit who dwells alone with the sun and moon, but insists on taking a rotten newspaper.[20]

Stevens's claim that Williams was a Romantic poet who gained insight from observing the "public dump" of the commercial world from his dwelling in the "ivory tower" was, ironically, the "key" to Williams's rhetorical strategy in *In the Money*. Stevens's observation that Williams's view of "advertising signs" fortified his imaginative writing is an accurate way to describe a structural principle that informs *In the Money*'s submerged plot. Indeed, Williams used the advertising method of "hidden persuasion" to wage a campaign of persuasion against literary rivals, a publicity strategy valuable to Williams because it accommodated his publisher's sense of the decorum of the modernist project. In the "hidden dialogue" with his rival in *In the Money*, Stevens was presented as a "fool" working for the usurious side of the printing industry. Williams parodied the image of Wallace Stevens as the capable business executive in the gray flannel suit, the vice president in insurance from Hartford. Through Stecher's example, Williams also transferred the prestige of the capable money manager toward himself (and away from Stevens, Eliot, and Pound, the insurance man, the banker, and the Social Credit theorist).

A working draft of the opening section of "Guitar Blues," Williams's *Nation* review of *The Man with the Blue Guitar and Other Poems* (1937), presents further evidence that Stevens's recent success as a commercially viable poet was on Williams's mind when he was composing *In the Money*. In the review, Williams pays attention to the importance of the commercial investment in and the marketing of modern letters before turning to an evaluation of Stevens's poetry.

> Money is power, a power. Without capital investment, the market for poetry, like every other market regardless of its intrinsic worth will slump. But Stevens has got himself published by a good firm. He is one of the few modern American poets to experience capital investment. Maybe there is money in it. Who knows? More power to him.
>
> They've given him a small attractive volume in bright yellow boards costing them perhaps, I don't know, say four or five hundred dollars to print. The price is two dollars. If they sell a thousand copies they'll

about clear expenses. How would you like to market an item entitled, *The Man with the Blue Guitar?* Counting colleges and libraries, maybe a fair bet.[21]

Besides projecting Stevens's fortunes with Knopf onto his own hopes for success with New Directions through the story of Stecher's receiving a "capital investment" from Lemon in order to print a form of money that Williams in the review says "is power, a power," the focus of much of the submerged literary "business battle" in chapter 3 concerns Williams's desire to dethrone Eliot. As the early signals from Washington send Wynnewood the message that Stecher has, indeed, underbid the international firm, "J. W." tries to gauge the scope of the damage to his printing empire. Wynnewood is "pretty sure [Stecher] hasn't tied up with any of the big companies." When the final news of Stecher's victory becomes official, however, Wynnewood's response to Stecher's victory suggests a personal wounding, as well as the response of a spirited competitor: " 'Well, I'm a son of a bitch. Where the hell do you suppose—? How the hell. . . ? Where is he going to print them? How in hell did he. . . ?' The old man was speechless."[22] When he returns to speech, Wynnewood brushes aside his son's advice to accept defeat.

> The sense of balance that I go by says, Don't get licked. And I don't get licked. Not by anybody. . . . Something tells me he's going to run into some pretty tough sledding before he gets through. Pretty tough going. If he's man enough, maybe he'll get by—maybe. If he's man enough. (*IM* 42)

Fearing that Stecher may be after "the whole God damn building," and unsure about "how far he's undermined my organization," Wynnewood vows to "kill that damned little bastard": "Who the hell owns this country? Him or me?" (*IM* 43).

It is not clear that T. S. Eliot was an equally engaged partner with Williams in their literary "business battle." Eliot, in fact, once said that Williams was only "of local interest, perhaps."[23] Williams, however, understood his position as a "nativist" poet after 1922 to be a maverick's response to Eliot's literary dominance. Leibowitz writes that Williams needed institutionally sanctioned enemies to rebel against, and Eliot was the perfect foil to his transgressive art.

Extremely competitive, when his insecurity was in the ascendancy he lashed out at his enemies with a nasty hysteria. He needed enemies, and the *Autobiography* contains many military images; he felt continually embattled. . . . His favorite villain or scapegoat was T. S. Eliot . . . As though it were a personal attack, *The Waste Land* felled Williams like a "sardonic bullet." Derailed, he must pick himself up from the ditch and start over. . . . Williams relishes his malice towards Eliot: it made him vow to resume the struggle and uphold his "rebellious" experiments. He would count on final vindication.[24]

Wynnewood's reaction to Stecher's renegade activity can be interpreted as the way Williams *would have liked* Eliot, who Fisher-Wirth writes thought Williams "too small to feud with,"[25] to have responded to his publication contract, if not with "one of the big companies" such as Stevens had with Knopf, then with Laughlin's new press.

Chapter 3 ends with Wynnewood ready to mount his campaign of "dirty work," as his lawyer Stevens calls it, to undermine Stecher's new printing house. Here Williams sets up the contrasting attitudes about business ethics that separates "honest" (Stecher's) from "corrupt" (Wynnewood's) versions of the printing and distribution of signs of wealth. Williams casts Stecher as the "innocent" printer out on his own who faces a conspiracy to undermine his professional success. Any unsavory or, possibly, illegal action Stecher takes to implement his printing house, therefore, is viewed in this novel as a necessary and ethically justified action. Stecher's "inside trading" is justified because the outcome is monetary reform that will benefit the national economy. Even though both sides are implicated in dishonest practices, "honesty" becomes a Stecher virtue. Corruption in order to maintain a wicked regime becomes the definitive Wynnewood vice, as this comment from Wynnewood suggests: "How you gonna get any work done if somebody's always yelling honesty, honesty at you. Honesty is the best policy, huh? Christ, who the hell ever cared about honesty but a lot of little craps that ain't in the money?" (*IM* 44). Wynnewood contrasts the honest but insignificant "little craps" with those willing to put ethics aside to get "in the money." This conflict between business ethics and the work of creating a reputation in an economy of scarce resources that appears to award dishonesty stands among the conflicts Williams, as a poet who was interested in getting "in the money," was exploring through the novel about Stecher's unsavory relationship to commercial publishing.

Stecher, like Williams in the New Directions phase, casts aside anonymity to put himself "in the money" by making a secret bid for renown through the critique of his former associates, Pound and Stevens, within his New Directions prose. Williams, like Stecher, had also gambled by entering into a publication agreement with Laughlin to write a number of books that he had planned and promised, but that he had not yet produced. In order to perform this separation from his former allies Williams had practiced what Wynnewood correctly accuses Stecher of engaging in: "double-crossing." Hence, the strategy that Stecher employed to win the government contract for the money orders resonates with a paradox that is at the heart of Williams's posture as an "innocent" writer who stood outside of both the commercial literary market and the institution of modernism.

The struggle in chapter 3 for the printing contract included hidden critiques of Stevens and Eliot. In the pivotal thirteenth chapter, Williams turns his attention to his disagreements with Pound about the role the American poet should play in the economic and political governance of the country. In chapter 13, Stecher is figured as deserving credit for his skill at printing the money orders on time and under budget. In order to make his case for winning the government account, Stecher visits Washington, D.C., to stand before no one less than President Teddy Roosevelt. Roosevelt is described in the novel as a muckraking reformer who opposes the kind of public abuse of funds enacted in this fiction by Wynnewood and Crossman. The president comes to trust Stecher, but at first Roosevelt wonders why the public printer isn't handling the job. "Because they don't know how," Joe tells the president (*IM* 177). Besides associating Stecher's activities in Washington with his own literary "know how," Stecher's successful bid to gain the support of Teddy Roosevelt also served as Williams's narrative reversal and critique of Pound's activities in Washington on behalf of the English economist Douglas's theory of Social Credit.

In April 1939 Pound had returned from Italy to lobby on behalf of monetary reforms before a second Roosevelt's administration in Washington. In the novel, Stecher comments to his wife Gurlie that he has been speaking about this idea with "Senator Platt and Chauncey M. Depew, men like that," and that he had been gathering the support that led to his successful meeting with Teddy Roosevelt and the four-year contract. Except for the outcome to these meetings in Washington, Stecher's journey is similar to Pound's.

Whether or not Williams knew it, Pound had also headed south for
Washington with his own inimitable cloak-and-dagger secrecy. Much
of what Pound did there is shrouded in mystery, but he did attend a
session of Congress and he did talk—as he reveals in the *Pisan Can-
tos*—with Senators Borah of Idaho (Pound's native state) and
Bankhead. . . . He also talked with Secretary of Agriculture Henry A.
Wallace. But he did not get to see Roosevelt and he did not avert
World War II. (*NWN* 427)

There is an essential difference between Pound's arguments for money
reform and Stecher's. Pound presented himself to Congress as an economist in 1939 on the eve of awesome and terrible shifts in world affairs,
whereas Stecher presented himself as a professional printer in 1903 who
appears before a president associated with repairing an existing political
institution. While Pound was using *The Cantos,* in Mariani's words, "to
show how the misuse of money was at the root of all modern evils"
(*NWN* 375), Williams, through Stecher's story, had created a plot about
how, literally, to make money to suggest the value of his attention to the
literary craft, rather than to abstract political or economic theory.[26] In
chapter 13, after the successful meeting with Roosevelt, Stecher enters
into an interior monologue. Here, the tenets of his printing practice
match Williams's ideas about literary nativism and precisionism.

My policy! what else? My policy. Nothing works efficiently any more
because of that idea. Church, government—the only thing that works
is one man that pays attention to what he is doing and knows what to
do about it. My brother plays the violin in Prague. My sister shows her
legs on the stage—I'm a printer. I hope we do our jobs all right.
Because if we don't—It's because it's to the advantage of someone or
other, my policy!—or we'd plant as much as we want and need and
we'd have a world worth living it.

Waste, waste, waste. There's the solution to everything. Just cultivate that land, just that little bit of acreage of New Jersey, just as far
as you can see on both sides of the train window, that is going to
waste. That's all you have to do. But really use it. And there'd be no
more poverty or misery in the entire world—Just put it to use. (*IM*
180–81)

This is a pragmatic, literally objective approach to monetary reform. It
is disinterested in abstractions, in praise of efficiency in design, advocates

a worker's expertise in one craft (musician, actress, printer), and is focused on reducing waste and poverty by gathering up the energy and materials of the local land. The theory of monetary reform, in other words, represents in displaced form the classic Williams philosophy of political and social change, as well as his program for the right form of the poem, as he stated in a 1951 "Symposium on Writing."

> We forget what a poem is: a poem is an organization of materials. As an automobile or kitchen stove is an organization of materials. You have to take words, as Gertrude Stein said we must, to make poems. Poems are mechanical objects made out of words to express a certain thing.[27]

From this point of view, Stecher's attention to details such as printing money orders that are difficult to counterfeit constitutes correct political action. Stecher's style resonates with Williams's use of what Anne Janowitz has called the "mechanical, manufacturing image for the 'creation' of a poem." The poem, Williams said, "will be an organization of materials on a better basis than it had been before."[28] In contrast to Stecher, Wynnewood and Crossman are enemies of this kind of pragmatic aesthetic reform through fidelity to detailing. From their point of view, reformation of the design of the money orders only cuts into profit margins. In chapter 5, Stecher explained to Gurlie that since Wynnewood had a monopoly on the contract he refused to listen to Stecher's ideas about how to prevent counterfeit orders. Here, the attention to the surface of the paper resonates with Williams's attention to the visual appearance of his poems.

> I wanted them to put in a new paper I found out about. But the old man wouldn't hear of it. It would stop the whole trouble with counterfeiting. If you change anything, it changes the surface of the paper. Well, that's where it started. I tried to sell it to him—for a year. I could see the advantages so when he wouldn't do it, I decided to see what I could do with it myself. I got a monopoly on it! (*IM* 59)

Williams argued that the streamlining of craft was an act of political reform appropriate to the poet's type of knowledge. Developing abstract theories about social and economic reform should be left to professors and political economists. Through Stecher's story, however, Williams did argue in favor of his own ability to publish literature for profit by applying to his situation ideas found in Douglas's books on determining new criteria for the awarding of public credit. Douglas argued that Social Credit (examples of which would be in Williams's case the New Directions contract and in Stecher's case the government printing contract) should only be offered to individuals who performed communally useful tasks with technical expertise. Douglas wrote that "the only claim which any individual or collection of individuals has to operate and administer the plant of society is that they are the fittest persons available for the purpose."[29] Stecher fulfills Douglas's characterization of an entrepreneur who deserves "real credit" because of his accomplishments in his special field. His "honest" practice is performed without the graft of the "international organization" that includes Legal Talent, Wynnewood, Crossman, and "Ink" Nesbit. These insiders are usurers in the sense that they skim profits off of every order book they produce, as Stecher explains later in the novel to Gurlie, about how the graft worked at Wynnewood's Mohawk Press.

> We got paid outside the contract. The old man asked for 6½ cents a book for delivery. Caldwell offered 4 cents. 4½ cents was agreed on finally. Even that was far beyond the cost. The boys got the difference, about 1⅙ cents a book. . . . We used to print books of 500 blanks but recently they never go out in any denomination higher than 200. That makes two and a half times as many books. Not a bad idea. (*IM* 168–69)

The conflict between Stecher and the international firm is not between backers of "hard" and "paper" currency, as might have been the case had Williams been writing *In the Money* during the age of Jackson and the bank wars of the 1830s. Instead, the conflict is between two attitudes toward the production of an abstract form of the distribution of wealth, the money order. It is efficiently produced by Stecher, and so presented as deserving of the public trust, but made usurious through graft and monopoly by Wynnewood and Crossman, and so presented as not deserving credit. In the novel, Williams does not assume the natural authenticity of money as a medium of exchange of value. Both in the area of finance and in poetry, his focus is on reforming the artificial instrument of exchange (the poetic line, the money order). In both cases, he promoted forms of social mediation that attempt to reflect without distortion the actual conditions of life in the social world, whether through the attempt to write a poem in the "American idiom" with a reduced metaphorical content and a prosody based in the oral practices of native speakers, or else in the form of money orders produced in an inexpensive way that does not tend toward the making of money from money (usury). Hence, in the novel, the boundaries between the two cultures of art and commerce becomes elastic, perhaps to the point where it is impossible to distinguish between aesthetic and economic forms of symbolic exchange.[30] Williams's mature iconography as a poetry technician and his theories about the value of poetry as a mediational instrument of social exchange are both found in the Stecher attitude toward the making of money.

We recall that in his letters to Laughlin, Williams thought of Eliot and Pound as "gang" leaders who were actively opposed to his advances in poetic technique. Williams's paranoia that other modernist writers were out "to keep the artist down" is reflected in the way Stecher must fight against efforts by Crossman and Wynnewood to sabotage his operation through the tactics of monopoly capitalism. First, they pay off the building inspector to claim that the warehouse Stecher rented was too weak to safely hold the presses (chap. 15). Then, in chapter 18, they issue a warning to any ink seller (Nesbit, in particular) that trading with Stecher will exempt that seller from other Wynnewood accounts. These attempts failed, they hire a group of thugs to bump Stecher off the Brooklyn Ferry (chap. 18). None of these schemes, however, keeps Stecher from fulfilling the government order by the December deadline. While fending off Wynnewood and Crossman's henchman presented an external challenge to Stecher's authority, the greatest challenge to his authority in the second half of the novel stems from internal doubts about his legitimacy as a printer and fledgling entrepreneur. Although Stecher tells Gurlie that because his bid was lowest the contract has "been awarded to me," he still feels inferior to Wynnewood and Crossman. He wonders if the work he has done will meet with approval by other printers. Although the wording of Joe Stecher's speech to Gurlie could be about Williams's fears that his New Directions writings will not meet the approval of literary critics whose judgment was sanctioned by their university affiliations, he is talking to her about the government officials who must approve the quality of the money orders: "To make it official it will have to have the approval of the department and I suppose I'll have to appear and prove to them that I'm properly equipped and qualified in other ways to complete the order. That's business" (*IM* 63). Stecher's paradoxical relationship to the establishment (i.e., the concomitant fear that the "insiders" are attacking his progress, as well as his need for "insider" approval in order to prove his qualifications) reflects Williams's paradoxical attitude toward university-sanctioned literary professionals in the 1930s and 1940s.

In the novel, Gurlie can't understand her husband's fear of failure. She assumes that even if Joe does not at the moment have the ink and the presses to form his own company, he will have the "best" press eventually. Joe describes to Gurlie his worry about being unable to "deliver": "This is government work. Suppose I break down in the first six months and can't deliver the orders. It's happened before. That's one thing about the old company. They have the equipment and they can always deliver" (*IM* 63). The fear that Stecher might "break down" before he could produce the work he promised Lemon resonates with Williams's fear of a personal "breakdown" that would disable him from delivering the literary work he had promised Laughlin for the 1940 New Directions Christmas catalog. When he was writing *In the Money*, Williams was also asked by Laughlin to put together a short pamphlet of his recent poetry. It was to be published in an inexpensive "poet-of-the-month" series that Laughlin proposed as another form of publicity for New Directions and for the forthcoming installment of the novel trilogy. Williams, however, had trouble coming up with even this modest amount of new material. He also had doubts about the quality of the work he finally did offer to Laughlin. A November 24, 1940, letter to Laughlin about the pamphlet of poems called "The Broken Span," which was published on January 2, 1941, suggests some of Williams's fears, which were magnified when he tried to write *Paterson* in the middle years of the 1940s.

I suppose it's too late to make any changes in the pamphlet of my poems you are issuing in January? I've been looking the work over and find that there is more than one spot in which it is weak. . . .

Such situations as this are bound to occur when work is gathered quickly together. A verse maker should never be in a hurry. The mind is a queer mechanical machine that allows itself to be caught in traps. A rhythmical jig takes hold of us forcing us to follow it, slipping in the words quite against our better judgement [sic] sometimes. We grow enamored of our own put-put and like to see the boat push ahead— even to its destruction sometimes: a heavy figure for a stupid happening. (*SL* 57)[31]

Perhaps the most important personal doubt of Stecher's that resonates with Williams's fears about breaking out on his own with New Directions after 1937, however, concerns the ethically questionable business practices of both the printer and the poet. In chapter 15, called "Final Offer," we can hear echoes of Williams's fears that his "hidden" selling strategy may not be deemed savory by other literary "insiders" who did not appreciate his irony. Sure now that he is "licked," Wynnewood makes a futile attempt to buy Stecher back by allowing him to "name his price," as long as he returns to the firm and drops his public accusations that the big firm was crooked. Stecher is now seriously concerned that the cost of winning a battle instigated by his own underhanded dealings may backfire. Wynnewood says: "Why didn't you come out into the open and tell me you were going to put in a bid on the contract? Then it would have been a fair fight. You didn't have the guts to do it, that's why" (*IM* 205). Stecher answers that accusation by making the obvious point that Wynnewood would have simply underbid him and taken a loss on this single contract if he had placed his bid in the open. Stecher becomes more agitated, however, when Wynnewood accuses him of stealing "all our training, all our methods, all our private knowledge" (*IM* 205). Stecher can only defend himself against this accusation by saying that he took "nothing out of your business that I didn't bring into it myself a hundred times over." Stecher cannot answer Wynnewood's cry that "you didn't have to smear our personal reputations to win your dirty little contract away from us. You didn't have to do that and you won't get away with it without paying." Accused by Wynnewood of "blackening our names" and stealing letters from the firm in order "to establish your fifth-rate little print shop in New York," all that Stecher can say is "Take that back" (*IM* 205). In terms of the covert depiction of the poetic competition that Williams was waging against Eliot and Pound, this was the accusation that Williams feared he could not answer about his own quest for literary renown through the "hidden critique" of Stevens, Eliot, and Pound.

In spite of the shaky moral ground upon which his new publishing firm was built, Stecher remained, in the last third of the novel, proud of his accomplishments. Like the *Autobiography*, which Fisher-Wirth describes as "a paean of success," and as the text in which Williams "fulfills the plan conceived in the radical innocence of his young childhood: the plan to do it all,"[32] "Lunch at the Club" (chap. 21) registers Stecher's overcoming of fear that forces, both internal and external to the self, would prevent his professional success. It is the last of the novel's important chapters regarding Stecher's professional struggle against the corporate sabotage. Although it leaves unresolved Stecher's response to Lemon's warning that the printing workers that Stecher now trusts in his closed shop might eventually threaten his new success, the tone of this chapter expresses Stecher's joy at success against great odds.

> "What do you really think of the whole business now that it's over? Was it worth it?" Mr. Lemon was speaking as if to the street in front of him.
> "Oh yes," said Joe.
> "Did you enjoy it? The fight, I mean."
> "Yes," said Joe.
> "I don't believe it," said Mr. Lemon laughing. "But you never can tell. And are they licked! You know I actually feel sorry for them sometimes."
> "Yah," said Joe. "So do I." (*IM* 287)

The fulfillment of Stecher's overcoming of personal and professional obstacles to "lick" the competition marked the final segment of the novel that Laughlin awaited for the New Directions Christmas catalog of 1940. By producing the story of Stecher's success under his own version of deadline pressure, Williams had, through the self-referential plot, overcome his own creative doubts and met his own deadline to produce a work that he hoped would bring him prestige, or, perhaps, the riches that would compensate for a lack of prestige. Now that he had the publisher and the assurance of a steady audience, Williams, like Stecher, proved that he could "deliver the goods" under the pressure of attention. For perhaps the first time in his career, Williams understood that his writing was destined to be read by an audience perhaps ten times as great as any that he had reached prior to *White Mule,* which Williams wanted badly to follow up with another "winner."

In spite of the spirited tone evident in "Lunch at the Club," we have also noticed a paradox at the heart of the book's moral critique of the corrupt practices of the established international firm of Wynnewood and Crossman. The paradoxes of Stecher's venture reflected the paradoxes of Williams's own situation as one of Laughlin's "literary saints." Williams used Pound's friendship to gain a publishing contract that, covertly, enabled him to define his public image in opposition to his former associates, especially Pound. Just as we have seen that Stecher's position as an innocent outsider was constructed through his manipulation of his commercial position, the plot of *In the Money* promoted Williams's position as the innocent outsider looking to reform a publishing monopoly that he claimed refused to accept innovative ideas. The presentation of Williams as a literary "innocent" from this point of view was an imaginative construction, a statement of Williams's literary strength enabled by his ambivalent relationship to literary markets. In the novel, Williams shows a nostalgia for producing a sign system in which the thing and the sign of value for the thing are aligned through Stecher's efficient (nonusurious) production of blank money orders. Williams's placement of this nostalgia within a narrative that has a secret alliance with another form of exchange (literary representation), however, reveals his version of the economy to be a cultural artifact. The money economy presented in *In the Money* is a cultural artifact to the same degree that the cultural artifact that Williams hoped to promote in the novel (his poems) are revealed to be commodities available for exchange.

NOTES

1. William Carlos Williams, *The Autobiography* (Norfolk, Conn.: New Directions, 1951), p. 158.
2. Ann W. Fisher-Wirth, *William Carlos Williams and Autobiography: The Woods of His Own Nature* (University Park: Pennsylvania State University Press, 1989), p. 33.
3. Herbert Leibowitz, "'You Can't Beat Innocence': *The Autobiography* of William Carlos Williams," *American Poetry Review,* March–April 1981, p. 36.
4. Lawrence S. Rainey, "The Price of Modernism: Reconsidering the Publication of *The Waste Land,*" *Yale Review* 78, no. 2 (Winter 1989): 294.
5. William Carlos Williams, *White Mule* (Norfolk, Conn.: New Directions, 1937), p. 13; Anne Janowitz, "*Paterson:* An American Contraption," in *William Carlos Williams: Man and Poet,* ed. Carroll F. Terrell (Orono, Maine: National Poetry Foundation, 1983), p. 301.
6. James Laughlin, introduction, *New Directions in Poetry and Prose* (Norfolk, Conn.: New Directions, 1939), p. xii.
7. Ibid., n.p.
8. *William Carlos Williams and James Laughlin: Selected Letters,* ed. Hugh Witemeyer (New York: Norton, 1989), p. 28; subsequent references are cited parenthetically, abbreviated *SL.*
9. Williams advised, "Zukofsky's *A* is another matter. It can't sell but may

bring the press a certain distinction" (*SL* 18). Besides repaying the debt he owed to Zukofsky for publishing his first collected poems with the Objectivist Press in 1934 and providing advice throughout this period, Williams is also saying that all New Directions authors will profit through association with an author involved in high-modern difficulty.

10. Although their interest proved transitory, Oxford University Press appeared willing to publish his *Complete Collected Poems*. Ronald Latimer's Alcestis Press and Laughlin from New Directions were also making serious offers to put together attractive packages of Williams's work.

11. Williams, for example, called the university the seat of the "worst scandal of our day" for refusing to accept poetry as an antitraditional "field of action" based on local language and local setting (Paul Mariani, *William Carlos Williams: A New World Naked* [New York: McGraw-Hill, 1981], p. 290; subsequent references cited parenthetically, abbreviated *NWN*).

12. William Carlos Williams, "The New Political Economy," *Poetry* 44 (July 1934): 223–24.

13. Alec Marsh, "Stevens and Williams: The Economics of Metaphor," *William Carlos Williams Review* 18 (Fall 1992): 37–49.

14. Neil Baldwin, "The Stecher Trilogy: Williams as Novelist," in Terrell, *William Carlos Williams*, p. 409.

15. Baldwin, "The Stecher Trilogy," pp. 460, 408.

16. James E. B. Breslin, *William Carlos Williams, an American Artist* (New York: Oxford University Press, 1970), p. 126.

17. Linda Wagner, *The Prose of William Carlos Williams* (Middletown, Conn.: Wesleyan University Press, 1970), pp. 124, 126.

18. Wendy Stallard Flory, *The American Ezra Pound* (New Haven: Yale University Press, 1989), p. 78.

19. Leibowitz, "You Can't Beat Innocence," p. 36.

20. Charles Doyle, *Williams Carlos Williams: The Critical Heritage* (London: Routledge and Kegan Paul, 1980), p. 126.

21. William Carlos Williams, "Guitar Blues," 1937. Typescript to a review of *The Man with the Blue Guitar and Other Poems,* Houghton Library, Harvard University, Manuscript collection: MS AM 1956 (2), unpaginated manuscript.

22. William Carlos Williams, *In the Money* (New York: New Directions, 1940), p. 41; subsequent references will appear parenthetically, abbreviated *IM*.

23. Quoted in Fisher-Wirth, *Autobiography,* p. 34.

24. Leibowitz, "You Can't Beat Innocence," p. 38.

25. Fisher-Wirth, *Autobiography,* p. 34.

26. On March 25, 1935, Williams wrote to Pound, "If you can't tell the difference between yourself and a trained economist, if you don't know your function as a poet, incidentally dealing with a messy situation re: money, then go sell your papers on some other corner" (*NWN* 375).

27. William Carlos Williams, *Interviews with William Carlos Williams*, ed. Linda Wagner (New York: New Directions, 1976), p. 73.

28. Janowitz, *"Paterson,"* pp. 301–2.

29. C. H. Douglas, *The Douglas Manual*, comp. Philip Mairet (New York: Coward McCann, 1935), p. 89.

30. I am indebted to James Livingston of Rutgers University for his commentary on a version of this paper that I gave at the "Economy of Literature" panel at the Central New York MLA Conference held at SUNY Cortland on October 21 and 22, 1991. The notion of elasticity among forms of exchange was part of Livingston's response to my presentation.

31. His January 6, 1941, letter to Laughlin reiterates this fear of being unable to produce new work: "I want to have a go at verse again. I haven't written any for years, it seems, and I know I shall never again write as I have written in the past. I want to know what's in there, I'm curious. Something has happened within me, perhaps a final catharsis of the whole material of verse. But if I'm empty at last I want to prove it" (*SL* 60).

32. Fisher-Wirth, *Autobiography*, pp. 35–36.

PART TWO
Voices at the Margins/Rereadings

Advertising Feminism: Ornamental Bodies/Docile Bodies and the Discourse of Suffrage

Barbara Green

There grew up an admitted policy of playing purely for effect, to excite the public curiosity, to fill the treasury. Tactics were adopted which seemed to indicate that militancy would be degraded to the purposes of advertisement and the movement reduced to the level of a spectacular suffrage show.

Teresa Billington-Greig

When militant activists trace the evolution of England's suffrage campaign in their autobiographical writings, they often mark a shift in the tactics of the Women's Social and Political Union from pageantry to militancy, from dramatic spectacles to guerrilla warfare. Typical are the comments of WSPU member Kitty Marion, who recollects an encounter with a bishop acting in behalf of the government during her imprisonment for militant activity:

The Bishop was sorry we had not continued our "beautiful processions." "When you had your beautiful processions you had everybody at your feet," he said, to which I replied, "Yes, but our beautiful processions didn't get us the vote, and we don't want anybody at our feet, we want the vote!"[1]

To Kitty Marion, militant activism was not just an alternative to the pleasing pageantry of the first half of the campaign, but a sign of its failure. WSPU leader Emmeline Pethick-Lawrence noted a similar opposition between spectacular activism and militant warfare in a 1908 essay published in *Votes for Women*: "We have touched the limit of public demonstration. . . . Nothing but militant action is left to us now."[2] In these writings militancy becomes the inverse of feminist exhibitionism and an indication of the ways in which radical street theater always collapses into a pleasurable but ineffective sensation.

When feminist historians tell the story of the women's campaign for the vote in Britain, they either write that history in terms of an opposition, not just between constitutional and militant activism, but between theatrical display and an outrageous and audience-aggressive activism—an activism that rejects the exhibition of the female body, an activism that goes underground[3]—or they collapse all versions of performative feminism under the umbrella term *theater,* seeing pleasing pageantry and violent scenes of torture as elaborate performances that depend on the celebrity of feminist actresses.[4] This tendency to separate out militant activism from the theatrical performances of the first half of the campaign, or to blur the distinctions between them, misses the complexity of the relationship between advertising and feminism when feminism advertises itself through an exhibition of tortured feminist bodies. This is especially so in the case of representations of the hunger-striking and forcibly fed bodies of suffragettes that circulated through London via first-person narratives and reconstructed images.

Through "spectacle," the impossible relations between "feminism" and "advertising" revealed themselves to militant activist Teresa Billington-Greig, who used these terms in her 1911 treatise, *The Militant Suffrage Movement: Emancipation in a Hurry,* to locate the militant suffrage movement both in a burgeoning commodity culture and in an increasingly technologized public sphere.[5] While other militant suffragettes also applied the term *spectacle* to a variety of performative strategies, they did so to separate recuperated from oppositional performances. Billington-Greig was unique in her condemnation of spectacle and in her tendency to read feminist activities ranging from pageantry to imprisonment as spectacular. These examples point to a vexed issue at the heart of the suffrage campaign: new feminist forms of performative activism depended upon modern methods of mechanical reproduction; however, these new methods link feminism firmly to the advertising culture that critics like Billington-Greig condemned.

For Billington-Greig, the term *advertisement* meant the depoliticization of spectacle.[6] While criticizing the Pankhursts' WSPU for its autocratic management, its commercial preoccupations, and thus its narrow focus, her most serious complaint was that the WSPU had taken up revolution as a performance and appropriated the methodology of advertising culture. Nostalgic for (the fantasy of) a utopian, carnivalesque, spontaneous form of resistance, she condemned the performative "spectacular suffrage show" of the WSPU for appropriating techniques of technological reproduction, thus mechanizing feminism. Although Billington-Greig grouped together the various strategies of the WSPU under the heading of "advertising feminism" (while I am trying to discern their complex relations), her critique of the connection between performative feminism and modern strategies of mechanical reproduction enables an understanding of *the benefits* for feminism of reduplicating the violated body. Countering Billington-Greig's charge of pure mechanism and co-optation with Walter Benjamin's insights into the subversive potential of mechanical modes of reproduction, I want to argue that the docile body produced through forcible feeding was *reproduced* in a distinctly modern way through the suffragettes' autobiographical narratives. Billington-Greig's refusal to "advertise feminism" should remind us of the often tense relations between modernism and mass culture. But where other essays in this volume revisit and revise a debate that has long been defined by the terms *high* (art) and *low* (culture), mine directs us to the political arena of suffrage, which defies such categorization. Neither strictly popular nor strictly avant-garde, the suffrage movement and its cultural products provide an instructive example for rethinking relations between the terms of this collection's title, *marketing* and *modernism*. Unlike many modernist figures who recoiled from the corrupting elements of advertising culture, the suffragettes struggled with advertising culture to locate its salutary effects.

My main subject of study will be an event—the forcible feeding of English suffragettes—and the discourse of painful embodiment it engendered—documents of forcible feeding that circulated through England via autobiographies, pamphlets, letters to the editors of major newspapers, and letters written on toilet paper to fellow activists smuggled from the prison. I shall examine the division between the pleasing spectacle of street theater that advertises feminism and the radical and audience-aggressive techniques of militant activism that (seemingly) reject spectacle, exhibitionism, and advertisement by rethinking the differences and connections between the two bodies those strategies produced: the ornamental body of street theater and the docile mechanized body produced through the macabre routine of forcible feeding.[7] In many ways Billington-Greig's opposition between the spontaneous force of rebellion and the mechanistic degradation of advertisement finds its parallel in these two bodies produced in the suffrage campaign. If we do not follow

Billington-Greig's lead and examine feminism's shift from ornamental body to docile body in the context of modernism's transformation under mechanical reproduction, we miss the larger consequences of that shift. A full examination of the shift from an ornamental body to a docile disciplined body would require seeing the suffrage movement in relation to a sequence of modern dilemmas: the disintegration of bodily integrity, the destruction of the notion of a unified public sphere, the recognition that history consists not of a chain of events but in (and made through) discourse. My focus will be, however, on a precise aspect of these transformations: the significance of mechanical reproduction as an innovative and vital feminist strategy of rebellion. Indeed, it is precisely the modern mode of mechanical reproduction that enables the creation of a new form of collectivity—a spectacular subculture—that is produced through participation in a shared narrative. The representation and reduplication of the event of forcible feeding ought to be read not as an alternative to suffrage's pleasing spectacles, but as a vital reworking of spectacle and of performative activism.

The shift from ornamental body to docile body is more than a mere change in tactics: the docile body signals both the destruction of the ornamental body and the sphere in which it operates. To unpack the implications of this shift, I will begin by considering the feminist bodies of the suffrage movement in the terms established by Peter Wollen in his theory of modernism's bodies, ornamental and functional.

To a certain extent, all of the major suffrage organizations—the Pankhursts' Women's Social and Political Union, Millicent Fawcett's National Union of Women's Suffrage Societies, Charlotte Despard's Women's Freedom League, Sylvia Pankhurst's East London Federation—participated in the radical street theater that made visible a feminist collective and women's desire for the vote.[8] Although the militant WSPU was not actively involved in producing the iconography of suffrage displayed in the banners, posters, and postcards that represented femininity to Edwardian England, its demonstrations, weekly Hyde Park meetings, and deputations to government officials were an integral part of the street theater of suffrage. However, it was not until Prime Minister Asquith demanded that women visibly *demonstrate* their desire for emancipation that two of the major suffrage organizations, the NUWSS and the WSPU, planned the theatrical marches through the streets of London that won the suffrage campaign its largest audience. Thousands of women prepared their audiences through savvy advertisement, then marched through the streets holding colorful banners and wearing dramatic costumes. Their aim was to present a disruptive display of femininity in the (male-coded) public spaces heretofore forbidden to them. In her comprehensive history of the iconography and representational strategies of the suffrage campaign, Lisa Tickner has demonstrated the ways in which activist women reworked dominant discourses of femininity to represent a challenging (yet appealing) woman to the public eye, such as the images of heroic womanhood (Sappho, Joan of Arc, Florence Nightingale) reembodied in Cicely Hamilton's Pageant of Great Women.[9] Making use of the new availability of photography in newspapers, women relied upon the sensation of femininity in the street to command a space in public discussions of citizenship and dominated the newspapers' front pages with discussions of the beauty, pageantry, grandeur, and organizational ability demonstrated by the spectacles of suffrage. Both militant suffragettes and constitutional suffragists quickly surpassed their initial theatrical efforts: for example, on 9 February 1907, three thousand women braved the rain and mud to march from Hyde Park to Exeter in the NUWSS's famous Mud March; by 13 June 1908 the numbers of marchers rose to at least ten thousand in a procession planned by the NUWSS. The pageants increased in size and beauty: on 21 June 1908 the WSPU presented their Woman's Sunday procession, an enterprise that involved thirty thousand women marching in seven processions (having trained into London on thirty special trains) and drew a crowd surpassing a quarter of a million spectators. Such efforts culminated in the Women's Coronation Procession of 17 June 1911, a collective endeavor in which militants and constitutionalists together brought Edwardian pageantry, imperialistic and nationalistic discourses, and invented traditions to feminist ends.[10]

The pageants of the suffragists and suffragettes brought together feminism, advertising, spectacle, and commodity culture in a variety of ways. Both militant and constitutionalist women performed a hybrid form of femininity, blending the image of womanly womanhood with the spectacle of activist women in the street and thus revealed their hope that traditional notion of femininity on display could be combined with traditional notions of citizenship. They manipulated the codes of a commodity culture that functions through exhibition by using storefronts and sandwich boards, by selling images of their leaders as radical celebrities, by marketing feminism through advertising the proper attire for a demonstration.[11] And, although they resisted representing themselves as "hyperfeminine" and saw limitations in the alignment of feminism with fashion culture,[12] the suffragettes cultivated a delicate relationship between activism and fashionable femininity, developing what I will call an "ornamental body."

However, that ornamental body was soon transformed into a docile body that rejected beauty, display, and visibility. Between 1903, when Emmeline Pankhurst and her daughters Christabel, Sylvia, and Adela founded their militant organization, the Women's Social and Political Union, and 1914, when they turned that organization to the task of supporting England at the onset of the Great War, the WSPU moved its location and articulation of struggle from the street to the prison, from pageantry to hunger strikes. It is impossible, of course, to transform what were in reality a series of shifts and simultaneous activities into a stark division between street and prison. For example, when the WSPU first launched what was to be a continuous, though varied, militant campaign, it was through an engagement with the prison: in 1905 Annie Kenney and Christabel Pankhurst interrupted a Liberal meeting at the Manchester Free Trade Hall and were subsequently arrested. That arrest put suffrage on the front pages of the daily papers. However, my point is that, as more and more women entered the prisons, street theater and its ornamental body gradually gave way to narratives of torture and their textualized and technologized bodies in the discourse of suffrage.[13] To understand this shift we must envision the prison as a space that invites and refuses the gaze simultaneously, and we must recognize the ways in which the prison enables a reproduction of the violation of the female body.

The story of the imprisonment, hunger striking, and forcible feeding of English suffragettes has been told many times but deserves to be repeated here. Briefly: on 5 July 1909, WSPU member Marion Wallace Dunlop, in prison for stamping a passage from the Bill of Rights on the wall of St. Stephen's Hall, began a hunger strike. Dunlop protested the criminal status assigned imprisoned suffragettes and insisted that, as citizens engaged in a political war, the suffragettes be awarded the privileges granted to political prisoners: namely, first-division status, the ability to send and receive mail, the ability to wear civilian clothing, and freedom from the rule of silence.[14] (The government's refusal to grant the suffragettes first-division status further demonstrated the incompatibility of femininity and citizenship as traditionally conceived—indeed, antisuffragists argued that the suffragettes' very imprisonment made them unworthy of citizenship.) The hunger strike swiftly became an official strategy for the WSPU, enabling suffragettes to short-cut the government's desire to separate activists from their leaders and isolate members of the militant organization.[15] By 24 September 1909, Gladstone, the home secretary, ordered tube feeding at His Majesties' request, and the WSPU members Mary Leigh and Charlotte Marsh became the government's first victims. Hundreds of women were forcibly fed over the next five years while physicians, government officials, suffragists, and concerned citizens debated the ethics of forcible feeding in the pages of the daily newspapers. In feminist journals, women tallied the numbers of activists imprisoned and published firsthand accounts of tube feeding for their readership. Concerned about the press the government received over the issue, yet determined that the militants would not "make martyrs" of themselves, Home Secretary McKenna introduced the Prisoners' Temporary Discharge Act in 1913 (renamed by suffragettes the Cat and Mouse Act), which forced women to leave the prison when their lives were in danger, only to be reimprisoned once the government decided the suffragettes had regained their health.[16] The Cat and Mouse Act worked effectively to extend the parameters of the prison and continue the disciplining of suffragettes recovering in friends' homes, private nursing homes, or their own bedrooms.

The terms *ornamental body* and *functional body* place the bodies constructed during the suffrage campaign's street theater and theater of punishment within a larger history of the evolution of modernist obsessions. Peter Wollen locates an ornamental and oriental modernism (exhibited in the popularity of Paul Poiret, Leon Bakst, and Henri Matisse) that precedes modernism's movement to function, mechanism, and technologism (exhibited finally in Fordism and Taylorism).[17] The ornamental/oriental designs of the Russian Ballet, Poiret's costumes for his Thousand and Second Night fête, and Matisse's odalisques defined a modern body without rejecting decoration. Thus these designers provide a striking midpoint on modernism's map: "To use Veblen's terms, an art of the leisure class, dedicated to conspicuous waste and display, gave way to an art of the engineer, precise, workmanlike and production-oriented."[18] If we follow Wollen's reading of the role of ornament in the development of modernism, we find an ornamental body of suffrage that positions the spectacular suffragette as celebrity, as decorative body, as exhibit. The association, then, is with surface, not depth, and consumption, not production. And if the ornamental bodies of women in the street maintain dominant notions of femininity while putting those notions to radically different purposes, the ornamental body of suffrage functions as a fetish and is positioned as object of a public gaze, thus accommodating "proper" (i.e., middle-class) images of femininity.[19]

The ornamental body, in modernism's history, gives way to a functional body, which we will see in suffrage's strategies as a mechanical, docile, and disciplined body. This is not to say that the ornamental body was not disciplined. Through corsets, luxury, finery, the ornamental body is made into a fetish that takes on the labor of fashionable display after the Great Masculine Renunciation. As Wollen points out, the functional body requires discipline of another sort: a regime of health ("exercise, sports, diet") disciplines the modern functional body through internal mechanisms.[20] The consuming feminine body, disciplined through corsets and artifice, is transformed into a new "female form," "unconfined, regulated and stripped down" (26). Wollen's essay places the feminine body in the center of a modernist (masculine) shift from ornament to function; however, limited as it is to the preoccupations of male designers, artists, and theorists, his narrative cannot fully explain the contributions female activists may have made to the creation of those categories.

Suffrage demands that we seek additional terms to consider the various relations that existed between feminist representations of the body and the struggle for equal representation in the public sphere. The disintegration of the female body in prison dramatizes the disintegration of both the dream of citizenship and the fantasy of equal participation in a traditional public sphere won through the (pleasing) performances of the ornamental feminist body.[21] In suffrage, functionalism's renunciation of ornament is exaggerated so that the modern, healthy body is "stripped down" to the point of ill heath. Through forcible feeding, the consuming feminine body is transformed into a machinelike, ascetic, feminine body that produces new meanings only when, through the rejection of consumption, it denies its conventional status as reproductive. The event of forcible feeding in which the female body is both violated and nourished by a "long red tube" brings technology to the scene of female embodiment and destabilizes the category of "femininity"; that is, the maternal body, which presumably exists only to feed others, erases itself and is sustained by mechanical (and masculine) science. The effect is an uncanny double move, whereby the female body as ground is both underscored and upset: the experience of the body gives the feminist text its authenticity, but the feminist body is no longer conventionally "feminine." The government's forced feeding of suffragettes by machine attempts both to preserve the continuity of the body that breaks down and to reinscribe femininity as maternity—an attempt doomed to failure.

The discourse of the docile body that emerges from the prison after the forcible feedings of suffragettes establishes a new structure of spectacularity, one in which not just the pleasing display of femininity, but also the "authentic" experiences of the body in pain, become performative.[22] Mary Leigh's narrative, published as the pamphlet *Fed by Force*, brings together the brutal dyad of performativity/authenticity in the experience of the body:

> [T]he wardresses forced me on the bed and the two doctors came in with them, and while I was held down a nasal tube was inserted. It is two yards long, with a funnel at the end—there is a glass junction in the middle to see if the liquid is passing. The end is put up the nostril, one one day, and the other nostril the other. Great pain is experienced during the process, both mental and physical. . . . The sensation is most painful—the drums of the ear seem to be bursting, a horrible pain in the throat and the breast. The tube is pushed down 20 inches. . . . The after effects are a feeling of faintness, a sense of great pain in the diaphragm or breast bone, in the nose and the ears. The tube must go below the breast bone, though I can't feel it below there.[23]

The narration of forcible feeding, which is more than a transcription of the transparent evidence of the body, destabilizes the category of "experience." That is, the scene of forcible feeding is already a gruesome performance when it takes place, a calculated and determined event that exists for the sake of its reproductive potential, and that exists for its audience only through its reproductions. Narratives like Leigh's organize the event of forcible feeding for disorderly woman and physician alike, scripting the oppressor and giving a plot to the oppressed. Thus the confessions of the tortured woman do more than intensify the publication of the private body (that is, making the internal external): they present a narrative that turns the dwindling body into an excessive textuality, allowing the event of forcible feeding to be restaged in autobiographies, plays, pageants, novels, and letters.

It is at the level of *re*production that the transformation in suffrage's *strategies* reveals itself. In creating the pageants of the campaign, the suffragettes devoted great energy to producing events that were then managed, regulated, and described by the public press. That is to say, the suffragettes performed for an audience who then controlled the reproduction of the event. (I should modify this claim—the pageants were described in the pages of suffrage journals as well as the daily newspapers.) The onset of forcible feeding and its textualization shifted the suffragettes' energy from producing events to reproducing them and managing the circulation of those reproductions. And the shift from ornamental to docile bodies required two different types of production: the suffragettes altered their subversive strategies from creating spectacles to restaging spectacular events in discourse.

The suffragettes reworked the feminist body as they narrated their encounters with forcible feeding, and that reworking carries the traces of modernist anxieties about the factory, its production of new (mechanized) social subjects, and the impact of technologies on the public sphere and the role of the citizen. In part, we can see those anxieties demonstrated in the suffragette's (proto-Foucauldian) descriptions of institutional discipline. However, as we shall see, the suffragettes' restaging of the body's torture also exploits the revolutionary possibilities contained in the distribution of information enabled by mechanical reproduction, revolutionary possibilities imagined by Walter Benjamin.

It is from Michel Foucault that we have a history of the disciplined subject produced through institutions of surveillance and management like the prison. In *Discipline and Punish,* he traces the ways in which the prison and the judicial system develop a docile body that is "subjected, used, transformed, and improved" through an "uninterrupted, constant coercion . . . exercised according to a codification that partitions as closely as possible time, space, movement."[24] Foucault's history makes sense of forcible feeding as a disciplinary institutional practice to which women were subjected in English prisons like Holloway and Walton Gaol; indeed, as it traces the ways in which the normativity of the public sphere is produced through disciplinary technologies, this history clarifies the suffragettes' attempt to read the issue of citizenship through the lens of the prison. Yet, though *Discipline and Punish* could describe the containment of rebellious femininity, this description of discipline cannot make sense of the *reproduction* of the prison in countless narratives of imprisonment and forcible feeding circulated through feminist journals, daily newspapers, letters, speeches and autobiographies.[25] In other words, how do performances and reproductions of docility provide (modern) strategies that resist the disciplinary project?

Feminist narratives of imprisonment and forcible feeding like Lady Constance Lytton's autobiography, *Prisons and Prisoners,* also mark the humiliating rituals of public baths and sartorial control that reposition individual activists as anonymous criminals.[26] That is to say, suffrage autobiographies (like Foucault's text) diagnose the habits, rituals, and modes of surveillance that produce the social subject. However, the suffragettes' narrations of these events become rituals themselves, dress rehearsals that produce a counterdiscourse as suffragettes represent their first encounters with the prison. The autobiographies of Hannah Mitchell, Christabel Pankhurst, Kitty Marion, and Sylvia Pankhurst all include descriptions of entering the prison that foreground the repositioning of female activist as "common criminal" through sartorial codes. Their descriptions are much like Lytton's, here detailing a prison shirt:

> It was very short, reaching barely below the hips and low at the neck, and the patches set in at random had added variety and counter design in many directions. It looked like the production of a maniac. For propaganda purposes it was an absolutely priceless garment and I determined that, if possible, it should accompany me out of the prison, for the enlightenment of those critics who are appalled at the leniency of the prison treatment of Suffragettes. (*PP* 78)

Lytton's interest does not lie with the garment itself and the role it plays in her subjection; rather, she contemplates the role it will serve in her feminist reproduction. As we shall see, the prison narratives written by suffragettes are constantly working out the performative predicament of their confinement. Separated from their audience, isolated from their colleagues, the suffragettes performed before invisible eyes and struggled to translate their experience into representation. That is, in moving from street to prison, they left the realm of the exhibit ("who wins the eye wins all") and arrived at a realm of surveillance, voyeurism, and invisibility. They countered that invisibility with autobiography, bringing life writing to the service of feminist activism, bending the contours of individual experience to the shape of a collective good.[27]

Much of Lytton's text concentrates not on the management of the female body but on the discipline of the female subject through a twofold scopic regulation, a regulation that develops official surveillance of the prisoner while controlling the prisoner's own gaze. For example:

> But my recollection of the two or three hours spent in this cell are vague and shadowy. I was at the end of my tether, and the craving to be alone overtopped everything else. . . . I noticed for the first time a curious aperture in the thick wall to the left of the door. A piece of grained glass near to the passage side of this hole shielded the light which was lit from outside. The cell was thus lit up with rays as from a bull's eye lantern. These details interested me very much. I was fascinated in a grim sort of way by the "eye" in the door of which I had heard so much. An oval wedge-shaped indentation in the thick nail-studded door, at about the height of one's head, was finished off in the centre by a small circular bit of glass about the size of a large eye-glass. On the passage side of the door this was overlaid with a bit of wood which could be turned aside like the flap over a key-hole, for the warders and others to take a look at the prisoner, unobserved, whenever they chose. (*PP* 69)

The cells are constructed to enable official scrutiny of the female prisoners, so that the suffragettes come to think of themselves as potential objects of a judgmental and punishing gaze. At the same time the prisoners' ability to look is regulated by wardresses who deny them access to a mutual gaze: "As a prisoner, it was almost impossible to look in the eyes of my keepers, they seemed to fear that direct means of communication; it was as if the wardresses wore a mask" (*PP* 75).

The prison, as public institution, disciplines the disorderly female body through enforced habit and surveillance, thereby becoming both a concentrated version of the street—a place where violence against dissenting women and official scrutiny can be more effectively managed—and the street's negation because the prison secludes the spectacular suffragettes from their audience. However, it is in their seclusion that the suffragettes become an intensely effective public sensation: Emmeline Pethick-Lawrence noted that "every prisoner means a harvest of converts."[28] How are we to make sense of the reversal that transforms cloistered woman into an exhibition? Lytton's text provides a clue, for it is, I think, through theatricalizing the prison, countering surveillance with performance, indeed transforming the category of experience into performance, that suffragette's discourse takes over and transforms the labor of constructing and representing the disciplined female body. Foucault has suggested that in the history of the prison the public spectacles of torture, execution, and the display of the mutilated criminal body give way to the invisible and institutional confinement, regulation, and surveillance of the imprisoned. This chronology provides a central question for a discussion of suffrage: how are we to understand the prison as a space that comes to exist for the suffragettes as a space to be represented?

The discourse of forcible feeding reworks the structure of performative activism established through the ornamental body in the first half of the suffrage campaign. If pageantry turns on the pleasing display of the decorative body, the discourse of forcible feeding refuses the transparency of the visible, undoes femininity as a natural category, and transforms "experience" into a category of performance. Rather than giving onlookers a spectacular activism represented through marches and pageants, the discourse of forcible feeding gives us a series of uncanny reduplications as woman after woman transcribes her "experience," each narrative constructed by the last and constructing the next. This is a feminist form of reproduction that takes over the work of duplication and circulation rather than staging a theatrical event for public consumption. Surveillance, the tool of containment and management for Foucault, is met by performance, creating the spectacle of the docile body.

Although it is often difficult to discern the differences between the techniques of displaying the ornamental body and restaging the sensational victimized body, it is in the issue of *re*production that the differences lie. Where the street theater of pageantry seems to decline in its effects through repetition, the event of forcible feeding depends on repetition for its effect (it is a kind of serialization).[29] Indeed, repetition is not the problem but the solution. The work of the pageants that theatricalize the prisoners or of the full-scale reproduction of a prison cell featured at the 1909 Women's Exhibition is to reproduce and make visible something prior, hidden, secret.[30] The narratives that restage the event of forcible feeding work differently: the various documents of bodily invasion foreground the issue of reduplication by binding together the mode of their own mechanical production and the new feminist strategies of repetition— feeding women into the prison as if on a conveyer belt.

This new form of feminist spectacle was met with both sympathy and condemnation, the latter demonstrated most forcibly in Teresa Billington-Greig's labeling the suffragettes' tactics a "spectacular suffrage show." Her critique of suffrage breaks into two parts: pre- and postprison. The period that preceded imprisonment was carnivalesque, characterized by the press and public as "a kind of hysterical hooliganism finding an outlet by variety show methods" (*MS* 163). Though suffragettes were "given Press notice on the same plane as that given to smart criminals and self-boomed variety performers," their outsider status made them uniquely capable of articulating revolt (163). Looking with nostalgia at the unregulated revolution of the period that preceded imprisonment, Billington-Greig seems to recoil from both organized rebellion and modern methods of reproduction. After the Pankhursts began to "ape" rebellion through deliberate imprisonments, activists lost their carnivalesque authenticity (and their status as outlaws) in the process of performing the part of injured femininity. As Billington-Greig tells it, suffragettes leaving the prisons entered a drawing-room theater.

> We were now met with unhealthy hero-worship and exaggerated devotion. New members tended to worship us rather than to understand and co-operate with us. The Press found sudden explanations for, and extenuations of, our unruly conduct. The pose of propriety was made almost inevitable by the obvious shock of surprise which showed itself when we were beheld in the social circles that had been barred against us. "These militant suffragettes are actually ladies!" was the gasping cry; and straightway most of us became ladies again and the rebel woman was veneered over or given hasty burial. (164)

Finally, in Billington-Greig's reading, spectacular activism based itself on a model of artificial reproduction so that the prison became a factory producing "artificial martyrs." Thus, the fatal flaw: the performance of victimization hides the British public *and the feminist activist* from the reality of "actual" suffering and prevents "authentic" revolution. What Billington-Greig condemns is the "small pettiness, the crooked course, the double shuffle between revolution and injured innocence" that necessarily accompany the project of advertising feminism (138).

It is the alignment of militancy, imprisonment, and advertisement that is particularly instructive, for this alignment indicates the ways in which the suffragettes took up the methodology of a technological society and introduced reduplication as an organizational strategy. Recalling her years working in the WSPU under Christabel Pankhurst, Mary

Richardson remembers Pankhurst as the consummate businesswoman, inaugurating a new mode of production.

> It was Christabel's genius, too, which inaugurated many of the new methods which we used and which, in years to come, were adopted by progressive business firms. She publicised the importance of publicity. She initiated the group system whereby one chief superintended each department and was responsible only to her. We had no argumentative committees in our organization. Everyone knew her job and did it.[31]

And when Teresa Billington-Greig critiques the WSPU for producing "artificial martyrs," she represents Pankhurst as more than businesswoman—she almost sees her as a factory owner.

> The very virtues of the movement have become dangerous to women; it is sapping their independence, their self-control, their scorn of small and dishonest things. It is blinding their eyes with passion and devotion. It is making them into tools. As a result of the system of autocracy great numbers of the militant women have ceased thinking, have ceased to feel the need for thinking, have become mere receptive vessels. Unstimulated and armed by original thought their advocacy is marked by crudity and ignorance. Half the suffragette speakers one hears reveal an amazing barrenness of matter and an utter lack of individual ratiocination. They repeat parrot-wise the speeches of other speakers. They make use of statements of which they do not know the origin and of which they cannot supply the proof. In the political world they play the game of follow-the-leader. (MS 196–97)

For Billington-Greig, the militant suffragettes become purely mechanized through their involvement with the WSPU; losing the means of independent thinking and articulation, they are emptied of substance, they become tools. Part of the machine that advertises the feminism upon whose behalf they labor, the suffragettes are truly docile, technologized bodies.[32]

> This policy has been put into practice; victims have been provided to move the hearts of the people. . . . Those who from the early days have kept in their own hands the control of the militant suffrage organiza-

tion decided upon a policy of making victims—of creating them spe-
cially to meet the need. . . . They made it a policy of the society to train
women to seek martyrdom in order that they might pose later to
waken enthusiasm among other women and to stir the sympathy and
admiration of the multitude. They abandoned the natural way of producing the forces of revolution and devoted themselves to an artificial
one. (*MS* 241–42)

The prison becomes a factory producing bodies as signs of resistance.
From a certain angle of vision, then, Christabel Pankhurst was a Tay-
lorite manager, producing workers that were as "predictable, regulated,
and effective as the machine itself."[33] Although Pankhurst is conventionally seen as a militaristic leader (even a fascistic dictator), Billington-
Greig's text suggests another model—Pankhurst as an all-powerful
industrial magnate who manufactures identical, inseparable, and interchangeable suffragettes.

Performativity and reduplication are the problem for Billington-Greig:
they drain activism of authenticity. But performativity and reduplication
seem to be precisely what is significant, and modern, about both the
process of acquiring the experiences of imprisonment, starvation, and
forcible feeding and the transformation of those experiences into narrative. The suffragettes deliberately took up a modernist form of mechanical reproduction and substituted it for the one-time event, the pageant, of
suffrage's street theater. As a theorist of modernity, Walter Benjamin
contemplated the ways in which technological reproduction and mass-
cultural artifacts could be taken up for revolutionary purposes. Claiming
that modern art must be industrialized, he took seriously what
Billington-Greig condemned. Bringing Benjamin's insights to a description of forcible feeding reveals what is distinctly modern about the suffragette's radical tactics; specifically, his essay, "The Work of Art in the
Age of Mechanical Reproduction," suggests two ways of rereading
Billington-Greig's critique of the production of "artificial martyrs."[34]
First, Benjamin noticed that the methods of technical reproduction
extend the fitness for exhibition of a work of art, thus enabling closer and
increased contact with a mass audience (225). Second, Benjamin argued
that mechanical reproduction enabled a new, more political, form of art
that is organized around its very reproducibility:

for the first time in world history, mechanical reproduction emanci-
pates the work of art from its parasitical dependence on ritual. To an

ever greater degree the work of art reproduced becomes the work of art designed for reproducibility. From a photographic negative, for example, one can make any number of prints; to ask for the "authentic" print makes no sense. But the instant the criterion of authenticity ceases to be applicable to artistic production, the total function of art is reversed. Instead of being based on ritual, it begins to be based on another practice—politics. (224)

Benjamin's suggestion that mechanical reproduction extends the exhibit, and thus enables a greater intervention into the workings of a public sphere, can illuminate the relation of spectacular street theater to reproduced scenes of torture, for the event of forcible feeding exists only in (and for) its reproductions—there is no original; there are only retellings. The narratives of forcible feeding extend the spectacular suffrage show by bringing it to the public through the copy: "The techniques of technical reproduction can put the copy of the original into situations which would be out of reach for the original itself. It enables the original to meet the beholder halfway."[35] As Wollen points out, the copy works as a "shock" to the urban dweller's system: "the copy jostles us in a crowd of other copies."[36] Thus the suffragettes brought the copy of the (shocking) experience of forcible feeding, through the publication of first hand accounts, into the everyday life of their audience. And they were successful because their command of the mechanics of publication and circulation was intense: the WSPU journal *Votes for Women* circulated at twenty thousand copies by 1909 with receipts and expenditures standing at over twenty thousand pounds. By 1914 the annual income of the WSPU rose to over thirty-five thousand pounds.[37] In addition to the militant journal *Votes for Women*, which was transformed into *The Suffragette* and edited by Christabel Pankhurst after the WSPU's break with Emmeline and Frederick Pethick-Lawrence, the WSPU published pamphlets and fliers, and its members wrote letters to the editors of major newspapers. By 1911 the WSPU moved its Women's Press (a press dedicated to the publication and republication of feminist texts) to Charing Cross Road. This feminist-publication industry created a space for feminist speech in the public arena, hence the increased participation of working-class women in the genre of autobiography. With an audience ready to receive their work, a place for its publication, and willing hands devoted to the mechanics of distribution, women began to envision themselves as writing subjects, and as participants in a specialized, invigorated, discursive community.[38] Indeed, by pointing out the ways in which

mechanical reproduction integrates consumers into the practice of producing art objects ("Any man today can lay claim to being filmed),[39] Benjamin locates the possibilities for resistance in mass art and, by extension,
in spectacular feminism as a form of mass-culture product.

Moreover, like mass-cultural artifacts, the narratives of forcible feeding mark a transition from ritual use and authenticity to mediation, commodification, and multiplication. The original act/artifact of forcible
feeding is invisible and unavailable (the public cannot enter the prison
and witness the scene of forcible feeding); what is available for public
speculation is the reduplication of that scene of trauma. Indeed, the reduplications of narratives of forcible feeding, when taken as a subgenre,
exist as reproductions without an originary text: there is no possibility of
locating a single text that sets the standards for the genre and reproduces
itself through imitation. Like Benjamin's prints made from a photographic negative, to ask for an "authentic" first narrative makes no
sense.[40]

As I have argued elsewhere, repetition is built into the subgenre of
forcible-feeding narratives and is, in fact, the distinct sign of this variety
of feminist embodied writing.[41] The testimony of Mary Leigh quoted earlier supplies a detailed account of invasion that parallels the accounts of
Lady Constance Lytton, Sylvia Pankhurst, Mary Richardson, Kitty
Marion, Annie Kenney, and many other suffragettes who turned body
into text for the good of the "Cause." Each of these accounts is organized
by the principle of itemization so that the ornamental body is broken
down into body parts that suffer, as in Sylvia Pankhurst's account of the
effects of a hunger strike.[42]

One's mouth and throat are terribly parched. One's tongue is dry, hot
and rough, and thickly coated. The saliva becomes more and more
thick and yellow and a bitter tasting phlegm keeps coming up into
one's mouth. It is so nasty that it makes one retch violently, as though
one were going to be sick, but sick one cannot be.

The urine is each day more scanty. It is thick and dark, and passed
with difficulty. The bowels do not move during the whole time one is
in prison.

There is great pain in the small of the back, pain in the chest, and a
sharp stinging liver pain in the right breast. Gripping pains come suddenly in the stomach and abdomen.

One sees each day that one has grown thinner, that the bones are showing out more and more clearly, and that the eyes are grown more hollow.[43]

The reproducibility of the experience is built into the event, which is, in effect, a string of *repeated* horrors. Mary Richardson's pamphlet, *Tortured Women: What Forcible Feeding Means: A Prisoner's Testimony*, foregrounds the number of times various suffragettes had suffered forcible feeding: Grace Roe over 160 times; Ansell 130 times; Mary Spencer over 120 times.[44] The principle of repetition governs the Cat and Mouse Act as well, so that the public watches English suffragettes enter and exit the prison as if on a turnstile—staggering out, dragged back in. But *Tortured Women* does more to foreground the significance of reduplication for suffrage narratives, for the document itself enacts a process of repetition. *Tortured Women,* a pamphlet of only four pages, is divided into a subjective "Letter" and an objective "Report." Despite their distinctive titles, the two halves mirror one another as a comparison of two quotations, the first from the "Letter," the second from the "Report," reveals.

It is a marvel to me how some of the others hold on, though they apparently have not the comfort of so innate a contact with active things. Grace suffers extremely from pain in her nose, throat and stomach all day and night, says she feels as if the tube were always in her body. That mentally this is telling on her and she sometimes feels as if something would crack in her brain.

Her worst suffering is mental, really, as she feels as if the tube were always in her body: that she is being constantly fed day and night. She cannot get rid of this feeling. She thinks she will collapse utterly when she comes out.

Although the "Letter" reveals the impact of Grace Roe's suffering on the speaker ("It is a marvel to me"), both "Letter" and "Report" insist on translating the experience of forcible feeding for an uninitiated public. Victims are statistical subjects (who appear in weekly charts in *The Suffragette* that calculated the number of imprisoned women and the length of their stay, whose injuries are documented in WSPU pamphlets) and unique, suffering individuals whose pain represents that of a group but cannot be adequately translated through a group account.

Thus the recirculation and representation of information is primary, for it reminds readers that the suffering is ongoing and duplicates the persistence of horror hidden within the prison walls. Take as an example the forcible feeding of Lady Constance Lytton/Jane Warton: that event generated speeches to Parliament delivered by her brother, Lord Lytton, speeches to suffragettes delivered by Lytton herself, articles written for *Votes for Women,* and finally the autobiography *Prisons and Prisoners,* written slowly and painfully with Lytton's left hand after she suffered the stroke that resulted from forcible feeding.[45] The recirculation of narratives of imprisonment flood the city with injured female voices; as Mary Richardson said of the militant activities of the WSPU in general, "we were everywhere."[46]

This emphasis on reproduction makes sense of the linkage suffragettes draw between the act of writing and the violation of their bodies. As bodies become texts that carry the traces of violation and record the histories of rebellion, suffragettes contemplate the project of writing the body—indeed, the project of writing itself.

> The effort to sit still, to do nothing, not to create anything with hands or brain, is almost superhuman to a woman—a woman who is accustomed to fill every moment of the day to overflowing. The only relief is her slate, and the prisoner takes it up and writes some diary of the day's events.
>
> First she has to rub out that of the day before, and with the rubbing out comes a sense of desolation. There is no excitement in the new now the old has gone, and the slate is soon filled even with the minutest writing she can achieve: it is a relief to let out the smallest thought; but it is soon over, and she is artist enough to hate rubbing that out just yet.[47]

What Helen Gordon notices is that the project of writing the body is both something to live for and an enliving practice denied the prisoner. In the prison, the suffragette cannot accumulate writings; anything she constructs will be erased—the "no surrender" Kitty Marion writes on her wall with soap scrubbed out the next day, the diary chalked onto the small tablet rubbed out for a new text. The act of writing a full account, a coherent protest, is deferred until the weakened body makes its way out of the prison, transferring its frailty into forceful words.[48]

In a section of her autobiography entitled "I Write with Red Ink,"[49]

Lady Constance Lytton records an attempt to trace her resistance on the body so that it cannot be erased: taking a needle, and then a hair pin, she begins to carve "Votes for Women" into her chest and up onto her face. She is found by the prison wardresses before the message is finished (only the V is victoriously carved into her chest) but she does enough to reposition her "observed" body in political discourse. Her confrontation with the Senior Medical Officer is telling.

> He and the ward superintendent, who ushered me into his presence and exposed the scratched "V" for his inspection, were evidently much put out. I felt all a craftsman's satisfaction in my job. . . . As I pointed out to the doctor, it had been placed exactly over the heart, and visibly recorded the pulsation of that organ as clearly as a watch hand, so that he no longer need be put to the trouble of the stethoscope. (*PP* 167)

Knowing that the physicians employed a medical gaze to limit hers (as an "observation case" Lytton, with her heart condition, could not join the other prisoners in the general cells), Lytton exaggerates her position as spectacle, literally engraving her body's secrets onto her skin so that medical inspection is made moot.

Lytton's attempt to trace rebellion onto the feminist body indicates the ways in which the docile body escapes its containment. Her body/text makes experiences of (self-)violation performative and theatrical: knowing that her body exists to be read, Lytton insists on controlling its meaning. Susan Bordo has argued that the disciplined bodies of anorexic women often subvert dominant images of femininity; their starved bodies exaggerate the slender body deemed valuable in dominant culture so that the hostile underpinnings of fashion culture are revealed.[50] Bordo's thesis shows us that the docile body produces alternative meanings even when the women carving their bodies into nothingness do not intend a feminist critique. It is a difficult but important step from the unintentional feminism of Bordo's anorexics to the activism of the militant suffragettes who performed a disciplined body. Covering that distance (to bridge the gap between a Foucauldian description of the ways in which technologies produce social subjects to a Benjaminian conception of the ways in which technologies are transformed through use) requires understanding the ways in which the suffragettes' self-representations negotiate and combine the analysis of subjection and the activity of resistance. What remains is a discussion of how these complex self-representations construct a collectivity out of isolated and disenfranchised voices.

The spectacular event of suffrage's pageantry enables and represents collectivity; the isolated, individualized, narratives of imprisonment should be the undoing of collectivity. Yet both the spectacle of feminist collectivity (the pageant) and the shared mode of self-representation of forcible feeding (the narrative that restages the event) image and imagine collective resistance.[51] The difference lies in the movement from the representation of collectivity to a collectivity forged through individual acts of (self)representation—the latter creating what Dick Hebdige calls a "spectacular subculture." For Hebdige the spectacular subculture both signifies disorder to outsiders and articulates a kind of community to itself.[52] I would argue that the reproduced narratives of embodiment extend the events that make collectivity visible by cultivating, through particular forms of embodied discourse, just such a spectacular subculture. The narratives of forcible feeding work not just as an advertisement of feminism to the outside world, but as a specific signifying practice that carries meaning for the suffragists themselves. As Hebdige argues when turning to contemporary subcultures, the various signifying practices of a spectacular subculture (sartorial style, modes of appropriation, specific forms of discourse) position the members of the subculture as something to be read, and work to cultivate a sense of group identity. It is, perhaps, through the notion of the spectacular subculture that we might distinguish the street theater of suffrage pageantry from the theater of torture of the narratives of forcible feeding, for though both practices enable the performance and creation of collectivity, one does so by performing collectivity, the other by making the collective discursive.

After the onset of forcible feeding, what the second half of the militant campaign gave London was the spectacle of torture, the representation of the punishment of the resistant female body and the detailed narratives of hunger, thirst, and a long red tube. The discourse and iconography of suffrage narrates and depicts the torture of forcible feeding to represent, record, and theatricalize not only the docile feminist body but the prison as a space of the female body. The prison, despite its regime of isolation and surveillance, enables a new form of collectivity, a spectacular subculture, that manifests itself through a feminist embodied discourse. Thus the prison is central for this reworking of feminist performance—despite its status as a space of concealment, official punishment, and withdrawal, it allows for a transformation of the very idea of advertising feminism. In Lytton's text, and in the testimonies of other feminists, the prison allows for a series of reduplications that reproduce and restage the disciplinary moment—the prison duplicates the privacy of the domestic sphere; the prison duplicates the conflicts of the street; and the street is transformed through images of imprisonment into a reproduction of the prison. The prison, which insists on the concealment and disciplining of the female body, instead produces new discourses of rebellion that write protest on the body, locating it within a modern collectivity.

NOTES

I wish to thank Stephen Watt for excellent guidance, and to thank Alison Booth, Ted Cachey, Julia Douthwaite, Holly Laird, Janet Lyon, Kathy Psomiades, and Ewa Ziarek for their insightful comments and conversations. David Doughan at the Fawcett Library, London Guildhall University, provided crucial assistance in locating testimonies of forcible feeding. This research is made possible in part by support from the Institute for Scholarship in the Liberal Arts, College of Arts and Letters, University of Notre Dame.

1. Kitty Marion, typescript autobiography, Box 639, 7/YYY6, Fawcett Library, London Guildhall University, 259.

2. Quoted in Lisa Tickner, *The Spectacle of Women: Imagery of the Suffrage Campaign, 1907–1914* (Chicago: University of Chicago Press, 1988), p. 98.

3. I am grateful to Janet Lyon for pointing out the ways in which histories of suffrage, particularly Tickner's, trace the evolution of feminist activism in terms of a *decline* from spectacle to militant activism; see her essay "Women Demonstrating Modernism," *Discourse* 17, no. 2 (Winter 1994–95): 6–25.

4. For this type of reading, see Andrew Rosen, *Rise Up Women! The Militant Campaign of the Women's Social and Political Union, 1903–1914* (London: Routledge, 1974); Mary Jean Corbett, *Representing Femininity: Middle-Class Subjectivity in Victorian and Edwardian Women's Autobiographies* (New York: Oxford University Press, 1992). Also see Jane Marcus, whose reading of militant activism, sartorial display, and modes of female identification as feminist fetishism does much to complicate discussions of the theatrical nature of suffrage: "The Asylums of Antaeus: Women, War, and Madness—Is there a Feminist Fetishism?" in *The New Historicism,* ed. H. Aram Veeser (New York: Routledge, 1989), pp. 132–51.

5. Teresa Billington-Greig, *The Militant Suffrage Movement: Emancipation in a Hurry* (1911, reprinted in *The Non-Violent Militant: Selected Writings of*

Teresa Billington-Greig, ed. Carol McPhee and Ann FitzGerald (New York: Routledge and Kegan Paul, 1987). Subsequent references appear parenthetically in the text, abbreviated *MS.* Billington-Greig began her career as a member of the Independent Labor Party, and was instrumental in the famous first split in the WSPU. One of the WSPU's first members, she joined Charlotte Despard and other suffragettes in a formal protest over the Pankhursts' tactics in 1907. The split was both political (Christabel had broken with the ILP and was drifting rightward, while Billington-Greig wished to cultivate ties to Labour) and ideological (Billington-Greig charged that the Pankhursts ran in a less-than-democratic fashion an organization that putatively sought to gain democratic rights for women). Out of the split came a new *democratic* militant organization, the Women's Freedom League, with Charlotte Despard elected president. Between the years 1905 and 1914 Billington-Greig developed a theory of nonviolent radicalism, a theory aimed at a complete social revolution; that is to say, she set her sights beyond the vote. Her ambitious vision placed her in an odd political position; she twice joined feminist organizations (the WSPU and the WFL) only to leave them in frustration. In 1911, after leaving both groups, she published a treatise critical of the militant suffrage movement that concentrated on the rhetorical and cultural productions of Emmeline and Christabel Pankhurst and on the actions of the WFL. Her treatise, *The Militant Suffrage Movement: Emancipation in a Hurry,* takes a rigorous look at the problem of feminist articulation, paying particular attention to those discourses and staged events that attempt to popularize feminist causes.

6. Teresa Billington-Greig's reading of the failure of spectacular politics predicts and predates the critiques of Marxist theorist Guy Debord, who traces the ways in which spectacle can only work to conscript social subjects into commodity culture, annihilating any possibilities for resistance, in *Society of the Spectacle* (1967; Detroit: Black and Red, 1983).

7. Thus I am locating myself between discussions of suffrage's pageantry as mass-culture artifact and of militant activism as avant-garde practice. For the former, see Tickner, *The Spectacle of Women.* For the latter, see Janet Lyon, "Militant Discourse, Strange Bedfellows: Suffragettes and Vorticists before the War," *Differences* 4, no. 2 (1992): 100–133.

8. Tickner's history, *The Spectacle of Women,* is devoted to the issue of feminist visual representations, especially as they appear in the street; Rosen's history, *Rise Up Women!* is focused on the practices of the Women's Social and Political Union. For other histories of the various suffrage organizations and their methods of persuasion, see Les Garner, *Stepping Stones to Women's Liberty: Feminist Ideas in the Women's Suffrage Movement, 1900–1918* (Rutherford, N.J.: Fairleigh Dickinson University Press, 1984); Brian Harrison, *Prudent Revolutionaries: Portraits of British Feminists between the Wars* (Oxford: Clarendon Press, 1987); Sandra Stanley Holton, *Feminism and Democracy: Women's Suffrage and*

Reform Politics in Britain, 1900–1918 (Cambridge: Cambridge University Press, 1986); Susan Kingsley Kent, *Sex and Suffrage in Britain, 1860–1914* (Princeton: Princeton University Press, 1987); Midge Mackenzie, *Shoulder to Shoulder: A Documentary* (1975; rpt. New York: Vintage Books, 1988); Martha Vicinus, "Male Space and Women's Bodies: The English Suffragette Movement," in *Women in Culture and Politics: A Century of Change*, ed. Judith Friedlander et al. (Bloomington: Indiana University Press, 1986), pp. 209–22.

9. Tickner writes: "With elegant sleight of hand, women responded to the accusation that they were 'making a spectacle of themselves' by doing precisely that, in full self-consciousness and with great skill and ingenuity. They were indeed part of the spectacle, but they also produced and controlled it; as active agents they need not passively endure the gaze of onlookers. . . . Their bodies were organized collectively and invested politically and therefore resistant to any simply voyeuristic appropriation" (*The Spectacle of Women*, p. 81). My description of the pageantry of the suffragettes derives from Tickner's reading; see especially her chapter entitled "Spectacle," pp. 55–148.

10. Note that for Tickner, the Women's Coronation Procession signals the end of spectacular politics: "With it, they [WSPU and constitutionalists] reached the limit of public spectacle not just as a political device, but as a practical possibility, and they never attempted to organize in this way or on this scale again" (*The Spectacle of Women*, p. 122).

11. The readings of the entanglement of feminist activism with commodity culture are varied. Tickner asks us to pay attention to the ways in which suffrage discourse was forced to function within the limits of available discourses of femininity and methods of circulation. Advertising feminism is a necessity, and her focus is on the ways in which feminist propaganda made itself available to a mass audience. Les Garner, on the other hand, argues that the militant suffragettes especially cut themselves off from working-class activists through a conflation of feminine consumerism and feminist activism: "What could working women have thought of the advertisements in *Votes for Women* and *The Suffragette*? These implored readers to shop at the exclusive Derry & Toms (*Votes for Women* November 19, 1909), or to buy fur coats at a mere 195 guineas (*Suffragette* October 18, 1912:12)—on a rough calculation about eight years' earnings on a working woman's average wage" (*Stepping Stones*, p. 47).

12. See Katrina Rolley on the relationship between feminism and fashion culture: "As well as being a central preoccupation in the WSPU's relations with the public and media, appearance was also vital to the Union's members. Many women were suffragettes in defiance of their families, their 'natural' impulses, and even the law. To counter this they needed an extremely positive image both of the WSPU and of themselves as members" ("Fashion, Femininity and the Fight for the Vote," *Art History* 13, no. 1 [1990]: 59).

13. But not completely. Katrina Rolley argues that as the militant WSPU went

underground, the new version of their journal, *The Suffragette,* exhibited a "modern" brand of femininity in its cover art. See "Fashion, Femininity," 56.

14. See F. W. Pethick-Lawrence on the struggle for first-division rights: "By common consent of civilized countries political prisoners receive different treatment from that of ordinary criminals. The object aimed at is not so much punishment as detention. They are accordingly generally allowed books, newspapers, writing materials, &c.; they are permitted to see their friends and to write to them. . . . *This practice of civilized nations, established by regular usage and defended by British Statesmen, is reversed by the present Liberal Government in dealing with the women who are their political opponents.* The Suffragettes have been put in prison in the second or third class and subjected to the indignities of ordinary criminals" ("Treatment of the Suffragettes in Prison," WSPU pamphlet No. 59, Pamphlet Collection, Fawcett Library, London Guildhall University).

15. See Christabel Pankhurst's discussion of the imprisonment of suffragettes: "I foresaw the day when the Government would imprison us, not for weeks or months, but for years, and by holding the leaders especially, in prison, would attempt to break and obliterate the movement. The hunger-strike, I felt, might be one of our measures in reserve for the frustration of such a policy" (*Unshackled: The Story of How We Won the Vote* [London: Hutchinson, 1959], pp. 134–35).

16. See the appendix attached to Jane Marcus's collection of militant essays for a record of Emmeline Pankhurst's imprisonments under the Cat and Mouse Act. They number ten releases and rearrests between April 3, 1913, and July 16, 1914. *Suffrage and the Pankhursts,* ed. Jane Marcus (London: Routledge and Kegan Paul, 1987), pp. 313–14.

17. For a discussion of an ornamental modernism, see Wollen's "Fashion/Orientalism/the Body," *New Formations* 1 (1987): 5–33; for a discussion of a mechanized modernism, see his companion piece, "Cinema/Americanism/the Robot," in *Modernity and Mass Culture,* ed. James Naremore and Patrick Brantlinger (Bloomington: Indiana University Press, 1991): 42–69.

18. Wollen, "Fashion/Orientalism/the Body," p. 5.

19. It is precisely this relation that Jane Marcus draws to our attention when she locates a form of feminist fetishism in suffrage's workings: "It seems to me that women's poster art, and its borderline status between commercial art and painting, should be as important to modern women's history as photography is to Modernism in general. Women naturally drew on commercial fashion art which was aimed at them and transformed it for political purposes—one might say they *translated semiotically the signs of commodity fetishism into a deliberate feminist fetishism*" ("The Asylums of Antaeus," p. 144). Also, Christabel Pankhurst detached her WSPU from Labour partly because the image of working-class women in the streets did little to promote her cause: "it was evident that the House of Commons, and even its Labour members, were more

impressed by the demonstrations of the feminine bourgeoisie than of the feminine proletariat" (quoted in Holton, *Feminism and Democracy,* p. 36).

20. Wollen, "Fashion/Orientalism/the Body," p. 26.

21. The issues here are complex: the ornamental historical bodies displayed in the streets of London in the Pageant of Great Women suggest that the public sphere merely requires expansion and can incorporate women into its workings: the history that runs from Sappho to Joan of Arc to Florence Nightingale to (presumably) the emancipated woman pretends to reconcile femininity and citizenship and supports the integrity of the public sphere. Yet, it is only through the celebrity status awarded suffrage leaders (Emmeline and Christabel Pankhurst, Emmeline Pethick-Lawrence) that the large collective event is made possible. The incompatibility of celebrity (the exception) and citizenship (the dream of equal participation) is played out not only in the public demonstrations of suffrage, but in the WSPU's support of a limited franchise and the organization's seeming indifference to the demands of working-class women. The examples of imprisonment and forcible feeding, which position woman as "common criminal" and mutilate her body, make visible that incompatibility and subvert the fantasy of an extended public sphere. I am grateful to Ewa Ziarek for discussing these issues; for a complex discussion of the intersection of femininity/technology/public sphere, see her essay "The Female Body, Technology, and Memory in 'Penelope,'" in the collection *Molly Blooms,* ed. Richard Pearce (Madison: University of Wisconsin Press, 1994).

22. For a contemplation of the performative nature of the category "experience," see Joan Scott's "Experience," in *Feminists Theorize the Political,* ed. Judith Butler and Scott (New York: Routledge, 1992), pp. 22–38.

23. Mary Leigh, *Fed by Force: How the Government Treats Political Opponents in Prison,* WSPU pamphlet No. 54, Pamphlet Collection, Fawcett Library, London Guildhall University.

24. Michel Foucault, *Discipline and Punish: The Birth of the Prison,* trans. Alan Sheridan (1975; New York: Vintage Press, 1979), pp. 136, 137.

25. Jana Sawicki has already brought Foucault's reading of the disciplined subject to a discussion of the intersection between technological reproduction and the female body; see her book, *Disciplining Foucault: Feminism, Power, and the Body* (New York: Routledge, 1991).

26. Constance Lytton, *Prisons and Prisoners: Some Personal Experiences by Constance Lytton and Jane Warton, Spinster* (1914; London: Virago Press, 1988). Subsequent references appear parenthetically in the text, abbreviated *PP.* Between 1908 and 1914, Lady Constance Lytton, daughter of a diplomat and sister to a member of the House of Lords, gradually involved herself in the Women's Social and Political Union. Though Lytton originally rejected the militant actions of the suffragettes, after studying the Union and its politics she became an active member of the organization—joining deputations, serving prison sentences, engaging

218 / Marketing Modernisms

in hunger strikes. Arrested twice as "Lady Constance Lytton," she became aware of the ways in which class differences affected her treatment as a suffragette. While other suffragettes at Holloway were treated with violence and disdain, some forcibly fed nearly to the point of death, Lytton was treated gently by officials, who were terrified of her family's power: she was deemed too weak to withstand the prison officials' "treatment" of forcible feeding. Determined to expose this kind of disparity, Lytton traveled to Liverpool disguised as "Jane Warton, Spinster," a "plain," lower-class suffragette, and was rearrested on January 14, 1910. After hunger-striking in Walton Gaol, Jane Warton underwent violent forcible feeding eight times, until prison officials began to suspect her true identity. For another reading of Lytton's autobiography, see Corbett, *Representing Femininity*, pp. 165–73. Also see Maud Ellmann, *The Hunger Artists: Starving, Writing, and Imprisonment* (Cambridge: Harvard University Press, 1993), p. 35.

27. Feminist theorists of autobiography have rejected discussions of isolated individual subjects. From the first, feminist critics of autobiography have resisted the idea of a coherent individual feminine subject tracing herself through life-writing. Either through discussions of alterity or intersubjectivity, feminist theorists have insisted that women write themselves through envisioning a relation with another: for the first, see Mary G. Mason, "The Other Voice: Autobiographies of Women Writers," in *Life/Lines: Theorizing Women's Autobiography*, ed. Bella Brodzki and Celeste Schenck (Ithaca: Cornell University Press, 1988), pp. 19–44; for the second, see Susan Stanford Friedman, "Women's Autobiographical Selves: Theory and Practice," in *The Private Self: Theory and Practice of Women's Autobiographical Writings*, ed. Shari Benstock (Chapel Hill: University of North Carolina Press, 1988), pp. 34–62. Poststructuralist theorists have dismantled the coherent (male) writing subject from another perspective: see Shari Benstock, "Authorizing the Autobiographical," in *The Private Self*; Sidonie Smith, *A Poetics of Women's Autobiography: Marginality and the Fictions of Self-Representation* (Bloomington: Indiana University Press, 1987); and Domna Stanton, "Autogynography: Is the Subject Different?" in *The Female Autograph: Theory and Practice of Autobiography from the Tenth to the Twentieth Century* (Chicago: University of Chicago Press, 1987), pp. 3–20. Only recently, however, have feminist critics moved from readings of individual authors to readings of collective feminine texts: see Regina Gagnier, *Subjectivities: A History of Self-Representation in Britain, 1832–1920* (New York: Oxford University Press, 1991); and Corbett, *Representing Femininity*.

28. Quoted in Rosen, *Rise Up Women!* p. 109.

29. The point is Tickner's: "Each new spectacle had, for its artistic and political effect (which were no longer quite the same thing), to transcend the last. To this end the tried and trusted formulae were reapplied (the nurses, the graduates, the prisoners' pageant was now almost 700 strong), but something different was needed too" (*The Spectacle of Women*, p. 124).

30. Indeed, this strategy of bringing the public eye to the private (taboo) realm of the prison may explain the entanglement Ray Strachey noticed between secrecy and exhibitionism in the WSPU: "'Deeds not Words' was the motto of the organization, and its deliberate policy was to seek sensational achievement rather than anything else. . . . [S]ince they [militants] deliberately put themselves in the position of outlaws dogged by the police, they were always wrapped round with secrecy and mystification, and planned surprises alike for their followers and for the public" (*The Cause: A Short History of The Women's Movement in Great Britain* [London: G. Bell and Sons, 1928], p. 310).

31. Mary Richardson, *Laugh a Defiance* (London: Weidenfeld and Nicolson, 1953), pp. 50–51.

32. For the significance of the factory to contemplations of the modern subject, see Wollen, "Cinema/Americanism/the Robot" and Mark Seltzer, *Bodies and Machines* (New York: Routledge, 1992).

33. Wollen, "Cinema/Americanism/the Robot," p. 43.

34. Walter Benjamin, "The Work of Art in the Age of Mechanical Reproduction," in *Illuminations,* ed. Hannah Arendt, trans. Harry Zohn (New York: Schocken Books, 1969). Jennifer Wicke brings Benjamin's discussion of mechanical reproduction to a reading of advertising. See *Advertising Fictions: Literature, Advertisement, and Social Reading* (New York: Columbia University Press, 1988), pp. 12–13.

35. Benjamin, "Work of Art," p. 200.

36. Wollen, "Cinema/Americanism/the Robot," p. 55.

37. See Tickner, *The Spectacle of Women,* and Rosen, *Rise Up Women!* for these statistics, passim.

38. See Marcus on the creation of a women's community: "At the height of the suffrage movement in 1911 there were twenty-one regular feminist periodicals in England, a women's press, a feminist bookshop, the Fawcett Library, and a bank run by and for women. The war decimated that impressive coalition" ("The Asylums of Antaeus," p. 136).

39. Benjamin, "Work of Art," p. 231.

40. Take as an example the images of forcible feeding that exist only as reproductions—as reenactments. See the artist's impression of forcible feeding originally published in the *Illustrated London News,* April 27, 1912, reproduced in Mackenzie, *Shoulder to Shoulder,* p. 123.

41. "Spectacular Confessions: 'How It Feels to Be Forcibly Fed,'" *Review of Contemporary Fiction* 13, no. 3 (1993): 70–88. Billington-Greig herself notices a similar repetition: "The purely personal story on 'I-went-to-prison' lines is re-told *ad nauseam* without historical or political background, philosophy or principle" (quoted in Harrison, *Prudent Revolutionaries,* p. 68).

42. By 1911 the conventions were so well established that Helen Gordon eschewed "details" for a discussion of "atmosphere": "it seems that in this sketch

I have left out details; but if so, it is in the effort to paint a certain picture, and I have used my power of selection with the distinct object of reproducing the atmosphere which surrounds the suffragette prisoner, especially when she is undergoing the last extreme of resistance and its attendant torture of forcible feeding. The details are now well known, but few can realize who have not undergone it the atmosphere that makes it into a torture" (*The Prisoner: An Experience of Forcible Feeding* [Letchworth: Garden City Press, 1911], p. v).

43. Quoted in Marcus, *Suffrage and the Pankhursts*, p. 259.

44. Suffragette Fellowship Collection, London Museum.

45. Take as another example a letter written by suffragette Katherine Getty onto a sheet of toilet paper, smuggled out of the prison for publication in the *Daily News*, then carefully placed in Maud Arcliffe-Sennett's collection of suffrage documents, a collection that functioned as a contemporary (private) history of the movement and functions as an archival resource today. See the Maud Arncliffe-Sennett Collection, British Library.

46. Richardson, *Laugh a Defiance*, p. 27.

47. Gordon, *The Prisoner*, pp. 14–15.

48. I am influenced here by Maud Ellmann's persuasive reading of the inverse relationship between bodies and texts in IRA prison writings. See *The Hunger Artists*, pp. 59–89.

49. See the manuscript, Suffragette Fellowship Collection, London Museum.

50. Susan Bordo, "Anorexia Nervosa: Psychopathology as the Crystallization of Culture," in *Feminism and Foucault: Reflections on Resistance*, ed. Irene Diamond and Lee Quinby (Boston: Northeastern University Press, 1988), pp. 87–117.

51. Corbett also notices that it is through autobiographical writings that imprisoned suffragettes recover the experience of collectivity: "Over time, it became one of the suffragettes' best weapons against the government: as an act of noncompliance, a protest against unfair imprisonment and unjust treatment, the hunger strike was an individual act that made, when undertaken by many, a powerful collective statement of solidarity" (*Representing Femininity*, p. 162).

52. Dick Hebdige, *Subculture: The Meaning of Style* (London: Methuen, 1979), pp. 100–102. I am not the first to bring a discussion of spectacular subcultures to earlier periods; see Rolley's "Fashion, Femininity" and Andrew Tolson, "Social Surveillance and Subjectification: The Emergence of 'Subculture' in the Work of Henry Mayhew," *Cultural Studies* 4, no. 2 (1990): 113–27.

Selling Taboo Subjects: The Literary Commerce of Gertrude Stein and Carl Van Vechten

Corrine E. Blackmer

> ... it is not improving, it is not amusing, it is not interesting, it is not good
> for one's mind. ... If this is the future, then the future is, as it very likely is,
> of the barbarians. But this is the future in which we ought not to be inter-
> ested.
>
> T. S. Eliot on Gertrude Stein's writing

The longtime personal and professional alliance between Gertrude Stein and her advocate, fellow author, and literary executor Carl Van Vechten represents, within literary modernism, an unparalleled instance of mutual cooperation, support, and good will between a woman and man of letters. This fact alone should qualify their relationship for the effort of appreciative understanding it has not thus far received, particularly since Van Vechten helped save Stein's writing from neglect in the years preceding and following her death. Their relationship, based on their mutual identification as subversive "ones" whose sexual identities made them reject societally defined feminine and masculine roles, found concrete expression in the advocacy of a pluralistic, nonhierarchical, and distinctly playful vision of modernism. Their project underscores the conservatism of male modernists such as Hemingway, Yeats, Faulkner, Eliot, and Pound, whose critical valorization and canonization often came at the direct expense of Stein, whose work was generally dismissed as offensively obscure, solipsistic, self-indulgent, or merely failed.

With the exception of a handful of iconoclastic writers and critics who, significantly, like Van Vechten, operated outside the academy, within the academy Stein was frequently positioned as the sphinxlike "Mother of Modernism," whose claims to genius were treated as pretentious and even infantile forms of self-advertisement. Academic criticism, moreover, often expressed an only thinly disguised fear of and animus toward her lesbianism.[1] This threat was contained by transforming Stein from an original literary Mother into an originary mothering figure whose primary value resided in her capacity to nurture and encourage the genius of her male modernist sons. The reformulation, repackaging, and simplification of such Steinian concepts as repetition within variation, self-contained movement, and the continuous present within, say, the works of Hemingway and Faulkner, excised the integral function that gender and sexuality played within her narrative, poetic, and critical practices. Within canonical male modernisms and earlier academic criticism, Stein became an object of literary exchange whose subversive sexuality served as an incitement to reconsolidate the male homosocial society of literary modernism and criticism.[2]

While the advent of poststructuralist, feminist, and queer criticism has brought perspectives and critical tools adequate to the measurement of Stein's achievement, Van Vechten has not fared well under any critical regime. This eclipsing of Van Vechten obscures understanding of the historical context in which both he and Stein elaborated narrative strategies and sexual vernaculars of queer existence not only capable of flying beneath the censor's radar but also, in Stein's case, of discarding the rules of referentiality and representation on which the battle between authors and censors was grounded. Apart from his advocacy of Stein, however, which is often reduced to naive boosterism bereft of substantial understanding of her literary project, Van Vechten is chiefly remembered as a photographer and the white male sponsor of the Harlem Renaissance. Few, either at that time or subsequently, have been able to read past the title of his 1927 bestseller *Nigger Heaven,* which refers to the segregated galleries of theaters and to black Harlem "looking down" at the spectacle of an all-white lower Manhattan. Although intended to arouse a sense of outrage over the injustices of racial segregation, this title has mainly succeeded in transforming Van Vechten himself into an object of scandal and embarrassment. In the move from substance to surface that Andy Warhol would later sardonically celebrate, the focus on Stein and Van Vechten shifted from the content of their work to the scandalous fascination of their personalities, as both became "famous for being famous."

Van Vechten's criticism, which has been dismissed as impressionistic and casual, helped to create audiences for neglected homosexual authors such as Ronald Firbank and Donald Evans, to popularize African-American culture, and to explicate and promote Stein's writing. As the precursor of the contemporary cultural critic, Van Vechten rejected the academic literary historian's practice of recounting a succession of dates and influences. Unlike modernist critics such as T. S. Eliot, F. R. Leavis, Edmund Wilson, and I. A. Richards, moreover, Van Vechten did not position himself as the steward of canonical traditions of Western culture that promised to rescue the reader from the "false gods" of modernity. While his criticism contains crucial elements of Paterian subjectivism, Van Vechten directs himself toward more inclusive, democratic, contemporary, and, above all, cosmopolitan cultural phenomena. Whereas Pater records his learned impressions of scholars of Greek antiquity like Winckelmann or High Renaissance art such as the Mona Lisa, Van Vechten dissolves the boundaries between high and popular culture. He gives equal attention and stature to Strauss's *Salomé* and Bessie Smith's blues; Stravinsky's *Firebird* and Scott Joplin's ragtime; Isadora Duncan and the cakewalk; Shakespeare and Yiddish theater; Ouida and Melville. As someone who has a personal investment in transforming settled cultural categories, Van Vechten strategically employed "originality" as his main criterion of excellence in the arts.

His novels, which lampoon moral earnestness, sexual prudery, racial intolerance, and "quick-fix" schemes of social amelioration, are particularly keen on the distinction between the disruptive originality of a lesbian writer like Stein and, for example, the nascent movie business, whose ersatz glamour and veneer of novelty conceal a bottom-line profit motive and social conservatism. Moreover, his novels expose the social practices that seem to liberate women and men but, in fact, offer them power at the expense of maintaining a facade of respectability and an ideology of romanticized, conventional heterosexuality that renders them victims. Furthermore, his narratives covertly represent the subversive potentials of queer sexuality in a world in which institutional heterosexuality enforces class, race, and gender power arrangements.

Stein, who had a shrewd understanding of the animosity and misconstruction her writing could evoke, selected Van Vechten as her literary executor, and, upon her death in 1946, he edited and introduced the *Selected Writings of Gertrude Stein,* which remains the best representative sampling of her work. He subsequently served as general editor of Yale University Press's eight volumes of her unpublished work. Moreover, in 1950, he arranged, with the assistance of Alice Toklas, for the first publication of Stein's early lesbian novella, *Q. E. D.,* which was slightly bowdlerized to disguise the identity of Stein's lover May

Bookstaver and titled *Things as They Are* after a line in the text. The publication of the original text in 1972 in *Fernhurst, Q. E. D., and Other Early Writings,* edited and introduced by Leon Katz, coincided with the emergence of the feminist and queer liberation movements, which created a discernible audience for Stein as a modernist lesbian author. These latter events served to gradually transform Steinian criticism into a field in which it has become increasingly difficult not to consider sexuality as central to her writing practices. How issues of gender and sexuality are handled in the criticism is an index of the changing aesthetic, social, and political valuations accorded women and queers in the past twenty years.

During the first half of the twentieth century, however, neither Stein nor Van Vechten could openly broach the subject of homosexuality without incurring censorship over their presumed "promotion" of criminalized sexual acts. In addition, both Stein and Van Vechten experienced an enormous chasm between their actual experiences as queer persons and the symbolic meanings attached to homosexuality by religious doctrine and medical sexology.[3] For example, Radclyffe Hall's melodramatic 1928 novel, *The Well of Loneliness,* which subscribed to Havelock Ellis's essentialist view of sexual inversion, pleaded for tolerance on the grounds that female homosexuals were "born that way," portrayed butch lesbians as "imitation" men, and underwent bruising censorship battles.[4] Furthermore, popularized versions of Freudian psychology positioned heterosexuality as the mature, adjusted state of adulthood and associated homosexuality with immaturity and infantile fixation. Thus, with the rare exceptions of novels such as *We Sing Diana* (1928) and *Torchlight to Valhalla* (1938), publishers demanded that authors pander to commercial interest in sensationalistic images of lesbians and demonstrate their moral disapprobation by representing them as maladjusted social outcasts.[5]

Confronted with censorship, stereotyping, and devaluation of lesbian sexuality, Stein responded by subverting the foundations of a linguistic and symbolic system that allied adult authority and propriety with male heterosexuality. Van Vechten, for his part, promoted Stein's cause and wrote novels that can be viewed as insider guides on how to covertly challenge and survive within heterosexist systems of domination. Hence, an array of social, legal, and cultural forces necessitated that Stein and Van Vechten enter the literary marketplace by thematizing the problematics of censorship, challenging dominant conceptions of literature, breaking down the opposition between high and popular culture, and blurring the linguistic boundary between metaphorical and literal treatments of sexuality. The fact that Stein and Van Vechten still hover as secondary, eccentric characters in the main plot of literary modernism indicates, ironically, the extent to which they succeeded in communicating these messages.

From Fin de Siècle to Modernist Aesthetics

Van Vechten began his career as a professional critic after he completed his B.A. at the University of Chicago and moved to New York City in 1906. Thus, he tentatively established himself as a critic during the same period that Gertrude Stein moved permanently to Paris and made the transition from the Jamesian realism of her unpublished lesbian novel *Q. E. D.* to the character typology, incremental repetition, limited vocabulary, and simple diction that characterize her early modernist works, *Three Lives* and *The Making of Americans*. Van Vechten landed his first job with Theodore Dreiser, who had become editor of *Broadway Magazine* in the wake of legal battles with Doubleday over their reluctant publication of an expurgated version of *Sister Carrie* in 1900. With Dreiser's enthusiastic support, Van Vechten wrote a lengthy and highly laudatory review of Strauss's *Salomé,* with libretto after Oscar Wilde's play. Olive Fremstad, the lesbian Wagnerian soprano, premiered the immensely challenging role of Salomé.[6] In the opera, Salomé is the daughter of Queen Herodias, who murdered her first husband in order to marry Herod, who now, along with most of the other men, lusts after his daughter-in-law. But Salomé, weary of the depraved decadence of the court, conceives an ambitious, perverse lust for John the Baptist, who has been imprisoned by Herod for preaching Christianity to the Jews. Salomé performs the erotically charged Dance of the Seven Veils at Herod's behest, and he subsequently promises to give her anything she desires. She requests that John the Baptist, whose steadfast refusal of her advances has enraged her, be beheaded. He complies reluctantly but becomes so terrified and repulsed at the spectacle of Salomé kissing the severed head of the Prophet that he orders her killed. Not surprisingly, *Salomé* was closed after one showing at the request of the directors, among them J. P. Morgan, who agreed to refund the entire cost of the production to prevent an encore performance.[7]

The *Salomé* fiasco suggested to Van Vechten that works that affronted bourgeois standards of morality in readily comprehensible terms, and that proclaimed a fascination with the very norms they rebelled against, were very likely to reconsolidate rather than undermine norms of judgment. For Van Vechten, who had escaped from the backwater of Cedar Rapids, Iowa, and who was fifteen when Oscar Wilde was imprisoned for homosexual offenses in 1895, an ironic perspective on provincialism and fin de siècle aestheticism forms the ground of his sceptical and anti-Romantic modernism. As a mature critic and novelist, Van Vechten assumes a stance of knowingness about the social and ideological traps awaiting those who, either from emotional naïveté, temperamental masochism, or a misplaced sense of personal heroism, make themselves martyrs by opening defying societal norms. Such martyrs, according to Van Vechten, are complicit in the ideology against which they rebel, for they perceive themselves as transgressors against an authority they still regard as authentic. Thus, Huysmans's Des Esseintes, perhaps the exemplary figure of *fin de siècle* literature, inevitably returns to the Church after his sexual adventures. Similarly, Oscar Wilde not only falls into sentimentality and bathos during his trial, but also publishes *The Ballad of Reading Gaol,* an abject apologia for his life, while in prison, thus transforming himself into the secular martyr of twentieth-century homosexual identity politics. Bisexual artists such as Wilde had delineated the contours of modern gay identity but, in facing persecution for publicly proclaiming the "love that dare not speak its name," had also strengthened the already medically essentialized opposition between homosexual and heterosexual identities. Van Vechten rejects oppositionality on the grounds that defiance plays by rules devised by the bourgeois majority, and he endeavors, rather, to *strategize* the closet by subverting and, hence, gradually eroding the entire system of heterosexist dominance. But such subversion, particularly when unnoticed or ineffective, faces the danger of devolving into even more insidious forms of ideological compliance and self-erasure. Van Vechten's entire career exemplifies the unresolved tension between covert subversion and overt obedience, a tension that frequently leaves his novelistic heroes in a state of painful isolation.

In countering the emotional costs of this ambivalent stance, Van Vechten sometimes takes comfort in imagining worse alternatives, which are most frequently embedded in a critique of the Gilded Age and projected onto female characters. For example, Countess Ella Nattatorrini, the central character of his 1924 novel *The Tattooed Countess,* exemplifies the heavy price of self-defeating, romantic self-abnegation. Her high-camp name is reminiscent of the fantastic appellations of the characters in Ronald Firbank's novels, a gay protégé of Oscar Wilde whose works Van Vechten promoted.[8] While her nymphomania and penchant for beautiful young men whom she, as an older woman, must attract through her financial largess make the countess an improbable portrait of an actual woman, "she" represents the kind of masochistic gay man whom Van Vechten both understands and seeks to distance himself from.

The countess, after a series of disastrous *affaires de coeur* in Europe following the death of her unlovable husband, decides to return home to Iowa in the wake of her most recent debacle with Tony, an inconsiderate, two-timing Italian tenor. Far from alleviating her broken heart, however, the smug provincialism and self-righteousness of the town only deepen her loneliness until she meets Gareth Jones, an ambitious, self-seeking young man who amuses himself with reading *The Picture of Dorian Gray*. In the end, Gareth realizes that he can forward his own literary ambitions by eloping with the countess, and in his subsequent novel, *Firecrackers,* Gareth reappears as a cynical, successful contemporary novelist who has long since abandoned his benefactress. *The Tattooed Countess* implies that romantic excess goes hand in hand with an equally excessive provincial moralism and either produces self-glorified martyrs or irresponsible, manipulative individuals who understand the "game" and are interested only in materialistic success. In fact, Gareth and the countess are as conventional and predictable in their way as the town from which they flee. For example, when asked of her opinion of the impressionists, the countess vehemently replies: "A side issue! A freak side issue! They amounted to nothing and now that they are finished they will soon be forgotten. Painting will go back to what is was before. . . . the world will soon return to the true art."[9]

While Van Vechten continued to write music criticism for the *New York Times,* he also began to write reviews of modernist dance innovators such as Isadora Duncan, Loie Fuller, Maud Allan, and Anna Pavlova, virtually creating dance criticism as a genre. As artistic forms, dance and music held particular attraction for Van Vechten because they allowed him to reconnect the body with language and to induce direct appreciation for sensuous aesthetic experience. In the meantime, Van Vechten made a definitive break with his Cedar Rapids roots and effected a workable compromise with societal expectations by marrying Fania Marinoff, a woman with an independent and established career as an actress with whom he maintained an equitable companionate marriage that allowed both of them the freedom to pursue their autonomous existences.[10] His marriage occurred at approximately the same time that Gertrude Stein broke her ties to her brother, Leo, and entered into her lifelong relationship with Alice Toklas. With this newfound freedom, the two women were able to open their apartment on 27 rue de Fleurus to sympathetic guests, among whom was the wealthy American patron of the arts, Mabel Dodge, who subsequently invited Stein and Toklas to her portable salon in Florence, Villa Curonia. Furthermore, Dodge, who sponsored "evenings" in Europe and New York City, and who knew most of the outstanding personalities of the day, was responsible for introducing Van Vechten and Stein.

The meeting between Van Vechten and Stein occurred shortly before an event that opened new possibilities for modernism. In 1913, Mabel Dodge sponsored the postimpressionist and cubist art show at the Sixtyninth Regiment Armory, which she later described as "the most important public event that has ever come off since the signing of the Declaration of Independence."[11] Van Vechten gained an important insight into the social dynamics of promoting modernism through the widespread reaction to the Armory exhibition. While the show invited the scorn and outrage of the public, no one seemed capable of ignoring, dismissing, or remaining silent about what they saw. Thus, rather than the fascination of *fin de siècle* artists with social and religious institutions that excluded them, the public became fascinated with works they felt incapable of comprehending, but that they nonetheless suspected of harboring subversive meanings. The show revealed to Van Vechten the power of sexuality, encoded in what Yeats called "the fascination of what's difficult," to offend, draw attention, and, most important, to garner publicity. Van Vechten later mythologized the Armory Show in *Peter Whiffle,* where it becomes a symbol of the power of modernist art to draw disparate groups of people together and to challenge the nineteenth-century genteel tradition.

> This show has now become almost a legend but it was the reality of that winter. It was the first, and possibly the last, exhibition of paintings held in New York which everybody attended. Everybody went and everybody talked about it. Street-car conductors asked for your opinion of the Nude Descending the Staircase, as they asked you for your nickel. Elevator boys grinned about Matisse's Le Madras Rouge,

Picabia's La Danse a la Source, and Brancusi's Mademoiselle Pogany, as they lifted you to the twenty-third floor. Ladies you met at dinner found Archipenko's sculpture very amusing, but was it art? . . . To sum up, the show was a bang-up whale of a success.[12]

This description indicates that when it came to interpreting modernist art, virtually everybody from elevator boys to society ladies was on the same rudimentary level, with no conventional critical perspectives to guide them, with the exception of standards of what constituted "proper" (i.e., moral) art. Modernist art could not be readily censored because it could not be accused of representing anything in particular. Indeed, in repeatedly refusing to explicate their creations, and in insisting that audiences rather than artists had the responsibility of interpreting their works according to their own lights, modernist writers and artists indirectly forced their audiences to examine the prejudices and preoccupations that informed their aesthetic judgments. Furthermore, the fact that the Armory Show drew spirited responses from a diverse array of people unaccustomed to sharing common cultural interests directly reflected the democratic amalgam of the arts Van Vechten championed in his criticism. This intermingling of diverse cultural forms was, in turn, reflected in the social composition of Mabel Dodge's famous "evenings," which Van Vechten describes enthusiastically in *Peter Whiffle*: "The groups separated, came together, separated, came together, separated, came together: syndicalists, capitalists, revolutionists, anarchists, artists, writers, actresses, 'perfumed with botanical creams,' feminists, and malthusians were all mixed in this strange salad."[13]

This dynamic and tension-filled drama of similarity and difference, grouping and regrouping, and identification and disidentification, made all the more potent by the continual play of sexual desire, resulted from bringing together people of vastly different backgrounds, interests, and ideologies who had heretofore been relegated to separate spheres. Needless to say, the academic critics whom Van Vechten opposed objected to these trends in modern culture precisely on the grounds that they would lead to "intermingling" and, hence, devaluation of unitary standards of taste and judgment. Van Vechten and Stein were drawn together because they both rejected the single center model of universality and perceived culture rather as a field with an infinite number of changeable centers. Each element in the field of culture matters equally and is not only centered in itself but is also in continual overlapping relation to every other element. Cultural analysis thus takes the form of noticing how what part of you and your group or groups overlap and interact with other elements in the field.[14]

By the time that Van Vechten, armed with a letter of introduction from Mabel Dodge, met Stein and Toklas in Paris in 1913, he had already read *Three Lives*, which had been published at Stein's expense by Grafton Press in 1909, as well as the word portraits of Picasso, Matisse, and Cezanne that appeared in the June 1912 issue of *Camera Work*. In addition, he had obtained a copy of Stein's *Portrait of Mabel Dodge at the Villa Curonia* from Dodge. Years later, Stein wrote an account of her meeting with Van Vechten in *The Autobiography of Alice B. Toklas* that began with her encounter with Anna Van Vechten, the "depressed and unhappy" wife who regaled Stein and Toklas with the "story of the tragedy of her married life."[15] Although the two women could not have possibly met Van Vechten at the performance of Stravinsky's *Le Sacre du Printemps*, as Stein reported in the *Autobiography*, this artistically "appropriate" backdrop lends their initial meeting an air of drama and significance associated with the uproar caused by Stravinsky's music. Furthermore, this setting enabled Stein to correlate her description of Van Vechten's highly eccentric appearance with the audience's outraged reaction to the dissonant, erotically charged music onstage.

> We looked around and there was a tall well-built young man, he might have been a dutchman, a scandinavian or an american and he wore a soft evening shirt with the tiniest pleats all over the front of it. It was impressive, we have never even heard that they were wearing evening shirts like that. That evening when we got home Gertrude Stein did a portrait of the unknown called a Portrait of One. (*AAT* 167–68)

According to Richard Bridgman's chronology, Stein wrote "One. Carl Van Vechten" in 1913, during the same period as *Tender Buttons* and the shift into her second stage of portraiture that occurred in "Portrait of Constance Fletcher."[16] This "portrait of the unknown" provides insights into Stein's deployment of the neuter pronoun *one* and takes the form of a commentary on the classic syllogistic definition of a man (i.e., All men are mortal. Socrates is a man. Therefore, Socrates is mortal). Stein provides the major and minor premises of the syllogism but omits the third-term conclusion and ends the portrait on "propositions" four and five.

This unusual form, however, turns out to have everything to do with the logical conclusions that can be drawn from Van Vechten's position as a "one" (as in one of *a* kind and *our* kind) rather than a "man."

The major premise is an extended meditation on the notion that clothes—and the accoutrements of power and grace—not only "make" the man but protect and disguise this "one" as well. In enumerating the qualities within Van Vechten and the elements that contain him, Stein begins with a highly riddling definition of, significantly, a closet: "In the ample checked fur in the back and in the house, in the by next cloth and inner, in the chest, in mean wind." A closet (or coatroom) is a place where "one" checks an ample fur coat—a protection against the harsh elements or "mean wind"—and also a permanent condition of existence that informs the relationship between "one's" inner being and outer appearance. Van Vechten may be *in* the closet, but his appearance in the fur coat and the "priestly" vestments of heavy watered silk ("best most silk") suggests his profound commitment to the notions that "the best might last and wind that." In other words, this "one" desires to preserve the best and has the power to persevere in the face of harsh opposition: to "wind that" or "win at that." The phrase "In the gold presently . . . unsuddenly and decapsized and dewalking" indicates that golden gifts or "presents" are now emerging or "coming out of the closet," so to speak, but they are doing so in a self-contained, "dewalking" or sedentary fashion that resists violent overthrow or destabilization. Hence, because this "one" is "none in stable" (i.e., not one unstable) and "none at ghosts" (i.e., not one haunted by apparitions), he is not one in the "latter spot," or last place. In other words, this "one," which also puns on "won," will indeed win.

The minor premise, announced when "one" transforms into "two," sets forth a "touching" description of Van Vechten colorfully attired in his "white shining sash . . . white green undercoat . . . white colored orange . . . [and] touching piece of elastic suddenly." His surprisingly "feminine" and decorative appearance "touches" Stein and establishes an intimate connection between them as "ones" of a kind. "A touching research," which refers both to Van Vechten's critical research and to his recherché or "dandified" appearance, "in all may day," or "aids" (from the French verb *aider*), Stein in *all* ways—personally and professionally. Van Vechten's "overshow" or outward style confers on him power and vulnerability, since his clothes reveal and conceal his queer self. "A touching expartition," or absence of a separation between the whole and its integrant parts, suggests both the amalgam of the "one" and the "man," and the relationship between Van Vechten and his work as a critic (i.e., his "beat"). As in *Tender Buttons,* the word "box," as a container that "houses," protects, and conceals things, among them presents, surprises, and sexual identity, becomes a metatextual metaphor for the entire portrait.

> A touching box is in a coach seat so that a touching box is on a coach seat so a touching box is on a coach seat, a touching box is on a coat seat, a touching box is on a coach seat.
> A touching box is on the touching so helping hand.[17]

This one's "touching box" is not only the closet that contains his queer sexuality but also the self-protective inner perspective from which he views things when seated (on a "coach seat"). The recognition that "one" and Stein have "boxes" and are "boxed in" by such inner knowledge of their "secret" difference constitutes the link between them—the "touching so helping hand."

The third concluding term of the syllogism, however, does not follow from the preceding portrait of this "unknown one." But the final section, which segues from "two" to "four," explains why. The problem of the disclosure of identity, as expressed in the closet and box metaphors, is constituted by *audience,* which mediates the relationship between the self and the public realm. The violent division or "hacking" of the subject, which also carries the connotation of "hack" writing, is associated with being in the "saddle," before a "dim judge" and a "great big so colored dog." Audiences are poor critics (i.e., "dim judge[s]") who seldom see beneath the gaudy, *colorful* appearances of persons or things. But this "dimness" has its protective advantages as well, for the metaphor of the dog, which Stein employs in her later writing to illustrate the problems of identification outside the self as well as the difference between "identifying" and "entifying" another person, is, in this context, "colored"; a word that for Stein connoted her practice of verbally encoding lesbian sexuality. Thus, the "colored dog" not only refers to Stein and Van Vechten's perception of each other as artists who "color" or encode their writing, but also to that portion of their audience who understands how to interpret—because they share in the practice of—encoding their queer sexual desires.

From Cultural Critic to Novelist:
The Problem of Genre

Once Stein and Van Vechten had established this "touching" connection, he arranged for Donald Evans's radical publishing house, Claire Marie Press, through which Evans had recently begun to serve "the seven hundred civilized people" in America, to publish *Tender Buttons*.[18] As the editor for the short-lived *Trend* magazine, which, as the title indicates, attempted to forecast and publicize new trends in the arts, Van Vechten began to explicate and introduce Stein to an American audience. His first lengthy analysis of Stein's writing style appeared in the same issue of *Trend* as his first article on African-American culture, a review of the play *Granny Maumee* entitled, "A Cockney Flower Girl and Some Negroes." This juxtaposition was far from coincidental, for Van Vechten perceived in Stein's writing and African-American culture analogous forms of unappreciated inventiveness, pure musicality, sexual expressivity, and childlike spontaneity capable of liberating Western culture from its repressive mores. The *Trend* article, "How to Read Gertrude Stein," established the genre of professional guides to her hermetic writing style. In a tongue-in-cheek tone, Van Vechten argues, on the one hand, that Stein has submerged the sexual meaning of her writing to evade the censors and, on the other, that her writing cannot be reduced to (or accused of having) a single, underlying sexual sense.

> The English language is a language of hypocrisy and evasion. How not to say a thing has been the problem of our writers from the earliest times. The extraordinary fluidity and even naivete of French makes it possible for a writer in that language to babble like a child; de Maupassant is only possible in French, a language in which the phrase, "Je t'aime" means everything. But what does "I love you" mean in English? Donald Evans . . . has realized this peculiar quality of English and he is almost the first of the poets in English to say unsuspected and revolting things, because he so cleverly avoids saying them.
>
> [Miss Stein] has really turned language into music, really made its sound more important than its sense. And she has suggested to the reader a thousand channels for his mind and sense to drift along, a thousand, instead of a stupid only one.[19]

The essay itself is an example of the problems of literary concealment and disclosure he thematizes. English-language writers are intensely aware of sexuality and expert in the various aesthetic modes of disguising it precisely because they are forced to cloak the body and provide critics and audiences with works that valorize moral didacticism. Van Vechten places Stein in a context of French culture not only because she lived in Paris and employed French puns in her writing, but also because her writing belongs in a tradition of French letters that extended back to Théophile Gautier's preface to *Mademoiselle de Maupin* (1835), which set out an antiutilitarian, antinaturalistic, and antibourgeois theory of aesthetics in the context of a novel that openly explores lesbianism and bisexuality. Van Vechten attributes to the French language qualities that actually adhered in French writers, whose presumably childlike "babble" refers to their more unself-conscious and, hence, "natural" treatment of sexuality. By contrast, English-language authors achieve literary maturity by treating sex as an infantile taboo; yet, because they cannot ignore the place of sexuality in adult human affairs, they become adepts in the rhetorical arts of "hypocrisy and evasion."

For Van Vechten, Stein has discovered an original method of evading the mechanisms of cultural censorship that goes far beyond cynically knowing, deceptive, and underhanded tactics. Principally, she overturns the game of representation and referent that had locked censors and writers in continual battle by refusing to play by the rules. Her encoded prose places the body and sexuality everywhere metaphorically and, hence, nowhere particularly or literally. Thus, her prose resembles music, which suggests a thousand images, associations, and moods to the individual listener, rather than a "stupid only one."

The subversive power of Stein's writing to evade the mechanisms of cultural repression is nowhere more evident than in the final poem of "Objects," the first section of *Tender Buttons,* in which Stein describes two lesbians "dressing up" to have sex—first cunnilingly and, finally and most daringly, with a dildo:

THIS IS THIS DRESS, AIDER

Aider, why aider why whow, whow stop touch, aider whow, aider stop the muncher, muncher munchers.

A jack in kill her, a jack in, makes a meadowed king, makes a to let.[20]

The archetypal item of women's apparel, a dress, is an emotionally charged object that invokes complex associations regarding gender roles.

This dress, in this context, arouses desire as well as recognition of neediness, vulnerability, and, distress. Thus, the title also reads "THIS IS DISTRESS, AID HER." The lady in the dress is in distress, but what is the nature of her "distress?" The French verb *aider* puns on Alice's nickname, Ada, but it is impossible to tell whether it is "Ada" who needs "rescuing" or Stein, who signals her sexual distress in pointing to this dress. The confusion over who is doing what to whom makes sense, however, in this context, in which both parties overturn dichotomized categories of subject and object, passive and active, and male and female. The first line of the poem, which may be translated as, "Aid her, why aid her (Ada) why and how?" continues this play of mutual seduction. "Whow . . . stop touch" indicates that one (or both?) of them is beginning to feel overwhelmed by powerful sensations. "Stop the muncher" is a double-edged order, as the person doing the "munching"—or "eating" in the slang term for cunnilingus—bears a name that orders the prohibited action; namely, munch her. The plural "munchers" engage in the mutual action of munching, a characteristic of cows that, in "As a Wife Has a Cow: A Love Story" and "Lifting Belly," Stein associates with female orgasm.

This play of dressing with dresses and munching arouses a "distressing" surfeit of feeling and touch insufficient to completely satisfy desire. Hence, the arousing foreplay leads to the desire for penetration. Imposing heterosexist categories of violent rape and sexual assault on this poem, some critics have seriously glossed "A jack in kill her" as "Ejaculate in her" and "kill her."[21] However, such interpretations are only ironically "accurate" in this context of intense lesbian sex. A "jack" is a rogue male, but here the figural term refers to a literal dildo, which in itself "refigures" the penis, just as lesbian sex retropes heterosexual practices. In brief, the "jack . . . kill[s] her," or gives "her" an orgasm (i.e., a "little death"). The dress, the munchers, and the jack "make a meadowed king," a metaphor for a male bull, or, more to the point, a "bulldagger," the slang term for a butch lesbian. "Makes a to let," if rendered as "makes a toilet," implies that the women are aware of having done something sexually taboo or "dirty" with the dress, the jack, and the English language that completely violates cultural codes of female sexual propriety. They may have been "dirty," but the dress (and the symbols attached to it), also allowed or "let" the action that follows. In French, however, this phrase translates as *faire une toilette,* or get washed and dressed, which suggests that the women must get "dirty" to get "clean."

For Stein, objects are "an arrangement in a system of pointing":[22] they "point" or refer to other things. Objects like the "jack" dildo are necessary prosthetic devices that enable one to *visualize oneself* (and one's sexuality) in the world. Objects like the dress not only "make the woman" (and man), but channel and provoke desire as well by playing on the illusion of naturalized gender difference. In brief, making our *toilette* reminds us that we are the clothes we wear.[23] As Van Vechten suggests in his article, Stein's encoded language in *Tender Buttons* does far more than escape censorship. Her poetry accurately renders the metaphorical richness of queer sexuality rather than misrepresenting it as having a single "stupid" or literal sense.

Although Van Vechten continued to produce music, dance, and literary criticism, he was able to escape the hackwork of journalism as well as the uncertain fortunes of small magazines like *Trend* when he met Alfred Knopf, a Jewish publisher who began his own firm in 1915. Knopf had earlier worked for Mitchell Kennerley, who had established an avant-garde monthly *The Reader* and had won victories in censorship battles against Anthony Comstock, whose New York Anti-Vice Society received generous support from tycoons such as J. Pierpont Morgan, William E. Dodge Jr., and Samuel Colgate.[24] Knopf represented a new breed of publishers that included Horace Liveright, Thomas Seltzer, Pascal Covici, Donald Friede, B. W. Huebsch, Harold K. Guinzburg, Richard Simon, Max Schuster, Bennett Cerf, and Donald Klopfer. As Jews, these men were particularly sensitive to the ideological and cultural interests of non-Anglo-Saxon readers who had been ignored by established publishing houses that upheld the socially conservative genteel tradition of American letters. Just as male modernists were to follow the example of Gertrude Stein, so these men followed the pathbreaking work of American lesbian publishers such as Margaret Anderson and Sylvia Beach, both of whom had lacked the financial resources that enabled subsequent publishers to build firms and fight costly censorship battles.

Knopf developed an impressive list of contemporary authors that included Conrad Aiken, Witter Bynner, Willa Cather, Max Beerbohm, T. S. Eliot, Kahlil Gibran, Ezra Pound, Robert Graves, E. M. Forster, Thomas Mann, Wyndham Lewis, and Dorothy Richardson. Perhaps with the intention of promoting an alternative to academic criticism and establishing an intellectual basis for the acceptance of modernist culture, Knopf published Van Vechten's *Music and Bad Manners* (1916). The reference to "bad manners" was aimed at those who believed that art should promote moral uplift and "good manners." The volume, an accessible and cosmopolitan series of short essays aimed at what Virginia Woolf called "the common reader," combined personal anecdote with critical interpretation, castigated the apathy and prejudice of traditional music critics, and discussed everything from opera technique to the use of musical scores for movies. His subsequent volume, *Interpreters and Interpretations*, was, as the title indicates, divided into two parts. "Interpreters" consisted of interviews with, and enthusiastic reviews of, the work of operatic and dance luminaries such as Olive Fremstad, Mary Garden, Yvette Guilbert, and Nijinsky. "Interpretations" considered the influence of music on modern literature and featured a series of reviews, "Modern Musical Fiction," which included an analysis of Willa Cather's fictionalized biography of Olive Fremstad, *The Song of the Lark*. In *The Merry-Go-Round*, Van Vechten continues his assault on pretentious academic criticism by taking a childlike ride around the various arts. "Our author mounts his wooden horse and dashes gaily round the circle of the merry-go-round of the arts," he cheerfully announces in the dust jacket note he prepared. While these volumes of criticism received generally favorable reviews from those who were sympathetic toward Van Vechten's efforts to promote contemporary culture, they sold very poorly. Perhaps Van Vechten, in attempting to create a new species of criticism, nonetheless faced unconscious resistance to essayistic criticism as a genre. He later claimed that he was surprised when the full-length "critical" text he wrote in 1921, *Peter Whiffle*, was not only called a novel but also became a best-seller. He later stated in "Notes for an Autobiography" that he did not "kn[ow] I was writing a novel. However, after it appeared, the reviewers began to declare that it was a novel and so, to my astonishment, I found myself a novelist."[25] Because he achieved far greater popular success as a "novelist" than as a critic, Van Vechten found himself in the curious position of viewing his second career as a "genuine" calling, for which his criticism had constituted a species of preparation. Rather than viewing his life as a series of "progressions," linked in a causal nexus of "development" or "maturity," however, Van Vechten purposefully stresses the casual and almost accidental fashion in which the narrative of his life unfolds.

Nevertheless, genre had an immense influence on the fate of Van Vechten's writing in the marketplace. While his impressionistic and personalized accounts of contemporary culture had sold poorly, similar observations rendered in novelistic form enjoyed great popularity. *Peter*

Whiffle and his subsequent novels, with the exception of *Parties,* were best-sellers. If Gertrude Stein subsequently gained best-seller status by ventriloquizing the voice of her lover Alice Toklas and composing a deceptively transparent and gossipy autobiography in *The Autobiography of Alice B. Toklas* that placed her in the center of modernism, then in *Peter Whiffle* Van Vechten popularized his critical aesthetic by splitting his persona into two male characters, the dilettante Peter Whiffle and his critic-friend, Carl Van Vechten. This plotless book narrates the artistic adventures of Peter Whiffle, a devotee of modern culture who wanders between Paris and New York City, obsessed with list making and catalogs as well as with various political and cultural enthusiasms. Van Vechten himself plays the part of the first-person narrator to whom Peter recounts the "story" of his all-consuming adventures. In this semifictional cross between a guide to modern art, a critical "autobiography," and a *roman à clef*, Van Vechten can represent actual persons and events disguised, according to the dust jacket, behind "thin, epithetical masks." As in most of his other novels, *Peter Whiffle* breaks down narrative patterns of beginning-middle-end and conflict resolution in order to present modern life as a series of interrelated events that have no overarching meaning outside themselves. As with Stein's *Autobiography, Peter Whiffle* appealed to fantasies of finding oneself in the midst of an original and daring circle of "movers and shakers" as well as to the game of guessing "who's who." As a novelist, Van Vechten seduced his contemporary audience by dramatizing the conflict between concealment and revelation that, as William Gass has noted of *Tender Buttons,* proves compelling "so long as the victory of concealment remains incomplete, so long as the drapery leads us to dream and desire and demand the body we know it covers."[26]

In his next book, the best-selling *The Blind Bow-Boy,* Van Vechten dramatizes his aesthetic philosophy through Campaspe Lorillard, an unflappable sophisticate whose mode of living teaches the reader the techniques of concealing subversive meanings behind a facade of respectability. Although married, Campaspe pursues an independent existence from her husband Cupid, a wealthy businessman who attempts, with notable failure, to arouse her jealousy by having affairs with women. But Campaspe's interest lies in her circle of friends, who revolve around the gravitational force of her person. Like Van Vechten the critic, Campaspe diverts herself with the discovery and promotion of hidden talent; in this case, an impoverished snake-charmer in Coney

Island whom she seduces, dresses lavishly, and, finally, guides to spectacular success as a motion picture star.

A pathetically naive young man named Harold Prewett is accidentally drawn into Campaspe's circle when his father, whom Harold has never met (having been brought up by a maiden aunt), decides to seduce his son into a life of "manly" conformity by giving him the wherewithal to pursue a decadent life. To this end, he hires Paul, a close friend of Campaspe. Here, Van Vechten elaborates the point found throughout his work; namely, that the prohibition of the father *creates* sexual disequilibrium and anxiety by prohibiting the unmanipulated, natural expression of desire. Hence, Harold, ostensibly bereft of a conventional plot to conform to or rebel against, feels confused and set up. He begins to suspect, without evidence, that Campaspe's "decadent" friends have designs on him. In a state of semipanic, he falls in love with Alice, a conventional young woman whose appeal to him grows in direct proportion to her father's opposition to him. Alice, it develops, is Campaspe's sister, and she arranges for them to go on what becomes a disastrous (and unconsummated) honeymoon after Harold discovers that Alice regards him only as a breadwinner. Robbed once again of his illusion of free will, at the end of the narrative Harold quietly leaves for England with Campaspe's friend, the duke of Middlebottom, who was in New York to stage a private play at the fantastically decorated home of two wealthy lesbians, and whose stationery bears the Wildean motto: "A thing of beauty is a boy forever."[27]

The fact that Harold's discovery of his homosexuality coincides with his escape from the manipulative narrative paradigm of the father (and the text of *The Blind Bow-Boy*) illustrates the limitations of Van Vechten's comedy of manners form: homosexuals must disappear from sight (and be invisible to most heterosexual readers) in order to be free. Hence, Van Vechten supplies his covert queer audience with the compensatory satisfaction of outwitting heterosexuals, who cannot "read" the signs of their existence. Van Vechten, as an author, shares in this compact of protective secrecy with his queer and female audience and has Campaspe expound on the wisdom of maintaining an appearance of conformity to outdo a "foolish" world.

Conform externally with the world's demands and you will get anything you desire in life. By a process of erosion you can dig a hole in two years through public opinion that it would take you two centuries to knock through. It is just as great a mistake to reject violently ideas that do not appeal to us. Rejection implies labour, interest, even fear. . . . The world . . . is a very pleasant place for people who know how to live. We are the few. The rest are fools, and all we have to do to persuade the fools to permit us to live our own lives is to make them believe that we, too, are fools. It's so simple, once you understand.[28]

Although Van Vechten achieved commercial success with his novels by perpetuating this ruse of "foolishness" on his major reading audience, this philosophy of sophisticated deception, which inevitably filtered homosexuality through nominally heterosexual and sexually aloof female characters, eventually became threadbare. Perhaps partly in response to complaints that *Nigger Heaven* sensationalized and demeaned African-American culture, in *Parties* (1930), his last and, by far, best novel, Van Vechten dispenses with the apparatus of fictional male homosexual "stand-ins" and explores the self-destructive violence that results from the taboo against homosexuality. Not surprisingly, *Parties* was a commercial failure that received polemically negative reviews that charged Van Vechten with nihilism, literary fraud, and immorality.

In *Parties,* the drunken excesses caused by Prohibition are treated as trivial and socially acceptable forms of ersatz rebellion against authority that mask a deeply conventional acquiescence to the social fictions of heterosexuality. The pressures on men to conform to heterosexual male roles causes an eruption of violent homosexual panic that results in the death of Roy Fern, a young, lower-class gay man who works as a runner for the bootlegger Donald Bliss.[29] The narrative elaborates the Steinian notion of the prolonged present inasmuch as the first scene forecasts, on the level of subconscious dream-memory, the violent action that finally occurs near the end of the book. Between the anxious prognostication and accomplished fact of Roy Fern's death, the narrative is a static frieze; a continuous, repetitive present of drinking, disputing, and partying. When asked, for example, what "happens" in New York City's social life, Rilda, the main character's unhappy wife, replies: "Nothing whatever. Just parties, that's all. The only happy people left in New York are the Lesbians and pederasts, and they are so happy they are miserable. Nobody else has anything."[30] In other words, the lesbians and pederasts at least have the satisfaction of knowing themselves, even if that knowledge confers on them the "miserable" status of social pariahs.

The text opens as Hamish Wilding, who seems to have no separate life apart from the role he plays as the ever-solicitous "third party" to the heterosexual dyad of David and Rilda Westlake, rescues David from a Harlem speakeasy, where he has gotten into a fight he cannot remember. His statement that "I've killed a man or a man has killed me" (*P* 1) turns out to be metaphorically and literally true. David is paralyzed by conflicting loyalties to Roy Fern, who loves him with mute, fatalistic passion, and his wife Rilda, who threatens to commit suicide if David runs off to England with Roy. Overmastered by an addiction to pleasing everyone even more fatal to rational self-understanding than his addiction to alcohol, David escapes by himself to England, where he repeats his customary patterns of drunkenness and obligatory sex with women. When he returns to New York City at the end of the novel, he and his wife are poised to return their usual life of drinking and sexual bickering.

In his absence, however, Roy, who has become the chaperone to the Grafen Adele von Pulmernl und Stilzernl, an amiable woman who finds American bootlegger society diverting, becomes increasingly anxious and irritable. During a sojourn to a Harlem nightclub, Roy becomes irrationally incensed when he spots Rilda dancing with Siegfried, a man to whom she has attached herself solely for the purposes of making David jealous. Roy, who has discovered that David intends to return to Rilda and who realizes his passion for David has no hope of fulfillment, decides to act on what he misconstrues as David's "order" to murder Siegfried.

> You and your guy! Roy cried. You'll get yours. You leave David alone. You stay away from David.
>
> Rilda swayed slightly, like a willow-tree in a breeze, as she said in a deadly calm tone: If I were you, I'd let David choose his own vices.
>
> Shut up, Roy, Hamish advised the boy testily. You don't know what you're talking about.
>
> I ain't goin' to talk no more, the boy responded grimly.
>
> Suddenly, before anybody could have an inkling of his purpose, he sprang forward, upsetting a chair. The knife flashing in his uplifted hand was buried a second later in Siegfried's breast. . . . Pausing a second to look back at his pursuers, Roy stumbled, and fell headlong, with a shriek of terror, to the very bottom of the flight of steps. (*P* 191)

The fact that Roy *falls* to his death, like an angel tumbling into hell, retropes the sexually encoded imagery that David, in the beginning of the book, employs to describe his "tussle" with two unnamed men.

In the bowels of the earth. Climbing, always climbing. . . . Nearer my
God to thee and Go down Moses! Well, I sat on the fellow's chest and
pummeled him and the stars began to fall. Chunks of dirt in his hair
bit my hands. Then we dropped. We musta tumbled in a well. There
was water. I died first. (*P* 1–2)

In this context, "die" refers both to orgasm and to passing out from
inebriation. Most important, however, it is David Westlake who has the
power to define the term as the differences between his pleasure,
Hamish's self-repression, and Roy Fern's death. Protected by his privileged social position (the stock market crash causes him only momentary
anxiety) and his marriage to Rilda, David can control the parameters of
what "passes" in this text, both metaphorically and literally, for male
homosociality and homosexuality. Charismatic men like David cause
tragic disruption because they are not obligated to know themselves. As
an African-American seeress informs him late in the text: "You do not
know yourself. . . . You don't know where you are, or who you are, or
what you are, or what you want" (*P* 232). Hamish Wilding, the third possibility of male homosexuality offered by this pessimistic novel, protects
himself from "ruin" by mediating his desires through the heterosexual
David-Rilda dyad and homosexual literary texts. In David's absence, he
consoles himself by reading about the training of boys for the Chinese
stage, and the lesbian Natalie Barney's memoirs, *Aventures de l'Esprit*.

Because literary narrative has traditionally linked male heterosexuality
with power, legitimate authority, and autonomy, Van Vechten, in this
sense like his character David Westlake, must suspend himself in an
ambivalent void between male homosociality and homosexuality. If *Parties* serves as any indication, Van Vechten was acutely aware of the dangers and privileges associated with such ambivalence that, on the one
hand, sentence his male protagonists to isolation but, on the other,
enable them to travel incognito through many worlds. Van Vechten does
not have at his artistic disposal a male analogue of Stein's signifier "Alice
Toklas," who, for Stein, interconnects the domains of female romantic
friendship and lesbianism. Although Van Vechten represents a Whitmanesque intersection between male romantic friendship and male-male
passion in *Peter Whiffle* through the critic-*flâneur* relationship between
the author-as-narrator and Peter Whiffle, he is nonetheless compelled to
mediate male homosexual desire through a female character. Peter has a
brief affair with an American opera singer hopeful whose sole narrative
function is to cancel the homoerotic threat implied by the intimacy

between the fictionalized author and his male protagonist.[31] Unlike the sometimes literally murderous conflict and division that defines the boundary between male homosociality and homosexuality, Stein can move with relative freedom within a wide range of overlapping sexual and gendered positions. This latitude enables Stein to dispense with traditional modes of autobiography, which present one-to-one subject and object relationships based on the dichotomy between present and past or truthful and fictional selves. Writing as a *lesbian* modernist, Stein adumbrates an ironic autobiographical mode that not only envisions the self as embedded in group and historical contexts, but also emphasizes the multiplicity of perspectivism.

Thus, in his relationship to Stein, Van Vechten occupies a position symbolically analogous to that of the "hero" D'Albert to the "heroine-hero" Madeleine/Theodore in the precursor text of queer modernism, Théophile Gautier's *Mademoiselle de Maupin*. Like Van Vechten, D'Albert marks his difference from conventional masculinity by wearing flamboyant clothing and displaying little interest in heterosexuality. The only person who attracts him is the cross-dressed Madeleine/Theodore, whom he thinks is a man. Hence D'Albert, like Gautier, can project the socially proscribed fantasy of male homosexual consummation onto the dual-gendered lesbian character, whom the text permits to act out her cross-dressed desires for another woman.[32] While Van Vechten's writings express a profound longing to escape the trappings of a societally defined masculine role, he nonetheless feels obligated to retain enough of the prerogatives of that role to serve as an effective mediator between public audiences and authors such as Stein. Thus, having reached a representational impasse in his novel writing, Van Vechten turned to the nonverbal realm of photography and the promotion of Stein's next, most popular, and most public stage of her literary career.

Making Modernist Monuments: Publicity and the Arts of "Colored" Autobiography

In 1932, the year after Van Vechten withdrew from the literary marketplace, Stein wrote, as a "joke," *The Autobiography of Alice B. Toklas*, the work that would transform her into a best-selling author and household name. When she composed the *Autobiography*, Stein was already fifty-eight years old and, despite thirty years of serious literary production, still an obscure and largely unpublished author whose distinctive style had achieved a dubious fame by being parodied in American newspapers and magazines. Despite his efforts, Van Vechten, like her other literary promoters, had been unsuccessful in convincing a major New York or London firm to publish any of her works, including *Three Lives, Tender Buttons,* or *The Making of Americans,* the latter of which Stein regarded as comparable to *Remembrance of Things Past* and *Ulysses,* and which she was particularly anxious to see published to establish her reputation as an important modernist.[33]

Until the *Autobiography* was serialized in *The Atlantic Monthly* and subsequently published by Harcourt Brace in 1933, Stein's work had appeared only in small magazines such as Stieglitz's *Camera Work* and Van Vechten's *Trend,* alternative houses such as Donald Evans's Claire Marie and Leonard and Virginia Woolf's Hogarth Press, vanity presses such as Grafton, and small firms such as Four Seas Company, Daniel Henry Kahnweiler, Payson and Clarke, and Seizen Press. The latter, generally operating on limited budgets, published but failed to publicize their small runs of her work; consequently, her titles fell quickly into obscurity.[34] Alice Toklas, frustrated by the seemingly insurmountable difficulties of finding publishers, began Plain Edition Press in 1930 and issued, in rapid succession, *Lucy Church Amiably* (1930), *Before the Flowers of Friendship Faded Friendship Faded* (1931), *How to Write* (1931), *Operas and Plays* (1932), and *Matisse, Picasso, and Gertrude Stein* (1933). Nonetheless, this modest effort at self-promotion did not, understandably, satisfy Stein's longing for broad public recognition.

Ironically, however, given the social condemnation of lesbianism, Toklas's position as confidante, witness, and promoter within the narrative of her and Stein's life was so crucial to the artistic design and the popular success of the *Autobiography* that, in the Harcourt Brace edition, Gertrude Stein requested that her name as author not be printed on the binding, the dust jacket, or the title page. Rather, a photograph by Man Ray, captioned "Alice B. Toklas at the door," appeared next to the title page to represent the intimate, collaborative context for the creation of this dual-authored autobiography. The photograph shows Stein seated at her writing desk, bent over her work, and Alice, haloed in light, entering the room, illuminating the murkily lit writing chamber. Although an unambiguous representation of domestic and artistic intimacy between two women, the general readership seized upon the diverting account of modernist alliances and rivalries, personalities and geniuses, and intrigues and social gatherings and failed to notice or wonder at the nature of the bond between Toklas and Stein. The text juxtaposes a linear, chronological narration of events—which tells of Toklas's childhood in San Francisco, her meeting of Gertrude Stein, the artistic activities centered around their atelier at 27 rue de Fleurus, their experiences of driving an ambulance during World War I, and their postwar literary and social activities—with a circular, overlapping structure of the "continual present" that, in withholding knowledge of Stein's authorship of Toklas's autobiography until the final page of the text, returns to the context of the photograph of Stein and Toklas at the beginning: "About six weeks ago Gertrude Stein said, it does not look to me as if you were ever going to write that autobiography. You know what I am going to do. I am going to write it for you. . . . And she has and this is it" (AAT 310).

Through a superb act of ventriloquism of Toklas's distinctive voice, Stein authorizes her claims of centrality within the narrative of modernism that takes shape around their "Saturday Evenings" and thus achieves literary and public recognition. Stein, through Alice's voice, can proclaim her own genius; more important, however, she can seize control of the processes of her own reputation making and impel critics to confront her on her own territory, from the standpoint of her own artistic assumptions and narrative of self-creation. Alice becomes a link between the domestic and public realms, an authorizing presence who permits Stein to state her claims for public recognition and refute the arguments of her detractors. Although many critics regard this text as uncharacteristic of Stein's writing, this judgment really points to the unusual popularity of the Autobiography, for the deceptively transparent style and quasi-sequential narration that Stein employs also inform her subsequent works in the autobiographical genre: Everybody's Autobiography (1937), Paris, France (1940), and Wars I Have Seen (1945).[35]

Nonetheless, if Stein places herself at the center of modernism in the Autobiography, this center is actually a convenient fiction, an artistic platform from which Stein, through Toklas, speaks in order to spur interest in a body of work that, because of its sheer multiplicity and complexity, cannot be reduced to a single, overarching center but rather must be considered as a collection of interrelated entities. Even the narrative structure of the Autobiography, with its shifting series of various centers of activity and interest that overlap with past and concurrent centers and anticipate future ones, indicates that the narrative of Stein and Toklas's shared life must be viewed as a series of self-contained movements, rather than as chains of causes and effects, or sequences of developmental progressions. A photograph in the Autobiography makes this exact point. It shows Stein as a young child, simply titled, "Gertrude Stein in Vienna," implying that Gertrude Stein, even as a child, has always been Gertrude Stein.

On the other hand, the very creation of an accessible center in the *Autobiography* around which the plots of modernism revolve has unwittingly contributed to the subsequent construction of what Marianne DeKoven has called the "Hollywood Life of Gertrude Stein."[36] This popularized "movie," which routinely disembodies and sentimentalizes Stein's sexuality, begins with her sitting for Picasso's portrait of her and ends when Stein, triumphant after the publication of the *Autobiography*, returns home to America after thirty years, a successful native daughter now able to drop the posture of unintelligibility and write clearly at last. As evidenced in *Everybody's Autobiography* and *The Geographical History of America*, however, Stein had an ambivalent reaction to the popularization that, while transforming her into an important figure on the landscape of modernism, focused on her personality to the neglect of her writings.[37] In her later work, Stein responded to this problem by distinguishing between "writing," or the kind that audiences were willing to purchase, and "really writing," or the challenging kind she had labored at continually throughout her career. Furthermore, apprehensive of being dismissed because of her lesbianism, Stein became preoccupied with the problems of audience, identity, and forms of knowledge, as well as the ways in which money and time can distort perception.

Having constructed a series of autobiographical platforms from which to address her times, Stein, understandably reluctant to take on directly the place of gender and sexuality in *displacing* her writings, attempts to unify the plurality of her work through an ambitious act of cultural nationalism. If her writings could not, by their nature, be assimilated or included in modernist literary canons, then she could at least make her writing representative of that diffuse, ahistorical anomaly, America. Thus, ranged alongside Stein's self-portrait as a proliferative American genius in the tradition of Whitman and Emerson, stands, in *Everybody's Autobiography*, a series of photographs of Stein by Van Vechten that have served to crystallize her public image: the monumental, inaccessible genius in profile; the unstylish, eccentric expatriate stepping off the Pan Am airplane with Toklas; the compelling hidden oracle surrounded by a rapt coterie of university students; and the recumbent pastoral figure, with her poodle, sunning herself at her country house in Bilignin, France.

There have been many and repeated complaints, particularly from both feminist and avant-garde critics, about Stein's anomalous position within the standard narrative of literary high modernism. At once central and marginal to the canonical plot constructed by academic critics, Stein's work, like Van Vechten's literary/critical practice, problematizes the entire notion of center and margin, and popular and high-cultural productions. Nonetheless, successful promotion through literary canonization has depended on creating a coherent narrative of an author's work and life that allow critics to make distinctions between categories of judgment such as good and bad, mature and immature, characteristic and uncharacteristic, and traditional and innovative, among others, and to group writing into genres such as novel, poetry, libretto, drama, short story, autobiography, criticism, novella, detective fiction, and so forth. Stein's oeuvre, like Van Vechten's critical/novelistic practice, resists received conceptions of valuation and generic classification, resulting in Stein's case in omission from anthologies and in Van Vechten's slipping through the cracks of early-twentieth-century cultural criticism. To cite but one example of the problems of judging maturity and immaturity in Stein's writing, there have been critics who have argued that her chronologically early lesbian novella *Q. E. D.* constituted her most "mature" (or, alternatively, revolutionary) act of writing, from which her subsequent productions, characterized by encodings and other obscurantist stylistic "ruses" forced upon her by censorship and homophobia, represent a regrettable regression.[38] Stein and Van Vechten did not write self-identified *as* lesbian or gay authors; rather, their *position* on the outskirts of normative structures of sexuality caused them to resist narrative paradigms that, allied with the notions of drama based on conflict-resolution, depth-surface models of subjectivity and on developmental progression, linked adult authority and canonicity with male heterosexuality. The impossibility of fitting Stein and Van Vechten into received conceptions of literary modernity suggests, at last, that we need to dispense altogether with the kinds of narratives and essentialist assumptions on which such canons are founded.

NOTES

1. This animus is evident in, for example, Edmund Wilson's "Things as They Are," in *The Shores of Light* (New York: Farrar, Straus, and Giroux, 1952); B. L. Reid's *Art by Subtraction: A Dissenting Opinion of Gertrude Stein* (Norman: University of Oklahoma Press, 1958); and Richard Bridgman's *Gertrude Stein in*

Pieces (New York: Oxford University Press, 1970). While Bridgman began the important practice of reading Stein's compositions through her personal experiences, he nonetheless often pathologizes Stein's lesbianism.

2. See Joan DeJean's *Fictions of Sappho: 1546–1937* (Chicago: University of Chicago Press, 1989), for an analysis of the manner in which generations of male literary artists joined the homosocial society of authors and, hence, achieved artistic majority by exchanging derogatory or sensationalistic images of Sappho among themselves. The ghostlike specter of Sappho's lesbianism serves as the incitement to contain her subversive potential through "fictions of Sappho." These male authors could appear to enlist themselves in Sappho's revolutionary challenge to the social order while actually reconfirming their culture's prohibition against a form of female sexuality that resisted exchange among men. An analogous form of literary exchange occurred around Stein, with the crucial difference that Stein, unlike Sappho, was able to refute her detractors, particularly in her autobiographical work.

3. Traditional Christian morality invokes the archaic, premodern image of the homosexual as a sinister, predatory, rapacious pervert who lures innocent victims to their moral doom. Medical sexology either sees homosexuality as a sign of inherited degeneracy (as per Richard von Krafft-Ebing's *Psychopathia Sexualis*) or as an inborn, but not necessarily malignant condition (as per Havelock Ellis's *Studies in the Psychology of Sex*).

4. See Edward de Grazia, *Girls Lean Back Everywhere: The Law of Obscenity and the Assault on Genius* (New York: Random House, 1992), pp. 165–208, for a complete account of Hall's costly and emotionally wrenching court battles over the purported obscenity of *The Well of Loneliness*.

5. Wanda Fraiken Neff's novel *We Sing Diana* (1928) explores the loss of freedom and unself-consciousness that accompanied the changes in attitudes toward female relationships that occurred before and after World War I. In 1913, the heroine has intense romantic friendships in college that are regarded as "great human experiences." When she returns to teach in the same school in 1920, however, the students have imbibed Freudian psychology and regard attractions among women with suspicion.

6. For a discussion of Olive Fremstad's and Mary Garden's identifications as lesbian divas and their significance within queer opera culture, see Wayne Kostenbaum, *The Queen's Throat: Opera, Homosexuality, and the Mystery of Desire* (New York: Poseidon Press, 1993).

7. Van Vechten retained a lifelong admiration for Fremstad and Garden, the latter whom premiered *Salomé* in French in Oscar Hammerstein's short-lived Manhattan Opera House and who created the roles of Melisande, Massenet's Sapho, and Cherubin. In 1952, Van Vechten wrote to Bruce Kellner and complained that "singers have deteriorated steadily and vastly." His faith in opera was only revived later that year with the advent of the African-American soprano

Leontyne Price. "After a respite of twenty years I am mad for opera again."
Significantly, Price had her debut in 1952 as Saint Therese in Virgil Thomson's
Four Saints in Three Acts, which has regularly featured an all-black cast, and for
which Stein wrote the libretto. (Bruce Kellner, *Carl Van Vechten and the Irreverent Decades* [Norman: University of Oklahoma Press, 1968], pp. 300, 287).

8. Such fantastically named characters include Mrs. Shamefoot in *Vainglory;*
Lady Laura de Nazianzi and Queen Thleeanouhee of the Land of Dates in *The
Flower beneath the Foot;* and Mrs. Almadou Mouth in *Prancing Nigger.* Such
names, although assigned to women characters, are part of the tradition of trans-
vestite queens.

9. Carl Van Vechten, *The Tattooed Countess: A Romantic Novel with a
Happy Ending,* introd. by Bruce Kellner (Iowa City: University of Iowa Press,
1987), pp. 213–14.

10. Bruce Kellner described the apartment of this companionate couple as
"small enough to serve Carl and Fania as an intimate and friendly home but still
large enough and suitably divided to allow them their separate lives" (Kellner,
The Irreverent Decades, p. 305).

11. Quoted in John Malcolm Brinnin, *The Third Rose: Gertrude Stein and Her
World* (Boston: Little, Brown and Company, 1959), p. 177.

12. Carl Van Vechten, *Peter Whiffle: His Life and Works* (New York: Alfred
A. Knopf, 1922), p. 123.

13. Ibid., p. 145.

14. I am indebted to these insights into Stein's perception of culture as a multiple, overlapping field to Judy Grahn, *Really Reading Gertrude Stein: A Selected
Anthology with Essays* (Freedom, Calif.: Crossing Press, 1989), pp. 8–9. The
lucidity, user-friendliness, and nonconformist intelligence of this guide—published by an alternative press and written by a lesbian poet for an audience of lesbians and feminists—places it in a direct line from Van Vechten's critical
approach to Stein.

15. Gertrude Stein, *The Autobiography of Alice B. Toklas* (New York: Harcourt, Brace and Co., 1933), p. 166. Subsequent references are to this edition and
appear parenthetically in the text, abbreviated *AAT.*

16. See Wendy Steiner's *Exact Resemblance to Exact Resemblance: The Literary Portraiture of Gertrude Stein* (New Haven: Yale University Press, 1978), for
an analysis that, despite methodological weaknesses involving the isolation of
Stein's portraiture from the sequence of her writings and the derivation of Stein's
theories of portraiture from her later writings, is still useful in describing features
of three portrait phases. According to Steiner, the first phase (1908–11) was
devoted to character typology, the second (1913–25) to visuals, and the third
(1926–46) to self-contained movement.

17. Gertrude Stein, *Geography and Plays* (New York: Haskell House, 1967),
pp. 199–200.

18. A letter that Mabel Dodge wrote to Stein warning her against publishing *Tender Buttons* with Donald Evans gives an idea of the dangers of association with those perceived as "decadent" (read homosexual): "Claire Marie Press which Evans runs is absolutely third rate, & in bad odor here, being called for the most part 'decadent' & Broadwayish & that sort of thing. . . . I think it would be a pity to publish with him *if* it will emphasize the idea in the opinion of the public, that there is something degenerate & effete & decadent about the whole of the cubist movement which they *all* connect you with, because, hang it all, as long as they don't understand a thing they think all sorts of things." Stein was sufficiently alarmed by this report that she requested her manuscript returned, but it was too late. *Tender Buttons* appeared in the spring of 1914. (*The Flowers of Friendship: Letters Written to Gertrude Stein,* ed. by Donald Gallup [New York: Alfred A. Knopf, 1953], pp. 96–97).

19. Carl Van Vechten, "How to Read Gertrude Stein," in *Trend* 7, no. 5 (August 1914): 553–57.

20. Gertrude Stein, *Tender Buttons* (New York: Claire Marie Press, 1914), p. 29.

21. See, for example, Lisa Ruddick, *Reading Gertrude Stein: Body, Text, Gnosis* (Ithaca, N.Y.: Cornell University Press, 1990), p. 216.

22. Stein, *Tender Buttons,* p. 9.

23. Stein's portrait also recapitulates the basic plot of Théophile Gautier's *Mademoiselle de Maupin* (1835), a novel that helped to inaugurate the modern consciousness of lesbianism and allied it with an antinaturalistic, antibourgeois, and antiutilitarian aesthetic. A young woman dresses up as a man in order to discover their true natures and subsequently loses consciousness of her sexual identity. Madeleine/Theodore acquires the desires of men through cross-dressing. In the end, her desires are aroused by a woman named Rosette who has made provocative advances toward "her," and the two make love.

24. See Chapter 8, "I Took a Girl Away from You Once" (pp. 128–49), in de Grazia's *Girls Lean Back Everywhere,* for a discussion of the proliferation of new American publishing firms in the 1920s.

25. Carl Van Vechten, "Notes for an Autobiography," in *Sacred and Profane Memories* (New York: Alfred A. Knopf, 1932), pp. 229–30.

26. William H. Gass, "Gertrude Stein and the Geography of the Sentence," in *Modern Critical Views: Gertrude Stein,* ed. Harold Bloom (New York: Chelsea House, 1986), pp. 162–63.

27. Carl Van Vechten, *The Blind Bow-Boy* (New York: Alfred A. Knopf, 1923), p. 117.

28. Ibid., pp. 71–72.

29. See Eve Kosofsky Sedgwick, *The Epistemology of the Closet* (Berkeley and Los Angeles: University of California Press, 1990), for a discussion of "homosexual panic" in the context of its use as a defense for a someone accused of antigay

violence. Sedgwick notes that this defense "implies that the [perpetrator's] responsibility for the crime was diminished by a pathological psychological condition, perhaps brought on by an unwanted sexual advance from the man whom he then attacked. . . . [This defense] rests on the falsely individualizing and pathologizing assumption that hatred of homosexuals is so private and so atypical a phenomenon in this culture as to be classifiable as an accountability-reducing illness. The widespread acceptance of this defense really seems to show, to the contrary, that hatred of homosexuals is even more public, more typical, hence harder to find any leverage against than hatred of other disadvantaged groups" (19).

30. Carl Van Vechten, *Parties: Scenes from Contemporary New York Life* (New York: Alfred A. Knopf, 1930), p. 70. Subsequent references appear parenthetically in the text, abbreviated *P*.

31. See Eve Kosofsky Sedgwick's *Between Men: English Literature and Male Homosocial Desire* (New York: Columbia University Press, 1985) for an extended analysis of the male-female-male triad that mediates male homosexual desire in "closeted" texts.

32. Also see Isabelle de Courtivron's essay, "Weak Men and Fatal Women: The Sand Image," in *Homosexualities and French Literature,* ed. Elaine Marks and George Stambolian (Ithaca, N.Y.: Cornell University Press, 1979), pp. 210–17. Courtivron remarks that "in leading [Madeleine] to the furthest stage of sexual androgyny, Gautier permits the acting out of his hero's forbidden and repressed longings, while managing to avoid what would prove a threatening self-confrontation" (218). An analogous pattern was played out, with obvious differences in the roles assigned, in the personal and professional relations between Stein and Van Vechten.

33. The publication history of *The Making of Americans* has been, to say the least, a checkered one and once again attests to the prejudice against perceiving lesbians as transformers of culture. *Transatlantic Review* published 150 pages of the manuscript, April through December 1924. Robert McAlmon (married, for a period, to the British lesbian writer, Bryher) printed a small run of the complete manuscript in 1925, although he and Stein had considerable disagreements concerning the costs of the printing, and she subsequently ended her dealings with him. Boni published an American edition of one hundred copies in 1926. Harcourt Brace, which had already brought out *The Autobiography of Alice B. Toklas,* agreed, although reluctantly, to publish an abridged version in 1934. Harcourt Brace subsequently issued a paperback edition in 1966, the same year that Something Else Press published a large run of the complete manuscript, approximately fifty-four years after Stein had written the text.

34. Four Seas Company (Boston) published *Geography and Plays* in 1922; Daniel Henry Kahnweiler (New York) published *A Book Concluding with As a Wife Has a Cow a Love Story* in 1926; Payson and Clarke (New York) published *Useful Knowledge* in 1928; and Seizen Press (London) published *An Acquain-*

tance with Description in 1929. The first two works are heavily inflected with queer themes, including erotic ones, while the last two, particularly *An Acquaintance with Description,* represent some of Stein's most challenging theoretical musings on the nature of knowledge, language, and literary representation. An important and, at least for queer readers, surprising exception to Stein's marginalization in the literary marketplace was "Miss Furr and Miss Skeene," a portrait of a lesbian couple, Mabel Squires and Ethel Mars, which appeared in *Vanity Fair* in July 1923.

35. In her fine essay, "(Im)Personating Gertrude Stein," in *Gertrude Stein and the Making of Literature,* ed. by Shirley Neuman and Ira B. Nadel (Boston: Northeastern University Press, 1988), pp. 61–80, Marjorie Perloff analyzes how popular-film and drama interpretations of *The Autobiography of Alice B. Toklas* manage to misconstrue, through oversimplification, sentimentality or bathos, this supposedly "transparent" text, thus showing that the *Autobiography* cannot be accommodated to traditional narrative strategies.

36. Marianne DeKoven, "Gertrude Stein and the Modernist Canon," in Neuman and Nadel, *Gertrude Stein,* pp. 8–20.

37. Employing vastly different styles of address, both *Everybody's Autobiography* and *The Geographical History of America* respond to Stein's comment that the focus on her personality rather than her writing deeply troubled her.

38. See Lillian Faderman, *Surpassing the Love of Men: Romantic Friendship and Love between Women from the Renaissance to the Present* (New York: William Morrow and Company, 1981), and Jane Rule, *Lesbian Images* (New York: Doubleday and Company, 1975). Faderman argues that "Stein's awareness of the threat of censorship probably accounts for her adoption of an unconventional style. . . . If she is difficult and often impossible to read, it is because she felt that one could not write clearly about homosexuality and expect to be published" (399–400). Rule notes that Stein, in *Lifting Belly,* "was reduced to coy code games to tease at rather than explore her domestic and erotic relationship with Alice B. Toklas. About all the insight that can be gained is that Gertrude thought of herself as a man in the relationship, referred to Alice as her wife, that they both played the intimate, inane sexual games in which most people indulge, fortunately without the temptation to record them and claim literary value for them" (69).

The Art of Self-Promotion; or, Which Self to Sell? The Proliferation and Disintegration of the Harlem Renaissance

Christopher M. Mott

Among the many schools and movements marketed during the modernist period, the Harlem Renaissance seems to have pursued most self-consciously its own promotion. Because the movement was so focused on exposing as widely as possible African-American artists and a new version of black experience in America, the Harlem Renaissance was particularly sensitive to market forces. At a dinner ostensibly given to celebrate the publication of Jessie Fauset's *There Is Confusion,* Charles S. Johnson skillfully brought together African-American writers and white publishers. For several reasons, not least of which was the commercial success of plays and stories featuring "black life," white publishers and editors such as Alfred Knopf, Paul Kellogg, and Horace Liveright were very eager to sign up these black artists who could give them what the public wanted. The market demand for the "exotic" life of blacks—especially as it was commodified as the cabaret nightlife of Harlem—made possible an unprecedented increase in the number of books, magazines, and essays written by blacks and published by major white publishers. The same market forces that led to an increase in black publications also resulted in a decrease after five or six years. Perhaps the stock market crash of 1929 left publishers and book buyers with less money to spend and led to a reactionary reduction of booklists; perhaps African-American artists and intellectuals turned their attention from race promotion to analyzing the shortcomings of capitalism; perhaps white patrons became bored or dissatisfied with the turn of Harlem art and thought. Whatever the reason, by 1933 the number of books written by blacks and published by large houses had fallen almost to none.[1] At the same time, the major promoters of the Renaissance—Johnson, Alain Locke, A. Philip Randolph, and

Chandler Owen—moved on to other pursuits; indeed, Johnson and Locke publicly pronounced the death of the Harlem Renaissance.

The narrative I have recounted above is a standard history of the Harlem Renaissance. Most historians of this movement acknowledge its sensitivity to market forces, its dependence on white capital, and its susceptibility to economic injury. Even those who argue that the Harlem Renaissance was not a failure, but left a legacy of race consciousness and artistic responsibility that remains with us today, admit that the force of the movement was severely curtailed by the reduced interest of whites and by the stock market crash.[2] However, a close study of the leading magazines of the Harlem Renaissance, edited by the men most responsible for promoting the movement, reveals that perhaps too much emphasis has been placed on bald market forces, that is, market forces that are understood simply in monetary terms. The content of *The Crisis, The Messenger,* and *Opportunity* indicates that a more complicated struggle was taking place, a struggle that included but went beyond financial viability into the realm of images and ideas—into the realm of ideology. The "marketplace" for the ideological efforts of Harlem Renaissance intellectuals was the consciousness of white and black Americans. The product was a "new" image of African-Americans. Profit would be measured in terms of racial uplift for blacks and racial sensitivity (or the eradication of racism) for whites. The battle waged within this ideological economy was more concentrated and briefer than the battle for financial support. The measure of its success cannot be counted in the number of black authors published or the number of black magazines distributed throughout the country. Instead, the success of the ideological endeavor undertaken by Harlem Renaissance intellectuals can only be measured by its continuing influence on the way we think now. In these terms, I have to agree with those who insist that the Harlem Renaissance was a (qualified) success. Renaissance intellectuals successfully changed race from a problem to a problematic, from an assumed set of definitive deviations to a complete rethinking of our assumptions about racial behavior. Harlem Renaissance intellectuals successfully questioned race, if they did not provide any answers—but, of course, the question of race might be unanswerable.

In this context, Renaissance intellectuals waged ideological war in two closely related fields: imagistic representation and the discourse of science. The science of race attempted to represent the truth about race. Harlem Renaissance intellectuals attacked this "pseudoscience," often from the perspective of representational skepticism or relativism. Yet they also seemed to advocate the very principles of representation and truth seeking found in the science of race. In practice, the science of race had been used to rationalize and provide evidence for a racial hierarchy, with whites on top in every category of human behavior and valuation: intelligence, morality, "willpower," reliability, and so on. The studies used to support such a racist apprehension of Americans were consistently and frequently attacked in the pages of Harlem magazines, as exemplified by Locke's critique of anthropology for not having established the link—the representational correspondence—between "physical character, and group behavior, and psychological and cultural traits."[3] However, the discourse of science—the rules of evidence, the establishment of an object of study, the assumption of an objective (in this case, biological) basis for (racial) phenomena, and the pursuit of truth—continued to attract Renaissance editors and writers. This complicated relationship to science paralleled the ideological campaign conducted by Harlem intellectuals. Their attack on the science of race corresponded to their attempt to undo racist thinking by whites; yet science also served the movement in providing the means to establish—with certitude—a (positive) racial identity, and a racial identity was deemed crucial to racial uplift. The complicated relationship between the discourse of science and racial uplift and antiracism was further complicated by the art-versus-propaganda debate that occurred at the height of the Renaissance. Those who sought to undermine the foundations of racial categories (found in the science of race and in racist thinking) argued for the total freedom of the black artist to depict whatever aspects of life interested him or her. Those who favored a program of racial uplift (which depended on a positive black identity) argued that only propaganda—art that portrayed only positive images of blacks—could help the cause of African-Americans. What makes the issue even more tangled is the fact that these different views were often held by the same person.

The cognitive dissonance that resulted from the attempt simultaneously to undo race and to promote racial pride created a great deal of tension in the movement. However, the impetus of the Harlem Renaissance was not lost because a consensus could not be formed, nor was it lost because the intellectuals tried to include too much diversity.[4] Rather, as is apparent in the retrenchment of *The Crisis,* the suspension of literary contests, Charles Johnson's resignation from *Opportunity,* and Chandler Owen's and Philip Randolph's departures from *The Messenger* and its almost immediate demise, the Harlem Renaissance lost its vitality not because of too much diversity but because of intolerance for diversity. While each of the magazines ran articles in 1925 and 1926 that praised diversity of opinion in the black community as a healthy development, by 1928 the editors had expressed much more conservative feelings. Indeed, these later articles and editorials suggest that the tension resulting from the effort to destroy race and promote it simply could not be sustained any longer.

Rather than judge the proliferation and dissipation of the Harlem Renaissance as an indication of its success or its failure, however, I propose to see this period as the beginning of our own. The dilemma faced by Renaissance intellectuals is a dilemma that still contorts our thoughts about race. They and we are fixed in a dialectical dilemma of race.[5] In this irresolvable dialectic one simultaneously seeks to deconstruct race, especially any features or characteristics that might distinguish whites from blacks, and to institute a race consciousness, a race identity for blacks based on their differences from whites. Although the manifestation of the dialectic dilemma particular to Harlem Renaissance intellectuals (i.e., their skeptical faith in science to establish the truth of race) is not so conspicuous today as it once was, we still struggle with the truth about race (or about sexual preference, the most recent battleground for science and social values). Unfortunately, even though the discourse of science promises an unbiased and objective reality that can serve as the basis for justice, none of its evidence or theories or narratives remain unsullied in the arena of social ethics. Even if science can prove that something is "natural," it cannot make the case that it is "normal." The correction of natural aberration is almost a characteristic feature of Western culture. In fact, in the case of the Harlem Renaissance, the scientific imperative to establish and enforce the truth led not to a consensus that created group cohesion but to greater intolerance that, in turn, led to group disintegration.

Despite the eventual dissipation of the Harlem Renaissance, those intellectuals left a legacy of public intervention that remains with us today. The common ground shared by W. E. B. Du Bois, Countee Cullen, Johnson, Randolph, Eric Walrond, Locke, George Schuyler, J. A. Rogers, and others appeared in their articles, reviews, editorials, and speeches: they constantly foregrounded the image of blacks circulating in the (white and black) American public mind. We share the same field with the Harlem intellectuals in our battle over the media image. The fact that Renaissance leaders chose to pour their energies into magazines indicates their awareness of the power of media representation to shape public opinion. They used the magazines to counter the negative images of blacks in the minds of blacks and whites by promoting positive images of African-Americans. While this strategy followed the campaign of uplift, a conflicting strategy appeared at the same time. To destroy racist assumptions of correspondence between race and any constellation of settled characteristics, the magazines proliferated images of blacks to the point where no stable correspondence between morphological features and behavior could be maintained. The three leading magazines multiplied occupational, intellectual, moral and artistic images and versions of African-Americans through photos, articles, studies, editorials, poems, and so on. In the magazines, blacks were represented as doctors, lawyers, nurses, teachers, farmers, streetwalkers, college students, college professors, sailors, soldiers, rioters, thieves, victims, instigators, and so on, almost indefinitely. Yet this proliferation of images, which coincided with the attack on the science of race, conflicted with the effort to promote a single, stable image of black life that could serve as a source of racial identity. Obviously, the structure and stability of science offers the perfect discourse to meet the need for racial identity. Many of the Harlem Renaissance intellectuals found themselves confounded in their attempts to destroy the pseudoscience that dominated public discourse on race by their feeling that a racial identity was necessary, and therefore a biological logic was also necessary. Charles S. Johnson provides a prime example of this conflict when he states in the same essay that "As the science of anthropology developed . . . a wider selection of subjects for study and more accurate instruments of measurement eliminated to an embarrassing degree the personal bias and preconceptions of the investigators," and that "it is so absurdly easy to prove almost anything where there exists a will to believe that the elaborate gestures of scientific thoroughness at times seems grotesquely out of place."[6] An unbearable tension arose between the recognition that the very bases for scientific investigation were suspect and the hope that science could still help to change market perception by producing truth.

The Ossification of *The Crisis*

In 1925 and 1926, *The Crisis* published a number of articles that criticized scientific studies of race, that is, scientific treatises on African-Americans. Every one of these essays concluded that race did not exist beyond a social category or scientific classification; in either case, race was an arbitrary construct created to benefit people outside the boundaries they set for the "Negro" race. The critiques argue that African-Americans exhibit the same broad spectrum of human traits—good and bad—that characterize any other group living under similar conditions. This sense of a permeable boundary between the races also appeared in a symposium that was published alongside these critiques. A wide variety of editors and writers representing a wide range of values and beliefs contributed to the symposium, suggesting—as had the scientific critiques—that not only was no consensus possible, it was not desirable.

Unfortunately this tolerance did not last long. By 1928, *The Crisis* no longer published the sorts of scientific critiques that intimated the impossibility of establishing a true identity. The magazine also suspended its literary contest and no longer conducted symposia. Instead, Du Bois mounted a campaign to spread the truth of the New Negro as he and his fellows understood it. In 1928, only one version of black experience was acceptable; the others were not only logically incorrect, they were morally wrong. To represent black experience as less than a wholesome struggle for education and income was to pander to the most prurient interests of white folks.[7] There was a thing—the Negro—that existed beyond culturally constructed social conditions and arbitrary significations and classifications. And *The Crisis* became adamant in its attempt to fix that thing.

In 1925, editorials in *The Crisis* not only approvingly cited many critiques of racialist science, but the journal also included several extended analyses of the scientific effort to settle a stable definition of race. Perhaps the foremost among these is H. A. Kelly's "Science, Pseudo-Science and the Race Question." Kelly was given six full pages to work out his thesis; in addition, his article was reproduced as a pamphlet that was promoted on the first page of the magazine and made available at *The Crisis* bookstore. Kelly's article reiterates the three main points emphasized by numerous critiques of "pseudoscience" published by *The Crisis* in 1925 and early 1926: first, science held no guarantee of objectivity, in part because scientists were human and subject to the same failings of perception and belief as the rest of humanity; second, "race" was an arbitrary classification, and the fact that scientists fought so hard to defend the boundaries of this category proved its tendentiousness; and finally, scientific instruments are not infallible and cannot overcome the failings of the people who use them. Indeed, scientific instruments can increase miscalculation when they remain unexamined.

In the conclusion to his article, Kelly compresses these three points into a powerful statement. He answers his own question, "what is a 'Race'?" with:

> The unbiased scientific conclusion seems now to be pointing to the fact that race itself is pseudo. A race is an artificial division of the human race for the purposes of classification just as science itself is artificially divided. Race lines apparently might just as well have been drawn in some other way, such as liability to measles, fondness for sour milk, or stature, all below five feet six might belong to the bronchic race and those above to the megalic. If all the red-headed people were classified as a race, all the racial phenomena could be found in them.[8]

The radical statement in this passage—that all race is "pseudo"—reflects the attitude of numerous other *Crisis* articles and editorials in 1925. "Race," then, according to the studies and reviews published approvingly by the editors of *The Crisis,* was an artificial category that could not be stabilized into a scientific truth; rather, it seemed to defy all attempts to settle on a group of definitive features. Thus, "race" was seen to serve the purpose of racial prejudice instead of the ideal of objective study.

The constant undoing of any constellation of racially distinctive traits that appeared in many issues of *The Crisis* for 1925 and 1926 paralleled the polyvalent attitude about racial typing in art and literature that appeared in two *Crisis* projects. In addition to the symposium that unsettled the question, "How to Portray the Negro in Art?" Du Bois himself invited participation in a series of writing and art contests sponsored by various white and black patrons, and promoted in *The Crisis.* While both projects bore the marks of Du Bois's moderate racial ideology—that blacks should be represented only as diligent, decent, respectable people—he was forced to welcome other viewpoints. Indeed, the conflict between Du Bois's insistence on promoting only a single image of black identity and the widely various versions of black identity that appeared in the contests and symposium created a great deal of tension.

In his announcement of the 1926 KRIGWA contest, Du Bois reveals both bias against and tolerance of the diverse images of blacks, the latter clearly overriding the former in the outcome of the contest.[9] Du Bois invited the participants to "write . . . about things as you know them; be honest and sincere. In THE CRISIS at least, you do not have to confine your writings to the portrayal of beggars, scoundrels and prostitutes; you can write about ordinary decent colored people if you want. On the other hand do not fear the Truth. Plumb the depths. If you want to paint Crime and Destitution and Evil paint it. Do not try to be simply respectable, smug, conventional. Use propaganda if you want. Discard it and laugh if you will. But be true, be sincere, be thorough and do a beautiful job."[10] Du Bois's paragraph is fraught with the tension of maintaining an open mind against the impulse to push the program he felt most capable of destroying racism. The *Crisis* contest was to be an open forum, and Du Bois's insistence that in his magazine one was not "confined" to representing beggars, scoundrels, and prostitutes fired a subtle shot at the white publishers Du Bois blamed for advancing a sensationalist representation of black experience in general and Harlem life in particular. For Du Bois, "ordinary decent colored people" were "the Truth" of the race. Yet, interestingly, he contrasts that representation—"on the other hand"—to "Truth." In yet another contravention, Du Bois then equates this "Truthful" version of black experience and identity with "propaganda," yet he felt that proper propaganda presented only positive images of blacks. In spite of his attempt to appear impartial, Du Bois cannot resist some kind of admonition about the representation of African-Americans: be "sincere." The call to sincerity supersedes and resolves the conflicting calls to Truth and to propaganda. Sincerity seems to transcend the clash of ideologies—or perhaps Du Bois wished it would: the strain of undoing and promoting race was telling.

The announcement of the 1926 contest reveals Du Bois's struggle to avoid insisting that any single representation of black experience and identity was any truer than any other, that any constellation of characteristics was more valid or more effective than any other. Indeed, Du Bois earlier expressed the limitations of promoting only the "respectable Negro" type: "It is said time and time again that when the Negro race exhibits real talent and genius, then it escapes the petty prejudice and annoyances which surround it in America. This is not only not true but often American prejudice actually pursues and attacks Negro genius."[11] While the attitude expressed in these lines may seem cynical—a black person who achieves in the United States provokes attacks by bigoted whites—it also has the air of a sophisticated assessment: simply relying on a single version of black identity to undo racist thought is naive and dangerous. In fact, by demanding that black identity appear by way of only one image, no matter how good that image is, one not only plays into the hand of bigots, but invites their attention; they know how to reinterpret the image to fit their purposes. On the other hand, by implication and by practice in the 1925 and 1926 issues of the magazine, to promote a boundless proliferation of images and meanings for black experience and black identity is to promote the destruction of racism by insisting that when it comes to racially distinct characteristics, "there is confusion."

Yet, while proliferation works well to undermine the logic of racism, it has the undesirable side-effect of undermining racial identity. Inevitably, it seems, one must choose either to undo racism or promote uplift. Du Bois chose no longer to sustain the stress of doing both by moving toward an unyielding and strict policy of representation. Three essays published in 1928 indicate the magazine's turn from proliferation. First, the magazine published an essay on New Negro intellectuals by Allison Davis in which the author followed the new old line established by Du Bois. In contrast to the open forum, which seemed to invite many perspectives on black identity, Davis attacked those who did not conform to the "old Negro" policy of putting the best foot forward. Second, Du Bois wrote a response to a letter by a young man who suggests that the word *Negro* has negative connotations. Du Bois uses an apodictic logic, a rationale that insists on our ability to perceive the "thingness" of an object despite the limitations of language adequately to represent that thing. The sensibility of the piece runs counter to the relativism in Kelly's highly promoted article. Finally, Du Bois wrote an approving, if somewhat inaccurate review of Melville Herskovitz's "scientific" study of race. According to Du Bois, Herskovitz established the existence of a New Negro all right—the mulatto population that had stabilized into a race. Ironically, Du Bois depends on the very group used previously to disprove categorical distinctions of race to serve as the example of the newest and truest race in the United States.

The increasing rigidity that marked Du Bois's ideas in the years following 1928, influenced his version of pan-Africanism, and led him to abandon *The Crisis*, the NAACP, and, finally, the United States seems to indicate a growing sense of futility about changing racist attitudes in the United States. The change that occurred in the magazine's policies in 1925 and 1926 may indicate a last blast at racism, a kind of desperate willingness to try anything, but that anything apparently proved to be at least as distasteful to Du Bois as the racism he hated. The notion that anything goes in promoting racial identity simply did not accord with his idea of race pride and race consciousness. But, to be fair, Du Bois was not the only intellectual leader who found it very difficult to negotiate the conflicting demands of destroying race and insisting upon it. Both Johnson, in *Opportunity*, and Randolph, in *The Messenger*, followed the same trajectory as Du Bois in their initial radical diversity to deconstruct race and subsequent retreat and abandonment of their promotional enterprises.

The Expansion and Reduction of *Opportunity*

While the trajectories of *The Crisis* and *Opportunity* are very similar, they are not, of course, exactly the same. Like *The Crisis*, *Opportunity*'s editorial staff waged an intense critical campaign against the "pseudo-science" that was being used to bolster the forces of racism. Like *The Crisis*, too, the conclusion reached by many of the scientific critics was that, according to true scientific examination, race did not exist apart from a classification or an arbitrary object of study. These critics often employed the tactic of counterexample to discredit the works they reviewed. For every constellation of traits assigned to African-Americans, these critics offered a differently inflected constellation, or, more commonly, several constellations. Eventually, under the pressure of so many "distinctive" attributes, the boundaries of the distinctive racial category gave way. This tactic of proliferating characteristics was mirrored in the editorial attitude toward the *Opportunity* literary contest. The editors at *Opportunity* encouraged a wide range of approaches to "Negro life," but they did insist that the short fiction at least be restricted to treating some aspect of Negro life; poetry could cover any topic. The contests were a great success, and the number of contestants increased from 1924 to 1926. Initially, the editors of *Opportunity* welcomed this increase and welcomed, too, the diverse points of view that such a large number of writings represented. However, by 1927, Johnson seems to have become overwhelmed by such diversity. In an important statement about the quality of materials submitted, Johnson completely reversed his laudatory comments about the high quality of all six hundred pieces and, instead, took to task those writers who felt they had something to say and the ability to say it just because they were black.[12]

Johnson's essay marks a turning point. The magazine continued to carry diverse viewpoints both in its social essays and its fiction, but the emphasis moved away from scientific critiques toward a more conservative censure of black writers who chose to write about the "underside" of black experience. However, unlike Du Bois and *The Crisis*, Johnson seemed to allow for the necessity of proliferation at the same time that he acknowledged his personal distaste for it. *Opportunity* did not undergo the kind of retrenchment that *The Crisis* did, but the optimistic vitality of a burgeoning movement in which all viewpoints are welcome had clearly disappeared. Johnson resigned from *Opportunity* in mid-1928, accepting a position at Fisk University as a researcher into social and economic conditions of African-Americans in the United States. Perhaps he felt safer trying to establish the certainty of race through statistics; perhaps he simply tired of the struggle to sustain a promotional attitude and maintain some stable standard of valuation. Whatever the explanation, Johnson left *Opportunity* at the height of Harlem Renaissance expansion—an expansion he engendered and nurtured through *Opportunity*.

Of the dozens of articles, reviews, editorials, and commentaries on scientific studies of race, "Race Prejudice" by Herbert Seligman encompasses most of the different themes treated in the other essays. Seligman's overarching thesis warns of the limitations of scientific study. In light of all of the "evidence" produced by dozens of scientific studies of race, Seligman tells his readers that "what is needed in this matter of race prejudice, is not more certainty, not more affirmation of fact. What is needed above all is doubt."[13] Further, he insists that the true scientific attitude is informed by uncertainty and suspicion—especially about its own instruments of perception: "the most enlightened among present day scientists would cause us to distrust that word [*race*]"; moreover, the scientific "attitude . . . is that anthropology is a descriptive, not a dogmatic science. That races as irreducible categories only exist as our fictions" (37, 39). Seligman concludes by asserting that "almost every general statement about races of men . . . is untrue" (39). Then no science of race is possible. One of the defining characteristics of scientific investigation is its attempt to establish laws—general rules of behavior or activity that allow for prediction and control. The only race that science establishes, Seligman reminds his reader, is the human race; any distinctive traits simply distinguish people with those traits. If a scientist studies mental ability, she will create a standard graduated according to mental ability; race becomes a category imposed upon such a standard, but, of course, race is not measured by or inherent to such an instrument of measurement. The critics of science in *Opportunity* constantly propose other features that might just as easily work as distinguishing features and apply them to scientific scales: the intelligence of redheads, the intelligence of left-handed people, the intelligence of people with big ears. The strategy here seems quite successful. By multiplying the features that could apply to a particular scale, the boundaries that constitute the exclusivity and accuracy of the measurement are simply destroyed.

This strategy of proliferation appeared in the magazine's approach to art as well. In a review of *Goat Alley,* Locke advises the reader that dramatists, especially Negro dramatists, must "learn how to cross-section scientifically the race life at this point." Locke recommends this approach against the "intelligensia of the Negro people [who] want uplift plays. They are wrong, I think, in wanting them to the exclusion of plays of other types, as well as wrong in complaining when others do not write them. . . . More plays then, of all kind [*sic*], but especially those by Negro authors, seem to be the only solution of the art problem produced for having for so long a time artificially restricted the portrayal of the life of the Negro in the arts."[14]

In an article that extends the observations of Seligman and Locke into the social sciences, Johnson emphasizes the importance not of facts but of interpretations in determining interracial attitudes and behavior. In "How Much Is the Migration a Flight from Persecution," Johnson identifies the political importance of interpreting African-American motives for the migration north. "After all, it means more that the Negroes who left the South were motivated more by their desire to improve their economic status than by fear of being manhandled by unfriendly whites."[15] This distinction is important to the economic survival of African-Americans: "The thought of flight from persecution excited little sympathy either from the practical employer or the Northern white population among whom these Negroes will hereafter have to live. Every man who runs is not a good worker" (274). Johnson's analysis is not only a pragmatic one, concerned with the outcome of the perception of images, but it also reveals a sophisticated understanding of the difference between a "cold, hard" fact and the consequences that result from the interpretation of facts. Since science could not stop people from interpreting experience, Johnson admonishes blacks to intervene in the cultural interpretations assigned to them. Johnson's work in *Opportunity* during this period was very much a promotional campaign to place multiple, even contradictory interpretations on the "facts" of black experience in the cities and hamlets of America.

The best example of Johnson's project is the *Opportunity* literary contest. In his announcement of the 1924 contest, Johnson appears to encourage as many viewpoints as possible about black life in America. Note the "Rules of the Contest": "The stories must deal with some phase of Negro life, either directly or indirectly; otherwise there are no restrictions."[16] In December, Johnson appeared to be very pleased at the great number and wide variety of submissions *Opportunity* received from the contestants: to date, "231 manuscripts have been entered. Stories, poems, plays, a sparkling colorful miscellany,—from the sophisticated centers of culture, from the rich veins of Negro life in the South, from tiny towns with unfamiliar postmarks, from the wide stretches of the West, from panama [*sic*] and the Virgin Islands. About them all is a passionate earnestness."[17] The telltale sign that links Johnson's and Du Bois's anxiety of diversity is "earnestness"—a guarantor of rightness along the lines of Du Bois's "sincerity."

In 1925, the winners were announced, and, true to the call put forth by Johnson, the stories represent a wide range of experiences and approaches to African-American life. First prize went to John Matheus for "Fog," a story that blurs the boundaries of absolute racial distinction. Indeed, the theme of the story is that the fog of tragedy—in this case a near-fatal trolley accident—can blind people to their racial differences and bind them in goodwill and mutual aid. Second prize went to a story that emphasizes the experience of poor, rural Southern blacks. Zora Neale Hurston's "Spunk" describes a powerful, sensual black man, Spunk, who pursues his passions no matter what—including killing the wimpish husband of the woman he loves. Hurston wrote the kind of story Du Bois would later warn his readers about. The third prize went to Eric Walrond's "The Voodoo's Revenge," which, as the title suggests, focuses on the exotic and spiritual elements in some blacks' lives. A reader would be hard pressed to create a consensus of opinion about black experience and black identity from these three stories. And, according to Johnson's "rules," that seems perfectly in keeping with the editor's promotional strategy and reason for having the contest in the first place.

Perhaps because he wanted to convince himself of the effect of these literary efforts, Johnson included an editorial in the very next issue that pointed out how white writers seemed to be getting the message. White poets, playwrights, and fiction writers were abandoning the limited stereotypes of blacks for a wide range of images depicting the diversity and possibility of black life. In the editorial entitled "New Pattern in the Literature about the Negro," Johnson reminds his reader of past white attitudes: Before, there was "one set of pictures,—a comic mask, rigid, forced, inflexible. That was permissible. There was another set describing various intensities or burliness. And for the gentler writers, there was permitted a small gallery of sentimental pictures which dealt with loyalty, religion, persecution, or the writer's sympathetic feeling toward helpless ignorance, poverty and hopelessness." However, "now . . . there has developed quietly but certainly, a new receptivity, a state of mind not only tolerable but hospitable to new pictures."[18] As examples, the editor cites Kay Boyle, William Carlos Williams, and others who had broken free from the limited and limiting stereotypes of just a few years previous and whose poetry includes a wide variety of "pictures" of black life, from stevedores to college professors, from old men stretched across a sun-dappled dock to young (female) nurses smartly and competently tending to the sick.

In the midst of this apparent success Johnson resigned. Why? The evidence suggests three possible answers. Johnson's final few editorials contend that he left because the goal he set out to attain as editor of the magazine had been achieved. On the other hand, Patrick Gilpin believes Johnson resigned because of a financial dispute with Eugene K. Jones. Jones had reduced the operating expenses of the journal, and Johnson felt that this reduction effectively blocked his efforts with the magazine.[19] Finally, for several months before his resignation the magazine tended toward the ideologically conservative, much as Du Bois had done with *The Crisis*. Perhaps Johnson moved to Fisk University to establish a more stable and more structured race object of study.

However, on first glance, Johnson's last editorials place him at odds with Du Bois. Indeed, where Du Bois wrote his editorial to a young black man suggesting that "Negro" was a thing in the world to be perceived and brought out, Johnson addressed his penultimate editorial "To Negro Youth," telling them that "the concept Negro is a variable: It never means the same biologically, geographically, historically, nor is it the same to different people of the same race, or period, or place."[20] In clear counterpoint to Du Bois and the "thingness" of "Negro," Johnson maintains the critical orientation by which "Negro" is a "concept": "The concept Negro is part of the concept 'stranger.' . . . And, finally, the concept Negro is part of the concept 'class.'" Moreover, Johnson anticipates the direction of black intellectuals of the 1930s and 1940s when he concludes his essay by making note of the "tendencies toward a crossing of racial lines when the common interests of class are concerned" (258). Finally, in his last editorial, Johnson discloses (but there is no telling how seriously) the irony that led to his resignation: "A quiet irony lies in the fact that the common interest which fostered many of the associations and working policies [at *Opportunity*],—an urge to uncover or see uncovered more and more of the richness and substance and spiritual purpose of Negro life at the matrix, makes inevitable this separation."[21] Ironically, the very project to uncover more and more of black life finally undoes the common interest of revealing black life.

When we read "To Negro Youth" in conjunction with "New Pattern in the Literature about the Negro" and Johnson's final editorial for *Opportunity,* we are hard-pressed to link Johnson's resignation to Du Bois's conservative retreat to a static version of black experience. And yet despite the differences between the viewpoints of the two editors, they shared the same fundamental frame of reference regarding race, and their different ideological trajectories can still be plotted on that frame. The work of both men was still encompassed by the dialectic of race; they found themselves needful of race as an object of study and a subject of activity, at the same time that they tended their activity toward the obliteration of the object. Perhaps Dr. Johnson needed to feel that the object of his work was a bit more scientifically ascertainable, a bit more certain, than "race," as it became dissolved in the proliferation and promotion of Harlem Renaissance writers. If our last supposition about Johnson has merit, then he shares more with Du Bois than a simple review of his editorials might indicate. Of course, we have evidence to link him to the ideology Du Bois began to promote in *The Crisis* after 1928: Johnson hired Countee Cullen, an ardent spokesman for the "best-foot-forward" school, to write a regular column on literature, and Johnson himself wrote a lengthy article praising the subtle and sophisticated antiracist strategies of Booker T. Washington, in addition to several articles condemning the "gutter-level" view of black life. At least part of the answer to our question about Johnson's resignation must be, then, that he, like Du Bois, could not abide the radical diversity of race that appeared in response to the very efforts he put forth to promote it. Despite the rhetoric of some of his editorials, Johnson finally seemed unwilling to part with certain racial characteristics that he favored and felt were definitive, which meant that he was unwilling to let race disperse amid a profusion of characteristics and traits. Du Bois finally retreated to a former ideological position; Johnson seems to have returned to his former interests as well—at Fisk he could pursue the social scientific studies he was trained to perform.

The Arrival and Departure of *The Messenger*

While the influence of *The Messenger* was neither so profound nor so consistent as that of *The Crisis* or *Opportunity,* the remarkable similarity between the advance and decline of Randolph and Owen's magazine and the other two leading journals of the Harlem Renaissance invites examination. Among the many intriguing correspondences between these journals, the most striking are the move, at the height of proliferating versions of black life, to an exclusive image of black identity; the sudden departure of the two editors in 1928 for more "real world" pursuits than running a journal whose battleground consisted almost solely of images; and a consistent attack on and undermining of scientific studies of race. More specifically, the trajectory of *The Messenger* began with the promotion of political and literary interrogations of race (including critiques of scientific race studies), which peaked in 1927 with the circulation of a "racial tactics and ideals" questionnaire and ended in the same year with the exclusive promotion of the New Negro as a union man—economically informed and willing to fight/strike for his rights.

The editorials written for June 1923 contain a trace of the ideological bent of the magazine for this period. In "The Youth Movement," the editors advise the "youth of the world" to run toward "a study of the problems of race, a sympathetic approach to and scientific understanding of which is imperative to the fashioning of a new society."[22] This emphasis on a scientific solution to race problems was quickly countered by a series of articles that attacked the validity of most of the contemporary scientific studies of race. Moreover, instead of mounting scientific, rational attacks on race studies, the writers for *The Messenger* resorted to literary techniques, especially satire. Schuyler joined the magazine at this time, and soon his column, "Shafts and Darts," found a ready target in "pseudoscientific" studies of race. In addition, *The Messenger* published a photographic satire of physiognomic and morphological studies that made full use of the new power of the media image (see fig. 14). Still, the 1927 questionnaire undermined to the greatest degree the scientific attempt to establish a single, true image of black Americans.

AMERICAN NEGRO TYPES

PLEASED

WISTFUL

EXPECTANT

THOUGHTFUL

MISCHIEVOUS

Mr. James L. Allen, a very youthful New Yorker, is one of those very rare photographers who knows how to photograph Negro types properly. Here we have five of his camera studies. In future numbers we shall reproduce many more studies made by this portraitist. Mr. Allen is on the staff of a large metropolitan concern.

216

The Messenger *never again ran a "gallery of types," although the magazine did regularly feature portraits with very definite individual identification.*

The questionnaire, which was first published in the January 1927 issue under the title "Group Tactics and Ideals," was "sent to Negroes in all parts of the country." The questionnaire consisted of eight questions asking if the development of race consciousness is compatible with the ideal of Americanism; if the ideal of social equality will result in "the disappearance of the Negro through amalgamation"; if amalgamation "is the solution of our problem"; if the respondent desired to see the "Aframerican group maintain its identity and the trend toward amalgamation cease"; and if the Aframerican group could maintain a separate group identity and consciousness and still obtain social equality.[23] The respondents were bankers, lawyers, school principals, ministers, leaders of clubs and organizations, journalists and editors, as well as "private citizens." The published responses to these questions present the reader with a variety that defies summary or consensus. As a brief example, some felt that race consciousness ran counter to Americanism and the American tradition of equality for all regardless of race. Others felt that race consciousness was a helpful political tool that inspired pride and therefore achievement but had no intrinsic value. Still others felt that race consciousness was simply a fact of racial life: to deny it would be like denying the color of one's skin. These responses appeared in three issues between January and October. By far the largest sample appeared in the January issue, and the amount of space devoted to the responses dwindled with each subsequent appearance.

The ink that had been given to the responses was used more and more to print articles and announcements for the Brotherhood of Sleeping Car Porters and Maids, which Randolph was leading through a difficult and unprecedented strike. In other words, multiple versions of black identity, black experience, and black politics gave way to a single, dominant version of black Americans as union folk. In the January 1927 issue, Randolph used negative rhetoric to create an image of the black man as a fighting union man.

> Negroes, least of all people, are not expected to revolt against opposition. However bitter their lot, according to tradition and custom running back through their history over a thousand years, Negroes, meekly and patiently, are supposed to bite their tongue and swallow it. ... Thus by all the gods of sanity and sense of Brotherhood men are a challenge to the Nordic creed of the white race's superiority. For only white men are supposed to organize for power, for justice and free-

dom. Only white men are supposed to face a long, hard struggle, to invite an exacting test, to encounter bitter opposition with unflinching courage, with a dogged stamina to work on and not grow weary, to fight on and not lose the faith. . . . Resistantly onward the Brotherhood marches.[24]

Despite the battle-heightened rhetoric of this speech, the image of the black union striker remains implicit in the negation of an image of white superiority. Randolph's example of white superiority is clearly a union striker. Randolph never questions the qualities of his mythical white man; his only complaint is that they are not also commonly attributed to blacks. His negative rhetoric is a response to the white union's exclusion of blacks, as was his decision to organize the Brotherhood along race lines, a strategy that he critiqued in previous issues of *The Messenger*. Now, Randolph's magazine will subsume all images of black Americans under the all-encompassing image of the black union worker willing and able to strike.

In March 1927, Randolph published an article by J. A. Rogers entitled "Who Is the New Negro, and Why?" Rogers described the New Negro as a man who is "satisfied with no concessions or patronage of any sort. He wants neither more nor less than his rights as a man and a citizen." He studies economics instead of the Epistles. He is determined to "make the whole weight of his presence felt while he moves on this earth." On the other hand, the "Old Negro" falls for the tricks that draw his attention from the race's "real problems" by minding the "over-stressing of Negro art, spirituals, piffling poetry, jazz, cabaret life, and the puffing into prominence of mediocre Negroes." The New Negro "realizes that the race question is almost solely an economic one."[25] Here, science is still at work; now, however, it is exclusively the socialist science of political economy. Race, especially as it was manifested in art, has given way to class: black working-class people (at least in the pages of *The Messenger*), like their white class-mates, insisted on an image and identity as a worker willing to fight for just wages and dignified working conditions. The attack on racism gave way to an attack on class exploitation, and the science of political economy formed the battle plan. By August and through to the final issue of the magazine (April 1928) most of the space in *The Messenger* that was not devoted to the promotion of the image of the black (union) working man were given over to letters from Pullman porters about the strike and about Randolph's leadership, updates on the negotiations, a new regular feature begun that year ("Brotherhood Activities,") and Randolph's schedule of public appearances.

Once again, we have to ask why the editors left the magazine just when it had provided a forum for a wide variety of African-Americans to address the race problem. What could explain Owen's move into mainstream politics or Randolph's decision to leave *The Messenger* rather than use it as an instrument of his union—the tendency indicated by the last several issues of the magazine? A possible answer arises from the parallel course run by the other two leading Harlem journals. While their initial efforts to promote alternative viewpoints resulted in a proliferation of images of black life, the editors later became more conservative, favoring—almost exclusively—a single, stable image of black identity near the end of their run. Owen and Randolph, like Du Bois and Johnson, seemed to need a "positive," reliable referent—one specifically suited to their ideology—that would enable them to continue to struggle against racism. Ironically, the very effort to promote a single, positive image led to the end of promotion altogether. Apparently, the editors felt that the realm of the image, the world of media images, was too precarious, too unsettled to provide them with a strong enough foothold to gain ground against racism.

Questionable Conclusion

While the trajectories I have described for Du Bois, Johnson, and Randolph tend downward at their conclusion, my own conclusion cannot rest easily on such a pattern. The very fact of my uneasiness about the formulation of a conclusion suggests that the trajectories do not finally crash to earth in defeat. Indeed, my uneasiness today resembles the tension that these intellectuals struggled with. The conflicting logics of race critique and race uplift, and the contradictory assumptions about representation implicit in each, continue to create tension in the battle against racism. This is not to say that Du Bois and Johnson, Owen and Randolph are unconditionally our contemporaries, but that the boundary we draw between the past and the present is not always so fixed as historical narratives might imply. Perhaps that border-crossing narrative *The Woman Warrior* provides us with a clearer explanation of historical narratives (including this one) that insist on crossing the chronological border that separates us from the Harlem intellectuals. In explaining why she has embellished the story of her no-name aunt who drowned herself because of an illegitimate pregnancy, the narrator tells us, "Unless I see her life branching into mine, she gives me no ancestral help."[26] How can we help but see ourselves in our precursors? My interpretation of the Harlem Renaissance, then, focuses on a problem that branches into our own: What logic will allow us to sustain the tension that results from the conflict between an identity politics and a politics of dissemination? How do we negotiate the differences and similarities between racial, ethnic, and class groups in the United States? How can we inflect difference without creating hierarchy? How do we suspend hierarchy without creating similarity? Can we actually live in a world without boundaries, or are borders an unavoidable aspect of human thought? From my perspective, these questions represent the legacy of the Harlem Renaissance. We are fortunate to inherit these questions. We are unfortunate to inherit these questions.

NOTES

1. For more details about the rise and fall of Harlem Renaissance publication, see Cary D. Wintz, *Black Culture and the Harlem Renaissance* (Houston: Rice University Press, 1988).

2. In *Harlem Renaissance* (New York: Oxford University Press, 1971), Nathan Huggins details white patronage of black artists and the strategic appeal to white publishers made by Johnson and others, esp. pp. 64, 118 and chap. 3. See also David L. Lewis, *When Harlem Was in Vogue* (New York: Alfred A. Knopf, 1981), and Wintz, *Black Culture*, p. 219. Houston Baker concludes *Modernism and the Harlem Renaissance* (Chicago: University of Chicago Press, 1987) by insisting that the Renaissance was a "resounding success" (107) because it fostered a way of "speaking *black and back*" (24) by engendering the strategies of "*the mastery of form* and *the deformation of mastery*" (15, and see 50) that continue to be effective for black artists today. However, Locke's *The New Negro*, Baker's prime example of Harlem Renaissance success, arose from Paul Kellogg's encouragement and the patronage of white publishers.

3. Alain Locke, "The Problem of Race Classification," *Opportunity* 1 (Sept. 1923): 262.

4. Wintz argues that the Renaissance declined because its leaders "never found any common ideology to bind together its adherents" (*Black Culture*, p. 222). In *The Novels of the Harlem Renaissance* (University Park: Pennsylvania State University Press, 1976), Amritjit Singh argues that the movement foundered because the writers did not "develop into a cohesive group" (21).

5. I have borrowed this term from Anthony Appiah. He introduces it in his essay "The Uncompleted Argument: Du Bois and the Illusion of Race," in *"Race," Writing, and Difference,* ed. Henry Louis Gates Jr. (Chicago: University of Chicago Press, 1985). The idea is common to students of the Harlem Renaissance. For example, see Huggins, *Harlem Renaissance.*

6. "Mental Measurements of Negro Groups," *Opportunity* 1 (Feb. 1923): 21.

7. I'm borrowing the concept of ossification from Claude McKay, who criticizes "the convention-ridden and head-ossified Negro intelligentsia, who censure colored actors for portraying the inimitable comic characteristics of Negro life, because they make white people laugh" *Liberator* 4 (Dec. 1921): 24.

8. *Crisis* 30 (Oct. 1925): 291.

9. KRIGWA was originally CRIGWA (Crisis Guild of Writers and Artists).

10. *Crisis* 31 (Jan. 1926): 115.

11. *Crisis* 31 (Dec. 1926): 87.

12. "Some Perils of the 'Renaissance,'" *Opportunity* 5 (Mar. 1927), see esp. p. 68.

13. *Opportunity* 3 (Feb. 1925): 37.

14. *Opportunity* 1 (Feb. 1923): 30.

15. *Opportunity* 1 (Sept. 1923): 272.

16. *Opportunity* 2 (Sept. 1924): 277.

17. *Opportunity* 2 (Dec. 1924): 355.

18. *Opportunity* 3 (June 1925): 162.

19. "Charles S. Johnson: Entrepreneur of the Harlem Renaissance," in *The Harlem Renaissance Remembered,* ed. Arna Bontemps (New York: Dodd, Mead, 1972), p. 243.

20. *Opportunity* 6 (Sept. 1928): 258.

21. "Valedictory," *Opportunity* 6 (Oct. 1928): 294.

22. "The Youth Movement," *Messenger* 5 (June 1923): 733.

23. *Messenger* 9 (Jan. 1927): 11.

24. A. Philip Randolph, "The Brotherhood and the Mediation Board," *Messenger* 9 (Jan. 1927): 17.

25. J. A. Rogers, "Who Is the New Negro, and Why?" *Messenger* 9 (Mar. 1927): 68.

26. Maxine Hong Kingston, *The Woman Warrior* (1976; New York: Viking, 1989), p. 8.

Making Poetry Pay: The Commodification of Langston Hughes

Karen Jackson Ford

In his first autobiography, *The Big Sea* (1940), Langston Hughes ironically titles a chapter "Poetry Is Practical," in which he describes meeting
his first literary friends and patrons through a sequence of events that
owed more to serendipity than to practicality. In fact, the chronicle of
those months in 1925 when Hughes was out of work and suffering from
hunger is a tale of fortunate flukes and unanticipated generosity rather
than one of pragmatics. Nevertheless, ten years later Arna Bontemps
would assert, with a surprising lack of irony, what eventually became a
favorite commonplace of Hughes scholars: "Langston Hughes is the only
Negro poet since Dunbar who has succeeded in making a living from
poetry."[1] The comparison to Paul Laurence Dunbar, who could find
work only as an elevator operator after graduating high school with honors, paid to publish his own first volume of poetry, was subsidized there-
after by white patrons, and died in his early thirties before it could reasonably be claimed that he had made a *living* at writing, is laden with
ironies that Bontemps seems to ignore. Indeed, Bontemps must overlook
the chronic financial hardships that Hughes endured in order to characterize his best friend's vocation as lucrative: "Poetry has turned a pretty
penny for the Negro who spoke of rivers the summer after graduating
from high school in 1920" (360). Yet despite his optimism about the earn-
ing power of poetry, Bontemps does admit that the poem must be commodified if it is to pay.

> But a poem must be used many ways to yield enough substance to
> keep a hearty individual like Mr. Hughes in the kind of food he likes.
> Therefore it is not surprising to find his poems being danced by Pearl
> Primus on the stage while they are sung by Juanita Hall in night clubs

and on the radio and television and by Muriel Rahn in Town Hall concerts and while Paul Robeson is reciting "Freedom Train" in the United States, West Indies and Central America. (360)

Hughes eked out a living writing poetry because he had the good business sense to understand that the poem could be "used in many ways"—that is, it could be commodified. Poems could be published individually in magazines and newspapers, gathered together for a volume, reprinted in later volumes or anthologies, interpolated in prose, sung on the stage, recited in personal appearances, submitted to writing contests, and recycled yet again for a *Selected Poems;* further, a poem could be revised, retitled, and even recalled like a defective product. Langston Hughes was a relentless marketer of his own poetry, successful because he recognized that promoting his poetry involved handling both the product and the consumer.

A chapter in his second autobiography, *I Wonder as I Wander* (1956), describes that latter task: handling the consumer. In "Making Poetry Pay" he recalls the "public routine of reading [his] poetry that almost never failed to provoke . . . some sort of audible audience response."[2] Reading to poor, uneducated southern blacks, Hughes would begin his program with a biographical introduction that established his humble background. He would then read some of his novice high-school poems to "show how [his] poetry had changed" and probably to demonstrate that poetry could be simple and accessible. Making fun of his own juvenilia, he would get the audience laughing, and then he would "read some of [his] jazz poems so [his] listeners could laugh more" (57). This comic opening put them at their ease and enabled him to lead them through a program of more challenging and troubling poetry: "By the time I reached this point in the program my nonliterary listeners would be ready to think in terms of their own problems" (58). If the attention of the audience wavered, he would recite "Cross," a provocative poem about miscegenation, with practiced theatrical flourishes. What Hughes describes here is working the crowd; he makes poetry pay with the right sales pitch and a shrewd presentation of the goods.

Hughes's attitude toward his nonliterary audience is not simply exploitative, however. In "The Negro Artist and the Racial Mountain," published in *The Nation* in 1926, he identifies these "common people" as the appropriate muse of the black poet: "They furnish a wealth of colorful, distinctive material for any artist because they still hold their own individuality in the face of American standardizations. And perhaps these common people will give the world its truly great Negro artist, the one who is not afraid to be himself."[3] The conflict that Hughes would have to confront is that the common people retain their individuality because they are outside of the commercial and academic institutions that impose standardizations. Since Hughes could not survive economically as a writer and remain independent of these institutions, his audience would have to include a much greater range of readers, specifically, more affluent black and white readers who would tend to hold "standardized" literary values.

Thus, the written record of Hughes's poetry indicates that in addition to creating an audience for his poems, he had to create poetry for a wide audience. These two impulses were in productive tension throughout his life largely because of the tremendous complexity of that audience. Over the forty-some years of his publishing career (from his first volume, *The Weary Blues*, published in 1926, to *The Panther and the Lash*, in press when he died in 1967), Hughes wrote for a diverse and contradictory range of readers. He worked through two major literary movements, the Harlem Renaissance in the 1920s and the Black Arts movement in the 1960s; published in exceedingly different political climates, from the socialism of the 1930s through the conservatism of the 1950s to the radicalism of the 1960s; rebelled against his New Negro elders in his youth and against the militant Black Arts poets in his old age; wrote on behalf of the poor black masses even as he did so at the behest of a wealthy white patron; sought readers among the uneducated and the educated, the poor and the middle classes, among political activists and the literati; and, of course, as an African-American writer, he wrote for a divided audience of black and white readers.

To hear Hughes in his most eloquent and influential statement about audiences, one would suppose he had escaped their conflicting demands. In the same essay where he casts his lot with the common people, he also proclaims his artistic autonomy.

We younger Negro artists who create now intend to express our individual dark-skinned selves without fear or shame. If white people are pleased we are glad. If they are not, it doesn't matter. We know we are beautiful. And ugly too. The tom-tom cries and the tom-tom laughs. If colored people are pleased we are glad. If they are not, their displeasure doesn't matter either. We build our temples for tomorrow, strong as we know how, and we stand on top of the mountain, free within ourselves.[4]

This powerful statement of indifference to the reactions of readers stands in curious contrast to Hughes's almost legendary adaptability to audiences; yet the difference between the proclamation of aesthetic independence and the record of capitulation and compromise in publishing is the difference between the making of the poem and the marketing of it. Throughout his career Hughes did indeed follow his moral and aesthetic instincts in his writing. However, when he *marketed* that writing, he made many concessions to audience, using the poems and reusing them, packaging and repackaging them, promoting and sometimes suppressing them. To the extent that poetry turned a pretty penny for Hughes, it did so by way of many other turnings.

Most of Hughes's commentators—reviewers, biographers, critics—acknowledge that he made, not just poetry, but much of his writing pay. For example, in a 1967 review of *The Best Short Stories by Negro Writers,* edited by Hughes, Robert Bone employs the language of commercialism to register his exasperation with the uneven quality of the volume and, thus, with what he takes to be Hughes's failure of judgment and discrimination: "He is *merchandising* these stories; to him they are commodities."[5] Bone complains that including too many stories is a marketing ploy; even more frequently, excluding material receives the same condemnation. Faith Berry, one of Hughes's biographers, recognizes this marketing impulse in the editing of two of the writer's collections, *The Langston Hughes Reader* (1958) and the *Selected Poems* (1959). By definition both books ought to represent the breadth of Hughes's work, yet both exclude his radical writings. Once again the charge is commercialism.

> There was nothing about the wide selection of poems to indicate a chronology, but obviously missing were any of his more radical ones from the 1930s; not even his revised version of "Let America Be America Again" [a poem Hughes had already sanitized] was included. Nobody knew better than Langston Hughes why they were not there. He had selected not his best poems, but those he thought would go over best with the public. He aimed to please. *Selected Poems* reflected that desire as much as *The Langston Hughes Reader.*[6]

In fact, Berry's biography, *Langston Hughes: Before and beyond Harlem* (1983), traces a lifetime of aiming to please an audience by altering or suppressing works.[7] Berry is especially interested in Hughes's radical poetry, meticulously documenting first his unequivocal commitment to leftist politics and then his gradual repudiation of much of his socialist writing. From his humiliating capitulation to McCarthy ("[The radical writings] do not represent my current thinking. . . . I have more recent books I would prefer") to his futile attempt to suppress the controversial "Goodbye, Christ" ("Goodbye, Christ does not represent my personal viewpoint. It was long ago withdrawn from circulation")[8] Hughes obviously acquiesced to the conservative tastes of the 1950s.

Arnold Rampersad's two-volume biography, *The Life of Langston Hughes* (1986, 1988), records several of these cases as well;[9] however, by 1993, in his two introductions to the reprinted autobiographies, Rampersad focuses much more aggressively on Hughes's evasions and exclusions, calling *The Big Sea* a "tour de force of subterfuge" and citing a string of contemporary reviewers who chide Hughes for his glaring omissions, and terming *I Wonder as I Wander* "provocative" for its "wise" blending of truth and untruth. And here again, wisdom is a euphemism for business sense.

> Indeed, Hughes was ceaselessly called upon to be a "wise" person, ever vigilant as he negotiated the space between the political right and the left, between the white race and the black, between the middle class who bought and read books and the poorer classes he deeply respected and wanted to reach, between the desire to speak his mind boldly and the restraint that his tenuous position demanded if he was to survive as a writer.[10]

What these and many other critics see as market-motivated survival tactics, Stanley Schatt considers aesthetic development. Schatt is the only scholar to make a systematic study of Hughes's alterations, and in "Langston Hughes: The Minstrel as Artificer," he insists that readers have underestimated Hughes's seriousness as a poet because "the general public and many critics are unaware of the vast number of revisions Hughes . . . made over the years."[11] Schatt confidently associates revision ("from minor alterations in punctuation to additions of entire stanzas") (115)—he doesn't mention the more troublesome *deletions* of entire stanzas—with artistic maturity. Hughes "revises," according to Schatt, to delete immature and derivative material (116), to remove outdated or obscure references (116), and to make a poem more specific (117). Many of Schatt's textual illustrations, however, reveal the inadequacies of these categories. For instance, Schatt's analysis of two versions of the controversial "Christ in Alabama" identifies only the poet's desire to make it more "universal and less personal" (118), qualities Schatt associates with greater artistry. The first version appeared in the December 1, 1931, issue of *Contempo* and was reprinted without change the following year in the political booklet *Scottsboro, Limited;* the second version appeared in *The Panther and the Lash* (1967).

Scottsboro	*Panther*
Christ is a Nigger,	Christ is a nigger,
Beaten and black—	Beaten and black:
O, bare your back.	Oh, bare your back!
Mary is His Mother—	Mary is His mother:
Mammy of the South,	Mammy of the South,
Silence your mouth.	Silence your mouth.
God's His Father—	God is His father:
White Master above,	White Master above
Grant us your love.	Grant Him your love.
Most holy bastard	Most holy bastard
Of the bleeding mouth:	Of the bleeding mouth,
Nigger Christ	Nigger Christ
On the cross of the South.	On the Cross
	Of the South.[12]

Schatt dismisses the typographical changes as insignificant and comments only on the ninth line in both versions, claiming that the substitution of "Him" for "us" shifts the point of view and removes Hughes from the poem: "It is still a social statement about the black man's plight in the South, but the revision makes it universal and less personal."[13]

In fact, however, a great deal more than point of view shifts in the revision. The italics in the earlier version indicate that there are at least two levels of discourse, that the voice of the poem is not unitary and stable as in the later revision. The alternating typefaces function visually and thematically as a call and response: the first voice asserts the ironic parallels between Christ and black people, and the response voice adapts that parallel into a highly ambiguous prayer refrain. Who shouts the italicized orders in the first two stanzas? Who urges black people to act like Christ (by silently submitting to beatings)? Such demands would typically issue from white racists, but here they seem also to come from blacks themselves in their effort to emulate the submission of Christ. These first two stanzas of the earlier version confuse the fact of oppression with the glorification of suffering that can result from it, especially in Christianity. The speaker here is both commentator and chorus, preacher and parishioner, whose voice blends in disturbing ways with the oppressor's. The capitalized nouns underscore these blurrings, visually pairing Christ and Nigger, Mary and Mother, God and Father. Schatt is right when he says that the shift from "us" to "Him" in line 9 alters the point of view, but if that revision makes the poem less personal, it also renders it less political. The speaker of the second version maintains a monotonous authority over the lines of the poem; he is aloof and sarcastic, able to register the similarities between Christ and southern blacks without being able to charge these parallels with tensions as the first version does. Indeed, this second poem tidies up the typography and punctuation, editing out the ironies created by the italics and capitalizations. Little wonder that the troubling ninth line is delivered flatly here, without the original implication of masochistic and confused loyalties. Finally, the second version recasts the last stanza, dismantling the metaphor of the South as crucifix in the last three lines. Indentation, line breaks, and capitalization indicate that the speaker has become too self-conscious of the metaphor in the later version. The phrases of the closing analogy are now doled out more deliberately, like a punch line or a clever afterthought. While the second version ends with a rhetorical snap, the first concludes with an expression of deeply internalized contradiction that only a more complex and ambiguous speaker could generate. And it is the original speaker who makes the greater political claim on us, for his discursive conflicts articulate a racism that cannot be reduced to one speaker or one stanza. The original version problematizes the speaker and therefore complicates the poem's "social statement about the black man's plight in the South."

The textual life of "Christ in Alabama" tells us a great deal about its status as a literary commodity. In 1932, the same year that Hughes signed an open letter backing the Communist presidential ticket, the poem identifies the pervasiveness of racism: the enemy without calls perniciously to the enemy within. The depiction of internalized racism makes it difficult to cast oppression in strictly racial terms. The early version of the poem, then, is an analysis of power relations as well as race relations. By 1959, "Christ in Alabama" is absent from the *Selected Poems,* along with many other fine poems from Hughes's leftist period. The attacks on Hughes from McCarthy and other conservatives and the general cold-war atmosphere induced Hughes to suppress his more militant work. But in 1967, the cultural marketplace has a new use for the poem. *The Panther and the Lash* reprints much of Hughes's militant verse excluded from the *Selected Poems.*[14] "Christ in Alabama" surfaces now, but with a less equivocal tone. The revised version is repackaged in subtle ways to reflect the certitude of the 1960s; its single typeface embodies the uniformity of the black nationalist vision and obscures the significantly more ambiguous representation of racism conveyed in the original version. If slight changes in typeface or punctuation or pronouns can work such important transformations on a poem, then readers of Hughes's poetry must take better stock of his incessant reworkings.

A record of the publication history of individual poems reveals that Hughes used and reused them this way with unprecedented frequency. While many of the cases may merely reflect Hughes's attempt to update the poems, as Schatt claims, or to work sympathetic magic by placing old poems in new books, other instances clearly indicate his effort to repackage his work to meet the shifting demands of his audience. The fate of one of his best-known poems, the famous "Refugee in America," is suggestive of what we would discover in a systematic investigation of the various incarnations of his poems.

> There are words like *Freedom*
> Sweet and wonderful to say.
> On my heartstrings freedom sings
> All day everyday.
>
> There are words like *Liberty*
> That almost make me cry.
> If you had known what I know
> You would know why.[15]

The poem first appeared in the *Saturday Evening Post* in 1943; it was anthologized twice during that year and soon after appeared in a volume of poems, *Fields of Wonder* (1947). The piece is clearly a product of the World War II period. It falls in a section of the book called "Words Like Freedom," clustered with poems about the war ("When the Armies Passed," "Oppression," "Today"). In "Refugee in America" the speaker recites the words that in 1943 constituted the promise of America to thousands of refugees fleeing the oppression and brutality of Europe in the 1940s. When these speakers say that words like *freedom* and *liberty* "almost make [them] cry," they are equating the acquisition of their new country's language with the achievement of that country's promised opportunities. In contrast to the rhetoric of the places they have just come from, the rhetoric of America sounds too good to be true. And, of course, it was.

"Refugee in America" retains its original title up until 1959, when it appeared without change in the *Selected Poems*. However, within a few years the militant black-liberation movement would ignite in America, and Hughes would feel at best ambivalent in the new, more aggressive political climate.[16] When Hughes compiled his last book of verse, *The Panther and the Lash*, in 1967, he attempted to refigure himself as a significant spokesman for the black movement. "Refugee in America" reappears in *The Panther and the Lash*, retitled "Words Like Freedom." In its new environment, in a context of more militant poetry, and with its new title, those former speakers of the poem are suppressed in favor of an implied group of specifically African-American speakers, who now take issue with "words like *Freedom*" and "*Liberty.*" Such words almost make *them* cry because they have endured the hypocrisy of the American dream. The redefinition and qualification of the speaker that the change of title signals amounts to a repackaging of the poem—a marketing technique that occurs with notable frequency in Hughes's work.

Not surprisingly, it is this repackaged version of the poem that Dudley Randall reprints in his definitive post-1960s anthology of African-American poetry, *The Black Poets*. A glance at the table of contents will make obvious to anyone familiar with these poets that Randall's principle of selection is highly political. The authors are represented by their most militant and nationalist works, even when, as in the case of Dunbar, such poems are not indicative of the author's canon. Such interested choices do, of course, determine the contents of all anthologies, and thus the significance of these choices lies not so much in the principle of selection as in the consequences of it: in the ways the poem responds to each new environment. "Words Like Freedom" occurs in Randall's volume amid a cluster of Hughes poems that all scrutinize language. Each poem suggests that America's clichés and catch phrases signify different things for black Americans and white Americans. "Children's Rhymes" asserts that even a black child can penetrate the hypocrisy of America's rhetoric. The poem ends,

> Lies written down
> for white folks
> ain't for us a-tall:
> *Liberty and Justice—*
> Huh!—*For All?*[17]

Immediately following "Children's Rhymes" is "Words Like Freedom" with its italicized *Freedom* and *Liberty* clearly related to the italicized words of the preceding poem. The next poem, "Justice" (87), takes issue with that word ("That Justice is a blind goddess / Is a thing to which we black are wise"). And "American Heartbreak" (87) similarly questions the meaning of the word *freedom* ("I am the American heartbreak— / The rock on which Freedom / Stumped its toe"). In this black-nationalist volume, amid other Hughes poems that interrogate the differences between black and white responses to America's most valued words, there is no trace of the original speaker of the poem—the refugee in post–World War II America. The opposition of the earlier poem, Americans versus refugees, both of whom might be any color, is discarded in favor of a specifically racial contrast: blacks versus nonblacks. The emphasis on African-American speakers is certainly more relevant in the 1960s, and Hughes's revisions demonstrate a keen responsiveness to this contemporary interest.

It is no coincidence that these two examples of commodified poetry—"Christ in Alabama" and "Refugee in America"—appear in the final volume of poetry, *The Panther and the Lash.* Compiled at the height of the Black Arts movement in a climate of militant black nationalism, the volume is a measure of Hughes's capacity to convert old poetry into a new cultural currency.

> He had written himself out about America's escalating war in Vietnam and the racial unrest at home. Knopf was soon to publish some of his poems about those events in his anthology *The Panther and the Lash.* With its forty-four new poems and twenty-six selected from previous

volumes, it was to be his final testament, the most militant book of
verse he had published since the thirties. He had considered calling it
Words Like Freedom, until the words didn't fit the times anymore.[18]

It is significant that Berry refers to the volume as an anthology, suggesting it is retrospective; Hughes, on the contrary, subtitles the book *Poems
of Our Times,* indicating the poems are not merely timely in their perti-
nence but also "of the moment" in their composition. Indeed, the book is
dedicated to Rosa Parks and casts itself as contemporaneous with the
Civil Rights and Black Power movements: "To Rosa Parks of Montgomery who started it all" (*PL* ix). Yet what Rosa Parks started in 1955
is here reflected in poetry composed over a thirty-five-year period, from
1932 to 1967. The advertising blurb from the 1992 reprinted edition of
Panther confirms that the historicity of these poems has been lost:

> In this, his last collection of verse, Hughes's voice is more pointed than
> ever before, as he explicitly addresses the racial politics of the sixties in
> such pieces as "Prime," "Motto," "Dream Deferred," "Frederick
> Douglass: 1817–1895," "Still Here," "Birmingham Sunday," "His-
> tory," "Slave," "Warning," and "Daybreak in Alabama." Sometimes
> ironic, sometimes bitter, always powerful, the poems in *The Panther
> and the Lash* are the last testament of a great American writer who
> grappled fearlessly and artfully with the most compelling issues of his
> time. (*PL* back cover)

Of the poems listed here as "more pointed than ever before," "explicitly
addressing the sixties," Hughes's "last testament" on the "issues of his
time," "Motto" was first published in 1951, "Dream Deferred" in 1959,
"Still Here" in 1943, "History" in 1934, "Warning" in 1951, and "Daybreak in Alabama" in 1940. By 1992 the poems of our times seem to have
eluded time and now stand outside the very history they helped to make.

Obviously Hughes compiled this last volume with the expectation that
the older poems would prove as relevant in their own ways as the new
ones were. Old and new poems alike deal with racial tensions and the
resulting social unrest. Yet the poems reprinted from earlier volumes
seem belated, nostalgic, and out of step with the times of *The Panther
and the Lash.* Still, they are the strongest poems in the book. The new
poems, while timely in their subject matter, are philosophically confused
and stylistically outmoded.

Take, for example, what might be considered the title poems of the book. "Black Panther" and "The Backlash Blues" are two of the only twenty or so poems published for the first time in this volume. "Black Panther" (*PL* 19) attempts to explain the logic of groups like the militant Black Panther Party, founded in 1966 when Hughes was compiling the book. The poem first imagines the Black Panther as a victim, who is "Pushed into the corner" in a series of periodic phrases by the enemy ("the hobnailed boot"), the desire to live (the " 'I-don't-want-to-die' cry"), and by the failed rhetoric of the mainstream Civil Rights movement (" 'I don't want to study war no more' "). These ineffective cries are transformed at last into the more militant "Eye for eye." While the poem seems to want to glorify the panther for "Wear[ing] no disguise," it concludes with a riddle that indicates the new pose is false as well: "Motivated by the truest / Of the oldest / Lies." Hughes believed that the Black Power movement merely perpetuated racism in the name of black pride,[19] and the poem registers his suspicion that the Black Panthers have become exactly what they claim to oppose. In its emphasis on black victimization, its distrust of militancy, and its retreat at the end into a riddle, "Black Panther" carries no political force. Likewise, "The Backlash Blues" (*PL* 8–9) takes as its structure a poetic form that the Black Arts leaders had already condemned as irrelevant. LeRoi Jones's infamous line from *Dutchman* (1964) had asserted, "If Bessie Smith had killed a few white people she wouldn't have needed [the blues]," and Ron Karenga had dismissed the blues as "invalid; for they teach resignation, in a word acceptance of reality—and we have come to change reality."[20] Here once again in this poem, the backlash against militant blacks by whites is finally indistinguishable from black militancy, which is itself a backlash against white racism.

Mister Backlash, Mister Backlash,
What do you think I got to lose?
Tell me, Mister Backlash,
What do you think I got to lose?
I'm gonna leave you, Mister Backlash,
Singing your mean old backlash blues.

You're the one,
Yes, you're the one
Will have the blues.

Both poems, in short, are deeply suspicious of the political developments they herald.

The riddle formula also structures "Stokely Malcolm Me" (*PL* 94–95) and again reveals that the most pressing question, how to speak to the times, cannot be riddled out.

I have been seeking
what i have never found
what I don't know what i want
but it must be around
since the day before last
but that day was so long
I done forgot when it passed
yes almost forgot
what i have not found
but i know it must be
somewhere around.

you live in the Bronx
so folks say.

Stokely,
did i ever live
up your
way?
???
??
?

The poem is a paean to confusion, beginning with riddles and drifting off into question marks, as though it has nothing left to say but cannot quit trying to say it. The relationship of the speaker to Stokely Carmichael and Malcolm X is posited in the title but not discovered in the poem. Perhaps they once lived in the same neighborhood, but even that possibility amounts to nothing here. One other new poem, "Go Slow" (*PL* 90–91), ends in a similar fashion, and here again the question marks seem to stand in for the poem's inability to say what it means. It ends:

Am I supposed to forgive
And meekly live

Going slow, slow, slow,
Slow, slow, slow,
Slow, slow,
Slow,
Slow,
Slow?
????
???
??
?

Ten or twenty years earlier we might have been tempted to read the question mark as a sign of resistance: "How long?" was the early battle cry of the Civil Rights movement, a refusal to wait any longer posing less threateningly as a question. But here in 1967, black militants are no longer troubling themselves with this question or with the posture of supplication. "Go Slow" is hopelessly belated in a time of extreme black militancy, when the only thing still "going slow" in 1967 is this poem.[21]

One final example will suffice to demonstrate the irresolution of the new poems in *Panther*. "Ghosts of 1619" (*PL* 26–27) figures the ghosts of slaves metaphorically resurrected in the persons of the rising black militants. When oppressed people refuse to acquiesce to their enemies, they gain substance and power. However, the concluding stanza wavers, seeming to confuse itself with its own questions.

How can one man be ten?
Or ten be a hundred and ten?
Or a thousand and ten?
Or a million and ten
Are but a thousand and ten
Or a hundred and ten
Or ten—or one—
Or none—
Being ghosts
Of then?

The answer to "How can one man be ten?" is found back in the second stanza, where the poem recognizes that "minority, / Suddenly became majority / (Metaphysically speaking) / In seeking authority"; that is, one person can have the moral authority of ten or of millions if he or she acts in accordance with ethical principles. Likewise, good deeds have their own authenticating power that evil deeds lack. If just one person takes right action, he or she will surely be joined by others. Why the third stanza fails to see the logic of its own formulations is puzzling. The lines appear to grow in confidence as the numbers increase; then suddenly there is a failure of nerve, a grammatical slip ("Or a million and ten / Are but a thousand and ten"—where "Are" should have been its near homophone "Or" and the numbers should have continued to increase), and then all is lost. The metaphysical additions come to nothing, and the ghosts dissolve back into the past.

Too many of the new poems in *The Panther and the Lash* are tentative, even unfinished, if we take a string of question marks to indicate a failure of vision. They seem to want to participate in the moment, yet they lack commitment and confidence. The volume was heralded then, as now, as Hughes's most militant poetry since the 1930s, but this is only true because the most militant poetry in it was written in the 1930s.

The old poems in the book are consequently more sure of themselves, but they speak of an earlier era and sound sadly out of place in *Panther*. "Motto" (*PL* 11), for example, expresses the Beat sensibility of *Montage of a Dream Deferred* (1951) and cannot possibly be mistaken for a militant political slogan: "Dig and be dug / In return." Likewise, "Warning" (*PL* 100), also first published in *Montage*, offers an extremely belated and nostalgic message for 1967. From its anachronistic use of the term *Negro* to its rural setting and complacent rhymes, the poem pitifully warns us about a change of mind that has long since happened.

Negroes,
Sweet and docile,
Meek, humble, and kind:
Beware the day
They change their mind!

Wind
In the cotton fields,
Gentle the breeze:
Beware the hour
It uproots trees!

In fact, many of the poems in *Panther* retreat in time like "Warning." The volume opens with a poem from the 1950s and closes not merely with one written in 1940 but with a poem that harks back to the rural, southern past of an even earlier decade. "Daybreak in Alabama" is a naive and nostalgic poem in which an innocent black speaker imagines an Edenic natural world populated by a beautifully integrated humanity; indeed, it is difficult to distinguish the people from the flowers.

> And the scent of pine needles
> And the smell of red clay after rain
> And long red necks
> And poppy colored faces
> And big brown arms
> And the field daisy eyes
> Of black and white black white black people
> And I'm gonna put white hands
> And black hands and brown and yellow hands
> And red clay earth hands in it
> Touching everybody with kind fingers
> And touching each other natural as dew. (*PL* 101)

The Panther and the Lash ends here with this idyll to nature and natural man and thus positions itself, despite its subtitle, well outside its time.

Hughes's last volume of poetry tells us a great deal about making poetry pay. In 1966, he and Knopf thought the time was right for a book of militant poetry;[22] however, he clearly did not have enough new poems for a volume. Even the ones he had were weak and hesitant about the 1960s. So he bolstered them with older poems, choosing to reprint many that he had excluded from his *Selected Poems* probably for the same reasons he was including them now. Several of the older poems are altered to heighten their sense of warning and anger. The word "colored," for example, is removed from the line "When I get to be a colored composer" in "Daybreak in Alabama." "Still Here" (*PL* 32), previously published twice with different degrees of dialect marking (it had been printed in mostly standard English in *Jim Crow's Last Stand* but then appeared in mostly dialect in 1949 in *One-Way Ticket*), retains all the dialect features, indicating an unassimilated, perhaps even separatist speaker. "Freedom" (*PL* 89) appears as the new title of a poem formerly called "Democracy," and that change registers a subtle shift from the socialist context and a concern with forms of government to the black-liberation context and a complete condemnation of America. "Who but the Lord?" (*PL* 16–17) adds two suggestive little words to the end of the poem, which transform it from a sarcastic admission of hopelessness to a thinly veiled warning—and with the warning comes new hope.

> Being poor and black,
> I've no weapon to strike back
> So who but the Lord
> Can protect me?
>   *We'll see.*

What Hughes had repackaged and commodified in 1967, Vintage Classics is marketing again today. The first Vintage Classics edition of *The Panther and the Lash* appeared in February 1992, just four months before the Rodney King trial in Los Angeles would force the country to acknowledge that racial tensions had once again reached explosive proportions. This is not Hughes's best book of poems—in fact, it is probably his worst—yet the most militant poems since the 1930s apparently make up in relevance what they lack in artistry. In the wake of the Central Park rape, the Crown Heights killings, the Rodney King and Reginald Denny beatings, and just in time for the Los Angeles uprising, reprinting Hughes's last book is a marketing coup.

Over the course of his writing career, Hughes packaged and repackaged his poems to suppress the perceived anti-Semitism of his second volume, to accommodate the pressures of the McCarthy era, and to embody the program of the Black Arts movement. Yet Hughes describes his poems as bursts of sheer, unmediated inspiration. In *The Big Sea* he characterizes his process of composition as spontaneous creation that involves almost no revision.

> But there are seldom many changes in my poems, once they're down. Generally, the first two or three lines come to me from something I'm thinking about, or looking at, or doing, and the rest of the poem (if there is to be a poem) flows from those first few lines, usually right away. If there is a chance to put the poem down then, I write it down. If not, I try to remember it until I get to a pencil and paper; for poems are like rainbows: they escape you quickly.[23]

Hughes, too, is like a rainbow, vanishing too quickly into such contrived accounts of himself. It is not surprising, then, that scholars have reproduced his elusiveness, ironically, often in their very efforts to define him. The anthology industry, for example, has canonized first a modernist Hughes, next an integrationist Hughes, then a black-nationalist Hughes, and more recently a Hughes who serves the significantly different demands of curricular multiculturalism.²⁴ Biographers have often constructed an African-American Everyman by suppressing or deferring questions about his political and sexual orientations.²⁵ And even the authors of reference aids, concordances and bibliographies, obscure crucial aspects of the Hughes record even as they presumably work to preserve it.²⁶

Most recently, when filmmaker Isaac Julien attempted to ponder these competing representations of Hughes in his 1989 film *Looking for Langston,* the executor of the Hughes Estate, George Bass, censored the film for its supposed depiction of Hughes's sexuality (the film is far too impressionistic and exploratory to be considered a depiction of Hughes; in fact, it is motivated by a fascination with the poet's elusiveness rather than by the desire to define him). The Estate succeeded in forcing Julien to cut three poems from the film and, hardly less restrictive, to release an altered version of the film to American audiences, a version that muted the voice of Hughes reading one of his poems in the opening sequence.²⁷

The battle waged by the Estate and Julien exemplifies the problem that Hughes poses for a commodity culture. Behind the commodification of Langston Hughes is the issue of representation, as Julien points out.

> [The Estate] can't stand the [homosexual] context of the film. . . . In effect they're saying, "What you're trying to do is construct [Hughes] as a gay icon and he's a black icon."²⁸

In "The Black Man's Burden" Henry Louis Gates Jr. proposes that we dispense at last with the "strictures of 'representation'" that such icons are made of: "The film, we should remember, is called *Looking for Langston;* it does not promise he will be found. In fact, I think *Looking for Langston* leads away from the ensolacement of identity politics, the simple exaltation of identity.²⁹" Citing the manifesto on the "new politics of representation" by Isaac Julien and Kobena Mercer, Gates deplores "representation as a practice of depicting and representation as a practice of delegation" (82) and tries to imagine a manner of representation that would be less mimetic than depiction (which places too much confidence in the "real") and less essentializing than delegation (which makes an individual work or person "stand for" a much more complex and varied group): "It has been argued that we should supplant the vanguardist paradigm of 'representation' with the 'articulation of interests.' In such a way, we can lighten the 'burden of representation,' even if we cannot dispense with it" (82). The difference between representation and articulation might serve as a model for drawing a distinction between commodification and marketing, where commodification entails the packaging of someone like Hughes as a stable icon while the marketing of him might merely involve the distribution of different versions of him—even competing versions. Julien suggests this when he indicates that the problem is not simply representation or mimesis but the ways in which these black images are commodified.

> But I'm more interested in questions concerning the commodification of black art and culture. I think questions such as commodification provide a more realistic analysis and critique of black art as we approach the end of the twentieth century. In the film I was pointing out the ways in which black artists were taken up and then thrown out like the ever-shifting tastes of fashion.[30]

The dominant culture's taste has traditionally demanded a heterosexual, integrationist Hughes who fills the post of the "poet laureate of black America," as he has often been called. More recently, because of interest in multiculturalism, he has also been recognized for his dialect poems and blues verses. Yet throughout his long and distinguished public sojourn, he has frequently wandered, to use his word, to the margins, where he has represented far more controversial positions.

The poet laureate of black America turns out to be a tremendously elusive figure and becomes only more so as efforts are made to define him. The project of defining and redefining Langston Hughes, a task he himself began, amounts to a continual packaging and repackaging of him. Each time the cultural marketplace attempts to make his poetry pay—by promoting him as a New Negro poet, radical poet, children's poet, black-nationalist poet, folk poet, gay poet—looking for Langston Hughes becomes an increasingly difficult job. If we want Hughes to be the poet of *our* time, we ought to acknowledge the multiplicity of his work. A capricious, changeful, uncertain, contradictory Hughes would be more difficult to commodify than an exemplary poet—but, by the same token, he would be far more valuable to market.

NOTES

1. Arna Bontemps, "Negro Poets, Then and Now," *Phylon* 11 (4th quarter 1950): 360.

2. Langston Hughes, *I Wonder as I Wander* (1956; New York: Hill and Wang, 1993), pp. 56–57.

3. Langston Hughes, "The Negro Artist and the Racial Mountain," *Nation* 122 (1926): 692.

4. Ibid., p. 694.

5. Robert Bone, review of *The Best Short Stories by Negro Writers,* ed. Langston Hughes, *New York Times Book Review,* 5 March 1967, p. 5.

6. Faith Berry, *Langston Hughes: Before and Beyond Harlem* (1983; New York: Citadel Press, 1992), p. 321.

7. For specific instances of such self-censorship, see Berry, *Langston Hughes,* pp. 53, 105, 126, 183, 197, 257, 294, 296–97, 316, 318–19, and 321.

8. Quoted in Berry, *Langston Hughes,* pp. 319, 296.

9. Arnold Rampersad, *The Life of Langston Hughes,* 2 vols. (New York: Oxford University Press, 1986–88), 2:357, for example.

10. Arnold Rampersad, introduction to *The Big Sea,* by Langston Hughes (1940; New York: Hill and Wang, 1993), pp. xvi, xix.

11. Stanley Schatt, "Langston Hughes: The Minstrel as Artificer," *Journal of Modern Literature* 4 (September 1974): 115.

12. Langston Hughes, "Christ in Alabama," *Contempo,* 1 December 1931, front page; *Scottsboro Limited: Four Poems and a Play in Verse* (New York: Golden Stair Press, 1932), n.p.; *The Panther and the Lash* (1967; New York: Random House, 1992), p. 37. Subsequent references to *The Panther and the Lash* appear in the text, abbreviated *PL.*

13. Schatt, "Langston Hughes," p. 118.

14. Some of the early political poems that were excluded from *Selected Poems* but included in *Panther* are "Still Here," "Christ in Alabama," "Bible Belt," "Florida Road Workers," "Justice," "Down Where I Am," "Oppression," "Color," "History," "Democracy" (reprinted as "Freedom"), "Where???" and "Vari-Colored Song."

15. Langston Hughes, *Selected Poems* (1959; New York: Random House, 1974), p. 290.

16. Rampersad discusses Hughes's uneasy response to the Black Power movement in the chapter "Do Nothing Until You Hear From Me," *Life,* esp. 2:407–12.

17. Dudley Randall, ed., *The Black Poets* (New York: Bantam Books, 1971), p. 86.

18. Berry, *Langston Hughes,* p. 327.

19. Rampersad, *Life,* 2:412.

20. Leroi Jones, *Dutchman and the Slave* (New York: Morrow Quill Paperbacks, 1964), p. 35; Ron Karenga, "Black Cultural Nationalism," in *The Black Aesthetic,* ed. Addison Gayle, Jr. (Garden City, N.Y.: Anchor, 1971), p. 36.

21. The practice of ending a poem with a piece of punctuation or a nonverbal sign may derive from a poem written in 1937 and also included in *Panther,* "Elderly Leaders" (7). In it, Hughes employs the dollar sign to indicate that the elderly leaders have sold out to a political system that generates only lies. In this poem, the dollar sign marks a retreat from language into monetary symbol that parallels the retreat from truth to lies.

> Elderly,
> Famous,
> Very well paid,
> They clutch at the egg
> Their master's
> Goose laid:
> $$$$$
> $$$$
> $$$
> $$
> $
> .

Even here, where the technique makes some sense, it risks appearing to be a failure of language. In the later poems, the question marks take the place of discourse the poems ought to be able to provide.

22. Berry, *Langston Hughes,* p. 327; Rampersad, *Life,* 2:409.

23. Hughes, *The Big Sea,* p. 56.

24. For a discussion of how the anthology industry has canonized Hughes, see my "Do Right to Write Right: Langston Hughes's Aesthetics of Simplicity," *Twentieth Century Literature* 38, no. 4 (Winter 1992): 436–56. In addition to mainstream anthologies, Hughes has been anthologized as a socialist poet in Granville Hicks's *Proletarian Literature in the United States* (New York: International Publishers, 1935); and as a gay poet in Michael J. Smith's *Black Men/White Men: A Gay Anthology* (San Francisco: Gay Sunshine Press, 1983).

25. For an illuminating discussion of homophobia in biographies of Hughes, see Scott Braverman, "Isaac Julien's *Looking for Langston:* Hughes, Biography and Queer(ed) History," *Cultural Studies* 7, no. 2 (May 1993): 311–23. See also Berry, *Langston Hughes,* app. A, "Breaking Silence: The Meaning of Biographical Truth" (359–67), and app. B, "The Challenge of Access: Archival Materials"

(368–76), where Berry wages war against the Hughes Estate and the official biographer, Arnold Rampersad, for suppressing and fabricating information about Hughes's political and sexual orientations.

26. Though the Preface to Thomas A. Mikolyzk's *Langston Hughes: A Bio-Bibliography* (New York: Greenwood Press, 1990) claims that "the annotated bibliography includes . . . virtually every critical piece published throughout the world" (viii), the bibliography does not contain a single reference to works dealing with Hughes's sexuality, many of which were in print well before 1990, when Mikolyzk's book was published. Similarly, Peter Mandelik and Stanley Schatt's *A Concordance to the Poetry of Langston Hughes* (Detroit: Gale Research, 1975) uses only "the most recent appearance of a poem as the standard edition" (vii) and excludes all of the children's poems from *The Langston Hughes Reader;* Mikolyzk rightly notes that such practices "eliminated most of the dialect used by Hughes" (113).

27. For accounts of Julien's conflict with the Hughes Estate, see Lisa Kennedy, "Listening for Langston," *Village Voice,* 14 November 1989, p. 49, and "Closeting Langston Hughes," *Village Voice,* 10 October 1989, p. 39; and Essex Hemphill, "*Looking for Langston:* An Interview with Isaac Julien," in *Brother to Brother: New Writings by Black Gay Men,* ed. Essex Hemphill (Boston: Alyson, 1991), pp. 174–80.

28. Qtd. in Kennedy, "Closeting Langston Hughes," p. 39.

29. Henry Louis Gates Jr., "The Black Man's Burden," in *Black Popular Culture,* ed. Gina Dent (Seattle: Bay Press, 1992), pp. 75, 81.

30. Hemphill, "Interview with Isaac Julien," p. 179.

Marketing Modern Poetry and the Southern Public Sphere

Walter Kalaidjian

Today's diversified literary market—which services readerships for African American, feminist, postcolonial, gay/lesbian, and cultural studies—has not only unsettled canonical foundations in the contemporary period but, equally important, has had certain recombinatory side-effects on our understanding of canonical modernism. The culture wars of our own moment, in particular, have recovered the contested public sphere at stake in the makeup and marketing of literary modernism. In this essay, I will trace the postwar reception and construction of modern poetry in the United States back to the conjuncture of the Southern Agrarian and New Critical movements. For it is precisely this conjuncture between the wars that has served to naturalize a key repression of America's cultural diversity.

In a somewhat unguarded boast that "the modernist canon has been made in part by readers like me,"[1] Hugh Kenner divulged in the mid-1980s the constructed, rather than transcendent, forces of canonicity. Contrary to T. S. Eliot's grounding of literary tradition in the "ideal order" of "the mind of Europe," Kenner's commercial troping in "The Making of the Modernist Canon" (1984), however ironic, points symptomatically to a thoroughly reified economy of valuation. Looking back on his graduate-student days under Cleanth Brooks at Yale, Kenner relates how he took up Ezra Pound in 1949 at the very moment when the Bollingen controversy threatened to destroy the poet's reputation by branding him as an anti-Semite and national traitor. "I was naive enough," he admits, "not to guess that I was mortgaging my future" against what at the end of the 1940s must have seemed a risky investment indeed. Nevertheless, Kenner reflects that, with the publication of *The Poetry of Ezra Pound* (1951), "Pound before long was a stock on the academic exchange: a safe 'subject' for the next two decades' academic expansion" (372).

Much of that twenty-year bull market can be attributed not just to the "intrinsic" value of Pound's art, but to inside traders like Kenner who, in the postwar academy, speculated on the sizable cultural capital already amassed by such literary magnates as Eliot, Pound, and Brooks. That story is normally told, as Kenner's is, in terms of a handful of "great men" (Yeats, Eliot, Pound, Joyce, Stevens, Williams) who fathered the modernist cultural revolution. Indeed, on Pound's insistence that "you have an obligation to visit the great men of your own time,"[2] Kenner dutifully made the pilgrimage in 1956 to Williams, Wyndham Lewis, and Eliot, among others, with introductions from *il miglior fabbro*. Such face-to-face bondings led each of these literary mandarins, in Kenner's subsequent critical campaign, to emerge as a trademark brand of high modernism. Yet this familiar lineage of "major" individual talents rests on a deeper genealogy whose social foundations are grounded in a specific conjuncture of national, racial, sexual, and class formations. Kenner's large claim that "International Modernism was the work of Irishmen and Americans" (367), however correct in its take on the reception and shaping of canonical modernism in the United States, betrays a key repression: one that elides the global diversity of the historical avant-gardes in Berlin, Moscow, and the Third World.

Kenner's postwar promotion of high modernism buttressed the critical and pedagogical edifice that his mentor Cleanth Brooks promulgated between the wars. In particular, Brooks's popular primer, *Understanding Poetry* (1938), codified for the classroom the emerging New Critical theory of such seminal volumes as his own influential study *Modern Poetry and the Tradition* (1939). In making his case for the kind of "difficulty," "allusiveness," "ironic indirection," and "complexity" in modern poetry that T. S. Eliot had advanced in his 1921 essay "The Metaphysical Poets," Brooks campaigned against the regnant anthology markets of the 1910s and 1920s. As Craig S. Abbott has shown, Fred Lewis Pattee's *Century Readings for a Course in American Literature* (1919, 1926), Harriet Monroe's *The New Poetry* (1917, 1923, 1932), Marguerite Wilkinson's *Contemporary Poetry* (1923) and *New Voices* (1919, 1921, 1928), and the six editions of Louis Untermeyer's *Modern American Poetry* (1919–50) shaped a readership for poets like Robert Frost, Edna St. Vincent Millay, Lizette Reese, Carl Sandburg, Sara Teasdale, Joyce Kilmer, Vachel Lindsay, James Oppenheim, Edwin Arlington Robinson, and such middlebrow talents as Katherine Lee Bates, Richard Covey, Josephine Preston Peabody, Ina Coolbrith, Eugene Field, Clinton Scollard, and other long-forgotten writers.

Until recently, the traditional story of modernism's reception between the wars placed these genteel anthologies in opposition to the Fugitive, and later New Critical, effort to move Eliot and Pound from the intellectual margins of the academic market to its center.[3] Yet this familiar take on high modernism's displacement of the genteel tradition cannot account for the full diversity of modernist aesthetic production. The clash between a formal, apolitical modernism with a tired, *fin de siècle* romanticism is not simply a reductive critical narrative but, as Cary Nelson observes, has served politically as a strategy of containment. "Once our image of the period," writes Nelson, "is contained and structured this way—once our sense of the discourses at work is limited to these choices—it is easy to feel that experimental modernism deserved to win this battle, for it is difficult to recapture the knowledge that these were not the only forces in play. But in fact they were not."[4] As a paradigm of twentieth-century literary history, the constituting binarism of the high/genteel divide not only represses the kind of cultural diversity that Nelson would recover. But equally important, it also naturalizes and sanitizes the messy ideological legacy of racism, sexism, classism, and anti-Semitism that shapes the high modernist and New Critical conjuncture in American literary culture between the wars.

In the wake of recent studies such as Nelson's *Repression and Recovery* (1989), Paul Lauter's *Canons and Contexts* (1991), Barbara Foley's *Radical Representations* (1993), and my *American Culture between the Wars* (1993), the discursive field of Eurocentric high modernism has been repositioned in political relation to, not transcendence of, the plurality of other, contemporaneous literary and cultural discourses at play in the international public sphere of the interbellum decades. The critical containment of modernism's cultural diversity, as I have argued, has typically relied on the figure of the author as valorized "agent"—to borrow from Kenneth Burke's grammatical pentad—to obscure the material "scene" of twentieth-century cultural production in the United States.[5] Such reigning tropes of individual talent have served to fix, regulate, and police modernism's unsettled social text, crosscut as it is by a diversity of transnational, racial, sexual, and class representations.[6] That policing of cultural modernism by the more restrictive literary canon of high modernism reaches back to a key repression of social modernization, again, by Kenner's mentors in the 1930s—Cleanth Brooks and his collaborators in the Fugitive, Southern Agrarian, and New Critical movements: Donald Davidson, John Crowe Ransom, Allen Tate, and Robert Penn Warren, among others. This line of reactionary cultural politics flourished throughout the Bush/Reagan era and survives to this day.[7] In the 1990s, however, an alternative survey of cultural modernity—one mapped through the materialist coordinates of what Antonio Gramsci theorized in the rise of fascism, Fordism, and Americanism between the wars—has exposed high modernism as itself a thoroughly ideological, rather than purely aesthetic, domain.

Although much work has been done on high modernism's various investments in Eurocentrism, monarchist Anglo-Catholicism, and Italian fascism, the persistence of these ideologemes in their American reception and, indeed, in the formation of postwar literary studies as such has been largely silenced.[8] The academic foundation for high-modernist studies was laid through New Critics like Brooks, who offered the first courses in twentieth-century literature at Yale in 1947. That institutional base, however, lies on deeper underpinnings in the Southern Agrarian platform for a genteel "squirearchy" of cultural domination. As its apologists advertised it in *I'll Take My Stand: The South and the Agrarian Tradition by Twelve Southerners* (1930), the Agrarian agenda was outspokenly political and, among other things, reacted against the burgeoning American consumer market conceived under an interbellum, Fordist economy in the United States. Anticipating the Frankfurt attention to the emerging *kulturindustrie*, Southern Agrarian ideologues such as Donald Davidson—longtime Vanderbilt mentor for the Fugitive movement—began to engage the question, as he posed it in his Southern Agrarian manifesto, "What is the industrial theory of the arts?"[9] Unlike, say, Walter Benjamin, Davidson was pessimistic about the new culture of mechanical reproduction. "Henry Ford's hired hands," he complained,

> do not hum themes from Beethoven as they go to work. Instead, the shop-girl reads the comic strip with her bowl of patent cereal and puts on a jazz record while she rouges her lips. She reads the confession magazines and goes to the movies. . . . The industrialists in art—that is, the Hollywood producers, the McFadden publications, the Tin Pan Alley crowd, the Haldeman-Julius Blue Books—will naturally make their appeal to the lowest common denominator. (*ITS* 35)

It is against this denigrated and feminized version of the mass-cultural market that the campaign for an elite, high-modern canon announces its classist and androcentric agenda. Building on T. S. Eliot's implicit critique of the alienating social effects of mass industrial society in *The Waste Land*, Southerners like Lyle H. Lanier looked forward to postwar critiques of advanced consumer society by analyzing what Hans Magnus Enzensberger would later characterize, from a Marxist vantage point, as the postmodern "industrialization of the mind."[10] Writing to the right of Enzensberger, Lanier in "The Philosophy of Progress" linked the Fordist techniques of factory production to the broader, ideological spread of consumer values throughout the social field: what Gramsci was simultaneously theorizing in *The Prison Notebooks* as "Americanism." "By 'industrialism,'" wrote Lanier, "is meant not the machine and industrial technology as such, but the domination of the economic, political, and social order by the notion that the greater part of a nation's energies should be directed toward an endless process of increasing the production and consumption of goods" (*ITS* 148). Beyond Lanier's somewhat undertheorized reading of Fordism, this new mode of industrial and cultural production, in Gramsci's more sophisticated analysis, effected a crucial turning point in the progress of advanced capitalism: one that demanded a radical rethinking of both Second International economism and the cultural politics of vanguard Leninism.

More powerful than either the legacy of the Soviet Revolution or the rise of Italian fascism, Ford's new industrial mode of production stood, according to Gramsci, as "the biggest collective effort to date to create, with unprecedented speed, and with a consciousness of purpose unmatched in history, a new type of worker and of man."[11] What was revolutionary about Ford's approach was its adaptation of Frederick W. Taylor's time-and-motion studies to the semiautomatic production line. This technical regime, in Gramsci's account, reduced workers to replaceable cyborgs within a production process driven by capital and managed by a new administrative class.[12] But equally important, the gigantic scale of Ford's mechanical infrastructure, documented in Diego Rivera's expansive *Detroit Industry* murals of River Rouge, was also very costly to maintain. Consequently, it demanded not only a speedup in the labor process but also a reliable market for its mass products. Ford's decisive advance lay in researching and surveillancing workers' habits of consumption as part of his productive calculus.[13] By targeting the domestic arenas and personal enclaves of consumption, he hastened the commodity form's penetration of everyday life, thereby setting the foundation for the postwar consumer society.

Significantly, the Fordist apparatus coupled a revolutionary principle of mechanization with a managerial strategy of planned consumption.[14] It is this conjuncture of the northern industrial mode of production and the mass-commodity market it serviced that Ransom, Brooks, and Warren anathematized as Southern Agrarians. The Southern critique of America's burgeoning consumer society, however, was doubly politicized in its proactive, anti-Communist agenda. Not just a front for cultural "squirearchy," agrarianism aimed to turn the tide of the emergent socialist culture that was gaining considerable momentum in America between the wars. Indeed, Andrew Lytle, Allen Tate, and Robert Penn Warren proposed *A Tract against Communism* as the original title for the biting agrarian manifesto *I'll Take My Stand.* "We therefore look upon the Communist menace," they proclaimed in the volume's collaboratively authored "Introduction: A Statement of Principles," "as a menace indeed, but not as a Red one; because it is simply according to the blind drift of our industrial development to expect in America at last much the same economic system as that imposed by violence upon Russia in 1917" (*ITS* xxiv). Thus, in the United States, the political struggle against the Comintern's Third Period push for a Soviet America would be spearheaded throughout the depression era by, among others, Donald Davidson, Frank Owsley, John Crowe Ransom, and Allen Tate.

Much of the Agrarians' reactionary social politics was theorized in essays published in the *American Review* (1933–37), whose editor, Seward Collins, advanced an American version of Italian fascism. Sharing many of the key discursive markers of Southern Agrarianism and English distributism, the native fascism that Collins espoused would support "the revival of monarchy, property, the guilds, the security of the family and the peasantry, and the ancient ways of European life."[15] Not unlike Collins's investments in tradition, family values, Eurocentrism, and what John Crowe Ransom called "squirearchy," the Southern Agrarians—like the Distributists Hilaire Belloc, Herbert Agar, and Troy Cauley—also saw the economic blight of the Great Depression as heralding the death of capitalism that had split humanity into monopolists and proletarians. Agrarians like Frank Owsley campaigned to redistribute land to small growers held by "loan companies, insurance companies, banks, absentee landlords," and bankrupt planters.[16] Such redistribution would foster an agricultural middle class that would, nevertheless, be discouraged from buying the new technologies and consumer goods from the North by punitive import tariffs. Politically, in the pages of the *American Review,* there was strong resistance to the spread of democracy among the proletarians. The distributionist plan was to limit the franchise to property owners or, in its more radical proponents, to adopt the kind of heirarchic rule witnessed in Mussolini's Italy.

Given the deepening economic crisis of the Depression era, the *American Review* espoused international fascism in reaction against the expanding democratic coalition of the Popular Front organized by the American left. Not insignificantly, the rhetoric of fascism and Southern white supremacy were imbricated in the work of such *American Review* contributors as Hoffman Nickerson, who in a 1935 essay entitled "Property and Tactics" argued that "what the Fascist march on Rome did for the Italian nation, Vigilance Committees of justly angry citizens have done for many an American city. . . . That is the story of the original Ku Klux Klan . . . which restored white supremacy in the South. . . . Should the day come when the silver-tongued oratory of the Kerensky-Roosevelt type is not enough to guard our civilization from Communist chaos, then the intelligence and virility of Christendom will produce more Fascist dictators . . . to diminish proletarianism and restore property."[17] Throughout the mid-1930s, the *American Review* ran articles that characterized Mussolini as "a man of tradition whom Aristotle or St. Thomas, or Machiavelli, might without too great difficulty feel at ease";[18] moreover, the journal featured articles, like Nickerson's, contrasting Karl Marx the "Jew, Mordecai" with Hitler, who restored "courage and hope" through the "resurrection of German National spirit."[19] By publishing their writing in the same venue as such anti-Semitic and pro-fascist ideologues as Nickerson and Ross J. S. Hoffman, the Southern Agrarians arguably aligned themselves with these troubling cultural politics.

Although the Agrarians ridiculed the American Left as mired in "propaganda"—their euphemism for social critique—Davidson, Ransom, Owsley, Tate, and the rest were no strangers to agitprop, as evidenced in such *American Review* contributions as Donald Davidson's "The Rise of the American City" (1933), "Lands That Were Golden" (1934), "Regionalism and Education" (1935), "A Sociologist in Eden" (1936), Owsley's "Scottsboro, The Third Crusade" (1933), "The Pillars of Agrarianism" (1935), "The Old South and the New" (1936), Ransom's "Happy Farmers" (1933), "A Capital for the New Deal" (1933), "Sociology and the

Black Belt" (1934), Tate's "The Problem of the Unemployed" (1933), "Where Are the People" (1933), "A View of the Whole South" (1933), "Notes on Liberty and Property" (1936), and "What Is a Traditional Society?" (1936). In standard versions of American literary and critical history, the social politics of Southern Agrarianism is either simply elided or contained in a *cordon sanitaire* from, on the one hand, the modernist poetics of the Fugitives and, on the other, the disciplinary formalism of New Criticism. Yet that figures such as Davidson, Ransom, Tate, Warren cut across these discrete, academic boundaries belies the supposedly apolitical transcendence that traditionally distinguishes literary from cultural studies.[20]

Consider, for example, the early career of, say, Cleanth Brooks. Typically viewed as a New Critic proper, Brooks is usually held at a formal remove from cultural matters by virtue of his close, "intrinsic" readings that are couched in sophisticated, theoretical registers. Nevertheless, the fact that Brooks was publishing in the mid-thirties in such reactionary journals as Collins's *American Review* reveals a certain positioning of his work within, not beyond, the political debates of his moment.[21] In fact, Brooks's reading of literary modernism is thoroughly implicated in an ideological, not just formal, critical stance. For example, in *Modern Poetry and the Tradition,* Brooks's constituting opposition between aesthetic "difficulty" and "sentimental" propaganda allowed him to valorize the high modernists under the first rubric and to denigrate, as its devalued "other," the poetics of Langston Hughes, Horace Gregory, Isidor Schneider, Genevieve Taggard, and the other contributors to *Proletarian Literature in the United States* (1935). "The characteristic fault," he charged, "of the type of poetry exhibited" [in *Proletarian Literature*] is *sentimentality. . . .* It requires no special definition of the term to convict poems of Genevieve Taggard, Langston Hughes, and others in the collection of just this vice."[22] In hindsight, the force and authority of Brooks's critical judgment is attributable less, certainly, to the internal logic of his position (whose constituting binarism rests on a wholly arbitrary criterion of value)—less, that is, to his reading's intrinsic, critical rigor—and more to the enabling, extrinsic cultural politics of an era rocked by the crushing blow delivered to the American Left by the 1939 Hitler-Stalin Non-Aggression Pact.

The culture war waged throughout the 1930s between, on the one hand, the loose confederacy of conservative agrarians, protofascists, neoscholastics, and English Distributists and, on the other hand, American Marxism shapes the social text, argues John Fekete, that positioned

"New Criticism as the ideological alternative to the Marxist criticism." It is no accident that the rise of New Criticism, witnessed in works such Brooks's *Modern Poetry and the Tradition* in 1939, is coincidental with the signing of the Soviet-German Nonagression Pact that same year. With this major setback to socialist culture in the United States, Fekete argues,

> The New Criticism was able to move in, not to combat a strong left-wing position, but rather to occupy the vacuum left by the failure of socialist criticism to realize its opportunities. . . . In other words, the cultural politics of the New Criticism are linked with the political culture of the period, and, as in the rest of the modern critical tradition, the cultural methodology reveals its politics directly.[23]

Part of the "political culture" largely ignored in Fekete's study, however, is the consolidation of a popular, consumer society underwritten by the new Fordist economy. Not insignificantly, what Fordism inaugurated between the wars was not just a revolutionary mode of factory production but, more to the point, a diversified consumer culture.

In its relentless search for new markets, capital bestowed broad cultural representation on a diversified buying public that, as consumers, decisively displaced the old-guard social representations of mandarin "squirearchy." The Southern Agrarian nostalgia for an idealized plantation economy not only protested the science and technology of Fordism's planned economy but, equally important, the leveling of social distinctions that subordinated blacks, ethnic groups, women, and the working classes to what Ransom described as the "Anglophile sentiment" (*ITS* 3) of the traditional Republic. In theorizing the South through what Benedict Anderson might describe as an "imagined community"—the narrative "fraternity" of a "deep horizontal comradeship"—Ransom charged that the newly industrialized South had "forgotten" its true self: its agrarian rootedness in "physical earth" and its "primary joy, which is an inexhaustible source of arts and religions and philosophies" (*ITS* 9).[24] "Communities," in Anderson's signal formulation, "are to be distinguished, not by their falsity/genuiness, but by the style in which they are imagined" (15). Promulgating a brand of southern nationalism, Ransom sought to deploy southern nostalgia for an idealized and largely imaginary tradition in ideological resistance to the forces of social modernization that went hand in hand with the spread of northern industry.

As spokesperson for a southern intelligentsia—"the historian and philosopher"—Ransom noted the damaging influences of capitalization and the "American progressive doctrine" on Southern living. His aim was to "reverse this order and find that the Southern idea rather than the American has in its favor the authority of example and the approval of theory" (*ITS* 3). Such a politics of "underdevelopment"[25] defended the kind of conservative cultural order espoused in T. S. Eliot's earlier framing of high literary tradition within the "mind of Europe": a key precedent for Ransom's own campaign for "European principles of culture."[26] Positioning Southern Agrarianism as heir to the "heredity" of Western culture, he warned that "the European principles had better look to the South if they are to be perpetuated in this country" (*ITS* 3). But more to the point, such Eurocentrism was lodged in Ransom's polemic, against what he stigmatized as the twin "Americanisms" of "Progress and Service."

In a tropology that imbricates nationalism and gender, Ransom links the former, "masculine" ideology of progress to the biblical typology of "Adam's Curse" of unbridled ambition and willful domination of nature. But more telling was Ransom's critique of progressive social "service" that he describes as the "feminine form" of the northern, urban economy. Ransom's tirade against the new social movements of the depression era reveals his own ideological melting pot of racism, sexism, classism, and ethnocentrism, against which he positions the "European principle of culture" in differential relation. Couched in misogynist and xenophobic stereotypes, "service," for Ransom, "means the function of Eve, it means the seducing of laggard men into fresh struggles with nature. It has special application to the apparently stagnant sections of mankind, it busies itself with the heathen Chinee, with the Roman Catholic Mexican, with the 'lower' classes in our society" (*ITS* 10).

Read as a reactionary nationalism, the Agrarian cause marks not just a turning away from the industrialized "new South," not just a recovery of an older confederacy "deeply founded in the way of life itself—in its tables, chairs, portraits, festivals, laws, marriage, customs."[27] But more troubling, the cultural logic of this Southern ideologeme rests on the differential rubric of race as its constituting ground of imaginary group identity. Not surprisingly, Southern squirearchy's regime of the same— what Tate defended as "white rule"—depends on an enabling community of others made up of its former slave class. Thus, the Southerners' critique of northern industrialism, their campaign for a refined Eurocentric and Anglophile canon, and their attempted restoration of a hierarchic cultural order were all inextricably interwoven with the specific historicity of the African diaspora coupled with the colonizing discourses and material praxes that would sustain "white supremacy."

The "social organization" of what John Crowe Ransom described as southern "squirearchy" entailed a cultural logic where "people were for the most part in their right places." But what does it mean, we may well ask, to be positioned in one's rightful place within a slave system? "Slavery," as far as Ransom was concerned, "was a feature monstrous enough in theory, but, more often than not, humane in practice" (*ITS* 14). Ransom's apology for a "humane" slavery, of course, is baldly oxymoronic and breaks down under squirearchy's commodification of persons as capital. Implicitly assumed here is what Ransom's colleague Frank Lawrence Owsley explicitly theorizes: that the slave plantation is the "right place" for African Americans due to their racial inferiority, primitivism, and savagery. Owsley is not only quite blunt about the bottom-line realities of such a chattel economy, noting that the North depleted the South of "nearly $2,000,000,000 invested in slaves." But more outrageously, he openly stigmatizes African Americans as subhuman brutes, "some of whom," he charged, "could still remember the taste of human flesh and the bulk of them hardly three generations removed from cannibalism" (*ITS* 62). It is precisely against this racial stereotype of the barbarous "other" that the South's own self-image as the latter-day exemplar of Western culture—the "seat of an agrarian civilization" (*ITS* 71)—is founded. In a symptomatic linkage of the American South to a venerable lineage of such precursor, slave-holding states as ancient Greece and the Roman republic, Owsley rationalizes slavery through the same cultural tradition that founds the Western canon.[28]

Although less blatant in its racial stereotypes than Owlsey's savage representations, Robert Penn Warren's "The Briar Patch" exploited Booker T. Washingon's version of the Tuskeegee work ethic to resist the emerging "New Negro" intelligentsia of the 1920s and to confine African Americans to the lumpenproletariat and semiskilled working classes. Black theorists of the so-called New Negro movement such as Alain Locke had five years earlier promoted the Roaring Twenties' renaissance in African American cultural expression celebrated in the salons, cabarets, and lecture halls of Harlem, Durham, Washingon, Atlanta, Hampton, Nashville, and Lincoln. Pockets of entrepreneurial success—as in, say, Durham's prosperous North Carolina Mutual Life Insurance

Company and its Mechanics and Farmers Bank—coupled with growing black enclaves in the professions and academy were sowing the seeds for the growth of an African-American bourgeoisie. And it was precisely against this emerging professional class that Warren advocated "an emphasis on vocational education for the negro" (*ITS* 250). This proletarianization of the emerging black professional class, moreover, was joined to the racial subtext of Warren's resistance to its call for social equality in, and desegregation of, the privileged spaces of the Southern public sphere—schools, restaurants, hotels, concert halls, and so forth. Warren sought to legitimate his take on desegregation by stigmatizing it as the agenda of the black "radical."

Linking his position to Booker T. Washington's famous Atlanta Exposition speech (1895) of the previous century, Warren allowed as how when Washington "lifted his hand and said, 'We can be as separate as the fingers, yet one as the hand in all things essential to mutual progress,' the hand he raised, in the eyes of such a radical, was the hand of treason" (*ITS* 254). Similarly, Warren argued against the integration of white trade unions, noting that while the American Federation of Labor had opened its ranks to blacks in the Atlantic City Convention of 1919, "there is a vast difference between that paper victory and a workable system which would embody its principles" (257). Through the clever argument that northern industry was relocating to the South to simply capitalize on cheap black labor, Warren maintained that African Americans would be better served under the South's traditional sharecropping economy.

Writing to the left of Warren, W. E. B. Du Bois had already critiqued the exploitation of pan-African labor worldwide. But differing from Warren, Du Bois's solution did not call on blacks to give up the new forces of industrialization to "white capital." Moreover, he challenged the force of racial propaganda installed throughout the modern culture industry that drives home capital's global wedge against labor. As early as 1925, in his contribution to Locke's *The New Negro* anthology, Du Bois had theorized that the "propaganda of poet and novelist, the uncanny welter of romance, the half knowledge of scientists, the pseudoscience of statesmen—all these, united in the myth of mass inferiority of most men, have built a wall which many centuries will not break down."[29] The same propaganda of the African American's racial inferiority is patent in Warren's patronizing claim that "the Southern negro has always been a creature of the small town and farm. That is where he still chiefly belongs, by temperament and capacity" (*ITS* 260).

For Warren, belonging to a southern "squirearchy" also meant an espousal of "a certain individualism" from which it sprang (*ITS* 257). In his idealized version of the agrarian economy, racial oppression and class subordination were obscured by such mystifying ideologies of earthy self-reliance and communal "personalism." "The rural life," he concludes, "provides the most satisfactory relationship of the two races which can be found at present. . . . in all cases—owner, cropper, hand— there is the important aspect of a certain personal contact" (262). Not coincidentally, Warren's defense of southern sharecropping as the best and most humane social alternative for African Americans comes after three decades of the so-called Great Migration of blacks to the urban North, which had the effect of eroding the South's cheap labor market. In fact, the real economic subordination of blacks served the interests of both wealthy southern planters and poor whites despite the latter's class differences.

Contrary to Warren's rosy picture of southern living, blacks had little incentive to eke out a subsistence wage under a racial caste system that also restricted them to separate and unequal facilities, disenfranchised them through discriminatory voting statutes, deskilled them in education, and exposed them to constant harassment and lethal levels of physical abuse. As a matter of fact, in response to these gross social inequities, some 170,000 African Americans made the exodus out of the South during the first decade of the twentieth century, while 450,000 followed suit in the 1910s, peaking in a flood tide of 750,000 black émigrés during the 1920s. One form of institutional racism that belies Warren's consoling myth of "personal contact" among owner, cropper, and hand was the covert system of black peonage practiced throughout the rural South. Although outlawed as early as 1867 and confirmed by a Supreme Court declaration of 1905, it was common for local judges and sheriffs to take blacks convicted of minor violations and contract them out to local plantations, where they were submitted to slave labor conditions for indefinite periods of time. Worked far in excess of their nominal fines, such prisoners were in some instances murdered, as on John Williams's twenty-seven-hundred-acre plantation, in local attempts to cover up this chattel economy. Chain gangs, prison camps, and urban vagrancy stockades compounded the inhuman conditions to which municipal offenders, 90 percent of whom were black, were sentenced.[30]

However disenfranchised at the voting booth, southern blacks nevertheless could vote with their feet by moving on to the urban, industrial

North. Out-migration was heaviest in such "Cotton South" states as Georgia and South Carolina, where African Americans were victims of longstanding racial violence. Between 1882 and 1930, for example, 1,663 African Americans were lynched by mobs of whites within the Cotton South alone, with another 1,299 legally executed on frequently trumped-up charges.[31] In Georgia, African Americans were terrorized by such infamous cases as Atlanta's mob violence of 1906. There, some 10,000 armed whites had rampaged through the streets of the city, torturing, mutilating, and shooting blacks during the harrowing weekend of September 22. Similarly, throughout the southern countryside, "legal" convictions of black Georgians on capital charges not infrequently degenerated into brutal spectacles that staged the message of racial subordination in the cruelest terms. In rural Georgia, writes James Dittmer, "there is truth in H. L. Mencken's statement that lynching often replaced the merry-go-round, theater, brass band, and other diversions found in the city."[32] Such was the case in Statesboro, where Paul Reed and Will Cato were sentenced to the gallows on the charge of murdering a white planter. Before the sentence could be carried out, however, a crowd of some 10,000 spectators violently seized the two prisoners from the custody of sixty-eight state militia, chained them to a stump, doused them with twenty gallons of oil, and burned them to death to the cheers of the mob.[33]

Not just a form of local entertainment, the southern spectacle of racial violence communicated in no uncertain terms the blunt message of the black underclass's social subordination at the very moment when new political antagonisms—coupled with revisionary representations of race and an emergent, cultural pan-Africanism—were shaking the foundations of white, Southern squirearchy. More is at stake here than a simple antiquarian glimpse back into the record of rural lynchings in the Deep South. For such racial subordination in social practice was also inherent in the ideological labor of the very figures who inaugurated the academic institution of modern literary studies. No less a founder of the Fugitive and New Critical movements than Allen Tate, in fact, advanced a rationale for enforcing "white rule" and "white supremacy" by any means necessary, including lynching. "I argue it this way," he wrote in Seward Collins's 1934 volume of the *American Review:*

> The white race seems determined to rule the Negro race in its midst; I belong to the white race; therefore I intend to support white rule.

Lynching is a symptom of weak, inefficient rule; but you can't destroy lynching by *fiat* or social legislation; lynching will disappear when the white race is satisfied that its supremacy will not be questioned in social crises.[34]

Such is the unsanitized conjuncture of racial and class oppression underwriting the Southern Agrarian campaign for an idealized, Anglo-American/Eurocentric squirearchy. But more to the point, it is precisely this barbarous social text which, in turn, stands as the foundational moment for the subsequent repression of history, social critique, and multicultural diversity in the New Critical shaping of postwar literary studies in the United States. For it is, after all, these same Southern polemicists who would later seek to position their project within the postwar academy, where they would carry on the ideological work of reactionary cultural formation as New Critics.

Beyond its shaping of the modernist literary canon, the New Critical agenda had wider cultural ambitions that—tied as they were to the social elitism and outright fascism of high modernists like Eliot, Pound, and Yeats—sought to intervene in the shaping of everyday life in twentieth-century America. For example, Brooks and Warren would complain in the 1950s that modern readers, as consumers of pop culture, showed little interest in or capacity for close textual reading: "Instead, they listen to speeches, go to church, view television programs, read magazine stories, or the gossip columns of newspapers."[35] Framed as it is here in the preface to the 1958 edition of *Understanding Poetry,* Brooks and Warren's project in this widely reprinted primer was arguably not just to popularize a set of rules for honing reading skills but, equally important, to intervene in the shaping of the wider emergence of the postwar information society. Operating, admittedly, at the academic margins of this new public sphere, Brooks and Warren nevertheless sought to secure it as what Bourdieu would describe as a privileged "habitus" of social distinction.[36] As an institution not just of knowledge but of power and domination, the literary canon that Brooks and Warren promulgated in *Understanding Poetry* would reproduce the social logic of squirearchy where, as Ransom had earlier written, "people were for the most part in their right places." Thus, of the ninety-four poets anthologized in the 1938 edition of *Understanding Poetry* not one is black; less than a handful are female; and not a single poet of the American Left is preserved.

To "save the text" of New Critical pedagogy, which is still an enduring, if not dominant, reading and teaching practice in the academy, one would have to argue that the canonical assumptions shaping *Understanding Poetry* reflect a moment where black literature, women's literature, and socially committed literature were simply absent from America's public culture between the wars. In the instance of race, to take just one of these social exclusions, one would have to argue that Brooks and Warren's erasure of black poetics was a disinterested oversight or blind spot toward race, not a willful silencing of racial discourse. Moreover, one would have to maintain that the New Critical core doctrine of eschewing from the study of literature proper (1) "paraphrase of logical and narrative content," (2) "study of biographical and historical materials," and (3) "inspirational and didactic interpretation" does not implicate that doctrine in a strategic politics of literary containment and social repression.[37] Yet, from the hindsight of our postmodern vantage point, none of these rationales is at all satisfactory. Indeed, the New Critical marketing of canonical protocols of reading in primers like *Understanding Poetry* implicates it in a seamless, ideological continuity reaching back to the Southern Agrarian cause. What Brooks and Warren's anthology plainly reacts against is the previous decade's initiative to grant cultural representation to African Americans in such precursor volumes as Louis Untermeyer's *Modern American Poetry* (1925) and Alfred Kreymborg's *Lyric America* (1930).[38]

Within the African-American community, intellectuals like James Weldon Johnson had theorized the necessity of valuing black culture on a par with white. "The status of the Negro in the United States," he wrote in the classic preface to *The Book of American Negro Poetry* (1922), "is more a question of national mental attitude toward the race than of actual conditions. And nothing will do more to change that mental attitude and raise his status than a demonstration of intellectual parity by the Negro through the production of literature and art."[39] Putting Johnson's cultural strategy into literary practice, Countee Cullen, in his foreword to *Caroling Dusk* (1927), rather self-consciously positioned his text within an authoritative African-American literary continuity. Here he cited its foundational precursors, including James Weldon Johnson's inaugural volume *The Book of American Negro Poetry* (1922), as well as Robert Kerlin's *Negro Poets and Their Poems* (1923), and Newman Ivey White's *An Anthology of Verse by American Negroes* (1924). Cullen's tactic was to popularize new black talents by joining them to a reputable body of "modern Negro poets already established and acknowledged, by virtue of their seniority and published books, as worthy practitioners of their art."[40] Thus, he linked Dunbar's dialect poetry and Johnson's sermon forms to Helene Johnson's "colloquial verses" and Hughes's blues lyrics, while noting Sterling Brown's fusion of vernacular idiom with sonnet forms.

Cullen revised somewhat the task of the black artist as Johnson had defined it five years earlier. "What the colored poet in the United States needs to do," Johnson had argued, "is something like what Synge did for the Irish."[41] Cullen, however, parted company with Johnson's nationalist paradigm as an inadequate, ideological limit to the emerging diversity of the new black canon. He resisted any "attempt to corral the outbursts of the ebony muse into some definite mold to which all poetry by Negroes will conform."[42] In this vein, Cullen foregrounded the role of black authors in advancing experimental modernism and the international avant-gardes. As examples, he cited Jessie Fauset's debts to the Sorbonne and Lewis Alexander's reliance on tanka and haiku forms. But equally important, Cullen shrewdly articulated Anne Spencer's "cool precision" to the new wave of imagist poetics, popularized in America by Amy Lowell. Differing from the often phallocentric bent of high modernists like Pound, Cullen, as a black bisexual editor, was open to the revisionary gender role inscribed in the poetry of Alice Dunbar-Nelson, Angelina Weld Grimké, and Gladys May Casely Hayford. He not only promoted art that challenged stereotypical relations between the races, but published works that subverted Victorian sexual norms.

All of this effort, however, was lost on Brooks and Warren, who, as arbiters of institutional literary tastes, simply erased the sophisticated linkages Cullen and many others had forged between literary modernism and the emerging black canon. Today, the standard "professional" gesture—which still gets played out in the classroom, at academic conferences, and even in print—is to dismiss such racism through the claim that modernists "didn't know better": that they were somehow innocent or unconscious of their racially motivated politics, that such racism was simply a reflection of modern culture.[43] This would be an understandable defense if modernism in its own moment was not so dialogic and contested a cultural terrain as our own period's panorama of competing social interests. But, as recent recovery projects have shown us, American culture was if anything even more politically inflected between the wars than it is today.

Despite the theoretical revolution of the post-Vietnam era, Brooks's cultural politics has proven a remarkably durable foundation for canonical institutions in the postwar era. Transmitted through such contemporary apologists for the Western canon as say, Allan Bloom, E. D. Hirsch, Arthur Schlesinger Jr., Diane Ravitch, Dinesh D'Souza, and Hilton Kramer among others, the Eurocentric cultural mission originally forged in the high modern/New Critical conjuncture of the 1930s made inroads via the Reagan/Bush presidencies into the Department of Education and National Endowment for the Humanities with the appointments of William Bennett and Lynne Cheney. Throughout the 1980s, both Bennett and Cheney exploited their government positions as bully pulpits to espouse the "transcendent" values of Western humanism.[44] Not surprisingly, their foregrounding of so-called great literature backgrounds the same multicultural constituencies that are marginalized in the formalist agenda of New Criticism.

For his part, Cleanth Brooks remained unwavering over the past half-century in his Eurocentric cultural platform, as evidenced in his 1991 *Partisan Review*–sponsored panel address entitled "The Remaking of the Canon." Reflecting back on his early schooling in a mostly male, white-only, "classical academy" in West Tennessee, Brooks recounted that his education naturalized the tradition of the "great" books as the unspoken norm. Although he pointed out that there was no semantic term for the canon as such, he admitted that "we read such books as Caesar's *Commentaries on the Gallic Wars*, Cicero's *Orations*, Ovid *Metamorphoses*, Xenophon's *Anabasis*, and the first three books of Homer's *Iliad*."[45] Moreover, Brooks quite frankly related that, as a depression-era teacher, he sought to reproduce this classical standard of taste with Robert Penn Warren in their *Understanding Poetry* text for modern students, who, he claims "could not distinguish between a good book and a bad" (353). Even as a defender of canonical values in the 1990s, Brooks still echoed the old-line Southern Agrarian platform, inveighing on behalf of the Western humanist tradition against the regime of science and vocational trends in the academy, as well as today's multicultural challenges to the Eurocentric canon of "great" books.

Repudiating those whom he maligned as the "New Revolutionaries" in feminism, Marxism, psychoanalysis, deconstruction, queer theory, and so on, Brooks would return literary studies to a prelapsarian moment where all "political, historical, and sociological information" would be excluded from its disciplinary purview.[46] In the 1930s, Brooks's colleague Robert Penn Warren had sought to discredit and exile the "black radical" from the interbellum republic of letters; in the 1990s, Brooks's target was the heretical subject of critical theory. Replayed here, albeit in a more guarded rhetoric, was the same cultural clash between, on the one hand, what John Crowe Ransom defended as the Eurocentric and Anglophile tradition espoused by T. S. Eliot and, on the other, the expanded social field of democratic representation forged by the new social movements of our postmodern moment. Today, from the hindsight of history, one cannot buy into the disciplinary formalism of the New Right—one cannot bank on its supposed transcendence of social struggle—without also investing politically in its barbarous legacy of cultural repression.

NOTES

1. Hugh Kenner, "The Making of the Modernist Canon," in *Canons*, ed. Robert von Hallberg (Chicago: University of Chicago Press, 1984), p. 374.

2. Kenner, "Making of Modernist Canon," p. 373.

3. For a discussion of the anthology market between the wars and its relation to the high-modern canon see Craig S. Abbott, "Modern American Poetry: Anthologies, Classrooms, and Canons," *College Literature* 17 (1990): 209–22.

4. Cary Nelson, *Repression and Recovery: Modern American Poetry and the Politics of Cultural Memory, 1910–1945* (Madison: University of Wisconsin Press, 1989), p. 21.

5. See Walter Kalaidjian, *American Culture between the Wars: Revisionary Modernism and Postmodern Critique* (New York: Columbia University Press, 1993); Kenneth Burke, *A Grammar of Motives* (Berkeley and Los Angeles: University of California Press, 1969), pp. 3–20.

6. On the theory of tropology as a constitutive ground for historical inscription, see Hayden White, *Metahistory: The Historical Imagination in Nineteenth-Century Europe* (Baltimore: Johns Hopkins University Press, 1973), pp. 31–38.

7. For a cogent discussion of the New Right's assault on progressive academic culture through such organizations as the Institute for Educational Affairs (IEA), the National Association of Scholars (NAS), and Accuracy in Academia (AIA), as well as in such generalist publication venues as the *Partisan Review*, the *American Scholar*, *Commentary*, and the *New York Review of Books*, see Michael Bérubé, "Winning Hearts and Minds," *Yale Journal of Criticism* 5 (Spring 1992): pp. 1–25.

8. See Elizabeth Cullingford, *Yeats, Ireland, and Fascism* (New York: New York University Press, 1981); Tim Redman, *Ezra Pound and Italian Fascism* (New York: Cambridge University Press, 1991); Robert Casillo, *The Genealogy*

of Demons: Anti-Semitism, Fascism, and the Myths of Ezra Pound (Evanston, Ill.: Northwestern University Press, 1988); Lucy McDiarmid, *Saving Civilization: Eliot, and Auden between the Wars* (New York: Cambridge UP, 1984); John Fekete, *The Critical Twilight: Explorations in the Ideology of Anglo-American Literary Theory from Eliot to McLuhan* (Boston: Routledge and Kegan Paul, 1977); Alexander Karanikas, *Tillers of a Myth: Southern Agrarians as Social and Literary Critics* (Madison: University of Wisconsin Press, 1966).

9. Donald Davidson, "A Mirror for Artists," in *I'll Take My Stand* (New York: Harper and Row, 1962), p. 28 (hereafter cited in the text as *ITS*).

10. See Hans Magnus Enzensberger, "The Industrialization of the Mind" (3–14) and "Constituents of a Theory of the Media" (46–76) in *Critical Essays,* trans. Reinhold Grimm and Bruce Armstrong (New York: Continuum, 1982).

11. Antonio Gramsci, *Selections from the Prison Notebooks,* ed. and trans. Quintin Hoare and Geoffrey Nowell-Smith (New York: International Publishers, 1971), p. 302.

12. For a discussion of the growth of what Daniel Bell, B. Bruce-Briggs, Everett Carll Ladd Jr., Norman Podhoretz, and others have discussed as the postwar "new class," see B. Bruce-Briggs, ed., *The New Class?* (New York: McGraw Hill, 1979), and Alvin W. Gouldner, *The Future of Intellectuals and the Rise of the New Class* (New York: Oxford University Press, 1979).

13. "During the period in which we largely increased wages," Ford wrote, "we did have a considerable supervisory force. The home life of the men was investigated and an effort was made to find out what they did with their wages." Henry Ford, *My Life and Work* (New York: Garden City, 1926), p. 263.

14. Buttressed by the pervasive spectacle of advertising, Fordism, according to Michel Aglietta, "marks a new state in the regulation of capitalism, the regime of intensive accumulation in which the capitalist class seeks overall management of the production of wage-labour by the close articulation of relations of production with the commodity relations in which the wage earners purchase their means of consumption. Fordism is thus the principle of *an articulation between process of production and mode of consumption.*" Michel Aglietta, *A Theory of Capitalist Regulation: The US Experience,* trans. David Fernbach (London: New Left Books, 1979), pp. 116–17.

15. *American Review* 3 (April 1934): 124; cited in Karanikas, *Tillers of a Myth,* p. 179.

16. Karanikas, *Tillers of a Myth,* p. 42.

17. Hoffman Nickerson, "Property and Tactics," *American Review* 5 (April–October 1935): 568–69.

18. Ross J. S. Hoffman, "The Totalitarian Regimes: An Essay in Essential Distinctions," *American Review* 9 (September 1937): 336.

19. Nickerson, "Property and Tactics," p. 565.

20. As a synechdotal instance of this tendency, Richard J. Gray's *American*

Poetry of the Twentieth Century not only represses the Southern Agrarian dimension of modern American verse but obscures and deflects its political subtexts through a more narrow focus on the symptomatic themes, say, of the individual's dissociation of sensibility and nostalgia for "unity of being." See Richard J. Gray, *American Poetry of the Twentieth Century* (New York: Longman, 1990), pp. 101–25.

21. See, for example, "A Note on Symbol and Conceit," *American Review* 3 (May 1934): 201–11; and "The Christianity of Modernism," *American Review* 6 (February 1936): 435–46.

22. Cleanth Brooks, "Metaphysical Poetry and Propaganda Art," in *Modern Poetry and the Tradition* (Chapel Hill: University of North Carolina Press, 1939), pp. 50–51.

23. Fekete, *The Critical Twilight*, p. 49.

24. See Benedict Anderson, *Imagined Communities: Reflections on the Origin and Spread of Nationalism* (London: Verso, 1983), p. 16.

25. On the use of nationalism to resist modernisation, John Breuilly has written that "some writers have linked nationalism to the maintenance of order, which might involve the avoidance of rapid modernisation." *Nationalism and the State* (Chicago: University of Chicago Press, 1985), p. 34. See also Gerald Heeger, *The Politics of Underdevelopment* (New York: St. Martin's, 1974), pp. 15–46.

26. T. S. Eliot, "Tradition and the Individual Talent," in *Selected Essays* (New York: Harcourt, Brace and World, 1960), p. 6.

27. Anonymous, "Introduction: A Statement of Principles" (*ITS* xxvi).

28. "The Greek tradition," he writes, "became partly grafted upon the Anglo-Saxon and Scotch tradition of life. However, it was the Romans of the early republic, before land speculators and corn laws had driven men from the soil to the city slums, who appealed most powerfully to the South" (*ITS* 70).

29. W. E. B. Du Bois, "Worlds of Color: The Negro Mind Reaches Out," in *The New Negro*, ed. Alain Locke (New York: Albert and Charles Boni, 1925), p. 407.

30. "Williams," writes Dittmer, "was a cousin of the Jasper County sheriff. Justice Department agents visited Williams's farm on February 23, 1921, to investigate allegations of peonage. They did not file charges. Several weeks later a black hired hand, Clyde Manning, confessed that after the initial investigation he and Williams destroyed evidence by murdering eleven blacks. Williams and Manning shot one victim, killed four others with an ax, and bound and weighted the other six men with stones before throwing them into the river. . . . Recalling conditions during his administration in the 1940s, former governor Ellis Arnall, admitted that 'the Georgia penal system was bad; it was evil; it was inhuman'" (*Black Georgia in the Progressive Era, 1900–1920* [Urbana: University of Illinois Press, 1977], pp. 81, 87).

31. See Stewart E. Tolnay and E. M. Beck, "Rethinking the Role of Racial Vio-

lence in the Great Migration," in *Black Exodus: The Great Migration from the American South,* ed. Alferdteen Harrison (Jackson: University of Mississippi Press, 1991), pp. 20–35.

32. Dittmer, *Black Georgia,* p. 132.

33. For an account of this burning see Dittmer, *Black Georgia,* p. 134.

34. Allen Tate, "A View of the Whole South," *American Review* 2 (February 1934): 424; cited in Karanikas, *Tillers of a Myth,* p. 90.

35. Cleanth Brooks and Robert Penn Warren, *Understanding Poetry,* 3d ed. (New York: Farrar, Straus and Giroux, 1958), p. xvii.

36. See Pierre Bourdieu and Jean Claude Passeron, *Reproduction in Education, Society, and Culture,* trans. Richard Nice (London: Sage, 1990); and Bourdieu, *Distinction: A Social Critique of the Judgement of Taste,* trans. Richard Nice (Cambridge: Harvard University Press, 1984).

37. Cleanth Brooks and Robert Penn Warren, *Understanding Poetry: An Anthology for College Students* (New York: Henry Holt and Company, 1938), p. iv.

38. For a detailed reading of race in the makeup of English studies between the wars see Paul Lauter, *Canons and Contexts* (New York: Oxford University Press, 1991), pp. 22–47.

39. James Weldon Johnson, "Preface to the First Edition," *The Book of American Negro Poetry,* rev. ed. (1922; New York: Harcourt, Brace, 1931), p. 9.

40. Countee Cullen, foreword, *Caroling Dusk: An Anthology of Verse by Negro Poets,* ed. Countee Cullen (New York: Harper and Brothers, 1927), p. x.

41. Johnson, "Preface," p. 40.

42. Cullen, foreword, p. xi.

43. This sort of apology, though traditionally made on behalf of high-modern figures such as, say, Pound, Eliot, and Fitzgerald, has also recently been invoked to "save the text" of writers like Djuna Barnes at her 1992 Centennial Conference held at the University of Maryland.

44. "I have the conviction," Cheney said, "that great literature, no matter whom it is written by, speaks to transcendent values that we all share, no matter what our time and circumstance. . . . In the West the first responsibility is to ground students in the culture that gave rise to the institutions of our democracy." Quoted in Richard Bernstein, "Academia's Liberals Defend their Carnival of Canons against Bloom's 'Killer B's,'" *New York Times,* September 25, 1988, p. 26E; and in Eve Kosofsky Sedgwick, "Nationalism and Sexualities in the Age of Wilde," in *Nationalisms and Sexualities,* ed. Andrew Parker et al. (New York: Routledge, 1992), pp. 237–38. Similarly, Bennett's famous manifesto "To Reclaim a Legacy" incorporates "culture" under the rubric of Eurocentrism that, in his metaphor, is the "glue that binds together our pluralistic nation." "That our society was founded upon such principles as justice, liberty, government with the consent of the governed, and equality under the law is the result of ideas

descended directly from great epochs of Western civilization—Enlightenment England and France, Renaissance Florence, and Periclean Athens." William Bennett, "To Reclaim a Legacy: Text of Report on Humanities in Education," *Chronicle of Higher Education,* 28 November 1984, p. 21.

45. Cleanth Brooks, "The Remaking of the Canon," *Partisan Review* 58 (spring 1991): 351.

46. Brooks, "Remaking of the Canon," p. 355. As a respondent to Brooks's paper, Gertrude Himmelfarb concurred with him. In a similar defense of such contemporary institutions of "close reading" as the "great" books program at St. Johns College, she betrayed New Criticism's hidden ideological agenda by discriminating between the representation of multicultural diversity and "merit"— her code word for canonical distinction. "I do not recognize," she proclaimed, "representation as a legitimate criterion. The final judgment has to do with merit—the worth and greatness of the idea or book. This was the criterion of the learned and wise in the past, and it seems to me we cannot do better than that." Gertrude Himmelfarb, "Response to Cleanth Brooks," *Partisan Review* 58 (spring 1991): 379. Resting her definition of a work's "greatness" on David Hume's criterion of "durable admiration," Himmelfarb implicitly discounts the materialist "contingencies of value" theorized in, say, Barbara Herrnstein Smith's critique of canonicity. See Barbara Herrnstein Smith, *Contingencies of Value: Alternative Perspectives for Critical Theory* (Cambridge: Harvard University Press, 1988).

The Fate of Gender in Modern American Poetry

Cary Nelson

In the opening pages of the October 1912 inaugural issue of *Poetry* magazine one of the senior figures of the previous generation extended a symbolic (and by then posthumous) greeting to the readers and writers of poetry who would succeed him. The author was William Vaughn Moody, and the poem, "I Am the Woman," took up pages 3 to 6 of *Poetry*'s first issue; it was followed by two poems by Ezra Pound. Moody had died exactly two years earlier—in October, 1910—and his widow Harriet had provided Harriet Monroe with "I Am the Woman." In retrospect at least, we can say that Moody's poem, in effect, linked the new poetry with the New Woman. Its opening stanza heralded a new gendered speech at the same time as it celebrated the overturning of the social restrictions that kept women silent so long.

> I am the Woman, ark of the law and its breaker,
> Who chastened her steps and taught her knees to be meek,
> Bridled and bitted her heart and humbled her cheek,
> Parcelled her will, and cried "Take more!" to the taker,
> Shunned what they told her to shun, sought what they bade her seek,
> Locked up her mouth from scornful speaking; now it is open to
>   speak.

Some have assumed the poem is straightforwardly feminist, but it is not that simple. If Moody's poem is partly celebratory, it is also obviously ambivalent. Woman, as he announces in the opening line, is at once the ground or repository of the law and the agent of its undoing. Her ambiguity is so great, he remarks in the next stanza—and here we can catch anticipations of the new poetry breaking on the scene—that the morning star itself is rendered mute, "scared at [her] manifold meaning." She is "the creature / Wrought in God's perilous mood, in His unsafe hour." She needs, it seems, to be both honored and contained. In the end Moody's essentializing but deeply divided investments in gender make the poem partly incoherent; the figure of the woman is rhetorically incapacitated by the contradictory messages it is required to bear. Invoking the same paradoxical claim that would soon capture William Carlos Williams's imagination, Moody has his Eve figure declare that she is simultaneously "harlot and heavenly wife." So too is she universal mother and pure spirit. In the end the multiple roles are too much for her, and she pleads with her "sleeping mother," the earth, to return her to her rightful place in unconscious matter: "Let me lie down with thee in the dark, and be slothful with thee as before."[1]

Twenty-six years later, in 1938, in the last decade of the modern era, Eugene Jolas opened the "Hypnologues" section of his poem and prose poem collection *I Have Seen Monsters and Angels* with the poem "Magna Mater."[2] Unlike Moody's poem, there is no acute social critique here, but both poems also claim to invoke a more fundamental reality that underlies and undergirds the social. In some ways, then, despite its wholly different rhetoric, its narrower thematics, and its open experimentalism, "Magna Mater" is not unlike Moody's "I Am the Woman."

> violetmountains and eveningfading and the torrent-blubber nearby
> and the halloohalali of the goatherd
> the sleepish eagle lazycircling over the jagcrest and the
> faroff snow fire and the cliffrocks and glacier
> a woman walked horizoning across the pass huge-fluttering her
> hair flamenetted and
> I saw the lustreyes upon her shineface moongleam-glowing
> nearer she came snowthudding through the quarter-light
> love-palsied shook the olivetrees the
> pneumawoman stopped
> there was a crash and clink
> trees nenuphars and roses sprouted from her body
> they brumeduskrose titanic
> her hair grew leaves her hair grew cypressleaves
> flitfluttering
> in the nearnightwind
> a silverbird lovenested in the branches
> a silverbird lovesang among the rustleaves and then

the woman walked bigmothering down into the
torrentgulch into
the drugworld of forgetting. (119)

Into a natural world untroubled by human or animal presences other
than an eagle, a goatherd, and presumably the goatherd's charges—a
natural world whose panoramic simplicity is nearly foolish, a world
called forth by the goatherd's "halloohalali"—comes a woman with
"lustreyes upon her shineface moongleamglowing." "Lustreyes"
invokes at once an inner animation that is both luminous and erotic and
an objectification within another's gaze. In any case, like the creature
who bursts on the scene in Lewis Carroll's "Jabberwocky," the woman's
arrival changes everything. The pastoral tableau is shattered, and from
her body sprout known and unknown plants and flowers. At first this
vitality seems beneficent; even its excesses provide nesting places for sil-
verbirds. But then her sexuality reveals its full portent; she and the poem
are drawn "bigmothering" down into a chaos of natural forces. The
poem and its readers at last are swept into "the drugworld of forgetting." Like Moody, Jolas begins affirmatively; the changes the New
Woman brings are welcomed; and, like Moody, Jolas soon voices com-
plementary anxieties. The special excesses of meaning that are gendered
female are, in effect, too good to be true, too rich to be borne. As with
"I Am the Woman," Jolas's Eve merges with the formless mothering
resources of the earth.

Between these two poems stretches, give or take a few years, what we
call modern poetry. Taken together, these two texts suggest there is reason to take on modern poetry not only in various developmental narratives but also as a certain space in which gendered themes undergo repetition and variation. There is reason, in other words, to make
comparisons and contrasts across the whole modern period and to ask
what gendered legacy modern poetry has bequeathed to subsequent generations. Such comparisons are impossible, however, unless we set aside
the long-honored division between experimental and traditional forms in
modern poetry. It is reasonable to claim, indeed, that our fixation on the
story of experimentalist triumph—the hallmark of modernism as it has
been marketed by academics for fifty years—has blinded us to other ways
of configuring modern poetry, including the divisions it exhibits in its
struggle over changing notions of gender. That is my aim here—to compare the efforts a variety of modern poets made to address sexual differ-

ence and ask what generalizations about the period they might lead us to make. As I should make clear at the outset, my use of the term *gender* signals what I believe to be at stake here—the social construction of the meaning of sexual difference—not necessarily what all the poets I discuss believe. Some of them clearly believe they are describing the inevitable and essential nature of men and women themselves. In addition, taking up the issue of gender in modern poetry most often means talking about women and about generalized notions of female identity and sexuality. For many poets, particularly male poets, though certainly not for everyone writing in the years 1910–45, only women possessed gender in any way that was distinctive and problematic enough to warrant conscious reflection. However imperiled it might have seemed, male gender was often, typically unconsciously and unreflectively, taken as a normative condition from which deviation was the only difference possible.

That distorted and unexamined assumption marks many of the poems of the modern period, though it is important not to let our awareness of it block our ability to recognize what variety and contradiction does exist in these decades. Despite what some recent criticism suggests, no simple dichotomy will account for the full range of poems that men and women wrote and published.[3] Men did not always, for example, write disparagingly about women, though they often did. Moreover, the range of sexist attitudes is so great that accounting for it may require distinct analytic categories rather than just a uniform category of misogyny or a description of a spectrum of deplorable stances.[4] Similarly, women did not by any means always write approvingly and sympathetically about other women, though they often did. When, for example, gender was articulated to class or politics, those concerns often either overrode or substantially complicated loyalties based on sexual difference; as might be expected, political or economic relations often took priority during the depression. Some poets, moreover, treated both maleness and femaleness as problematic. And in some cases poets wrote poems so troubled and unstable that any effort to fix the positions they take is likely to curtail the cultural work the poems can do. To begin to get a fair picture of the status of gender in modern American poetry, however, one must go substantially beyond the extraordinarily restricted (and exclusively male) canon of American modernism that came to dominate academic literary study in the 1940s and 1950s and that has been aggressively marketed as the entirety of modernism ever since. It is only then—after, say, Eliot's and Pound's sometimes startling misogyny is countered by other poets' work—that something of modernism's troubled but varied work on gender begins to be available.

One key reason gender is such a vexed subject in modernism is that it frequently does double duty in many poets' work. As always, gender was radically overdetermined, so much so that it is unwise to imagine we can sort out various relevant historical forces and assign specific weight to each of them. It is thus fair to say not only that numerous cultural processes destabilized and altered gender roles, but also that thinking about gender became a way of representing, reflecting on, and either promoting or containing general cultural change. Gender is at once its own subject and a stand in for other anxieties about cultural life. In America, gender differences were destabilized both by overt polemics over issues like birth control and women's suffrage and also by massive immigration and urbanization. Then the First World War intervened. Once again, war exaggerated every tendency in masculinity, while simultaneously teaching men and women how to live without one another and making it difficult to return to prewar gender relations. In the meantime women had entered the workforce and become rather different social and economic agents. The economic forces that had periodically helped to fix gender identities were thus doing precisely the opposite. Moreover, the powerful religious consensus about gender, long threatened, was largely overturned for many constituencies by the time of the heyday of modernism. When modern poets tried to deal with all of this in their work, they were hardly in full control of either the historical context or their own take on it. The result is that gender is both symptom and subject; it is also central to a great many poets' work, so much so in fact that to ignore its presence is to misread modern poetry and the legacy it gives us.

Since I opened with two quotations by men, I should make clear that I am not trying to return to the early phase of contemporary feminist literary criticism that involved mainly interrogating what male writers had to say about women. Nor am I, obviously, exclusively committed to the continuing project of examining women's writing in detail. My aim here is to do both and in doing so to open up a general discussion of the struggle over the meaning of gender in modern American poetry. A full discussion of these issues would, I should add, range still more widely than I have here. It would have to compare work in different countries, and it would have to consider in detail bodies of work that I have left largely outside this paper, such as the continuing presence of the genteel tradition. Finally, I am limiting the discussion to poems that deal explicitly with what it means to be male or female, leaving outside the discussion poems that are more obliquely gendered.[5]

There is one body of poetry that must be cited, however, even if it cannot be reviewed in detail, because it is probably modernism's most concentrated poetic exploration of the trials of masculinity—the poetry about World War I. Though even that poetry cannot be credited with altogether decentering masculinity, it does leave modernism with an unforgettable anxiety about masculinity's essential character and social effects. Thus Carl Sandburg's "Vaudeville: 1916" treats the war partly as a violence carried out by men against one another's bodies. Women are victims as well, but it is men's bodies that are the specific focus of violent intent. Moreover, it is not anonymous, long-distance slaughter by artillery bombardment that he forces on our attention but rather the intimate violence of close combat: "how long will French and Prussians cut each other, faces and guts, in the trenches and tunnels. . . ?" In "Planked Whitefish," a poem he may have deemed too raw to publish, the aggression is both gendered and sexual: "He saw near Ypres a Canadian soldier fastened on a barn door with bayonets pinning the hands and feet . . . . The genital organ of the victim amputated and placed between the lips of the dead man's mouth."[6] It is at this point that war becomes something like masculinity's fate, the final state of an identity grounded in violence. With armies of men set against one another, masculinity becomes its own enemy, an antagonism in which the other is never really different but instead the same; its public violence displaces a will to self-mutilation.

If there were essentialist views of femaleness in circulation, then, there were also comparable views of masculinity at work. One economical way to complicate the pattern suggested by the problematic essentialism of my first two quotations, then, is to cite equivalent reflections on male identity. Indeed, in this case it is possible to move again to the last decade of modernism and cite a counterexample from one of those same two poets' work. Jolas, as it happens, closes the "Hypnologues" section of *I Have Seen Monsters and Angels* with what seems structurally and thematically an explicit companion piece to "Magna Mater," the poem that opened the section. It is called "Firedeath," and in it a male figure initiates a kind of planetary apocalypse.

crackleflame and the circle the snapop and the
implosion the volleybang the whirtatoo in the sandring
the man stood up and yawned his cheeks roseflickering

his hands drumrapping the atlas and
  his hair began to simounflash it bonfired Africa red
blazesheaves sweltered then his
  clothes seethesmouldered summer there was a terra
caliente fume sirroco sheets twirled upwards and
  his head fell off it parchflushed on the ground his
upper muscles twitchboiled chest abdomen and genitals
    in rose
  a legstump danced in sheetflame
  it flitflew into rumbarhythms til it nothinged and the
sandring moved
  birds flipwinged low they aerocruised right to the
edge they dipped and lipped and driftdripped to the
flame they
  wingfared to the firefingers in the cauldron they
were heatwafted in a whirlflight then the cinders and
  the birdsong incantating plantcarols in a burst of
phoenixmusic. (124–25)

Unlike with "Magna Mater," nature here does not subsist in its bucolic silliness until the gendered figure breaks upon the scene. The man rises up into an already burning world that is duplicated in his body and that seems his only destiny. In "Firedeath" the male body self-destructs and takes the world with it. When his hair burns, continents catch fire; his smoldering clothes are the seasons the planet wears. Nothing could be truer to the history of war or to the atomic age this poem predates and anticipates. If the birds in "Magna Mater" nested and sung in the woman's exfoliating body, the birds here risk everything in wild flight that broaches the fires burning everywhere; their song is caught up in the flames that consume them. The great mother of the first poem was partly a dangerous figure of dark fertility; here we have a still more dangerous (and perhaps more threatened) Adam whose body sprouts fire rather than leaves. Both poems take up clichés of gender and make them fresh with their coined words and incantatory rhythms. Both give us these clichés in extremis, as figures of apocalyptic destiny. Yet whatever critique of gendered notions of destiny they muster is productively complicated by the poetry's verbal appeal. The reader wants to sing with these poems, to carry through with these figures of gendered destiny and break through on their far side. In part we may feel that way because both poems are so cheerfully overstated; gender in them is placed hyperbolically on stage. In the midst of Jolas's half-frivolous coinages, gender here seems as much as anything else a kind of linguistic performance, a verbal part that potentially anyone can play.

There would not be much reason to recode Jolas's two poems into any simple judgmental system of politically approved and disapproved poems. They are playful, willfully overwritten in a style that seeks partly to press Hopkins's alliterative experiments to their furthest limits, and irreducibly double not only when taken together but also in their internal implications. Jolas mounts a critique of monolithically gendered destiny—showing absolute maleness and absolute femaleness to have disastrous inner logics—at the same time as he lets those models of ultimate maleness and femaleness retain a certain lyrical and libidinal appeal.

Jolas, of course, is hardly a well-known figure. Even those who know his name from the journal he edited, *transition,* or in the context of studying American and British expatriates in Paris, are not likely to have read his poetry carefully. As I suggested above, part of the problem in thinking through the issue of gender in modern poetry is that we lose a sense of the full range of historical practices when we limit ourselves to canonical poems. Sandburg's unpublished poems about World War I and Jolas's little-known pair of poems about gender in extremis, about as small a sample of unknown or forgotten poems as one could make, already present a suggestive alternative case. That is not to say that noncanonical poets were all by any means writing radically innovative reflections on gender. But any conclusions we might reach about how gender plays itself out in modern poetry are complicated and enriched by wide reading in the forgotten poems of American modernism.

There is also good reason to judge the record of the canonical male modernist poets as a depressing one. There certain misogynist stances recur often enough to justify codifying them into types. For some poets an attack on women became a kind of set piece of their early careers, almost a necessary apprentice undertaking, one of the decorously validated components of an appropriately marketed literary career. The two most famous instances are no doubt Eliot's "Portrait of a Lady" (1911) and Pound's "Portrait d'une Femme" (1912), poems that embody attitudes quite characteristic of their authors' work at that time. In both cases the poets have apparently come to believe that Western civilization, in a period of decline, has erroneously given over to women the authority to maintain its threatened traditions. Yet women's essential being itself either threatens or diminishes everyone who becomes entangled with them. For Eliot, women's precious triviality makes for a life of empty, gestural anxiety. Pound admits these creatures have their allure; one alas repeatedly turns to them in fascination to see glittering "trophies fished up," bright riches that distract but have no substance. Indeed that is the core of female being—gaudy found objects masking an inner emptiness: "In the whole and all," the speaker in Pound's "Portrait d'une Femme" concludes, there is "Nothing that's quite your own. / Yet this is you."[7]

Yet neither of these two poems is quite uniformly or simplistically mysogynist. Eliot's is a historically specific engagement with the early-twentieth-century culture of female patronage, salons, and hostessing and thus partly a class- rather than gender-based critique. Nevertheless, its picture of a certain time and class is clearly gender differentiated, and the structural maintenance of this fragile world of empty forms seems to fall distinctly to women. What Eliot implies in his style of partly self-reflexive revulsion Pound explicitly projects and personifies. Thus the two poems are written in quite divergent voices. Eliot, whose quintessential male protagonist at this time was Prufrock, adopts that voice of self-incriminating critique; he returns to sample the very social world he savages. Pound, on the other hand, casts out and castigates the alluring if vacant sirens whose voices would drown him. Pound's prototypical male figure at the time was Mauberley, and unlike Eliot he saw himself as a man of action. Eliot to some degree shows us both men and women implicated in the world of fallen social relations women have come to oversee; Pound here is Odysseus trying to get past the sirens. Both, however, can be seen as revising and reversing Henry James's map of gender relations in *The Portrait of a Lady* (1881), which offers us a woman who in some ways is the one uncorrupted, if assimilated, figure in a corrupted world. Thus Eliot in his much looser, more meditative and dialogic "Portrait of a Lady" and Pound in his rhetorically focused and almost univocal "Portrait d'une Femme" both show us women of baubles and bric-a-brac who lead men and their civilization to its collective doom.

That is not to say that there is nothing to admire in these poems. Eliot presents a world in which no position external to social life exists from which we might securely critique it, a stance many contemporary theorists would endorse. And there is unquestionably pleasure to be had in the layering and counterpointing of elegance, exhaustion, and wit in his rhetoric. Pound on the other hand offers a bravura performance that elevates complex metaphoricity to something approaching declamatory public speech: "For all this sea-hoard of deciduous things, / Strange woods half sodden, and new brighter stuff." Yet both poems are also instances, whether deliberate or not, of the backlash discourses that swept across America in the wake of nineteenth-century feminism's gains and that would intensify in response to early-twentieth-century feminism. It is not anachronistic, then, to question what sort of cultural work these poems do; there would have been good reason for a reader sensitized to feminism to have found them offensive when they were first published in journals or later reprinted in books by Eliot and Pound. In tracking grounds for both approval and disapproval, in recognizing that both textual and sociohistorical complexities are at stake in any full evaluation of the poems, I am of course undermining any purely aesthetic response to them. Marketed for decades by academic readers as unproblematically aesthetic objects, the poems in their own time were arguably efforts to reach out to audiences troubled by women's changing roles and identities. Indeed, the poems are clear enough in their distaste for women that some readers of this essay have found anything other than their unqualified rejection unacceptable. On the other hand, a more conservative reader thought my criticism of them seriously misguided. Such are the politics of contemporary criticism; it may be that I can please neither of these camps. It is the conservative reader, however, whose position seems to me to be the least defensible.

In case such a reader were inclined to underread the attitudes toward women unhesitatingly put forward in these and other poems, or to find some exculpatory explanation for them—note, for example, Pound's "Canto II" and his gendered offer to breathe a soul into New York ("a maid with no breasts") in his poem "N.Y."—one could turn to Pound's most remarkable programmatic statement of his misogyny, his substantially more than half mad introduction to his translation of Rémy de Gourmont's *The Natural Philosophy of Love*.[8] In putting forth the notion that the human brain is basically "a great clot of genital fluid held in suspense or reserve (p. vii)," Pound allows that this is so obvious and reasonable a hypothesis that it needs little proof. In human creativity and on the evolutionary scale, of course, men predominate. The brain is, after all, essentially male seminal fluid. Insects, on the other hand, are inherently female: "the insect chooses to solve the problem by hibernation, i.e., a sort of negation of action" (ix). Men act, "the phallus or spermatozoid charging, head-on, the female chaos. . . . Even oneself has felt it, driving any new idea into the great passive vulva of London" (viii). It takes Pound eleven pages to lay this all out in detail and by the end it is quite impossible to take it as Swiftian satire. By now, of course, the effect is partly comic, at least in part because Pound mixes his overwrought paeans to phallic creativity with a clubby, chatty style that implies he is casually gathering representative anecdotes from the limitless evidence available to all of us. But make no mistake about the bottom line: Pound believes all of this, and the arguments here underwrite his poetry.

This piece is, one hopes, at the outer edges of any imaginable sexism in the poetry of the modern period. I would be disinclined, moreover, to read its assumptions wholesale into the many unquestionably biased poems about women written in the first half of the century. Other poets whose work is compromised by the binary clichés about gender that underlie so much of our history, some of which Pound echoes here—female passivity versus male aggressiveness being an obvious instance—do not believe an evolutionary hierarchy runs from female insects to male artists. Nor are they likely to persuade themselves the brain is inherently male. So Pound is partly a special case, but some constitutive elements of his madly elaborated misogyny find their way more broadly into twentieth-century poetry.

It did not, therefore, require immersion in Pound's intense, idiosyncratic, and energetically inventive misogyny for him to use the adjective "slut-bellied" when seeking to express revulsion and contempt in the version of "Salutation the Third" published in *BLAST* in 1914. Images like that are readily available as a resource within the general culture. Even Langston Hughes, who so often wrote sympathetically about women, including prostitutes, found himself castigating the South as a "Honey-lipped, syphilitic" whore in *The Weary Blues*.[9] Reaching for an image like that amounts almost to a reflex gesture in our culture. That was arguably the situation Harry Crosby faced when he began writing "Target for Disgust," one of the poems of hyperbolic invective he published in *Mad Queen* (1929).[10]

Crosby was sometimes inclined to write poems that involved a significant amount of gender reversal and gender ambiguity. His obsessive sun-worship, embodied not only in dozens of poems but also in his own sometimes ritualistic behavior, moreover, took as one of its avatars the female figure of the "Mad Queen," a personification of the visionary excess he held as his highest ideal. But in writing from Paris a tirade against his native Boston, "City of Hypocrisy," he did more than echo the culture's existing sexism. He found instinctively that this decaying "City of Tea Rooms" with its "constipated laws" could best be excoriated by elaborating images of a degenerating female body.

I curse you

In the name of Aknaton I curse you
in the name of Rimbaud I curse you
in the name of Van Gogh I curse you

your belly is a nest of worms
your breasts tubercular
you have a falling of the womb
you are an ulcer on the
    face of the earth
    leprous

hogs vomit when they approach you
    City of Stink Stones
    City of Dead Semen
with your Longfellows and your Lowells.

Written in a style that amounts to a kind of incantatory, Whitmanesque invective, "Target for Disgust" is remarkable for pressing poetry toward a social function we have largely forgotten it might serve. Like a good deal of Crosby's work, its energy is striking; one wishes he could have avoided the conventional impulse to personify the city as female and certainly avoided the frenzied misogyny at the poem's core. But he did not. He curses Boston as the "City of Swan-Boats" and the "City of Frog-Ponds," but he also announces to Boston that he "would rather defile a / dead body than uncover / your nakedness." He curses Boston for having a library full of wretched tracts while having none of Gertrude Stein's books, but he also declares to the city that he "would rather spill out / my seed upon the ground / than come near to you." That is not to say that any poet who draws on the culture's stereotypes of gender to address social issues can be accused of fundamental antagonism toward either men or women. Positive and negative gendered images of cities and countries, for example, should not simply be collapsed into one another. The problem here is that Crosby is relentless in deploying diseased or dismissive images of women as a weapon, one he assumes instinctively will resonate with his readers. What the poem helps prove, in the end, is that a certain hatred of women is one constitutive element in Crosby's work. It is by no means present in all of his poetry, but it undermines any general investment we might now make in his career. Moreover, because Crosby deploys an essentialized femaleness both as a site of idealization and as an object of disgust, the two impulses—even when parceled out to different poems—become interdependent within his whole body of work.

It may be strategically useful to suppose that it was not only in response to the dominant culture's values but also in response to such poems (and such poets) that a number of modern writers mounted a substantial critique of conventional gender stereotypes in their own work. Grouped together now, the wide range of poems taking up issues of gender from different vantage points amounts not only to a coherent and thorough analysis of the effect of gender difference in identity, discourse, economics, and social relations but also to a sustained body of speculation about the origin and destiny of gendered subjectivity. Like the misogynist poetry of the period, this work depends on and responds to the first wave of modern feminism. Pound in his introduction to Rémy de Gourmont either blindly or disingenuously declares that he is "certainly neither writing an anti-feminist tract, nor claiming disproportionate privilege for the spermatozoid" (viii), but it is evident he is doing both. The presence of modern feminism also underwrites the poems that counter, rather than reinforce, the dominant culture's sexism. Even poets who rejected feminist activism and politics often made significant contributions to this emerging long-term project. There was, to be sure, nothing like a continuing, coordinated effort to conceptualize the social construction of gender in modern poetry, but we can in retrospect recognize a recurrent impulse to reflect on, critique, and rethink assumptions about gender throughout the period and, as a result, make links between poems and poets that would have been difficult to make at the time.

Perhaps no poem better exemplifies the complexity of this enterprise than Louise Bogan's notorious 1923 poem "Women".[11]

Women have no wilderness in them,
They are provident instead,
Content in the tight hot cell of their hearts
To eat dusty bread.

They do not see cattle cropping red winter grass,
They do not hear

Snow water going down under culverts
Shallow and clear.

They wait, when they should turn to journeys,
They stiffen, when they should bend.
They use against themselves that benevolence
To which no man is friend.

They cannot think of so many crops to a field
Or of clean wood cleft by an axe.
Their love is an eager meaninglessness
Too tense, or too lax.

They hear in every whisper that speaks to them
A shout and a cry.
And like as not, when they take life over their door-sills
They should let it go by.

This is the same poet who in 1923 also spoke in the harsh persona of
Medusa and who six years later stood with Cassandra, declaring herself
"the shrieking heaven lifted over men, / Not the dumb earth, wherein
they set their graves" (33). Yet in "Women," at least on the surface, it
seems she writes a poem with which Pound would find himself comfortable. Certainly it seems to elaborate the same generic metaphors of
female passivity and male vitality. In this case, however, a great deal
depends on whether we credit the female signature above the poem; if we
acknowledge that a woman wrote the poem or that the speaker can be
considered female, then the poem is less stable than it appears. Yet gendered authorship cannot actually constrain or guarantee the semiotic
effects a poem can have. Actually, as long as any woman who attempts
to read the poem aloud is not struck dumb, an unlikely eventuality, then
the gender of the speaker is at least demonstrably reversible. And as soon
as a woman reads the poem, almost everything the poem says is proven
untrue.

If a woman speaks "Women"'s lines, then the poem in most of its
figures undoes all its apparent propositions and assertions. "They do not
see cattle cropping red winter grass," the line that opens the second
stanza, exhibits exactly the precise visually observed detail that the line
asserts women cannot see. Moreover, the detail is sufficient to equip any
reader—male or female—to imagine the scene it describes. Much the

same is true of the sound of snow water in the lines that follow, lines that themselves paradoxically enact and enable the very capacity they rhetorically deny. Two stanzas later we read that women "cannot think of so many crops to a field / Or of clean wood cleft by an axe." Yet here too the reader of either gender is provoked to visualize exactly what the lines describe—to enumerate the crops a field can grow, to imagine the fresh wood exposed by a sharp axe. Similarly, the opening stanza, which declares that women have no wilderness in them, speaks knowingly of the wilderness that it claims women do not know. And if their hearts are really "tight hot cells," then something of wilderness energy and watchfulness has found its way into the home. Indeed, if women "stiffen, when they should bend," then they are capable of resistance, not compliant, as a more conventional image would suggest. Finally, to hear "a shout and a cry" behind "every whisper" is not simply to be fearful but to recognize a hidden wild energy in every domesticated impulse.

This is not to say, however, that there is any perspective from which the poem is likely to seem unambiguously feminist in its assertions; it mounts every feminist claim as a counterassertion, written against the grain of (and at work within) every patriarchal cliché about femininity. The poem is poised to reverse itself, and it powerfully demonstrates how every sexist utterance is undermined from within. The poem's subject is more properly understood not as "women" themselves but rather as masculinist discourses about women, the declarations about women that our culture habitually makes. Those discourses, the poem shows, inevitably contradict and disqualify themselves. Yet it also puts these discourses in circulation again and reminds us—with excruciating precision—of women's culturally imposed self-containment and self-denial. Moreover, the poem finally leaves these matters to our intervention, to the work readers must do. And the last lines—with their ambiguous advice about letting life go by—remain irreducibly open to multiple interpretation.

Bogan's bid to disentangle resistance from within prevailing commonplaces—a project I believe to be too rigorous in this poem to be unintentional—has often been misunderstood. But then misrepresentation and dismissal have been the fates of many of the radical modern rereadings of gender. Another attempt to work from within the dominant codings of sexual difference is the Baroness Else von Freytag-Loringhoven's "MINESELF—MINESOUL—AND—MINE–CAST-IRON LOVER." A German national who was part of the American scene for a time and who wrote and published some poems in a willfully Germanic English, Freytag-Loringhoven explodes the formulas of romantic passion from the inside.

Published in *The Little Review* in 1919, the poem is partly a rather unconventional version of a traditional motif—a dialogue between body and soul.[12] Notably, the body is rhetorically (but not necessarily physiologically) gendered male and the soul female. The body is at once her own body and the body of a lover, and the ensuing conversation thus simultaneously interrogates the inner and outer dimensions of gender relations. On one level, the poem is also a masturbation fantasy: "Alas—mine body—use thine fingers desirous to see! pray—caress—flame—burn deep—mark the place— — —dance in laughter and dizziness— — — come back with fingers strong—steady—wise—shining stars!"—"To arouse it I will probe deep"—"Surrender to NOTHINGNESS!" As the excitement increases, the soul objectifies the body and sings of it ecstatically—"HIS HAIR IS MOLTEN GOLD AND A RED PELT"—and the body tenses, becoming figuratively phallic.

At that point masturbation leads to a series of reflections on male identity as the culture has constrained and constructed it. Muscles tensed, the body becomes a "cast-iron animal," a "toadking" who is "full of suspicious fear" and "STIFF pride"—"usurperpride." The toad king, majestic but wary, hides in darkness, squatting in his cave under his crown in the center of his crimson throne, and dreams of flight. But the toad king does not know himself or know his limits. He is hidden from himself and hidden in himself. He cannot fly like a bee and is better off being what he is, a toad who dreams "TOADDREAMS!"

Filled with ambivalent but ecstatic admiration for the male archetypes she critiques, Freytag-Loringhoven at once puts forward and demolishes romantic conventions. In this case she contains within herself identities sufficient to encompass both genders, and it is thus an autoerotic reverie that enables her to reflect on the psychic economy of masculinity. Like Bogan, she knows within herself every male capacity the culture would deny her. Like Whitman, whose style she partly emulates, she contains multitudes.

The other notable form of gendered self-sufficiency in the period involved women loving other women and writing poems about them. Amy Lowell's series of poems from 1919—including "Decade," "Opal," "Madonna of the Evening Flowers," and "Venus Transiens"—are among the most elegantly passionate love poems in modern American poetry. As we can tell from its first stanza, "The Weather-Cock Points South" is remarkable for the way it fuses an eroticized spirituality with explicit physical references.[13]

> I put your leaves aside,
> One by one:
> The stiff, broad outer leaves;
> The smaller ones,
> Pleasant to touch, veined with purple;
> The glazed inner leaves.
> One by one
> I parted you from your leaves,
> Until you stood up like a white flower
> Swaying slightly in the evening wind.

The leaves are put aside at once by a disrobing and by a probing embrace. The poem involves a pursuit of psychic intimacy—a drive to know and celebrate another's inwardness—and an explicit vaginal caress. The flower with its petals and bud is thus both body and spirit, but there is no severing the two. And the woman she describes seems both the object of her gaze and the flower of her own unfolding affection. The flower is both the center of the lover's body and the center of the self, for it becomes the site from which the subject seems to speak. It is also the center of the gardens coalescing in the poem and, implicitly, of nature as a whole. Her unwavering concentration on it gives it the transience of wax and the permanence of stone—"of jade, of unstreaked agate; / Flower with surfaces of ice."

"The stars crowd through the lilac leaves / To look at you," Lowell writes, so it is clear she would have no patience with a criminalized notion of the gaze. There seems little reason, indeed, to impose a contemporary prudishness either on her or on other modern poets. An objectifying look or verbal representation does not preclude a variety of other perspectives; indeed it is both a form of celebratory play and a form of concentration that can be empathic. That may be the case, for example, in Claude McKay's 1917 "The Harlem Dancer."[14]

> Applauding youths laughed with young prostitutes
> And watched her perfect, half-clothed body sway;
> Her voice was like the sound of blended flutes

Blown by black players upon a picnic day.
She sang and danced on gracefully and calm,
The light gauze hanging loose about her form;
To me she seemed a proudly-swaying palm
Grown lovelier for passing through a storm.
Upon her swarthy neck black shiny curls
Luxuriant fell; and tossing coins in praise,
The wine-flushed, bold-eyed boys, and even the girls,
Devoured her shape with eager, passionate gaze;
But looking at her falsely-smiling face,
I knew her self was not in that strange place.

Of course there is no guarantee that the speaker in the poem reads the dancer's feelings accurately, facial expressions being notoriously open to multiple interpretation. Gender here is caught up in other systems of value—as it necessarily always is—and here those other values include the moral system that frames the poem and prejudges the prostitutes and the night club or brothel setting. Nonetheless, McKay does insist that the dancer is both an admirable symbolic figure and an individual, dual recognitions crucial to the other context that energizes this text—race. The phrase "grown lovelier for passing through a storm" reaches beyond her skilled triumph over the dance hall setting to reverberate throughout black history, or so the poem urges us to believe, and the dancer's pride and beauty stand for everything black Americans have won from adversity. Yet her mastery of the dance—along with its suggestions of materially constrained and compromised transcendence—is also specified and limited in a crucial way, for she has triumphed at the historical intersection of gender and race. Indeed, gender and race here are inseparable from history; they are social values, not unchanging essences.

If McKay's poem is somewhat compromised by its unself-consciously judgmental opening and closing lines (and by a formalism that does not altogether serve this subject well), one finds few compromising elements in Langston Hughes's poems about women. Hughes's notable fairness in writing about black women is facilitated, certainly, by his thorough understanding of their history and their current social positioning. From the outset of his career he was adept at creating concise portraits of women that manage to treat them as representative figures while providing enough detail to make them seem distinct individuals as well. Nor are his women simply interchangeable with black men. They face special discrimination and have their own distinctive triumphs. Hughes was thus capable of recognizing how gender intersected with and complicated race, something not all modern black male writers have been capable of doing. Part of this may have been due to his rumored homosexuality, which perhaps left his poetry free of any compromising will to power over women. But Hughes was also broadly tolerant and nonjudgmental. He also knew his limits and never attempted greater psychological intimacy than he could make plausible.

Significantly, Hughes's portraits of men are equally fair—sympathetic, critical, bemused, aware of behavior that is socially produced and encouraged. Throughout his career, he never succumbs to the bourgeois fantasy of a wholly distinctive subjectivity for either men or women but instead realizes that the pleasures and pitfalls of gender are substantially given to us by the culture in which we live. It is worth underlining this characteristic here, because Hughes might be faulted by some readers who are uncritically wedded to an ideal of bourgeois individuality. Indeed, one of the recurrent complaints about politically and socially committed writers is that they depict types, not individuals, a complaint that sometimes says more about the critic's assumptions than about the work being discussed. In many of Hughes's early poems, to be sure, individual differences are registered very lightly—a name, a few verbal inflections, a slight narrative specification, and nothing more. Recognizing this carefully wrought balance between types and individuals requires us to credit a more socially and politically grounded notion of identity. Indeed, there would be little reason for poets to interrogate gender without some conviction about its social construction. The only alternatives are to treat gender as irrelevant or to adopt Pound's mad biologism.

There are portraits of a wide range of men and women in Hughes's poems. Among the women are dancers, businesswomen, the young and the old. In *The Weary Blues,* almost uniquely among male poets—but following upon comparable work in fiction and drama—he also writes sympathetically about prostitutes without sentimentalizing them. Here is "To the Dark Mercedes of 'El Palacio de Amor.'"[15]

Mercedes is a jungle-lily in a death house.
Mercedes is a doomed star.
Mercedes is a charnel rose.
Go where gold
Will fall at the feet of your beauty,

Mercedes,
Go where they will pay you well
For your loveliness.

Years later, Hughes will have a speaker in a poem assert that "a woman does the best she can." "So does a man," someone else answers.[16] Recognizing how severely choice is constrained at the intersection of gender, race, class, and ethnicity, Hughes anticipates one of the central arguments of feminist historiography. Here Hughes wants to insist that Mercedes, whose racial and ethnic identity is unspecified, is one among many women in different roles who can serve as figures for all oppressed people of color. The opening line, with its image of the "jungle-lily in a death house," of course also invokes black history and the slave trade, since the ships that served the middle passage were precisely death houses for many, as were the slave quarters in the American South. As a "doomed star" Mercedes takes up her place in a fatalistic history that long precedes and follows her. It is that history, in part, along with her beauty, that lends her a certain figural invulnerability. The concluding advice is at once practical—if this is your only choice, make the most of it, gain what honor you can in the only tender that is relevant—and symbolic, for the gold coins honor more than her service. As he writes in another poem, "When Sue Wears Red," "a queen from some time-dead Egyptian night / Walks once again." If these lines from the same book echo in this poem, it is partly because of the form Hughes uses. The first three lines in particular, with their serial recitation of the same declarative form, lend the poem a ritualistic, incantatory quality, so that when the gold coins fall in the next two lines they do so at the feet of a figure who is necessarily more than she seems.

Here and elsewhere in his work, an understanding of economic hardship leads Hughes not simply to empathize but also to differentiate and to specify. Part of that effort to differentiate—especially in the midst of the hourglass economy of the 1920s and the Great Depression of the 1930s—cuts across gender to produce loyalties based on class difference and economic interest. It led Hughes to speak for the poor of all races. It also led many poets to speak out against privilege.

The privilege and power that were culturally decisive were overwhelmingly male. But some poets extended their critique to the privilege possessed by wealthy women. Thus Lucia Trent placed a series of poems attacking upper-class women in her 1929 book *Children of Fire and*

Shadow, including "Lady in a Limousine," "Little Lady of Comfort," and "Society Woman." Muriel Rukeyser's "More of a Corpse Than a Woman," first published in *Partisan Review* and then collected in *U.S. 1* (1938), predicts that all the special escapist retreats and decathected prisons devised for protected women of wealth and privilege will be done away with when other "women are ready and rich in their wish for the world."[17] And Tillie Olsen in her 1934 poem "I Want You Women Up North to Know" warns the women who buy embroidered children's dresses at northern department stores of the social conditions under which those dresses are produced, namely the exploited labor of Mexican-American women in the Southwest.

Women, of course, were not running corporations, and they did not control the U.S. Congress. But by the time these poems were written women had taken a variety of jobs during World War I and they had finally won the right to vote. Thus the options for women, however constrained in the postwar world and in the depression, no longer seemed immutable. Poets on the Left were therefore less tolerant of those women who were indifferent to the poverty around them and who led lives that seemed self-indulgent or trivial. Again, the critique is gender specific, and there were certainly many more poems published that attacked the power men wielded. But the special roles available to upper-class women came under specific scrutiny, particularly by other women poets.

In trying to create a women's tradition, then, it is important not to limit our recovery efforts to poems that are uncritically and universally supportive of other women. People's historical commitments were finally more complex and productive than that. There is certainly a sisterly appeal across class difference in many of these poems—Tillie Olsen, for example, implicitly asks financially secure women to recognize that it is other women whose suffering and exploitation secures their own material comfort—but such appeals are not based on covering over real inequities and ignoring distinctions in social practice.

The critique of privileged gender roles is also entangled with a broader analysis of the roles available to men and women. Joy Davidman's "This Woman" urges women not to "put a ribbon in your hair . . . nor twine / a flower with your strength: go bare, go bare." Recognize instead, she urges women in a suggestive but open-ended metaphor, the special forces that "carved your body like a tree of earth."[18] Alice Dunbar-Nelson in a 1927 poem bemoans the fact that she must "sit and sew—a useless task it seems," while dreaming of "the panoply of war, the martial tread of men." But she also makes it clear what the battlefield harvest of absolute masculinity is: "wasted fields, and writhing grotesque things / Once men."[19] And Georgia Douglas Johnson, in the 1927 poem "The Heart of a Woman," reminds us that women's imaginations are restless in an imposed domesticity. They roam far afield "in the wake of those echoes the heart calls home," she writes, perhaps allowing "wake" to serve as a wishful pun, suggesting reverberations at once of the constricting hearth and its demolition.[20] Finally, Lucia Trent opens the 1929 poem "Breed, Women Breed" with a blistering mock-injunction for women to produce children for male ends.[21]

> Breed, little mothers,
> With tired backs and tired hands,
> Breed for the owners of mills and the owners of mines,
> Breed a race of danger-haunted men,
> A race of toiling, sweating, miserable men,
> Breed, little mothers,
> Breed for the owners of mills and the owners of mines,
> Breed, breed, breed!

Although Trent's poem moves forward relentlessly through three more stanzas tonally in keeping with the one above, it is clearly grounded in an unstable mix of anger, anguish, and contempt—emotions directed not only at the men who manage the institution of motherhood within capitalism but also at the women who collaborate with it. Only by wholly rejecting both capitalism and patriarchy can we gain any relief from the gender dynamics she critiques, and that is precisely the recognition she seeks. Biology, economics, and male power are part of one interlocking system, one overarching productive and constraining mechanism. If we are to change any of it, we must change it all. Trent is willing to risk offending part of her audience because there is nothing to lose. No modest gains, no hedged alliances, can alter the mutually reinforcing structures she describes.

All these poems attacking conventional gender roles and power inequities are also implicitly written against conventions for representing male and female interests and identities. Occasionally representation becomes the explicit focus of critique, and sometimes the weapon is satire. There is certainly a satiric impulse behind Trent's "Breed, Women Breed," even though it is not the only sentiment informing the poem, and the risks inherent in satire are apparent not only in the aggressive triple command that ends the stanza but throughout. One of the risks, of course, is that the poem becomes merely an instance of the thing being satirized. Herman Spector takes on exactly that danger in "A Wohmmn," his 1929 satire of a blues homage to male lust.[22]

i wann, i wann a wohmmn
whose touch hrts.

no mere alyin en allayin drab.
no cynico-mundane dust,
no haddit befaw . . .
i wann a wite wide wohmmn,
promising maww.

o, sing r softly under me now!
i know the banked caress,
the side-to-side weaving.
her womb is wide,
her flesh is swift with tenderness . . .

reech me in my agony!

tears r no damn good;
but things to eat r good.
a continually eaten wohmmn
with vast hungriness . . .

(on cool days, the streets are bare.
walking; her skirt blows
around firm legs.
the sun glos over er.)

Since embittered satires were a staple of Spector's poetry, one can be reasonably confident in reading this poem that way. The demand that is the poem's leitmotif—"i wann a wohmmn"—uses a pun on woman and womb to make the wish both commodifying and infantile. It thus undermines adult masculinity with a wish to crawl back into the womb or to be consumed. Textually, however, the poem is a good deal less determinate. As always, commodification and parody risk exemplifying the contempt they would critique. As a result, it is also readable as a sexist and

344 / *Marketing Modernisms*

racist faux blues poem, and no amount of biographical or extratextual information can prevent it from being so. Since exaggeration alone will not insure that the poem is taken as satire, Spector works instead to underline its inauthenticity by self-consciously mixing different rhetorics. Note, for example, the use of "cynico-mundane" in the second stanza and the more neutral descriptive voice at the end. All this adds up to a poem that is in many respects hopelessly conflicted, though it has moments of telling satire that help make its struggle to do productive cultural work still instructive six decades later.

Equally conflicted is Hart Crane's "National Winter Garden," one of three poems about the cultural and psychological meaning of gender that comprise the "Three Songs" section of *The Bridge* (1930).[23] It is a poem that critiques a striptease as an emblem of male/female relations. Crane takes up this setting because it stages the economy of illicit desire in its most uncompromising form. There are, he writes in the opening stanza, "no extra mufflings here." We get "bandy eyes" and "outspoken buttocks" in a form concentrated enough so that "the world's one flagrant, sweating cinch." Even here, however, there is planned displacement. The performer provides stimulation, while the men in the audience wait the women who are fair game and then "rush the nearest exit." Meanwhile, even the apparently elemental libidinal encounter with the figure on stage is revealed to be an assemblage of artifices. Her pure whiteness—"shall we call her whiter than the snow"—is a staged spectacle, an artifice of the harsh lights, which in turn become red and green.

Although Crane has no special respect for the male patrons, it is of course primarily the woman who is on display and who demonstrates the nihilistic core of heterosexual relations as they are institutionalized here. The critique of heterosexuality is thus mounted primarily at her expense, even though he wants to leave the stripteaser herself some unreadable inner life that is not accounted for by her performance. Detached and unrevealing, her visage is "least tearful and least glad" of all those here. "Who," indeed, can claim he "knows her smile?" But Crane also wants to explore his own ambivalent revulsion as thoroughly as he can, more thoroughly, say, than McKay did in "The Harlem Dancer." In the end he turns to the woman on stage to figure "the burlesque of our lust"; that voided space of valueless substitution, he tells her, is centered in the "empty trapeze of your flesh."

Her eyes exist in swivellings of her teats,
Pearls whip her hips, a drench of whirling strands.

Her silly snake rings begin to mount, surmount
Each other—turquoise fakes on tinselled hands.

We wait that writhing pool, her pearls collapsed,
—All but her belly buried in the floor;
And the lewd trounce of a final muted beat!
We flee her spasm through a fleshless door.

Although one could try to argue that this is not a description of the
dance itself but rather of its image in the minds of the men in the audience, in fact Crane could have credited her with some skill and grace had
he wanted to make such a differentiation. Despite an element of evenhanded critique, therefore, "National Winter Garden" arguably does at
least as much misogynist as any other sort of cultural work; the woman
in the poem pays the price for the poem's judgment about the culture of
heterosexuality.

Elsewhere in the modern period, however, what should pass as satire
sometimes intends nothing of the kind. I refer specifically to the rear-
guard actions, the various efforts to secure the traditional terms of sexual
difference at the very moment they were disintegrating. One might innocently assume satire was at work in opening John Crowe Ransom's
Selected Poems and discovering the titles he gave to its two main sections:
"The Innocent Doves" and "The Manliness of Men."[24] It does not take
long, however, before one realizes that these categories are meant seriously, despite his wry tone and bemused perspective on all human
endeavor. In the 1924 poem "Miriam Tazewell" a woman weeps when a
thunderstorm breaks and afterward walks out to see "her lawn
deflowered" (3). Apparently this is the sort of sophomoric joke Ransom
imagines his male readers enjoying together. It seems to her "the whole
world was villain, / The principle of the beast was low and masculine."
In "Lady Lost," first published in 1925, in which a bird serves as a figure
for all women, the speaker asks, "has anybody / Injured some fine
woman in some dark way?" If so, it represents no real problem.

Let the owner come and claim possession,
No questions will be asked. But stroke her gently
With loving words, and she will evidently
Return to her full soft-haired white-breasted fashion
And her right home and her right passion. (10)

His poems are full of foolish girls and worldly men. When Ransom's men commit errors of pride, the price paid is manly and imposing: solid oaks split, winter storms strike, or battlefields are strewn with dead. Ransom's women flirt and flutter and give themselves over only to romance or its rejection. Despite all this, his sexism is not unself-conscious. It is rather a deliberate and witty effort to articulate what he sees as the differences between men and women. Yet of all the well-known modern American poets his oeuvre may be the most thoroughly constituted by misogyny, for his whole poetic project is founded on an exaggerated and absurdly stereotypical view of sexual difference. Subtract these views and there are few poems left, no career to speak of remaining. Nonetheless, the poems are too intricately crafted, their diction too surprising, for Ransom's sexism to warrant simple outrage. And often enough the rhetoric of his wit offers pleasures that counter the pettiness of his subject matter and his attitude toward it. But his career is finally wholly circumscribed by clichés about men and women that he could not see beyond.

A conservative reader might attempt to defend Ransom by noting that some of the more condescending poems are written to young girls, not mature women, but the effect of his *Selected Poems,* which mixes poems devoted to women of a variety of ages, is to make older women and young girls interchangeable. The additional poems in his individual books, moreover, add significantly to the sense that a frustrated idealism underlies a generalized misogyny in his work.[25] On that relational ground, improbably enough, one may compare Ransom with Crosby, one a dignified southern traditionalist, the other a willful iconoclast and expatriate outlaw. They could hardly be less similar figures otherwise, despite the comparable intensity of their very different obsessions. Yet on the issue of how gender functions in their poetry they display a fraternal bond. Underlying this similarity, however, are different social conditions. Although one would not know it from the surface of Ransom's poems, for example, their constitutive rage at women is again historically grounded. In Ransom's despair at the changes he saw in the country and in his regret at the passing of the old South is also a distress about destabilized gender relations.[26]

One of the most succinct and telling indictments of the relationship between frustrated idealization and misogyny, interestingly enough, is a poem that appears to be exclusively about an earlier age, H.D.'s 1924 "Helen." The poem in fact also addresses its own historical moment, not just the period of the Trojan War. It is about the anger some in the culture feel now that women are not simply beautiful objects.[27] "Remembering past enchantments," Greece now "hates / the still eyes in the white face." Only death, it seems, can relieve this tension and recompense the culture for the changes women have wrought.

> Greece sees unmoved,
> God's daughter, born of love,
> the beauty of cool feet
> and slenderest knees,
> could love indeed the maid,
> only if she were laid,
> white ash amid funereal cypresses.

If one sets against Ransom's trivializing and contemptuous injunctions to women—"think no more of what will come to pass / Than bluebirds that go walking on the grass"—the articulate passions one finds in H.D's poetry and in Lowell's love poems—"When I am with you, / My heart is a frozen pond / Gleaming with agitated torches"—it is possible to conclude that modern poetry amounted to a pitched battle between male and female poets. Even this survey, however, suggests that the record was more varied and complex. Certainly modern poets were frequently preoccupied with undermining, redefining, or consolidating notions of gender, enough so that it can be counted one of the core topics that shaped modern poetry and led poets to write in the first place. But no easy gendered categories—or any other categories I am aware of—warrant grouping Langston Hughes with Ezra Pound or John Crowe Ransom. Nothing seems less relevant than that they were all men. Nor is our understanding enhanced by grouping together all the women who wrote about gender.

In some cases, indeed, individual poets were so divided in their attitudes as to preclude assigning a single consistent identity for even one writer. There seem, for example, to have been at least two Edna St. Vincent Millays. They sometimes overlapped, but not so thoroughly that we can extract from her work one view of relations between the sexes. There are sonnets like "I, Being Born a Woman and Distressed," which argues clearly to a man that a woman's status alone does not warrant wishing "to bear your body's weight upon my breast" (601).[28] She thus vows not to season "scorn with pity." Or like "Oh, Oh, You Will Be Sorry for That Word" (590), which might as well have been written to Ransom.

Responding to a man's jibe of "What a big book for such a little head!" the speaker promises never again to read a book or "tell you what I think" and hereafter "be called a wife to pattern by"—until she walks out never to return. And of course there is the sequence "Sonnets from an Ungrafted Tree" that focuses on a woman watching a dying man she never really loved: "Gazing upon him now, severe and dead, / It seemed a curious thing that she had lain / Beside him many a night in that cold bed" (622). This is the articulately antiromantic Millay that the culture has largely chosen to forget. But the rhapsodically romantic Millay who has been both remembered and belittled has also left us poems written from her perspective. What makes this dichotomy problematic is the fact that the two Millays are not notably in dialogue with one another in individual poems. Within any one poem, the opposite perspective is there only as a rejected and exteriorized other. Only if we take her work as a whole can we say that Millay carried on in her own poetry the debates about the meaning of gender that have raged throughout our century in the public sphere. Both points of view, however, could obviously be occupied by a single person at different moments in her life. Indeed, this is the dichotomy that many heterosexual women live within every day of their lives.

The poet who most thoroughly fulfilled Millay's antiromanticism— anticipated it, in fact—was Mina Loy. Yet if Millay's "Sonnets from an Ungrafted Tree" are elaborate and often even realist in their narrativity, Loy's 1915–17 "Love Songs" are elliptical and minimalist in their own. In her "Feminist Manifesto," unpublished but probably written shortly before "Love Songs," Loy argues that "woman must destroy in herself the desire to be loved" and urges that "honor, grief, sentimentality, pride and consequently jealousy must be detached from sex."[29] The "Love Songs" accomplish that and more. Loy concludes that all the values embedded in masculinity and femininity are perilous and destructive. Idealization of female purity and virtue, for example, is "the principle instrument of her subjugation."

As the sequence begins, the speaker has already failed at conventional romance—steeped in all the drama of stereotyped emotions—and opts instead not for unreflective animal sexuality but for something like a verbally inventive biological union. The sequence repeatedly offers up the illusory dramas of gender ("I am the jealous store-house of the candle-ends / That lit your adolescent learning")[30] only to reject them; repeatedly, in their place, Loy offers us versions of intercourse that invent figures for bodily fluids and anatomy:

laughing honey

And spermatazoa
At the core of Nothing
In the milk of the Moon

Shuttle-cock and battle-door
A little pink-love
And feathers are strewn.

Some critics have concluded that these are images of degraded lust; they seem instead to be antiromantic but celebratory.[31] Moreover, their variety and surprising capacity to recode the rhetoric of romance ("honey," "the milk of the Moon," "pink-love," and "feathers" above all reposition romance tropes) demonstrate that a degendered human sexuality—one freed of cultural clichés about men and women—need not be impoverished.

Loy, I believe, is a good deal clearer and less ambivalent than she is often taken to be. A poet whose work is, however, arguably more fundamentally indeterminate is William Carlos Williams. Along with Hughes and Frost, Williams is one of the three better-known modern American male poets whose work includes a wide range of portraits of individual women. The difference, however, is that Williams's interest is consistently both social and erotic. Like Ransom, women are indispensable to Williams's work; without their presence in his poetry, his oeuvre would be substantially impoverished.[32] Unlike Ransom, however, his perspective on women is rich and varied and generally affirmative; moreover, Williams often treats men and women in much the same way, something Ransom is disinclined to do. That does not exempt Williams from charges of sexism. No doubt many contemporary readers would be troubled by the characterization of women at various points in his work and find many of his "affirmations" reifying. Indeed no one who has grown up in a sexist culture will be entirely free of sexism, but Williams's work often partly triumphs over these limitations, and it is, if anything, strengthened by comparison with other men and women writing at the same time.

Williams regularly wrote poems about men's and women's interactions and love poems to women throughout his long career; their approach can be sacralizing, irreverent, erotic, mythologizing, or realistic. His brief imagistic portraits of individual women remain among the best-known poems he wrote. These portraits are often sexually charged, but then almost everything Williams describes is. Like Amy Lowell's flower imagery, for example, or Georgia O'Keefe's flower paintings, Williams's flowers are charged with sexuality. Indeed, even his most spare descriptions of natural objects, as in the 1927 "Young Sycamore," are highly sensual.[33] It is possible that the human body (and, more specifically, a woman's body) is the implicit object underlying many of the individual things he celebrates. Notably, however, his physical descriptions of men, as in the 1919 "The Young Laundryman," are also quite sensual and equally focused on telling details:

> his muscles ripple
> under the thin blue shirt; and his naked feet, in
> Their straw sandals, lift at the heels, shift and
> Find new postures continually. (122–23)

Williams certainly fragments men's and women's bodies to describe them, but he most often does so in order to assemble either telling portraits of whole persons or representative characterizations of people's social positioning. If there is a hint of objectification in the process of representation in Williams's work, then, it seems relatively harmless; that is a cultural and political judgment on my part, but I am willing to make it. Representation wholly without objectification may in fact be impossible. When it predominates and when there is nothing else, that is another matter. But treating any trace of it in earlier periods as a fatal heresy is irrational. Recent fervor about objectification may be a contemporary neurosis we would be better off not imposing on our predecessors. At the very least, there is the chance that such charges are hopelessly anachronistic. On the other hand, as I suggested earlier, the arguments disseminated simultaneously with modernism by the first wave of modern feminism give more than sufficient warrant to read Pound's and Ransom's sexism severely and consider it misogynist even within its historical context. Williams, again, presents a more complex and nuanced case.

Part of what sustains poems like Williams's 1916 "The Young Housewife" (57), in which the woman observed "moves about in negligee behind / the wooden walls of her husband's house," beyond its spare, precise description, is Williams's willingness to acknowledge and mock his presence as an observer. As with "Woman Walking" (66–67), the poet is never simply an invisible figure who wields the power to name and describe but rather a speaker whose voice effects a relationship in verse. And that relationship typically includes a genuine if sometimes whimsical reflection on the ontological issues at stake in the poet's role.

> At ten A.M. the young housewife
> moves about in negligee behind
> the wooden walls of her husband's house.
> I pass solitary in my car.
>
> Then again she comes to the curb
> to call the ice-man, fish-man, and stands
> shy, uncorseted, tucking in
> stray ends of hair, and I compare her
> to a fallen leaf.
>
> The noiseless wheels of my car
> rush with a crackling sound over
> dried leaves as I bow and pass smiling.

The poem masquerades at once as a piece of literal reportage and a fantasy surveillance, a celebration and critique of voyeurism. We may credit the speaker with some sensitivity to women's social status when the house is described as the husband's property, but we may also wonder (as one of my students suggested) if we can hear "negligent" and "negligible" judgmentally echoing within the negligee she wears, a garment as well that suggests more corporeal property rights. Whether the speaker would protect her, take advantage of her, or merely observe her in her shy vulnerability we cannot say. We cannot even be certain whose innocence wanes most notably in the poem's autumnal season, the speaker's, the young housewife's, or even the reader's, for we too are implicated in the poem's final recognition. Is it guilty self-recognition, mutual recognition, an exchange of glances, shame, regret, or delight in transience that sounds in the crackling leaves of the last stanza? One critic suggests that "the young housewife is metaphorically crushed in the last stanza," since, in the previous stanza's Shakespearean conclusion, she is herself compared to a fallen leaf.[34] But it is as easily the moment and the fantasy relationship that give way as the car passes. Moreover, the only real pressure exerted is the poem's descriptive act of possession. Indeed, no fixed reading of Williams's short poems will survive sustained reflection, for—

despite their straightforward narrativity—they remain so ambiguous and unresolved that one interpretation continually displaces or reverses another. Thus a particular poem may from one moment to the next seem distinctly sexist and generously understanding.

As many of Williams's critics have noted, there is also a strong mythologizing element in the image of women in his longer poems, from "The Wanderer" to *Paterson.* The woman who is his guide in "The Wanderer" is both young and old, virgin and whore. The latter identity, moreover, is partly celebratory; she is a "reveller in all ages— / Knower of all fires out of the bodies / Of all men." For Williams, anticipating an argument that I do not accept but that some feminists would later make explicitly, women have stronger links to the transformative natural processes that all of us must undergo if we are to rise above the pettiness and violence of so much of human history. Though they are closer to nature, at least as some cultural feminists would claim, women are of course in no way unconscious figures. Rather they have special knowledge that men must seek to share and that Williams would bring into his poetry. Williams is also aware that not every mythic vision of women is beneficial. In *In the American Grain,* in a journey that Pound completed in the opposite direction (minus the monarchist component, which Pound left to another American expatriate), Walter Raleigh fantasizes himself on a voyage on the body of his queen when he plunges "his lust into the body of a new world."[35] It is a fantasy that ends in disaster.

What Williams shows us, finally, is one route to a substantially affirmative and generous heterosexuality in poetry. Williams clearly believed that sexual relations could reorient people toward restorative natural processes and away from the destructive tendencies in modern culture. This differentiates him from Eliot, for example, for whom failed sexual relations in *The Waste Land* and other poems exemplified the modern condition; indeed, for Eliot nature itself no longer offered any hope. In a culture whose inherited and active linguisticality is permeated with gendered binarisms, Williams sorts out these meanings and reconfigures and resemanticizes them. There were certain binary metaphors of gender he found productive and life enhancing, others he considered destructive and demonic. That all these gendered binarisms were fantasmatic—artifices of cultural process with no necessary grounding in the facts of nature—Williams may never have realized. But if we wish to judge him, we had best realize that all of us live partly by way of myth and ideology.

What one does not find in Williams, however, is a thoroughgoing critique of patriarchal culture and all the gendered binarisms by which it sustains and reproduces itself. We get a glimpse of what such a critique might entail in Marianne Moore's 1935 poem "Marriage."[36] On one level it is a strikingly evenhanded demolition of the illusion that either party to a marriage can so divest himself or herself of self-absorption and self-interest to make a union possible.[37] "He loves himself so much," she writes, "he can permit himself / no rival in that love." And she brings a comparable investment to the marriage contract: "She loves herself so much, / she cannot see herself enough." But the poem is much more than an analysis of the pitfalls in gender relations. It actually moves centripetally and centrifugally at the same time, treating marriage not only as a site on which individuals and the culture as a whole act out their contradictory investments in independence and community but also as a figural resource that informs all compromised institutions in the culture. Thus the poem is at once about the marriage two people make and about the marriage the states made to form one country—"Liberty and union / now and forever." Both require "public promises / of one's intention / to fulfil a private obligation," and both "can never be more / than an interesting impossibility." Marriage is an institution constructed by contractualized idealization and a model for comparably problematic institutions of other sorts. Marriage is effectively both victim and purveyor of illusions within the culture, and gender relations are both constituted by and constitutive of impossible binary amalgamation everywhere in public and private life.

Moore's double subject makes her paradoxical and characteristic use of decontextualized but footnoted quotation particularly apt here, for we can thus take every statement about negotiated or contested difference as informed by notions about gender relations. It is not, therefore, that Moore is simply borrowing statements from other writers' work and making them mean something else, but rather that she is teasing out the pattern of ideological reinforcement that underlies apparently diverse utterances about persons and institutions. Interestingly, Gertrude Stein sometimes uses the opposite technique to perform related work, managing to make almost every phrase feel like a quotation without using quotation marks. To go significantly beyond Moore's project, indeed, one must turn to Stein and to one of the great poems of the modern era, her forty-page "Patriarchal Poetry." It is a 1927 poem that did not make its way into print until decades later.[38] Yet it may be the only fully realized and rigorous deconstructive poem in American modernism.

Can the poem, the title questions behind its unruffled nominalism, be *about* patriarchal poetry, or is it to be an *instance* of patriarchal poetry? The parameters of that question are immediately ruptured. For the "poetry" referred to here is not just a literary genre but rather the poetics of everyday thought. "Patriarchal poetry" is the metaphoric logic ruling the meanings that make our culture what it is. The ambiguity of the title thus reflects Stein's judgment that everything one writes will be in some ways patriarchal. A critique of patriarchal poetry cannot be mounted from a position wholly outside the poetics it would critique. The only sure strategy of demolition available is a defamiliarizing burlesque from within.

> Patriarchal Poetry might be withstood.
> Patriarchal Poetry at piece.
> Patriarchal Poetry a piece.
> Patriarchal Poetry in peace.
> Patriarchal Poetry in pieces. (281)

Using witty and strategically staged repetition, variation, and rhyme, Stein exposes hierarchical gendered biases built into the most unassuming usages.[39] Repetition short-circuits the sense that words and phrases can function as neutral syntactic units and frees us to recognize patterns of semantic association that all language carries with it in use: "They said they said they said when they said men. / Men many men many how many many many men men men said many here" (280). "Men," we hear here, is always a statement, always an assertion, always a cultural imprimatur. In patriarchal poetics "they said" always says "men" for "they" and always says "men said" for "said." In the poetics of patriarchy, difference is really the repetition of the same: "there is a very great difference between making money peaceably and making money peaceably" (259). Or as she writes at another point: "Made a mark remarkable made a remarkable interpretation made a remarkable made a remarkable made a remarkable interpretation" (284). A re-*mark*able interpretation is not remarkable at all. It is the honorific imposition of the law of male priority. It is "patriarchal poetry as signed" (286), another interpretation that is marked and that we are linguistically prepared to remark.

Repetition and variation let Stein successively place a variety of words, phrases, and concepts under pressure so that all the components of a statement are shown to be individually permeated with the ruling assumptions of patriarchal poetry. This technique also isolates and decontextualizes words and phrases, seeming at first to turn them into unstable echolailic nonsense, but thereby severing them from their syntactical functionalism and making it possible to see them as counters in a very different semantic game. On the other side of nonsense is the broader ideology that patriarchal poetics continually reinforces: "Patriarchal poetry makes no mistake" (263); "Patriarchal poetry is the same" (264); "Come to a distance and it still bears their name" (264); "Patriarchal Poetry is the same as Patriotic Poetry" (264).

Patriarchal poetry is the poetics of unreflective reason and order, of officious segmentation and classification—"Patriarchal in investigation and renewing of an intermediate rectification of the initial boundary of cows and fishes" (258)—often to comic effect: "Patriarchal poetry and not meat on Monday patriarchal poetry and meat on Tuesday. Patriarchal poetry and venison on Wednesday Patriarchal poetry and fish on Friday Patriarchal poetry and birds on Sunday" (259). Patriarchal poetry is therefore a poetics of marching: "One Patriarchal Poetry. / Two Patriarchal Poetry. / Three Patriarchal Poetry" (274). It is the signature of the authority of the nation-state and of the corollary authority of the individual subject: "signed by them. / Signed by him" (274). Patriarchal poetry is the self-evident logic of culture transforming itself into natural fact: "If any one decided that a year was a year when once if any one decided that a year was a year" (260). Extended in time, it is thus the reiterated story of our collective origin and the linear history that fictitiously unfolds from it: "Able sweet and in a seat. / Patriarchal poetry their origin their history their origin" (263). And patriarchal poetry also cuts the other way, interdicting every impulse that deviates from the norm and its radiant myth of origins: "Patriarchal Poetry originally originate as originating believe believing repudiate repudiating" (282).

Stein's poem does not proceed in any obvious linear way; to do so would be to adopt the armature she wants to disavow. So she works by indirection. But the poem does have signal moments of disruption and revelation. The first of these occurs as a serial eruption of the phrases "Let her be," "Let her try," and "Let her be shy." They are simultaneously pleas for space for women's freedom and commands disseminating differences through the language. "Let her be" is, of course, also the letter *b*, whose supplementarity and secondary character Stein offers in place of patriarchal claims for priority and origination.

So what, we may ask, does the perspective we gain from Stein's work teach us about some of the other gendered poems of the modern era? In part, that is what this whole essay has been about. Consider, for example, that when Williams in the end of "The Wanderer" merges with the river under the tutelage of his timeless female guide he clearly partly revises the gendered fate Moody put forward a few years earlier in "I Am the Woman." Far from a uniquely female destiny, the river is a space the male poet too must take into himself. Moreover, it is not only a natural force but also a symbol of social dissolution and decay. And the shape-changing woman in "The Wanderer" is herself conscious and articulate, not merely a figure for a natural energy still present within culture. But it is still the male poet who tells the story of the journey, and thus still the male, as in Pound's essay, who is the ultimate avatar of high culture. Williams and Pound are hardly interchangeable, nor is it simply a question of degree. No spectrum of gradual differentiation will take us from Pound's or Ransom's unqualified misogyny to the whole range of gendered projects in Williams's work. Yet they share elements of patriarchal totalization, elements, moreover, that remain disabling even when they are radically resemanticized.

Part of what this tells us, I believe, is that totalizing, ahistorical myths of gender—whether men figure positively or negatively, whether women are valorized or degraded—are always self-undermining and reversible. Perhaps we are better off with no master narratives of the fate of gender that claim to transcend history. It is not only poets but also literary critics who have been enamored of such overarching stories about the essential nature of men and women. The simple fact of such totalizing narration often persuades critics that a transformative, spiritualizing project is in view. Certainly critics writing about Williams's "The Wanderer" or *Paterson*, or Crane's *The Bridge*, have regularly felt that larger mythic structures either right all local wrongs or literally render them invisible. Of all the poets we have discussed, it is striking to note, perhaps only Stein, Loy, and Hughes fully realize that it is culture, not the eternal and essential nature of men and women, that is at stake in interrogating the nature of masculinity or femininity. That is a proper and salutary focus for a poetics of gender—the linguistics of our inherited prejudices. But in the modern period—while gender undergoes a continuing struggle of critique, redefinition, and consolidation—the terrain is rarely clearly refocused from nature to culture. Most poets persisted in thinking they were dealing with men's and women's innate natures and capacities rather than with identities made available by the culture. The work of reorienting our awareness in that way is a task, finally, that is left to us.

What modern poetry does give us is a rich body of texts that can energize and enable such cultural work. Working from the canon and its nearer provinces, we see first the risks of inherited bias. In Ransom we see how condescending idealization can evolve into an oppressive but deceptively elegant system of gender differentiation. It is a model of sophisticated prejudice that no nonpoetic discourse could give us in such perfected form. In Pound we see a hierarchical binarism of gender at its fantasmatic extreme, patriarchy in a poetic frenzy. Yet suggestive forays against the gender system also abound. They range from Bogan's successful demolition of clichés about women to Millay's casting of a cold gaze on gender relations to Spector's outrageous mimicry of blues sexism to Jolas's and Freytag-Loringhoven's wild versions of masculinity and femininity in extremis. They include Lowell's demonstration that women can be the object of other women's erotically charged idealization. We also learn from modern poetry's treatment of gender the limits of individual imaginative effort within given historical conditions; to visit Williams's work in that light is to see what could be done in the way of a restorative poetics of heterosexuality in the first half of the century. Finally, despite the limitations of historical perspective, certain totalizing but historically grounded narratives do survive intact, such as Hughes's lifelong effort to show that, within time, in our world, when gender and race intersect, they can indeed be destiny.

NOTES

1. In *Estranging Dawn: The Life and Works of William Vaughn Moody* (Carbondale: Southern Illinois University Press, 1973), Maurice F. Brown argues that "the word *slothful* is deliberately chosen to suggest the latent potentiality of mere matter, the antithesis of the masculine creative energy Moody located in the element of fire" (187). For Moody's poetry and plays, see *The Poems and Plays of William Vaughn Moody* (Boston: Houghton Mifflin, 1912). In *Harriet Monroe and the Poetry Renaissance: The First Ten Years of Poetry* (Urbana: University of Illinois Press, 1977), Ellen Williams points out that "I Am the Woman" was given to *Poetry* by Harriet Moody (27).

2. Eugene Jolas, *I Have Seen Monsters and Angels* (Paris: Transition Press, 1938).

3. For a consistently dichotomous view of modern men and women writers see Sandra Gilbert and Susan Gubar, *No Man's Land: The Place of the Woman Writer in the Twentieth Century* (New Haven: Yale University Press, 1987). For groundbreaking and wide-ranging approaches to American women's poetry that acknowledge greater diversity, see Suzanne Clark, *Sentimental Modernism: Women Writers and the Revolution of the Word* (Bloomington: Indiana University Press, 1991); Mary Loeffelholz, *Experimental Lives: Women and Literature, 1900–1945* (New York: Twayne, 1992); and Cheryl Walker, *Masks Outrageous and Austere: Culture, Psyche, and Persona in Modern Women Poets* (Bloomington: Indiana University Press, 1991). Finally, for an indispensable collection of modernist texts, see Bonnie Kime Scott, *The Gender of Modernism: A Critical Anthology* (Bloomington: Indiana University Press, 1990). In addition to making many pointed comments on some of the writers I discuss, these books take up other relevant traditions outside the scope of this essay.

4. I use the term *misogyny* to signal a more constitutive and thoroughgoing antagonism toward women than that suggested by *sexism*. In each case, therefore, the decision about which term to apply to a particular poet's work is open to debate.

5. For an analysis of how the work of the canonical male modernist poets is substantially—but often unconsciously—gendered, see Frank Lentricchia's *Modernist Quartet* (New York: Cambridge University Press, 1994).

6. Carl Sandburg, "Vaudeville: 1916" and "Planked Whitefish," in *Billy Sunday and Other Poems,* ed. George and Willine Hendrick (New York: Harcourt Brace, 1994), pp. 22, 19–20. Neither poem was published during Sandburg's lifetime.

7. Ezra Pound, *Personae: The Shorter Poems*, rev. ed., ed. Lea Baechler and A. Walton Litz (New York: New Directions, 1990), pp. 57–58.

8. Rémy de Gourmont, *The Natural Philosophy of Love,* trans. Ezra Pound (London: Neville Spearman, 1922).

9. Langston Hughes, "The South," in *The Weary Blues* (New York: Alfred A. Knopf, 1926), p. 54.

10. Harry Crosby, "Target for Disgust," in *Mad Queen: Tirades* (Paris: Black Sun Press, 1929), pp. 7–9.

11. All of Bogan's poems are quoted from Louise Bogan, *The Blue Estuaries: Poems, 1928–1968* (New York: Ecco Press, 1977). "Women" is on p. 19.

12. Elsa Von Freytag-Loringhoven, "MINESELF—MINESOUL—AND—MINE— Cast-IRON Lover," *Little Review* 6, no. 5 (September 1919): 3–11.

13. Amy Lowell, "The Weather-Cock Points South," in *Pictures of the Floating World* (New York: Macmillan, 1919), pp. 51–52.

14. Claude McKay, "The Harlem Dancer," in *Selected Poems of Claude*

McKay (New York: Bookman Associates, 1953), p. 61. The poem was originally published in *Seven Arts* 2 (October 1917): 741.

15. Langston Hughes, "To the Dark Mercedes of 'El Palacio de Amor,'" in *The Weary Blues*, p. 90. In *The Life of Langston Hughes—Volume I: 1902–1941* (New York: Oxford University Press, 1986), Arnold Rampersad reports that the poem was inspired by a night Hughes spent at a brothel at Las Palmas in the Canary Islands during his 1923 trip to Africa (76–77); Hughes was a crew member aboard a ship.

16. Langston Hughes, "Sister," in *Montage of a Dream Deferred* (New York: Henry Holt, 1951), p. 7.

17. Muriel Rukeyser, "More of a Corpse Than a Woman," in *The Collected Poems of Muriel Rukeyser* (New York: McGraw-Hill, 1978), p. 115.

18. Joy Davidman, "This Woman," in *Letter to a Comrade* (New Haven: Yale University Press, 1938), p. 54.

19. Alice Dunbar Nelson, "I Sit and Sew," in *Caroling Dusk: An Anthology of Verse by Negro Poets*, ed. Countee Cullen (New York: Harper and Brothers, 1927), p. 73.

20. Georgia Douglas Johnson, "The Heart of a Woman," in Cullen, *Caroling Dusk*, p. 81.

21. Lucia Trent, "Breed, Women, Breed," in *Children of Fire and Shadow* (Chicago: Robert Packard and Company, 1929), pp. 78–79.

22. Herman Spector, "A Wohmmn," in *Bastard in the Ragged Suit: Writings of, with drawings by, Herman Spector*, ed. Bud Johns and Judith Clancy (San Francisco: Synergistic Press, 1977), p. 53. The poem was originally published in Charles Henri Ford's magazine *Blues* in 1929.

23. Hart Crane, "National Winter Garden," in *The Complete Poems and Selected Letters and Prose of Hart Crane*, ed. Brom Weber (New York: Boni and Liveright, 1966), pp. 100–101. For a related and very suggestive reading of "National Winter Garden" see Thomas E. Yingling, *Hart Crane and the Homosexual Text: New Thresholds, New Anatomies* (Chicago: University of Chicago Press, 1990), pp. 215–19.

24. All quotations by John Crowe Ransom are from his *Selected Poems* (New York: Alfred A. Knopf, 1969).

25. For comments on misogynist elements in some of Ransom's other poems, see Cary Nelson, *Repression and Recovery: Modern American Poetry and the Politics of Cultural Memory, 1910–1945* (Madison: University of Wisconsin Press, 1989).

26. On Ransom and the South see his essay "Reconstructed but Unregenerate" in *I'll Take My Stand: The South and the Agrarian Tradition* (New York: Harper and Brothers, 1930).

27. H.D., "Helen," in *Collected Poems, 1912–1944*, ed. Louis L. Martz (New York: New Directions, 1983), pp. 154–55. See Susan Stanford Friedman's analysis

of "Helen" in her *Psyche Reborn: The Emergence of H.D.* (Bloomington: Indiana University Press, 1981), pp. 232–36.

28. Edna St. Vincent Millay, *Collected Poems,* ed. Norma Millay (New York: Harper and Row, 1956). All of Millay's poems are quoted from this edition.

29. Mina Loy, "Feminist Manifesto," in *The Last Lunar Baedeker,* ed. Roger L. Conover (Highlands, N.C.: Jargon, 1982), pp. 269–71.

30. Mina Loy, "Love Songs," *Others* 3, no. 6 (April 1917): 6–7. This version is more reliable than that published in *The Last Lunar Baedecker.*

31. See Virginia M. Kouidis, *Mina Loy: American Modernist Poet* (Baton Rouge: Louisiana State University Press, 1980).

32. For a helpful and very positive analysis of Williams's view of women see Audrey T. Rodgers, *Virgin and Whore: The Image of Women in the Poetry of William Carlos Williams* (Jefferson, N.C.: McFarland, 1987).

33. All poetry by Williams is cited from A. Walton Litz and Christopher MacGowan, eds. *The Collected Poems of William Carlos Williams: Volume I— 1909–1939* (New York: New Directions, 1986).

34. Yingling, *Hart Crane,* p. 244.

35. William Carlos Williams, *In the American Grain* (New York: New Directions, 1925), p. 59.

36. Marianne Moore, "Marriage," in *The Complete Poems of Marianne Moore* (New York: Macmillan/Viking, 1980), pp. 62–70.

37. See Taffy Martin, *Marianne Moore: Subversive Modernist* (Austin: University of Texas Press, 1986), pp. 21–24, for an analysis of gender relations in "Marriage."

38. Gertrude Stein, "Patriarchal Poetry," in *Bee Time Vine and Other Pieces* (New Haven: Yale University Press, 1953).

39. I have learned a good deal about Stein's poetry in general (and specifically about repetition) from Karen Ford's 1989 University of Illinois dissertation, "Moments of Brocade: The Aesthetics of Excess in American Women's Poetry."

Contributors

Corrine E. Blackmer is Assistant Professor of English at Southern Connecticut State University, where she teaches American literature, gay and lesbian literature, and critical theory. She has edited the anthology *En Travesti: Women, Gender Subversion, Opera* (Columbia University Press, 1995). Her first book, *"The Presence of the Thing Not Named,"* is also forthcoming from Columbia University Press. She has recently completed a book on race and lesbian desire in American women's literature and film.

Maurizia Boscagli is Associate Professor of English at the University of California, Santa Barbara. Her book, *Eye on the Flesh: Fashions of Masculinity in the Early Twentieth Century,* was published in 1996 by Westview Press. She has published essays on European feminism and the politics of the emotions in *Differences, Discourse,* and *College Literature.* She is currently translating a volume of political theory by Antonio Negri.

Kevin J. H. Dettmar is Associate Professor and Director of Undergraduate Studies in the Department of English at Clemson University. He has published a number of essays on modernist and postmodern fiction, especially the texts of Joyce and Beckett, and is editor of *Rereading the New: A Backward Glance at Modernism* (University of Michigan Press, 1992). His study of the stylistics of Joyce's texts, *The Illicit Joyce of Postmodernism: Reading against the Grain,* was published by the University of Wisconsin Press in 1996.

Leonard Diepeveen is Associate Professor of English at Dalhousie University in Halifax, Nova Scotia. He has published essays on modern and contemporary American poetry and is the author of *Changing Voices: The Modern Quoting Poem* (University of Michigan Press, 1993).

Enda Duffy is Associate Professor of English at the University of California, Santa Barbara. He is the author of *The Subaltern Ulysses* (University of Minnesota Press, 1994), and has published essays in the *James Joyce Quarterly*, *College Literature*, *The South Asian Review*, and *Diaspora*. He is currently working on a project on tourist aesthetics.

Karen Jackson Ford is Assistant Professor of English at the University of Oregon in Eugene, where she teaches American, African-American, and modern poetry and poetics. She has published another essay on Langston Hughes in *Twentieth Century Studies* and has completed a series of essays on African-American poetry and poetics that includes pieces on Jean Toomer's *Cane*, the blues, and elegies of Malcolm X. She has recently completed a book-length manuscript on feminist excess and marginal aesthetics.

Barbara Green is Assistant Professor of English at the University of Notre Dame. She has published essays on militant suffrage narratives in the *Review of Contemporary Fiction* and *Discourse,* and is at work on a study of the British suffrage movement that focuses on the role of the feminist body in performative activism.

Walter Kalaidjian is Professor of English at Emory University. His books on twentieth-century American poetry include *American Culture between the Wars: Revisionary Modernism and Postmodern Critique* (Columbia University Press, 1993), *Languages of Liberation: The Social Text in Contemporary American Poetry* (Columbia University Press, 1989), and *Understanding Theodore Roethke* (University of South Carolina Press, 1987).

Timothy Materer is Professor of English at the University of Missouri, Columbia. He is the author of *Wyndham Lewis, the Novelist* (1976), *Modernist Alchemy: Poetry and the Occult* (Cornell University Press, 1995), *Vortex: Pound, Eliot, and Lewis* (Cornell University Press, 1979), and editor of two volumes of the letters of Ezra Pound. He has received grants from the ACLS, NEH, and the Guggenheim Foundation, and reviews "Modern Poetry: 1900–1940" for *American Literary Scholarship*.

Daniel Morris is Assistant Professor of English at Purdue University. In addition to publishing essays on Ernest Hemingway, William Carlos Williams, and Charles Simic, his study of Williams, *The Writings of*

William Carlos Williams: Publicity for the Self, was published in 1995 by the University of Missouri Press. His own poetry and reviews of contemporary poetry have appeared in *Agni Review, Western Humanities Review, Poet Lore,* and *Harvard Review.* He is currently working on a book on self-portraiture in the wake of postmodernism.

Christopher M. Mott is Lecturer in the English department at UCLA. He is interested in modern and postmodern literature, as well as theories of representation that affect cultural, political, and psychological issues. He has recently completed a book-length study of the postmodern narrative strategies of Don DeLillo; his work in progress examines the cultural logic in various traditions that allows for and promotes intercultural exchange.

Michael Murphy is a visiting Assistant Professor of English at the State University of New York–Oswego. He has published articles on theoretical approaches to the teaching of writing and is, at present, finishing a book on popular art called *Camp Happens: Modernism, Postmodernism, and Recyled Culture.*

Cary Nelson is Jubilee Professor of the Liberal Arts and Sciences, and Professor of English and Criticism and Interpretive Theory, at the University of Illinois, Urbana. Among the most recent of the books he has either authored or coedited are *Marxism and the Interpretation of Culture* (with Lawrence Grossberg, 1988), *Repression and Recovery: Modern American Poetry and the Politics of Cultural Memory, 1910–1945* (1989), *Cultural Studies* (with Paula A. Treichler and Lawrence Grossberg, 1992), and, with Michael Bérubé, *Higher Education Under Fire* (1995). His book *Manifesto of a Tenured Radical* is forthcoming in 1997.

Stephen Watt is Associate Professor of English at Indiana University, Bloomington. For the academic year 1992–93 he was a Fellow of the Howard Foundation at Brown University. In addition to publishing essays on drama and Irish culture in *PMLA, James Joyce Quarterly, Comparative Drama,* and other journals, he is the coeditor of *When They Weren't Doing Shakespeare: Essays on Nineteenth-Century British and American Theater* (University of Georgia Press, 1989) and *American Drama: Colonial to Contemporary* (Harcourt Brace, 1995), and author of

Joyce, O'Casey, and the Irish Popular Theater (Syracuse University Press, 1991). He has recently completed a book-length manuscript, *Postmodern/Drama.*

Joyce Wexler is Associate Professor of English and Director of the Honors Program at Loyola University of Chicago. Her book *Laura Riding's Pursuit of Truth* was published by the Ohio State University Press in 1979; she has published articles on Conrad, Riding, Hemingway, and other modernist writers in such journals as *Psychoanalytic Review, Sewanee Review,* and *The Georgia Review.* Her book entitled *Who Paid for Modernism?* is forthcoming in 1997 from the University of Arkansas Press.

Jennifer Wicke is Associate Professor and Chair of Comparative Literature at New York University, where she teaches literature, film, and cultural theory. She is the author of *Advertising Fictions: Literature, Advertisement, and Social Reading* (Columbia University Press, 1988), and has written on Joyce, modernism and postmodernism, feminist theory, and contemporary critical debates. Her forthcoming book is a study of consumption and gender in the twentieth century.

Index

obscenity, 24, 25, 91–95, 97–99, 101,
103, 105
Olsen, Tillie
"I Want You Women Up North to
Know," 341
Opportunity, 254, 255, 262–65, 267,
268
ornamental bodies, 191, 193, 194,
196–98, 200, 203, 208
Owen, Chandler, 254, 255, 268, 272
Owsley, Frank, 302, 303, 307

pan-Africanism, 261
Pankhurst, Adela, 196, 204
Pankhurst, Christabel, 196, 201, 204–7
Pankhurst, Emmeline, 192, 194, 196,
204
Pankhurst, Sylvia, 194, 201, 204, 208
Pater, Walter, 223
patriarchy, critique of, 353–55
patronage, artistic and literary, 5, 22,
62, 83, 329
Pawling, Sidney, 95, 96
Perloff, Marjorie, 27, 28, 32
Petacci, Claretta, 33
Pethick-Lawrence, Emmeline, 191,
202, 207
Pfeiffer, Pauline, 84
photography, 62, 133, 135–58, 195,
207, 208
Picasso, Pablo, 7, 63
Pinker, J. B., 98, 99
piracy, literary, 94, 105
Poetry magazine, 22, 23, 321
pop art, 66
Popular Front, 303
portraiture, 146, 147
postmodernism, 65, 66, 80–82
poststructuralism, 222
Pound, Ezra, 4, 7, 8, 17–28, 32–34, 37,
39, 50, 51, 54, 55, 99, 100, 162–64,
166–72, 174, 177, 178, 181, 183,
184, 221, 297–99, 321, 324, 329–31,
334, 339, 347, 350, 352, 356, 357
"Canto II," 330
Cantos, The, 26, 33, 178

Hugh Selwyn Mauberley, 33, 329
"N.Y.," 330
"Portrait d'une Femme," 328–30
Postscript to *The Natural Philoso-
phy of Love* by Rémy de Gour-
mont, 330, 331, 333
"Salutation the Third," 331
Pratt, William, 19
Prisoners' Temporary Discharge Act
("Cat and Mouse Act"), 197, 209
private publication, 101–7, 129
public sphere, 194, 195, 198, 200, 207,
297, 299, 311
Punch, 136, 138
purity, artistic, 2, 3, 8, 10, 64–70, 76,
79, 81, 83, 85, 92, 97, 163

queer criticism, 222
queer liberation movement, 224
queer sexuality, 223, 232, 236, 292
Quinn, John, 21, 22, 25–27

Rabelais, François, 24
race "science," 254–58, 261–64, 268
racism, 10, 254, 255, 257, 260–64,
270–72, 282, 285, 286, 291
Rainey, Lawrence, 6, 162
Raleigh, Walter, 352
Rampersad, Arnold, 279
Randall, Dudley, 283
Randolph, A. Philip, 253, 255, 256,
262, 268, 270–72
Ransom, John Crowe, 300, 302–7, 311,
315, 346, 347, 350, 356, 357
"Lady Lost," 345
"Miriam Tazewell," 345
readership, modernist, 43
Reagan, Ronald, 129
Reid, B. L., 28
repetition, narrative use of, 203, 208,
209
Richards, I. A., 223
Richardson, Mary, 205, 208–10
*Tortured Women: What Forcible
Feeding Means: A Prisoner's Tes-
timony*, 209